REASONS AND INTENTION
AND PRACTICAL AGE

This collection of new essays explores in depth how and why we act when we follow practical standards, particularly in connection with the authority of legal texts and lawmakers. The essays focus on the interplay of intentions and practical reasons, engaging incisive arguments to demonstrate both the close connection between them, and the inadequacy of accounts that downplay this important link. Their wide-ranging discussion includes topics such as legal interpretation, the paradox of intention, the relation between moral and legal obligation, and legal realism. The volume will appeal to scholars and students of legal philosophy, moral philosophy, law, social science, cognitive psychology, and philosophy of action.

GEORGE PAVLAKOS is Research Professor of Globalization and Legal Theory at the University of Antwerp and Professor of Globalization and Legal Theory at the University of Glasgow. He is the author of *Our Knowledge of the Law* (2007) and has edited several collections of essays including *New Essays on the Normativity of Law* (2011).

VERONICA RODRIGUEZ-BLANCO is Senior Lecturer in the School of Law at the University of Birmingham, UK. Her publications include *Law and Authority Under the Guise of the Good* (2014).

REASONS AND INTENTIONS IN LAW AND PRACTICAL AGENCY

Edited by

GEORGE PAVLAKOS

University of Antwerp and University of Glasgow

VERONICA RODRIGUEZ-BLANCO

University of Birmingham

CAMBRIDGE
UNIVERSITY PRESS

CAMBRIDGE
UNIVERSITY PRESS

University Printing House, Cambridge CB2 8BS, United Kingdom

One Liberty Plaza, 20th Floor, New York, NY 10006, USA

477 Williamstown Road, Port Melbourne, VIC 3207, Australia

314-321, 3rd Floor, Plot 3, Splendor Forum, Jasola District Centre, New Delhi-110025, India

79 Anson Road, #06-04/06, Singapore 079906

Cambridge University Press is part of the University of Cambridge.

It furthers the University's mission by disseminating knowledge in the pursuit of education, learning and research at the highest international levels of excellence.

www.cambridge.org
Information on this title: www.cambridge.org/9781107642928

First published 2015
First paperback edition 2018

A catalogue record for this publication is available from the British Library

Library of Congress Cataloging in Publication data
Reasons and intentions in law and practical agency / edited by George Pavlakos, Veronica Rodriguez-Blanco.
pages cm
ISBN 978-1-107-07072-1 (Hardback)
1. Law–Philosophy. 2. Intention. 3. Normativity (Ethics) I. Pavlakos, George, editor. II. Rodriguez-Blanco, Veronica, editor.
K272.R43 2015
340′.1–dc23 2014027893

ISBN 978-1-107-07072-1 Hardback
ISBN 978-1-107-64292-8 Paperback

CONTENTS

CONTRIBUTORS

JOSHUA P. DAVIS is Associate Dean for Academic Affairs, Professor, and Director of the Center for Law and Ethics at the University of San Francisco School of Law.

WILLIAM A. EDMUNDSON is Regents' Professor of Law and Philosophy at Georgia State University. He is the author of *Three Anarchical Fallacies* (1998) and *An Introduction to Rights* (2nd edn 2012).

KENNETH M. EHRENBERG is Assistant Professor of Philosophy and Adjunct Professor of Law at the University of Alabama.

MATTHEW HANSER is Professor of Philosophy at the University of California, Santa Barbara.

ANTONY HATZISTAVROU is Senior Lecturer in Philosophy at the University of Hull. He is the author of *Ancient Legal and Political Philosophy* (2014).

ULRIKE HEUER is an Associate Professor in Philosophy at the University of Leeds.

HEIDI M. HURD is the David C. Baum Professor of Law and Philosophy at the University of Illinois. She is the author of *Moral Combat* (Cambridge, 1999).

A. J. JULIUS teaches philosophy at the University of California, Los Angeles.

BEN LAURENCE is an Assistant Professor in the Philosophy Department at the University of Chicago.

GEORGE PAVLAKOS is Research Professor at the Faculty of Law, University of Antwerp and Professor at the School of Law, University of Glasgow.

VERONICA RODRIGUEZ-BLANCO is Senior Lecturer at the University of Birmingham School of Law, UK. She is the author of *Law and Authority Under the Guise of the Good* (2014).

ORI SIMCHEN is Professor of Philosophy at the University of British Columbia. He is the author of *Necessary Intentionality: A Study in the Metaphysics of Aboutness* (2012).

SERGIO TENENBAUM is Professor of Philosophy at the University of Toronto. He is the author of *Appearances of the Good* (Cambridge, 2007) and the editor of *Desire, Practical Reason, and the Good* (2010).

MANUEL VARGAS is Professor of Philosophy and Law at the University of San Francisco. He is the author of *Building Better Beings: A Theory of Moral Responsibility* (2013) and a co-author of *Four Views on Free Will* (2007).

BRUNO VERBEEK is Senior Lecturer at the Institute for Philosophy at Leiden University and a fellow of the Centre for Political Philosophy. He is the author of *Instrumental Rationality and Moral Philosophy* (2002) and *Reasons and Intentions* (2008).

ACKNOWLEDGEMENTS

We should like to thank for valuable comments and unmitigated support the contributors to this volume, most of whom also participated in the IVR Workshop on 'Legal Normativity and the Philosophy of Practical Reason', which was held in Frankfurt on 15–18 August 2011. The editing of the volume would have been a much more difficult task had it not been for the help of Özge Akarsu, a doctoral researcher at the University of Antwerp. Anthea Connolly has offered invaluable suggestions and advice on matters of English style. We are further grateful to Hilary Gaskin, our publishing editor, for believing in our project and offering plenty of wise advice in preparing the manuscript. George Pavlakos acknowledges the generous support of the long-term strategic development financing of the Institute of State and Law of the Academy of Sciences of the Czech Republic (RVO: 68378122).

Finally we would like to dedicate the book to our loved ones, who yet again have tolerated our demanding passion for philosophy: Thomas, Estelle, Eleonora, and Charlotte.

Introduction

GEORGE PAVLAKOS AND VERONICA RODRIGUEZ-BLANCO

Outline

Can an agent act out of normative considerations without engaging with the moral quality of their actions? Contrary to common understanding, a lot of philosophical work assumes a positive answer to that question. Accordingly it is not unusual to read in philosophical accounts that practical agency can be understood in the relation between some (normative) fact and a token of conduct; or in the relation between some mental state and a token of conduct. As long as an explanation of conduct can be plausibly offered in the light of either facts or mental states, an account of practical agency is considered successful. Such accounts of practical agency abound: 'Mary takes her umbrella because it rains'; or, to take another example, 'Mary evades paying her taxes, because she intends to free-ride on her fellow citizens.' No doubt these accounts fit well the model of theoretical explanation, yet they remain markedly insufficient for capturing what is practical about normative agency.[1] *For, in all those cases, there is a lingering sense that a fully-fledged practical account would need to demonstrate how the cited facts or intentions feature in agency qua agency-guiding items.*

The collection of essays at hand questions – for the first time in such explicit terms – the plausibility of accounts of normativity that eschew the link between agents and reasons for action. In challenging these accounts it illustrates the inadequacy of partial explanations of action, such as those that take normativity to reside in normative facts or outside agents, or to be reducible to psychological items, which pay no heed to mind-independent standards of action. The contributors, all leading or emerging scholars working in legal and practical philosophy broadly conceived, engage trenchant arguments to demonstrate the shortcomings of such views in respect of three key aspects of any account of practical

[1] Besides being mutually incompatible.

normativity: the normative meaning of action; the grounding of legal authority; and the relevance of social institutions to any such account. What emerges, far from some joint doctrine common to all contributors, are the ingredients of a theory in whose core resides the idea that a successful account of practical normativity needs to integrate intentions with reasons for actions. It is envisaged that the strong appeal of the suggested solution will invite thinkers in law and philosophy to engage further in the debate.

The standard picture

Arguably, a key controversy surrounding accounts of normativity concerns the understanding of what renders such accounts *practical*. While all sides in the debate claim to offer a 'practical' account, opinion as to what counts as 'practical' diverges considerably. Yet, even taking this divergence into account, most – if not all – accounts seem to be in broad agreement about the explanatory tasks involved in such an enterprise. The first task involves demonstrating how normative items (reasons) are linked to agents as authors of their actions; and the second task relates to the constraint imposed by the need to show that normative reasons concern the merit of an action, independent of the subjective psychology of an agent.

The first task can be brought under the scope of 'internalism'. While the term 'internalism' was coined within the Humean tradition of accounts of practical philosophy (Williams's 'reasons internalism' is the most prominent such account) it has since then gained wider plausibility, even though it is still resisted by the more ardent moral realists:[2] they prefer to explain away internalism by assuming that knowledge of practical reasons is independent of and prior to any intentional items, including acting intentionally.[3]

For all its laudable contributions, internalism is for the most part grounded on agents' psychology. In other words, internalist accounts (especially those that remain close to the Humean tradition) frequently

[2] See D. Parfit, *On What Matters* (New York: Oxford University Press, 2011); T. Scanlon, *Moral Dimensions: Permissibility, Meaning, Blame* (Cambridge, MA: Harvard University Press, 2008).

[3] In particular with respect to reasons internalism the argument runs that moral reasons, once cognized by the agent, ought to cause her to develop the appropriate intentional states, unless there exists some defect in their moral psychology.

operate under the assumption that what makes anything 'practical' or 'action-pertinent' is its capacity to motivate the agent in a straightforward manner, free of reliance on any non-motivational items. While the requirement of motivation can be developed in different ways, many accounts impose the following stringent condition: for any practical standard to remain internalist in an appropriate manner, it must be the kind of thing that is psychologically efficacious and to which agents have unmediated access when they reason – namely, a mental state. This condition comes at a high price, however, since if practical reasons are confined to mental states, it is difficult to see how they could offer anything more than (causal) explanations of action. Reasons, in this context, would rather be accounts of mere causal links between the action undertaken (*explanandum*) and some intentional state of the agent (*explanans*), and would be in isolation from anything that may feature as explanation qua normative standard for the action undertaken.

The second explanatory task involved in an account of practical normativity is to spell out the relationship between reasons as 'explanations' of actions, which do not collapse into the subjective psychology of agents, but instead derive their authority from their capacity to justify the action under consideration. That justificatory dimension of normativity features prominently in cognitivist accounts of practical reasons, such as those advanced by moral realists. Simplifying somewhat, moral realism considers normative reasons to explain actions in virtue of their being (agent-independent) facts about what ought to be done. In so arguing, realists take the justificatory task of normative reasons to be antecedent to the explanatory one.

Some refinement is needed here, lest one jump to the conclusion that realist accounts eschew any connection between reasons and the agent's intentional environment. Rather, the realist account requires that the agent be in some cognitive mental state (belief or, should one subscribe to the view that it is a mental state, knowledge), which puts them in touch with the appropriate normative reason. To that extent it is true that the explanation of action, under the realist model as well, requires the presence of agential mental states. It is arguable, however, that cognitive mental states do not contribute any additional practical input to the explanation of action other than the propositional content of the normative reason which they (purport to) represent. To that extent it is the normative reason that explains the relevant action, rather than any intentional state of the agent. That is why, on the proposed understanding, it is antecedent belief/knowledge of a reason which can, by itself, explain the action performed. Accordingly, if I believe/know that there exists a normative fact R, such that 'I ought to Φ', then intending to Φ is merely what I ought to do if my Φing is to be explained appropriately.

Among the problems emerging from that account is that if normative reasons provide the required justificatory reasons for action independently of the explanatory reasons for actions from the agent's point of view, then it becomes difficult to explain the persistence of complex actions over time. Moral realists can explain justificatory reasons for action but not reasons in the action and when the agent acts. In other words, they cannot explain the reasons that the agent had and on the basis of which he persisted in his actions. Furthermore, control and guidance are interconnected. The reason needs to be transparent to the agent from the deliberative point of view in order to be able to guide the agent and for the agent to be in control of his reasons *during the action*. Furthermore, the realist account has the tendency to portray normative knowledge as theoretical. Given that in order for agents to connect to reasons they are required to acquire some relevant cognitive state, it is hard to see how the realist account of normativity can fail to turn into a theoretical one.

Towards an integrated account of intentions with reasons

It would seem that a key shortcoming of both the internalist and moral realist accounts of practical normativity is a tendency to focus either only on states of agents which causally determine the origin of actions, or only on normative facts which, in determining permissibility, function as external constraints to agency. By contrast, a practical account of normativity – as several contributors to this volume suggest – should aim to integrate intentions with reasons in a twofold manner: on the one hand, it is not the case that intentions should, or could, be confined to internal states of agents when it comes to accounting for action. Increasingly philosophers have come to realize that intentions are wedded to the actions they explain in a manner that encompasses the normative meaning of those actions. For, as Anscombe notably remarked, a practical account of intention entails that to intend to act is already to be in the process of doing the action. Intending to act is thus not something that could be the efficient cause of that whole process but, conversely, needs to be informed by it.

Mutatis mutandis there is a parallel case to be made about realist accounts of reasons. Standards of permissibility or normative correctness, unless they form part of the agents' intentionality, will fail to determine the meaning and, further, provide an explanation of the act they are called to explain. Stripped of their explanatory power, realist reasons would cease to be about this or that action, when it happens, but would merely relate to it as a token act relates to a type act. Yet the kind of explanation provided by token type correlations fails to capture the *practical difference* that reasons for action make; that is, their contribution to the meaning of action and agency in a manner that is asymmetric to the contribution of other non-practical or speculative items, which for that reason cannot replace an account in terms of practical reasons.

Producing an integrated account, however, is no small task, and surely not one within the scope of this collection. For present purposes, some signposting should suffice. The task of an integrated account will most certainly appear too demanding, or even insoluble, if one approaches it as a theoretical or speculative task. For, in that case, one would be starting with isolated intentions, reasons, and actions, and seek to establish connections between them only at later stage. As we saw earlier, this two-stage model assumes the existence of self-standing items – intentions, and reasons – which are *practical* antecedently to their connection to agents and their actions, and which proceed to explain[4] action as being practical on the basis of those items: either because it can be causally explained by them, as in the case of internalist accounts, or because it can be subsumed under them, as in the case of realist justification.

It would seem, then, that an integrative approach ought to part with the kind of theoretical knowledge that undergirds the two-stage model of normativity and seek to offer an account in terms of *practical knowledge*. Practical knowledge has been a recurrent theme in philosophical debates on reasons despite the lack of a uniform treatment of the term. Aristotle and Kant, to name the two most prominent defenders of the idea, seem to place great importance on the existence of a special kind of knowledge which pertains to our grasp of reasons for action. Yet many philosophers have argued that the lack of any uniform understanding of practical knowledge by those thinkers suggests that there exists no single useful

[4] Recall that, in the case of internalist accounts, explanation takes the form of causal explanation, where intentions function as sufficient causes for action. Conversely, in the case of moral reasons qua facts, on which realist accounts rely, the explanation takes the form of a 'justification' which is generated by subsuming a token act under a type act. This kind of justification counts as theoretical in that it requires assertion of a (moral) fact independently of the agent who acts and the action undertaken.

concept of practical knowledge: Aristotelian accounts (especially in their Anscombian variation) place the emphasis on the capacity of the agent to know what they are doing. Conversely, Kantian accounts focus mainly on the capacity to know what it is right to do.

Careful consideration of the two seemingly opposing positions might suggest that they merely represent different aspects of a single capacity or power: that is, the power to act through reasoning.[5] Acting through reasoning can accommodate Aristotelian and Kantian intuitions in a coherent manner. The key supposition here is that when we act through reasoning we are involved in two operations. On the one hand, we are reflecting upon what is good to do, *simpliciter*. On the other, we attend to reasons *as we engage in the process of doing the action intentionally*. Such an interpretation would suggest that practical knowledge, through the capacity to act through reasoning, combines knowledge of what the agent is doing with knowledge of what it is good to do. If the picture adumbrated here can lay claim to plausibility, practical reasoning and the capacity to act through it emerge as crucial ingredients of practical knowledge. While this is neither the time nor the place to develop that idea further, it seems that practical reasoning ought to occupy centre stage in accounts of practical normativity, and can certainly be considered an implicit theme unifying most of the contributions in the present volume.

Positioning the volume within the current debate

The unappealing picture of the fragmented relationship between reasons, intentions, and action, which is supported by the two-stage model, has

[5] For this idea and an illuminating development of it see the excellent paper by Sebastian Rödl, 'Two Forms of Practical Knowledge and their Unity', in A. Ford *et al.* (eds.), *Essays on Anscombe's Intention* (Cambridge, MA: Harvard University Press, 2011), 211–41. Rödl's arguments build on more foundational work on the role and nature of powers in practical reasoning, to be found both in classical and contemporary authors. See, among others, Aristotle, *Physics, Books III and IV*, trans. E. Hussey (Oxford: Clarendon Press, Clarendon Aristotle Series, 1983); Aristotle, *Metaphysics Book Θ* with commentaries and introduction by S. Makin (Oxford: Clarendon Press, Clarendon Aristotle Series, 2006), 133; T. Reid, *Essays on the Active Powers of Men*, ed. Knud Haakonssen and James Harris, a critical edition (Edinburgh University Press, 2010); U. Coope, 'Change and its Relation to Actuality and Potentiality', in G. Anagnostopoulos (ed.), *A Companion to Aristotle* (Oxford: Wiley-Blackwell, 2009); T. Pink, 'Power and Moral Responsibility', *Philosophical Explorations* 12 (2009), 127–49; H. Steward, *A Metaphysics for Freedom* (Oxford University Press, 2012); G. Yaffe, *Manifest Activity: Thomas Reid's Theory of Action* (Oxford University Press, 2004).

led many philosophers to question – in more or less explicit terms – its premises. While there is no unified approach emerging as yet in the literature, the most common strategy is to side with either intentions or reasons with an eye to articulating a more appealing alternative. Thus a number of authors have attacked the relevance of intentions to questions of permissibility (Scanlon), or otherwise undermined the importance of intentional accounts of normativity (Raz, Scanlon). Conversely, others have placed the emphasis on intentions over reasons (as normative facts) in order to illustrate what is practical about normative agency (Bratman). Exceptions to such dualistic approaches are those accounts of neo-Aristotelian or Kantian orientation that argue that reasons and intentions are constitutively interconnected through practical reasoning. Their merit notwithstanding, such accounts are often strongly indebted to the intellectual tradition of Aristotle or Kant, failing to articulate arguments that appeal to those working outside these traditions.

Nowhere does the disparity between the two models of normativity play out more strongly than in the domain of law. While the richer debate in the philosophy of normativity has made significant progress in exploring connections between intentional action and reasons, scholarship in law has shunned direct inquiry into the relationship between reasons and intentional action. As a result, despite the new vindication of old (and interesting) ways of understanding practical reason and reasons for action in philosophy, the connection between practical reason and law remains elusive in contemporary legal theory.

The contributions in this volume, some originating in legal philosophy and others in the general philosophy of agency, are linked to one another by making law their implicit or explicit focus. As such, in addition to advancing important new philosophical positions, they also generate fresh argument on a number of topics in the domain of legal philosophy and the legal doctrine. The volume comprises three parts: Part I, 'The normative meaning of actions'; Part II, 'Normativity of legal authority'; and Part III, 'The social dimension of normativity'.

In Part I the authors raise questions about the relevance of intentions and reasons in determining the normative meaning of actions. The task is carried out in a number of ways including by asking how intentions and reasons contribute to the normative content of actions (Ulrike Heuer); by assessing the model of rationality that underlies standard accounts of intentional action (Sergio Tenenbaum); and, finally, by scrutinizing a particular understanding of the contribution of intentions to the meaning of legal authoritative enactments, which is traditionally employed in so-called originalist accounts of the semantic content of legal propositions (Heidi M. Hurd; Ori Simchen).

The contributions in Part II aim to challenge the standard picture of legal authority. Legal obligation, in involving different orders of agents (those who issue and those who incur the obligation), displays a seeming asymmetry of structure: there is a sense in which a person acceding to another person's order or request does that person's will rather than his own. Yet the order or request does not override his will: he chooses to do the other's bidding, and he presumably has his reasons for doing so. To that extent an adequate account must capture both the sense in which he does this other person's will and the sense in which he does his own. Matthew Hanser, Veronica Rodriguez-Blanco and Antony Hatzistavrou tackle the asymmetry in contradistinction to Joseph Raz's service conception of authority. In the remainder of the second part of the volume the authors take issue with the stand-alone model of legal obligation, which is often taken to presuppose the idea of coercion. Painting with a broad brush, the claim is that because legal obligation conceptually requires some fact or instance of authoritative imposition by institutions (coercion), the law generates special obligations which are distinct from other reasons we have. This assumption is scrutinized, and eventually rejected, in the chapters by A. J. Julius, William A. Edmundson, Ben Laurence, and George Pavlakos.

Part III of the volume collects essays by Kenneth M. Ehrenberg, Joshua P. Davis and Manuel Vargas, and Bruno Verbeek. All three contributions engage in some form with the question about the possibility of an account of legal normativity in terms of social facts. While such accounts might prima facie be considered bad candidates for practical accounts of normativity, the contributions do not aim to dismiss the practical element of normativity. Rather, they propose to offer accounts of social practices which explain how such practices generate reasons for their participants, while retaining the explanatory neutrality of social sciences.

PART I

The Normative Meaning of Actions

1

Intentions, permissibility, and the reasons for which we act

ULRIKE HEUER

If you injure me, it matters morally whether it was an accident or you did it intentionally, and whether you did it because you thought it would be fun. I take it that any ethical theory will have to include some explanation of why this is.

There are two dominant views in the current debate about the moral significance of an agent's intentions: one is that the intention with which someone acts at least sometimes determines whether what she does is right or wrong (permissible or impermissible). Proponents of the so-called doctrine of double effect (DDE) hold that an action which has certain bad outcomes may be permissible if the bad consequences are only foreseen, even if the same action would be morally wrong if they were intended as a means. This is not the only way in which intentions could make a difference to an action's permissibility, but it is the best defence that they do.

According to the second view, intentions do not matter in this way: they do not determine the permissibility of an action. They do matter, but in a different dimension of normative assessment: they determine whether the agent is a good or a bad person; or, alternatively, they determine the 'moral worth' of an action[1] or its 'meaning', including its praiseworthiness or blameworthiness,[2] or the severity of a wrong-doing.[3]

I presented earlier versions of this paper at a workshop on 'Legal Normativity and the Philosophy of Practical Reasons' at the World Congress of Philosophy of Law in Frankfurt, a conference on 'Practical and Theoretical Rationality' at the Institute of Advanced Studies at the Hebrew University in Jerusalem, and at the Moral Philosophy Seminar in Oxford. I would like to thank all those audiences for very helpful discussions, questions, and comments. I am particularly grateful to David Enoch, Matthew Hanser, George Pavlakos, Joseph Raz, Veronica Rodriguez-Blanco, and Fiona Woollard for their thoughtful and probing written comments.

[1] Julia Markovits, 'Acting for the Right Reason', *Philosophical Review* 119 (2) (2010), 201–42.

[2] Thomas Scanlon, *Moral Dimensions* (Cambridge, MA: Harvard University Press, 2008).

[3] Judith Jarvis Thomson, 'Self-Defense', *Philosophy and Public Affairs* 20 (4) (1991), 283–310.

The main thesis is what Thomson called 'the Irrelevance-of-Intentions-to-Permissibility Thesis' (*IIP* for short).

> [IIP] It is irrelevant to the question whether X may do alpha what intention X would do alpha with if he or she did it.[4]

IIP is driven in part by scepticism about DDE: since – according to proponents of IIP – DDE is false, we must explain the relevance of intentions and reasons in a different way. Proponents of IIP tend not to consider the possibility that intentions might matter to permissibility in ways that are different from DDE.[5] In this chapter I will not focus on the arguments for or against DDE, but investigate IIP itself more closely, and look at some of the arguments for and against it.[6]

Some preliminary clarifications

I will start from some assumptions that I am not going to argue for – but which, I hope, will appear innocuous. They will also explain why I am looking at intentions and the reasons for which we act at the same time.

(1) *Reasons for actions.* I will assume that we have reasons for actions, and that those reasons are facts (rather than beliefs or belief–desire pairs). I do not think that this begs the question against any of the major theories of practical reasons. Even reasons internalism can be, and – I think – should be, interpreted in a way that is perfectly compatible with this assumption.[7] Since reasons are facts, we can

[4] Ibid., 294.

[5] Matthew Hanser, 'Permissibility and Practical Inference', *Ethics* 115 (3) (2005), 443–70, expounds such an alternative: according to him, permissibility traces the quality of a person's deliberation. He explains both how his view differs from Scanlon's account of the meaning of an action (i.e. why it does not simply replace 'meaning' by 'permissibility'), and how it differs from DDE.

[6] For recent defences of DDE, see Jeff McMahan, 'Intention, Permissibility, Terrorism, and War', *Philosophical Perspectives* 23 (2009), 345–72; Ralph Wedgwood, 'Scanlon on Double Effect', *Philosophy and Phenomenological Research* 83 (2011), 464–72; and Ralph Wedgwood, 'Defending Double Effect', *Ratio*, special issue on Deontological Ethics, ed. Brad Hooker, 24 (2011), 384–401.

[7] Take the following interpretation of reasons internalism: the fact that *p* is a reason to Φ for agent, A, if and only if there is a sound deliberative route from A's existing motives and *p* to the conclusion that A has a reason to Φ. Compare Williams' famous gin–petrol example: Ralph wants a gin and tonic, and believes that the liquid in the bottle is gin. It is, however, petrol. Ralph does not have a reason to mix the stuff in the bottle with tonic and drink it. Instead he has a reason not to drink it, Williams tells us. Why? There is no sound deliberative route from Ralph's desire for a gin and tonic, and the fact that this is petrol, to the conclusion that Ralph has a reason to Φ. The view that reasons are facts can

generally be mistaken about what reasons we have. The *reasons for which a person acts* are the reasons she *believes* to have and for which she acts. It follows that the reasons for which a person acts may not be reasons for so acting at all in case she is mistaken about the facts.

(2) *Acting for the right reasons.* This expression has at least two different senses. One is that the 'right reasons' are simply the reasons that there are. So a person acts for the right reasons when her beliefs about her reasons, her reasoning, and the intention it leads to do not contain any mistakes. But there is also a different sense of 'right reasons': some Kantians, for instance, use 'right reasons' to refer to moral reasons (rather than, say, merely self-interested ones). The 'right reason' in this sense will be identified by the moral content of the proposition that describes it. A person may act for the 'right reason', and yet be mistaken about her reasons (i.e. she may believe that there is a moral reason for acting as she does, even when there is no such reason). I will use 'right reason' in the first sense.

(3) *Intentions.* A further assumption concerns intentions. The intention with which a person acts – i.e. the intention that guides her action (or the 'intention in action', as it is sometimes called) – is based on the reasons the person believes to have. There is no algorithm which explains how a person's intentions relate to the reasons she believes she has. It is not true, for instance, that a person necessarily intends to do what she believes to have most reason to do. Weakness-of-will cases prove the point.

(4) *Acting intentionally / acting with an intention.* 'Intention in action' contrasts with a different sense of acting intentionally. Acting intentionally is more basic than 'acting with an intention'. It may only require that the person is aware of what she does, or perhaps that she can become aware of it and can control it. Take scratching one's head, or biting one's fingernails: as opposed to falling down the stairs these are actions, but they are not done with any intention. I will not be concerned with this broader and more basic sense of acting intentionally, but only with 'intention in action'.[8]

make sense of Williams' verdict about the case. Note that Williams does not even require that Ralph could have known that the content of the bottle is petrol – it is simply the fact that it is that explains why Ralph does not have a reason to drink the mixture, and has a reason not to drink it. Bernard Williams, 'Internal and External Reasons', in *Moral Luck* (Cambridge University Press, 1981), 102.

8 For a similar distinction see Joseph Raz, 'The Guise of the Good', in S. Tenenbaum (ed.), *Desire, Practical Reason, and the Good* (Oxford University Press, 2010), 111–37; and Scanlon, *Moral Dimensions*. For a more comprehensive discussion see my 'Intentions and the Reasons for Which We Act,' *Proceedings of the Aristotelian Society* 114 (3) (2014), 291–315.

How intentions might matter for permissibility

This brief sketch by itself may suggest that the reasons for which someone acts cannot be directly relevant to the normative assessment of her action: in particular, they cannot determine whether her action was morally permissible. After all, whether an action is morally permissible depends on the reasons that there are for or against the action, and not on the reasons that an agent *believes* herself to have. If an agent is mistaken about her reasons, but could not have been expected to know better – i.e. if the case is one of non-culpable ignorance – she may be excused and not be blameworthy, in case the action is wrong. The reasons for which the person acts are normatively relevant in this way. But whether the action is wrong would seem to be independent of her beliefs.

If intentions are based on beliefs about reasons (as I assume they are), you might expect something similar to be the case: they are not directly relevant to the permissibility of the actions. If an agent's beliefs about her reasons and her reasoning are correct and she forms an intention based on her reasoning, then the intention she forms is the intention she ought to have formed, and the subsequent action is the action she ought to have undertaken. If her beliefs or her reasoning involve mistakes, the intention may not be the intention that she ought to have formed, and the action she performs may not be the one she ought to have performed. ('May not' because it is possible that a person does what she ought to do incidentally and as a result of flawed reasoning.) What is wrong with *both* the intention and the action would be explained by the reasons that there are – and not by any mental states of the agent.

Even so, it would be false to conclude that if the relations between the reasons for which a person acts, her intentions, and the reasons that actually bear on the situation are as I described them, neither the reasons for which a person acts nor her intentions could be relevant to the permissibility of her actions. It does not follow from my initial assumptions that IIP is true.

What follows from the assumptions is, rather, that if the reasons for which someone acts or her intentions *are* relevant to the permissibility of her action, it must be because there is a reason (not) to act with a certain intention (or there is even a reason not to act in some way unless it is done with a certain intention). Call reasons of this kind 'reasons to act (or not to act) with a certain intention', or RAWCIs.

One form this may take is that, while there is a reason to act in a certain way, there is also a (sufficient) reason not to perform the action with a certain intention. Take an example: Peter is drowning; Caligula considers rescuing Peter in order to torture him to death more slowly. If it would be wrong to rescue Peter with this intention, then it must be true that (a) even though there is a reason for rescuing Peter, (b) there is also a sufficient reason for not rescuing Peter with the intention of torturing him to death more slowly. If Caligula were to rescue Peter to get him out of danger, he would rescue him with the right intention, thereby complying with both (a) and (b). If he rescues him to torture him, he does not comply with (b), and assuming that (b) defeats (a) when there is a conflict, his action is morally wrong. (I am not suggesting that this is the right analysis of the example; I use it only to illustrate how the agent's intentions might determine the action's permissibility.)

This explanation of the relevance of intentions to permissibility does not appeal to DDE, since it does not rely on the foreseeing/intending distinction. But does it entail the truth of DDE nonetheless? It may seem so, because if there is a reason not to act with a certain intention, then presumably this is not a reason against acting in the very same way while foreseeing the outcome. But this, while true, is not enough to support DDE. DDE involves the much more specific claim that a bad outcome which is foreseen as a side-effect may be morally acceptable when the balance of good over bad is favourable, even when the same action would be impermissible if the bad outcome had been intended. Furthermore, the claim that there may be reasons against acting with certain intentions does not entail that it is wrong to act with these intentions. Whether or not it is depends on the other reasons for and against acting in this way. Thus, my suggestion is much more modest than DDE: I am not proposing an absolute restriction on acting in certain ways. The entailment does, however, hold the other way around: DDE entails that there are RAWCIs, but the existence of RAWCIs does not entail DDE.

Let us take a closer look at certain staple examples used by proponents of DDE: examples of actions where our moral assessment seems to vary depending on the agents' intentions. Take an example of Scanlon's: 'Drug – Transplant – Drug/Transplant'.[9]

DRUG. There is not enough medicine to cure everyone who needs a certain drug: it could be used to either cure one who is in an

[9] Scanlon, *Moral Dimensions*, 15 f.

advanced stage of the illness, or five who are in earlier stages. (All who do not get the drug will die.) There is a reason to, and it is permissible to, give the drug to the five.

TRANSPLANT. Five people are in need of organ transplants. It is impermissible to kill one who happens to be an ideal match for all of them.

DRUG/TRANSPLANT. Same situation as in TRANSPLANT, except that the one whose organs could be used needs a drug which is in short supply (same as DRUG) to cure his illness.

Many believe that it is impermissible in DRUG/TRANSPLANT to withhold the drug from the one in order to then use his organs as transplants. Based on RAWCIs, the explanation could be the following: there is a reason to withhold the drug (i.e. that it will cure the five), and there is a reason for procuring organ transplants, but there also is a sufficient reason not to let a person die with the intention of making use of her organs.

A proponent of DDE would describe the case differently: in DRUG, you may withhold the drug, foreseeing that the one will die, because the good of rescuing the five outweighs the bad, the death of the one. In DRUG/TRANSPLANT, you may not withhold the drug because you would do it with the intention of letting the one die, even though you further intend to help the five who need the drug, as well as the five who need organs. According to DDE, the crucial difference between DRUG and DRUG/TRANSPLANT is that in DRUG/TRANSPLANT you intend to let the one die as a means to acquiring the organs, whereas in DRUG you merely foresee that she will die. You may balance the outcomes only when the death is foreseen but not when it is intended.

Putting it in terms of the relevant reasons is different: (1) there is a reason to help the five; (2) there is a reason to procure transplants; but (3) there is a reason to not let one die with the intention of harvesting his organs, and (3) defeats (1) and (2), or excludes them in some other way. I am not making the case that this is the right way of judging the case, but only describe how things would have to be for it to be true that withholding the drug in DRUG/TRANSPLANT would be wrong because of the intention with which it is done. We need a substantive argument to establish the truth of (3). (3) invokes the intention in determining the normative status of the action, but it does not turn on either the intending/foreseeing distinction, or the claim that balancing may come in when the bad outcome is not intended.

This gives us the basic shape of a view (different from DDE) that takes the reasons for which a person acts, or her intentions, to be relevant to permissibility. Denying that they matter in this way is denying that there can be reasons like (3); or, more generally, that there can be reasons (not) to act with a certain intention (RAWCIs).

Why deny it? Proponents of IIP believe that we should explain the apparent role of intentions in different ways, rejecting not only DDE, but also RAWCIs. They also offer direct arguments for IIP. In the following three sections, I will first consider some alternative explanations for the apparent role of intentions, and then Thomson's and Scanlon's arguments in favour of IIP.

Towards IIP

A conflation?

There is a challenge that any defender of IIP will have to meet. She will have to explain the apparent relevance of intentions to permissibility as in DRUG/TRANSPLANT. Both Thomson and Scanlon take on the challenge.[10]

Scanlon offers not only an alternative explanation of the moral differences in the examples, but also an explanation of why the assessment of intentions and the reasons for which people act plays an important role in evaluating actions: he offers an account of their normative significance. As he sees it, intentions matter morally, just not for the permissibility of actions. Those who believe that intentions are relevant to an action's permissibility conflate two different kinds of normative assessment.

A similar suggestion has been pursued by Thomson early on: intentions matter if we ask ourselves whether someone is a good or a bad person. They are crucial for assessing the agent's character, as well as for determining whether she was at fault in acting as she did.[11]

Scanlon's view differs in some respects. He distinguishes between two usages of moral principles: a deliberative (first-personal) one which settles the question what to do in a certain situation. Intentions are irrelevant here. But there is also a critical (third-personal) use of moral

10 For a more detailed (and cautious) interpretation of Scanlon's view, see Nico Kolodny, 'Scanlon's Investigation: The Relevance of Intent to Permissibility', *Analytic Philosophy* 52 (2011), 100–23.

11 Judith Jarvis Thomson, 'Physician-Assisted Suicide: Two Moral Arguments', *Ethics* 109 (3) (1999), 497–518, at 517; Thomson, 'Self-Defense', 297, n. 10.

principles which usually takes place after the fact. As Scanlon sees it, intentions matter in this second dimension of moral assessment: they determine the meaning of actions. Thus they are not only relevant to assessing the agent's character, but the action itself.

Thus one explanation why intentions appear to be relevant is that they are relevant – just not to assessing the rightness or wrongness of actions, but the character of agents or the meaning of actions, and we tend to conflate these different dimensions of assessment.

The apparent role of intentions: alternative explanations

We still need an explanation of the staple examples which seem to show that the permissibility of an action sometimes does depend on intentions. The general strategy is to find an explanation that does not depend on attitudes, but on objective differences. To illustrate the strategy, here is an example of Scanlon's.

Buying rat poison is generally permissible. But is it permissible if you buy it in order to supply your neighbour, who – as you know – will use it to poison his wife? If the answer is no, does this not show that intentions do indeed determine permissibility in this case? Here is the alternative explanation: buying rat poison is generally permissible. But it is wrong to facilitate another person's wrongdoing. On this view, what is wrong with the buying of the rat poison is that it facilitates wrongdoing. But does it matter that you give it to the neighbour with the intention of assisting him? The defender of IIP denies this. Your action would have been wrong whether or not you intended to supply your neighbour. The intention with which you do it determines the meaning of your action (or its moral worth). If you intend to help him, your intention reveals that you did not count being involved in the killing of an innocent person as a (decisive) reason against the action.

This case is meant – at a stretch – to cover the following: you are buying rat poison with the intention of killing your own wife. This again is wrong, not because of your intention, but because it facilitates wrongdoing – your own wrongdoing this time.

Is this alternative explanation better than its competitors (i.e. explanations according to which wrongness depends on the intention)? Not obviously. It does not provide an argument for IIP. It just shows that – if there are independent arguments for IIP – its proponents may be able to deal with counter-examples. Of course, this illustration of the strategy does not suffice to show that it can deal with all apparent counter-examples.

Thomson's arguments

Thomson offers a number of direct arguments for IIP. As a first approach to showing what is wrong with the idea that intentions determine permissibility, Thomson tries to bring out the absurdity of DDE. It is absurd, she claims, that an action, which has O_1 and O_2 among its outcomes, may be permissible if the agent intends O_1, but impermissible if she intends O_2.[12] Why would intentions have this role? Why would it depend on the agent's state of mind whether her actions are wrong? Take DRUG/TRANSPLANT again: the outcomes of withholding the drug from the patient are that the patient will die (O_1), that the drug will be used to cure five others (O_2), and that the organs will be used as transplants (O_3). A defender of DDE would claim that the action is permissible if the doctor intends to bring about O_2, but impermissible if she intends O_1 – and therefore impermissible if she intends O_3 because she cannot realize O_3 without making O_1 happen, and would be rationally required to intend O_1 as a means.[13] However, if the doctor only intends O_2, and as a foreseeable consequence O_1 happens, and she later decides to use the deceased patient's organs as transplants (an intention she had not formed when deciding to withhold the drug), her actions may be morally permissible. Thomson finds this unacceptable: we are not interested in the doctor's state of mind when trying to determine whether or not she may withhold the drug from the one.

Claiming that DDE is absurd is not helpful. But Thomson makes clear that we need an explanation why intentions would play any crucial role in the assessment of the permissibility of actions.

Thomson offers two further arguments for her view: intentions are crucial for determining fault. But fault is neither necessary nor sufficient for impermissibility. An agent can act impermissibly without being at fault. The ordinary practice of offering excuses is based on this assumption. More controversially, an agent can be at fault without acting impermissibly (if, say, a person intends to poison someone, spooning what she believes is poison into the would-be victim's tea, although in

[12] Thomson, 'Physician-Assisted Suicide', 515.

[13] Fiona Woollard suggested to me that a defender of DDE may deny that the doctor must rationally intend O_1 as a means to O_3 even though O_1 is a condition of permissibly performing O_3. Thus, DDE may permit withholding the drug after all, even if it is done with the intention of getting the transplants. This suggestion is based on Frances Kamm, 'The Doctrine of Triple Effect and Why a Rational Agent Need Not Intend the Means to His End', *Proceedings of the Aristotelian Society*, supplementary vol. 74 (1) (2000), 21–39.

fact the substance she takes to be poison is sugar). Thomson assumes that intentions have run their course in determining fault – and since fault and impermissibility can come apart, there is no role for them to play in determining permissibility. Recently, Matthew Hanser has rejected this argument by pointing out that intentions may well have more than one role to play: as Thomson rightly claims, they determine fault, but they may also be relevant to determining permissibility.[14]

Thomson's third argument is that when a person deliberates whether a certain action would be permissible, she would not ask herself which intention she would be doing it with. She would ask about the consequences of the action, or whether in acting in this way she would be violating someone's rights. She would not look 'inwards' but 'outwards'. But this argument again seems doubtful: on the one hand, an agent may well look 'inwards', as, for example, when, being suspicious of her own motives, she asks herself 'really, what would be my reason for doing this?' On the other hand, it is not clear that, if permissibility depended on intentions, a deliberating agent would be required to think in terms of her reasons or her intentions.[15]

Scanlon's argument

Scanlon's guiding question is whether what we ought to do is the right thing for the right reasons. In one sense this is trivial: not making mistakes about one's reasons is a good thing. But this is not enough to defend the view that actions are permissible if and only if they are done for the right reasons. Scanlon rejects this view.

Let us focus on the following case: '[Adèle] hates [Bernie] who needs help, and would be happy to see him die, but she saves him anyway because she does not want him to die right then, since that would mean that his heir, with whom she is locked in a bitter political contest, would have more money to spend on his campaign.'[16] Would it be impermissible for Adèle to save Bernie? Hardly. You may even think

[14] As Hanser, 'Permissibility and Practical Inference', sees it, Thomson's argument is question-begging: while she is right that intentions determine fault, and fault does not track permissibility, intentions could *also* be directly relevant to the permissibility of actions.

[15] For a more comprehensive discussion of this argument see ibid., 458–64. David Enoch, 'Intending, Foreseeing, and the State', *Legal Theory* 13 (2) (2007), 69–99, develops a version of Thomson's argument which he calls 'the appropriate question test'.

[16] Scanlon, *Moral Dimensions*, 57.

she is morally required to save him. But why not think: she is required to save him for the *right* reason?

Scanlon offers the following argument against this suggestion. The answer to the question 'is it permissible?' guides the agent's choice. 'Permissible' applies only to options that an agent can choose – otherwise they are neither permissible nor impermissible. But Adèle cannot choose to save Bernie for the right reasons, because she cannot choose her reasons. Thus if the only permissible option were rescuing Bernie for the right reason, this would be an option Adèle cannot choose. But there must be a permissible action that Adèle can choose. Scanlon contends that it is permissible for her to rescue Bernie, even if she does it for a very bad reason. Her reason for doing so does not affect the action's permissibility. He writes:

> This conclusion about choice and reasons explains why it is odd to say, in the case of the person who thinks that *the only good reason* to save a person is the advantage to her of that person's staying alive, that the only permissible course of action for her is to save the person for the right reason. Saying this is odd because it presupposes that it is open to her to choose to act out of concern for the person's well-being. It is open to her to choose whether to save the person or not, but not open to her to choose to see a certain consideration as a reason for doing so.[17]

The argument rests on the assumption that an option that an agent cannot choose is neither permissible nor impermissible for her. Answers to questions about permissibility must be at least potentially action-guiding. An option that an agent cannot choose is just not one of the options to be considered when deciding what to do.[18]

(1) 'Permissible' applies only to the actions an agent can choose.
(2) An agent cannot choose her reasons.
(3) So, an agent cannot choose to Φ for a specific reason, R.
(4) Therefore, 'permissible' does not apply to options of the form: to Φ for R.
(5) An agent can choose to Φ or not to Φ.
(6) 'Permissible' only applies to options of the form: to Φ.[19]

[17] Ibid., 61 (emphasis added).

[18] Scanlon contrasts the 'ought' of (im)permissibility with Thomson's 'objective ought' which is based solely on the relevant facts with no consideration of whether an agent could know about or be guided by them.

[19] For a somewhat different analysis (and criticism) of Scanlon's argument, see Kolodny, 'Scanlon's Investigation', and Hallvard Lillehammer, 'Scanlon on Intention and Permissibility', *Analysis* 7 (3) (2010), 578–85.

(1) is a claim about the meaning of ' permissibility' that I will simply assume to be correct for the sake of the argument. (I will, however, come back to some ambiguities in (1) below.) (2) seems innocent enough in one interpretation: if Adèle does not believe that there is a reason to rescue Bernie out of concern for his well-being, then she cannot choose to believe that there is such a reason.[20] This is simply an instance of the more general, plausible claim that we cannot choose what to believe, i.e. it may be based on a rejection of doxastic voluntarism. I take it that this is what Scanlon has in mind: in general, no one can simply choose to believe that there is a reason R to Φ.

But, on this interpretation of (2), (3) is problematic. Why can Adèle not choose to Φ for R? Is that not exactly what she does: she chooses to rescue Bernie for the reason that doing so is, at this time, advantageous to her? (2) does not support (3) if (3) is meant to exclude that Adèle chooses to rescue Bernie for her self-interested reason. If the point is that Adèle cannot rescue Bernie for the reason that doing so will save his life, since she does not believe that there is such a reason, the claim is true, but of limited relevance. Scanlon's opponents – those who defend DDE, for instance – do not maintain that agents should act for reasons they do not believe they have. The claim is, rather, that they should act for certain reasons that they believe to have, and not for others that they also believe to have.[21] Since Scanlon takes his argument to show that we should reject DDE (and other principles that make permissibility depend on intentions) he has to show that this kind of choice is impossible too.

Here is how the argument might go: when Adèle chooses to rescue Bernie for the reason she believes to have (that it would be advantageous for her to do so), she only chooses to Φ – she does not

[20] It may seem extraordinary that Adèle does not believe that there is a reason to rescue Bernie to save his life. Lacking knowledge of a common reason of this kind may show the agent to be a psychopath.

[21] I am not sure whether this is really what the proponent of DDE thinks, since the view is normally not stated in terms of the reasons that the agent believes she has. Does an agent who follows DDE acknowledge, in DRUG/TRANSPLANT, that there is a reason for procuring organ transplants, as well as an instrumental reason for letting the one die because it is a means to procuring transplants, but maintain that these are reasons the agent must not act for, and they must not determine her intention? Or does she deny that there are those reasons, which, in turn, may explain why an intention formed on the basis of these considerations would be objectionable – it would be an intention formed for no reason? Since the latter would be a very odd way of explaining what is wrong with the impermissible action (is it impermissible to act for no reason at all?), I take it that the DDE proponent affirms the former – but I am not very confident about this.

choose [to Φ for R]. Of course she chooses to Φ for R (that is: R explains her decision), but she does not choose the reason for which she acts. And, as (3) tells us, she cannot do that. If this is how we should read (3), then it does not follow from (2) (on the interpretation of (2) that I suggested above). We need to interpret (2) quite differently to get to (3):

(7) If an agent believes she has a reason R_1 and a reason R_2 to Φ, then she cannot choose to Φ for R_1 alone.[22]

That is, even if less-wicked Adèle believed that there is not only reason R_1 (to rescue Bernie because it is advantageous to her), but also reason R_2 (to rescue Bernie to save his life) she could not rescue Bernie just for R_2 (the right reason), but any of the reasons she believes to have will be a reason for which she acts. It does not matter that Adèle sees only one reason for acting as she does – it is not because of that that she cannot choose her reason (and therefore cannot choose to act for the right reason). It is because of the general claim expressed in (7) that agents cannot choose to act for one reason rather than another when they consider Φing, and believe that both reasons count in favour of it. It is not, as it were, that you could survey the reasons you believe you have for a particular action, and then choose one of them as the one for which you act.

We can now complete an argument that Scanlon may have had in mind.[23] (7) supports

(8) For any agent whose beliefs about her reasons are partly mistaken, she cannot choose to act for the right reasons.

And from (1), (7), and (8) we get:

(9) It is false that an action is permissible only if done for the right reasons.

[22] Scanlon explicitly endorses something like this: 'when one sees several considerations as counting in favor of the same action, one cannot choose to act on one of them rather than another . . . there is no such thing as choosing, or "singling out," one of them as *the* reason that one is acting on' (*Moral Dimensions*, 60).

[23] While (7) is presumably the relevant interpretation of (2), (3) does not follow from it either. After all, (7) only applies to cases in which an agent sees more than one reason for acting in a certain way. (3) would apply to cases where the agent believes herself to have only one reason. Might it be possible that she can decide to act for that reason? I am doubtful that it makes sense to speak of choosing to φ when there is no alternative. But I do not think that settling this is relevant to Scanlon's argument, and I will therefore not pursue (3) any further. Thanks to Matthew Hanser for pressing me on this point.

(7), if true, might indeed undermine DDE. The proponent of DDE may have to assume that agents can choose to act for some reasons they believe to have but not for others. Take DRUG/TRANSPLANT again: the agent believes that one reason for withholding the drug is that it is necessary for saving the lives of the five. Another reason to withhold it is that if you do so, the five who need organs can also be saved. Now perhaps, the defender of DDE would want to deny that withholding the drug to save the five who need organs is a reason for doing so.[24] But we only need an agent who falsely believes that there is such a reason: such an agent could not choose to act for the right reason if (7) is true, and since an action is permissible only if the agent can choose it, it cannot be impermissible for our partly mistaken agent to act for the wrong reason.

But should we accept (7)? (7) may rest on the assumption that 'acting for a reason' is a causal notion. The reasons for which a person acts are those that are causally efficacious. But whether a reason is causally efficacious is not a matter of choice. Causes cannot be turned on and off like taps.

Nonetheless, (7) does not seem very plausible to me. It often appears as though we can choose to act for certain reasons, and not for others. I could promise you, for example, not to act for some reason R – and I think that it is within my power to keep this kind of promise. Thus if R is a reason to Φ, and I know that, and I Φ, it may still be true that I did not Φ for R. Imagine I promise you that I will not abandon my work for your charity for the reason that I can make more money elsewhere. Let us assume that I believe both that I can make more money elsewhere and that I have a reason to earn more money. When I stop working for your charity, is it not nonetheless at least conceivable that I did not stop because of the money, but for quite a different reason: because I found that the charity's work is really inefficient and does not benefit those whom it is meant to help (say)? But for it to be even possible that I kept my promise in this case, (7) has to be false. I'm not denying that we are prone to self-deception in cases of this kind. I am only denying that it is conceptually impossible that I could have kept my promise.[25]

But if (7) is false, then a proponent of DDE need not worry about Scanlon's argument, because it might then be possible for an agent who believes that she has several reasons to Φ, to choose to Φ for one particular reason. And if the right reason is among the reasons she

[24] Cf. n. 21.

[25] For a different criticism of (7), see Alec Walen, 'Choosing Your Reasons for an Action', available at: http://papers.ssrn.com/sol3/papers.cfm?abstract_id+1447042.

believes to have, then she can also choose to Φ for the right reason. Thus, if (7) is false, so are (8) and (9).

But we are still stuck with Adèle: she believes that she has only reason R_1 for rescuing Bernie. So even with (7) gone, *she* cannot act for the right reason since the only reason she believes she has is not the right one. But can she not at least choose to rescue Bernie but *not* for the wrong reason? This may be irrational – choosing to act for no reason. But it would still be enough to provide her with a choice to not act for the wrong reason. But this is impossible too, as Scanlon sees it, because he endorses a further premise:

(10) An agent cannot choose to act for no reason.[26]

Should we accept (10)? I think we should – at least in one sense. While agents can probably *act* for no reason, they cannot *choose* to do so. It is not just that we make choices for reasons – this may generally be true, but perhaps we can 'just choose', for no reason, to buy this particular can of tomato soup (say), rather than its brother to the right. However, the relevant choice for our purpose is not the choice (for no reason) to act in a certain way – but a different kind of choice: the choice to Φ for no reason. If the question is about choosing reasons, and not about choosing actions, then Adèle cannot choose to act for no reason. Choosing 'no reason' as one's reason is perhaps not something that an agent can do.[27] If (10) is true, then Adèle cannot even choose not to act for the wrong reason (granted, anyway, that she cannot choose to act for the right reason).

Hence, she cannot choose to Φ for R, because there is only one reason that she believes she has for Φing,[28] and even with the crucial premise (7) gone (but the quite plausible (10) added) there is no choice *of reasons* open to her. So we get

(11) For any agent whose beliefs about her reasons are thoroughly mistaken: she cannot choose not to act for the wrong reasons (understood as a choice of reasons, not of actions).

However, as Scanlon rightly notes, even Adèle can choose to Φ or not to Φ – i.e. (5) is true of her. Her only rational choice is of course to act for the only reason bearing on the situation that she believes she has. But she

[26] 'One can adopt an end only if one sees some consideration as counting in favour of it' (Scanlon, *Moral Dimensions*, 59 f.).

[27] It is not clear to me, however, that a proponent of DDE would need to make a case for (10) in this interpretation. It may be sufficient for her purposes that Adèle can choose to rescue Bernie for no reason (i.e. there is no reason for her choice), even if she cannot choose 'no reason' as her reason.

[28] I simply assume here that choice requires options. Cf. n. 23.

could make an irrational choice: that is, she cannot choose to Φ for a different reason, but she can choose not to Φ. Thus, as far as Adèle goes, Scanlon is right (even if we abandon (7)): she can choose to act or not to act, but she cannot choose to act for a reason, let alone for the right reason.

Does Adèle's case pose an insurmountable problem for the view that an action may be permissible only if it is done for the right reasons? Is it sufficient to show that the reasons for which an agent acts are irrelevant to permissibility?

This question brings us back to (1): the concept of permissibility, and one further claim which seems to be implicit in Scanlon's discussion – something like:

(12) Every agent at any time has at least one permissible option.

So we get:

(13) It is not true that Adèle's action is permissible only if not done for the wrong reasons.

If we reject (1), the argument breaks down anyway – but it also breaks down if we reject (12). Perhaps for Adèle, and those like her, who are thoroughly misguided, there is no permissible option that they can choose without acquiring different beliefs. This is, at any rate, what opponents of IIP may want to say in reply to Scanlon's argument.

There is a related problem with (1), which concerns the interpretation of 'can'. (1) helps Scanlon's argument only if we understand 'can choose' as 'can choose, given her current beliefs'. But it is far from obvious that this is the right way to understand the claim. Of course an agent can choose to act for a reason only once she is aware of it. But 'not being aware' is not enough for 'cannot'.

I conclude that Scanlon's argument does not, in the end, help IIP. So thus far we lack a convincing argument for IIP. In the remainder of the chapter I will consider objections to IIP.

Counter-examples to IIP? Actions which have intentions as constitutive parts

Some philosophers think that actions which have intentions as constitutive parts (e.g. murder, forgery, wrongful attempts) are clear counter-examples to IIP.[29]

[29] The examples are Douglas Husak's, 'The Costs to Criminal Theory of Supposing that Intentions are Irrelevant to Permissibility', *Criminal Law and Philosophy* 3 (2009), 1–70.

I will focus on wrongful attempts. What it is that a person attempts when she tries to do something, but fails, depends on her intention: someone fires a gun, but the bullet does not hit anyone or anything. If she fired because she intended to kill a person, the action may have been attempted murder. Attempted murder is wrong; firing a gun with a different intention may not be wrong. Is that enough to show that the permissibility of attempts depends on intentions? Is the action wrong, because – while the agent did not cause any harm – had things worked out as she planned, she would have murdered someone?

Imagine someone intends to kill another by sticking needles into a voodoo doll which represents the intended victim. This too may be attempted murder. After all, had things been as the agent believed them to be, and had they worked out as she intended, she would have murdered someone. But, in this case, it is much less obvious that the action is wrong. If it is not, then attempted murder is not wrong simply qua attempted murder. One difference between the two attempts is that in firing a gun the agent endangered other people, but by sticking pins into a doll she did not. Thus, perhaps, attempts are wrong only if what the person actually does creates a risk and endangers others.

Husak[30] objects that we would not 'label' some (perhaps unintentional) endangering of another person 'attempted murder'. And that is, of course, right. An action is not attempted murder unless the agent intends to kill someone. We cannot identify what an agent attempts without referring to the intention. But when a person attempts, but fails, to do something, there is always something else that she does. We are asking whether what she does is wrong – not whether what she failed to do would have been. Firing the gun may be wrong because you endangered others, but in that regard it is not different from firing a gun accidentally. That too endangers others.

Is attempted murder worse than the accidental firing of a gun? If so, the endangering of others cannot explain why that is. So, again, we need the intention to explain the difference. But even if the one is worse then the other, both are impermissible. Hence the intention, which marks the difference, is not needed to explain (im)permissibility. This is true if the impermissibility of the endangerment simply depends on the risk of harming that the action creates. The intention may explain the *gravity* of the wrongdoing. Why would intention make this kind of a

[30] Ibid.

difference if it does not affect permissibility? The answer may be the one that Thomson and Scanlon offer: the gravity of a wrongdoing concerns how blameworthy the agent is – and that does depend on the reasons for which she acts, as well as her intentions, and the availability of excuses. In this way, the proponent of IIP may well be able to explain why and when attempts are wrong.

In general, even if the intention is a constitutive part of an action, it does not follow that the intention explains the action's wrongness (when it is wrong). It may be other features of the action that do. Thus I take it that the observation that certain actions have intentions as constitutive parts does not, by itself, provide an objection to IIP.

Objections to IIP

Let me raise two objections to IIP that seem more powerful to me.

The 'meaning' of actions

Scanlon explores a dimension of the moral assessment of actions (not just of persons) under the heading 'the meaning of actions'. Take Adèle's case again: the reason for which she rescues Bernie gives her action a certain meaning (for Bernie, and potentially for others).

The meaning of an action is what the action indicates about the agent's attitudes to others and her relationship to them. It can vary without change in the permissibility of the action.[31] But is it not at least possible that an action could be impermissible in virtue of its meaning, and therefore – since the meaning depends on the reasons for which she acts – in virtues of those reasons?

Take friendship as an example. You are (I believe) my friend, and I am ill. You come to visit me. But you do not come to visit me because you want to cheer me up or help me, but because you have, unbeknownst to me, accepted a bet that you will win if you visit me. If I find out that this is your reason for visiting me, I may be outraged, and take our friendship to be over. I may also think that what you did was wrong.

Extrapolating from Scanlon's response to what he calls 'expression- and expectation-cases',[32] his analysis of the case might be the following. When I learn about your reasons, the meaning of our relationship

[31] Scanlon, *Moral Dimensions*, 52 ff. [32] Ibid., 39 ff.

changes: I find out that you are not a true friend, and I downgrade our relationship as a result. But was your action wrong? Perhaps. After all, you misled me to consent to your visit, knowing that I would do so only because I would misinterpret your intentions. Your intentions are derivatively relevant, because the misleading (which makes the action wrong) is done by allowing me to be mistaken about your intentions. The basic wrong is 'misleading' – the relevance of intentions to mislead is an incidental feature of the example.

Something seems to be missing here: the meaning side of the evaluation and the deontic judgement may not be as unrelated as the analysis suggests. As Scanlon sees it, I believed that you were my friend, but then I discover that I was mistaken. The subsequent downgrading of our relationship is an adjustment to reality. But there is a different way of understanding what happens: perhaps you are my friend (I am not mistaken), but you act wrongly as a friend – and not only in misleading me (which would be wrong even if I were a stranger) but in failing to act like a friend. This very possibility seems to be excluded from Scanlon's analysis. For this kind of complaint, the reasons for which you acted are directly relevant. As a friend you ought to have acted for certain reasons but not for others. This can be a failure within a friendship, rather than a failure of friendship.

Scanlon has to deny that, as a friend, you *ought to* have acted differently (i.e. for different reasons). The view is, instead, that as a friend, you *would* act for certain reasons but not others – otherwise you are not a friend. This flies in the face of the quite common understanding of friendship as being in part constituted by obligations to one another – at least if those are obligations (not) to act for certain reasons: if they involve RAWCIs.

Exclusionary reasons

Above I suggested that an intention can be relevant to the wrongness of an action if there is a reason (not) to Φ with the intention, a RAWCI. If such a reason is conclusive because it defeats other reasons for or against Φing, then it would determine the action's rightness/wrongness: the action would be wrong if (or unless) done for a certain reason.

It seems that there is no argument for the impossibility of such reasons, and the friendship case may even suffice to show that they exist.

There is a further class of reasons that requires that agents act (not) for certain reasons (or with certain intentions): 'exclusionary reasons'. Joseph Raz introduced the term to explain the nature of authority, the reasons we have to follow orders, legal reasons, and reasons from obligations and duties.[33]

Sometimes, so runs the idea, an action is wrong if done for certain reasons, but may be acceptable if done for others. This is so when there is an exclusionary reason – a second-order reason – against acting for certain reasons. The excluded reasons are excluded only as reasons for which to perform the action – the same action, when done for other reasons, may well be permissible.

Take a rather mundane example: you have a reason to give your child the best education available, but you also have a reason to take the costs to yourself into account. However, you promised the child's mother not to act for reasons to do with your own convenience when deciding which school to send the child to. (Let us imagine you are a single parent and in charge of these decisions.) The reason to keep your promise is an exclusionary reason: it is a second-order reason, a reason not to act for certain reasons. Thus it is not a reason for or against sending the child to a particular school. It does not conflict with the first-order reasons for or against particular schools directly, allowing you to send your child to any school as long as you do not do it for a particular reason. It may turn out that an inexpensive neighbourhood school is the best school available. If you send your child to that school because it is the best, you comply with the exclusionary reason, even though it is also convenient for you to send her there.

Reasons of this kind bring back the structure I started with: the idea that the reasons for which we act can be relevant to an action's rightness or wrongness if there is a reason for (not) acting with a certain intention, or for certain reasons. Exclusionary reasons exhibit precisely this structure. And if there are such reasons, then the reasons for which we act can determine the rightness and wrongness of actions. Thus, some exclusionary reasons provide counter-examples to IIP.

Since we need only one counter-example for IIP to be false, I conclude that IIP is false. But is the principle nonetheless broadly on the right track, since actions whose wrongness or rightness depends on intentions are only few and far between? I see no reason to think so. We still lack a comprehensive answer to the question how intentions are relevant to the rightness and wrongness of actions.

[33] Joseph Raz, *Practical Reason and Norms*, 2nd edn (Oxford University Press, 1999; first published 1975).

2

Acting and satisficing

SERGIO TENENBAUM

I am searching for new shoes. I go to the first store, look at the selection and prices, move to the second store, find a pair a bit cheaper and nicer than my favorite in the first store, and buy it. My friend comes to me and says: 'This might come as a surprise to you, but there are many more shoe stores in Toronto; in fact, dozens of them. The chances that you'd find an even nicer pair for an even cheaper price in one of these stores are very high. Fortunately, you still have time to return these shoes and continue searching; I expect you will do much better.' Sensible words indeed. But I reply: "Thanks for your insightful remarks, but these shoes are *good enough*. I shall keep them." My response seems perfectly rational, and such examples seem to speak for the correctness of satisficing as a standard of rational choice. According to a general satisficing theory of rationality, an agent is rational if (and only if) her choices are good enough, and thus an agent's choice can be rational even if the agent recognizes that there is another choice that is (or is expected to be) better.[1] My expectation of finding better shoes were I to continue my shopping adventures does not show that my decision to buy the second-store pair was unreasonable; it is perfectly rational for me to turn a deaf ear to my friend's advice.

Satisficing is thus supposed to be an intuitive alternative to maximizing theories of rationality which would require me never to choose an option if there is any other option I can choose that has a higher expected value or utility.[2] Almost no one doubts that, given normal background

Many thanks to Niko Kolodny, Erasmus Mayr, Jennifer Nagel, and an audience at the November 2013 meeting of the DFG Netzwerk in Stuttgart for excellent comments on a draft of this chapter. This research was supported by the Social Sciences and Humanities Research Council of Canada, and a Visiting Fellowship at Magdalen College, Oxford.

[1] In some ways of understanding this definition, this would be a rather strong form of satisficing. I will refine the view as I continue.

[2] It does not matter to my purposes whether "expected value" in our understanding of maximization is a function of the agent's preference or a function of belief or some belief-like attitude towards objective value. I will alternate between these understandings in the chapter.

assumptions, it is perfectly rational for me to keep my new shoes. Yet, it is dubious whether such examples really pose a challenge to a maximizing conception of rationality. Maximizers will easily come up with ways of representing the intuitively permissible course of action as a maximizing action. In our case, maximizers could say that the reasonableness of stopping our search short of the expected best shoes is due to the overall expected gain in utility rather than being due to some supposedly rational attitude of frugality towards value as such. After all, if I were to keep shopping for shoes I would need to forego meeting my friend for coffee, have unpleasant interactions with other sales clerks, feel the agony of not knowing what my full outfit will look like for a few more hours, etc.

However, advocates of satisficing do not merely rely on examples. They often try to provide some kind of rationale that together with such examples would show a satisficing theory of rationality to be a well-motivated theory. Defenders of satisficing mainly rely on the limits of human cognitive faculties, special features of human agency, or certain types of values in generating such rationales.[3] But these theoretical defenses of satisficing face challenges of their own. In this chapter, I present in broad outlines the problems that satisficers typically face in defending their views. Then I present a very different kind of rationale for satisficing – one that does not depend on any of these limits, or peculiar features, of human agency. Rather, the defense of satisficing I propose depends only on very general features of practical rationality. For this very reason this view is not prone to any of the typical difficulties encountered in various attempts to make sense of satisficing. In particular, I argue that once we move our attention to rationality in *action* proper (rather than desires or preferences), especially long-term actions with indeterminate ends, we see that satisficing has a very important role to play in our understanding of rational agency.

A dilemma for satisficing

Most plausible versions of satisficing rules *permit* rather than obligate; no one claims that you ought to forego a (known) maximizing option

[3] Many proponents of satisficing argue in favor of ethical satisficing as a form of consequentialism that can survive the "demandingness objection." I am not concerned with such views. I am only concerned with satisficing as a general decision rule. For a survey and criticism of various possible versions of ethical satisficing, see B. Bradley, "Against Satisficing Consequentialism," *Utilitas* 18 (2) (2006), 97–108.

because a suboptimal option clears a certain acceptable threshold. Advocates of satisficing generally claim only that it is not irrational to do so.[4] So here are two possible satisficing rules:

> **General Satisficing Rule** (GSR): For any choice set C, there is an option O^t such that for every option O at least as good as O^t, if O is in C you may choose O (even if there is another option O^+ that is better than O in C) simply because O is at least as good as O^t.[5]

> **Restricted Satisficing Rule** (RSR): In some choice situations (you may) choose option O, even if there is an option O^+ available such that O^+ is better than O simply because in such a context one is allowed to choose any option that is at least as good as O^t and O is such an option.

GSR and RSR do not cover all the possible versions of satisficing; for instance, they eschew comparative versions in favor of absolute ones.[6] However, sticking to these principles allows us to avoid various complications that are ultimately irrelevant to the argument below. It is worth focusing on the explanatory clause to understand the difference between the two rules. GSR claims that rationality allows for the existence of basic "value thresholds"; that is, for the rational pursuit of certain actions in face of better options simply because these actions are "good enough." RSR, on the other hand, is not committed to the view that actions can be

4 Not all versions of satisficing formulate the rule as a permission. P. Pettit, "Satisficing Consequentialism," *Proceedings of the Aristotelian Society*, supplementary vol. 58 (1984), 139–76, for instance, proposes a rule that tells us to choose, roughly, the first choice above a certain threshold. However, in proposing a dilemma for satisficing, it is worth noting that it arises even for weaker views. It will also be clear in what follows that in the positive proposal I defend, the satisficing rule is indeed the only possible rational rule to follow, not because you are *required* not to maximize in these contexts, but because it is not *possible* to maximize in these contexts.

5 Neither O nor O^t needs to be in the set, so it is compatible with GSR that there are certain choices that you need to maximize, since you cannot reach the "good enough" threshold. A more precise definition would specify that O^t cannot be defined in terms of the maximizing action in each choice set or the maximal point in the agent's preference ordering, so that the maximizing rule does not turn out to be an instance of satisficing rules. An obvious way to do this would be to stipulate that O^t is never the maximal point in the agent's preference ordering and that replacing an option from C with another of higher utility does not change the value of O^t. Alternatively one could change the order of the quantifiers and stipulate that there is no unique value for O^t (other than the maximal point) across all choice sets. But it is easier to work with the simpler formula, so I will simply assume that one of these (or similar) stipulations hold.

6 See T. Hurka, "Two Kinds of Satisficing," *Philosophical Studies* 59 (1) (1990), 107–11, for the distinction. Nothing significant in our argument would be affected by looking into the comparative version.

made rational simply by being good enough; rather, RSR claims that particular features of a choice situation justify a permission to choose an option that is suboptimal. It is easier to see the difference between the two principles if we think of items in a choice set ranked in terms of a certain value. So, let us say C's members are all aesthetic experiences (let us say that this is a choice among contemplating various paintings). Now suppose that GSR determines for this case that any aesthetic experience that is as good as contemplating painting P is "good enough." Then, according to GSR, whenever I choose to contemplate a painting that is at least as good as P I am rational, even if I could have as easily chosen to contemplate a better painting instead.[7]

RSR, on the other hand, does not imply anything nearly as general. It will, perhaps, allow me to choose to contemplate a painting that is "good enough," if it would be difficult to deliberate about the various options on this occasion, or if I am under time pressure and I tend to be a terrible reasoner in pressure situations, etc., but it would not give me a blanket permission to choose a less valuable option over a certain threshold.

With this distinction in mind, we can put forward a basic dilemma for arguments for satisficing. GSR seems extremely implausible. It is hard to get behind the idea, for instance, that, in the absence of any competing considerations, I could choose the (equally priced, equally fattening, etc.) WORSE QUALITY ice-cream over the PREMIUM QUALITY one simply because WORSE QUALITY is good enough. On the other hand, if we do specify certain features of the context, satisficing becomes more plausible. If, as I am about to leave the store after having bought the WORSE QUALITY ice-cream, I see that a new shipment of PREMIUM QUALITY has arrived, it seems rationally permissible that I forego the opportunity to take advantage of their "Easy Refund, No Questions Asked" policy.

Similarly, to use one of the classic examples in support of satisficing, if I am trying to sell my house, it seems permissible that I settle for a certain monetary offer on the grounds that, say, \$150,000 is good enough, even if I expect that if I were to hold out for a better offer, I could probably get a larger amount. On the other hand, were a buyer to write down two offers, one of \$150,000 and one of \$160,000, it would be obviously irrational, *ceteris paribus*, to take the lower offer. The advocate of GSR cannot explain this difference; after all, if what made the first offer rationally permissible was simply the fact that it was good enough, it

[7] I am assuming that the choices are exclusive. In most situations, you would probably have a chance to look at both paintings.

should also make my choice of the lower offer permissible in the second scenario. The advocate of RSR has no problem, at least in principle, explaining the difference. The context that makes satisficing rational was present in the first case, but absent in the second. More specifically, in the first case, holding out for a better offer involves prolonged anxiety, unsettledness, etc.

However, once we made the advantages of RSR clear, we also made it apparently easy for maximizers to accounts for the phenomena. The maximizer can say that the agent is satisficing only from a *local* perspective: that she is, in our example, settling for a sale price that is merely good enough *relative to how much she could get for the house.* But getting as much money as she can for the house is only one of her goals and reflects only one aspect of her preference ordering. She also wants peace of mind, to avoid wasting her limited resources, etc. She is a local satisficer, but a *global* maximizer. In other words, she is settling for a good enough price since this way she maximizes her expected utility by taking into account also her preferences for not wasting too much time in the sale of the house, reducing anxiety, etc. The maximizer will gladly make a concession here. It might be that adopting a strategy of satisficing some goods is the best deliberative strategy. Given our limited resources, calculating expected utilities is prohibitively expensive; a global maximizer should often use local satisficing as a decision procedure.[8]

At first, this response seems to miss the mark. After all, the intuitive claim is that someone is permitted to choose from a large range of options that are good enough but not required. The idea is not that an agent *must* sell her house once she reaches a certain price, while knowing that she could get a better price. She *may* do so, but she is not required to do it. The intuitive thought is that it would be no less rational if she held out and waited to get a bit more money, and this would be as rational as if she held out for even more money, etc. Maximization would require either an implausible indifference curve among these options or that only one such action (or at least many fewer actions) would count as rationally acceptable.

[8] For this strategy, see D. Schmidtz, "Satisficing as a Humanly Rational Strategy," in Michael Byron (ed.), *Satisficing and Maximizing: Moral Theorists on Practical Reason* (New York: Cambridge University Press, 2004); H. A. Simon, "A Behavioral Model of Rational Choice," *Quarterly Journal of Economics* 69 (1) (1955), 99–118; and H. A. Simon, *Administrative Behavior*, 4th edn (New York: Free Press, 1997). Schmidtz and Simon are not defending what I will be calling "proper satisficing," so this is not a criticism of their views in particular.

But the maximizer can also reply to this objection. First, the need for a heuristic itself can already justify some kind of leeway in the range of options that will count as rationally optimal. If using a certain kind of heuristic is optimal, and the heuristics do not distinguish between various options that would otherwise have different utilities, then it is rational to choose any of the options that would be recommended by these heuristics. Moreover, arguably our ranking of states of affairs is incomplete or imprecise. The fact that none of these stopping points is rationally required might be just a reflection that our attitudes do not fully determine a precise tradeoff between, say, profit and convenience.

We can now see that there are at least three different rationales for satisficing that are fully compatible with a more general maximizing theory of rationality. First, *local* satisficing in relation to a certain good (trying to get enough money, bake a good enough cake, etc.) is compatible with *global* maximizing when all the agent's preferences are in. Second, a maximizing general theory can allow that we have *limited resources*, and thus satisficing might be an optimal decision procedure; that is, the decision procedure that has the highest expected utility. Finally, satisficing might be allowed in cases within "gaps" and "imprecisions" within our preference ordering.[9] Given the high level of idealization involved in the assumptions of orthodox expected utility theories, it is hardly contentious that they are not suitable to be universal decision procedures for actual agents. Thus, it is relatively easy to agree that, at least in some contexts, satisficing rules are our best guides. Given human agents' resource limitations and imperfections, an agent who adopts satisficing rules might do better, even if "doing better" is understood as "maximizing expected utility." We can assume widespread agreement with the claim that it makes sense for agents in certain circumstances at least to be *guided* by a rule of satisficing. However, insofar as the correctness of a satisficing rule depends on the fact that following such a rule maximizes expected utility, it is not, in my terms, a "proper" satisficing rule. A "proper" satisficing rule is a rule of instrumental rationality whose validity does not depend on its maximizing potential. From here on, I examine the possibility of proper satisficing rules.

[9] Strictly speaking, orthodox rational choice theory requires that one's preference ordering be complete. However, many of those who are otherwise sympathetic with maximizing theories of rationality have expressed doubts about the validity of this requirement. See, for instance, J. M. Joyce, *The Foundations of Causal Decision Theory* (New York: Cambridge University Press, 1999), and M. Kaplan, *Decision Theory as Philosophy* (New York: Cambridge University Press, 1998).

When to satisfice

A difficulty for satisficing arises from the above discussion. Suppose I identify, in a choice situation, an outcome O_s that is "good enough" and another one, O_m, with greater utility or value, that is the optimal point. Given that I know that O_m is better than O_s, how could it be rational to choose O_s over O_m? Here it seems that saying that O_s is good enough is completely unsatisfactory. Rather than insisting that rationality requires only that we choose an outcome that is good enough, most advocates of satisficing try to identify features of certain choice situations that are not given their due by the maximization procedure. So perhaps there is a virtue of moderation that requires us not to maximize;[10] perhaps our psychology is such that we evaluate things from perspectives not fully accounted for by maximizing;[11] perhaps satisficing (or at least some version of it) might make it easier to accommodate value incommensurability.[12] These views have a common strategy: they accept that, from a certain perspective, maximizing provides the correct choice of action, but given peculiar features of human psychology or the nature of value, the maximizing conception turns out to be a partial one. A maximizing conception, on these views, makes certain important considerations invisible to the rational agent. However, these approaches have some shortcomings: they depend on substantive assumptions about the nature of value or about our "evaluative psychology," or they need to defend satisficing as a second-best strategy for beings with limited cognitive powers. I propose here a different view. It is part of the very nature of the instrumental theory of rationality that a maximizing conception cannot be a general theory of instrumental rationality, especially if we focus on the rationality of *actions* rather than of *decisions*. We need only very minimal assumptions about ends to show that maximizing is an option only for a subset of actions and that a more general theory of rationality must incorporate at least certain permissions that are incompatible with a general maximizing theory. I hope to show that a rational agent could not obey the principle of instrumental reasoning in most circumstances without being guided by a rule of satisficing.

[10] M. Slote, "Satisficing Consequentialism," *Proceedings of the Aristotelian Society*, supplementary vol. 58 (1989), 139–63. Slote has changed his views on this matter since: see Slote, "Two Views of Satisficing," in Byron, *Satisficing and Maximizing*, 14–29.

[11] M. Weber, "A New Defense of Satisficing," in Byron, *Satisficing and Maximizing*, 77–105.

[12] M. Byron, "Simon's Revenge: or, Incommensurability and Satisficing," *Analysis* 65 (288) (2005), 311–15.

Orthodox rational choice theory requires that our preference ordering must be fully determinate so that for any lotteries L_1 and L_2, either $L_1 \geq L_2$ or $L_2 \geq L_1$. As we said above, this is an assumption that many philosophers find suspect. It is often agreed that a rational agent need not have a definite preference between some outcomes, let alone between probability distributions over outcomes. There is widespread agreement that the agent's attitudes such as preferences or ends might be fully rational without being fully determinate. More importantly, orthodox rational choice theory idealizes away an important set of ends and projects we have: namely, indeterminate (or not fully determinate) ends that are pursued not in a moment but through a long series of momentary actions.[13]

All, or at least nearly all, our ends are indeterminate and need to be pursued through actions that extend through time. Even rather simple actions such as baking a cake cannot be completed in a single momentary action. Given that I have no access to a miracle mixture, I must bake a cake through a series of actions that will span intervals in which I will be doing nothing that is instrumental to baking a cake (taking a break, answering the doorbell, etc.).[14] Moreover, our end in baking a cake will be in various ways indeterminate or vague: what counts as an edible cake (or a cake at all), how long it should take to bake, how large it should be, etc., is not precisely determined.

Suppose, for instance, that Mary has the end of running a marathon. There is a great deal that is indeterminate about her end. First, of course, there are many opportunities to run a marathon. Doubtless, if she waits too long to do it she will not achieve her end; however, there is a range of time in which any marathon she completes within that time would count as reaching her goal. She also does not necessarily set on a particular time she thinks she needs to complete a marathon, even if there are obvious

[13] I discuss these ends in S. Tenenbaum and D. Raffman, "Vague Projects and the Puzzle of the Self-Torturer," *Ethics* 123 (1) (2012), 86–112, and S. Tenenbaum, "Akrasia and Irrationality," in T. O'Connor and C. Sandis (eds.), *A Companion to the Philosophy of Action* (Malden, MA: Wiley-Blackwell, 2010), 74–82. They are often referred to in these papers as "vague ends" or "vague projects." My view is that vague ends constitute a proper subset of indeterminate ends, but nothing here depends on this. The discussion below is a summary of the more detailed discussion in these papers.

[14] On this issue, see K. Falvey, "Knowledge in Intention," *Philosophical Studies* 99 (1) (2000), 21–44. Tenenbaum, "Akrasia and Irrationality," and S. Tenenbaum, *Appearances of the Good: An Essay on the Nature of Practical Reason* (Cambridge University Press, 2007).

scenarios in which she would not have achieved her goal of running a marathon simply because it took her too long to cover 26.2 miles. Moreover, in such cases, how to achieve the goal is also vague and indeterminate. It is not clear how many minutes of training Mary needs to be ready to run a marathon, and when her training will happen; she needs a balanced diet, but she can sometimes eat cake and ice-cream; as she is running the marathon, she might start very fast, or somewhat fast; etc. In fact, we might notice something important about Mary's momentary decisions as she is pursuing this end. Suppose she needs to decide whether she is going to go out right now for a run. Given the indeterminacy and vagueness of the situation, it seems that at any time she might, say, spend one more second singing instead of going out for her run.

Of course, if she does this continuously, at some time it will be too late to go for a run on this day, but since one missed day of running is unlikely to make a difference to her chances of being ready to run a marathon, these choices will not be incompatible with successfully running a marathon. Surely, if she does this every day, at the end she will no longer be in position to run a marathon in a way that would count as successfully fulfilling her goal. But there might be no precise point at which this happens, or if there is, Mary might never be in a position to know that she is at that point. And, of course, if she is past the point at which she can still get herself ready to run a marathon, it would be perfectly rational for her to keep on singing; after all, since she has already failed in her end of running a marathon, there is no point in missing out on an opportunity to sing. In such a case, the following might obtain: given that postponing running for a second does not make a (significant) difference to her aim of being ready to run a marathon, and given that, say, at any moment **m** she prefers singing at **m** over running at **m**, it might be that for a certain interval, at each moment it is rational for her to sing rather than run. However, if she chooses to sing at every moment during that interval, she will not be ready to run a marathon, and she might prefer to be able to run a marathon than to sing on any number of occasions, and this preference might be one that she has stably throughout this whole interval. Assuming that there is nothing wrong with Mary's ends and preferences,[15] if Mary always chooses to sing, her

[15] One might think that we have already indicated what is wrong with Mary's ends and preferences: they are vague and indeterminate. However, given that nearly all our ends are indeterminate in this way, one needs to give a compelling reason why indeterminacy or vagueness suffices to make an end irrational.

choices will be overall irrational without any of her momentary choices being irrational. After all if she never trains for a marathon her choices lead her to an outcome that she regards as clearly unacceptable, given her original options.[16]

Given these facts about Mary's ends, we can say that her ends allow for the possibility of *top-down irrationality*;[17] namely the possibility that the rationality of a set of momentary actions does not supervene on the rationality of each momentary action. But since Mary's end does not *require* that she runs at any particular moment, but if she fails to do this at every moment she will not have pursued efficient means to her end, it seems that what instrumental rationality demands with respect to such ends is that she be permitted to run even if running is not her most preferred momentary action, since the cumulative effect of always choosing her most preferred action leads to the choice of a less preferred option. I propose that actions that one performs within a range of time when one is pursuing a long-term, indeterminate end or project need to be evaluated from two distinct (but compatible) perspectives; a perfectly (instrumentally) rational agent is never deemed irrational by either perspective. A punctate perspective evaluates whether a momentary choice or action is rational, given the agent's various preferences and ends. For our purposes, all that matters is that a punctate perspective will permit the agent to choose her most preferred momentary action, but will also permit the agent to forego her most preferred action in favor of pursuing actions that are constitutive of the pursuit of the agent's long-term, indeterminate ends. Were it not for such permissions, the agent in the above example would need to sing at every moment, and thus would not be able to run a marathon (an option that, according to our stipulation, the agent considers to be unacceptable at every moment in the relevant time interval).

The *extended* perspective evaluates whether enough of these permissions have been exercised and thus the end has been achieved. So if our

[16] One must tread carefully here, given that, if I am correct about Mary's ends and preferences, her preferences are not transitive. I think the right thing to say here is that Mary is irrational if she never trains for a marathon because she ends up with a choice that she knows to be *unacceptable*. For the notion of acceptability in question, see Tenenbaum and Raffman, "Vague Projects."

[17] I discuss the possibility of top-down irrationality in S. Tenenbaum, "The Vice of Procrastination," in Chrisoula Andreou and Mark White (eds.), *The Thief of Time* (New York: Oxford University Press, 2010), 130–50; Tenenbaum, "Akrasia and Irrationality"; and Tenenbaum and Raffman, "Vague Projects." The points I make in the rest of this paragraph are discussed in more detail in these works.

agent does not train on enough occasions, she will be unable to run the marathon. Although at each point she will have chosen something that from the punctate perspective she was permitted to choose, she will have violated a requirement from the extended perspective: the requirement to take the means to an end that she held stable through the whole extent of the time interval in question. So although we cannot locate her irrationality at any particular moment in time, the extended perspective deems that she has acted irrationally by failing to take the necessary means to one of her long-term ends. This is obviously just a very rough sketch of how principles of instrumental reasoning apply to long-term, indeterminate ends, but hopefully it will be enough for our purposes.

Getting some satisficing

Nothing we have said so far rules out the possibility that Mary could also train for the marathon non-stop and never spend any time singing. The punctate perspective allows an agent to exercise permissions not to choose her most preferred action. But since we imposed no limits on how often those permissions can be exercised, Mary could *always* choose to go running rather than singing. Given what we know of human nature, this is rather unlikely, but nothing we have said so far would make it irrational for Mary to choose this alternative. But assuming that Mary does have singing as one of her ends, always exercising such permissions would also be a violation of instrumental rationality.

Let us look for a moment at what seems to be an intrinsic limitation of the principle of instrumental reasoning, at least if we think of that principle as the sole principle of instrumental rationality. Mary has two ends: singing and running a marathon (or the instrumental end of getting ready to run the marathon). At this level of abstraction, these ends are fully compatible. But each of these ends has a certain internal structure: for each of them there are better and worse realizations of the end. As far as the end of running a marathon is concerned, a faster marathon is better than a slower one, certain courses are better than others, etc. If no other end were relevant to one's life, one would train as much as one could without risking injury, would eat only those foods that would not interfere with one's training, would never wear uncomfortable shoes, etc. One's life purpose in this case would finish as one crossed the finish line.

We can think of the somewhat different end of being a marathon runner, in which this gloomy outcome would not be necessary. The end of a run would only signal the beginning of a new training regimen in preparation for the next one.

Like being a marathon runner, singing has an internal structure that never fails to give meaning to one's life. There is no point at which singing reaches its natural stopping point, but it is always "complete" at any point when one stops singing. If I stop my marathon training too early, I will have failed to achieve the end for which I was training (namely, completing a marathon). But no matter when I stop singing, I will not have failed to realize the end of singing. And if I keep training for a marathon after I have run it, I will just be wasting time (unless I aim to run another one); but if I keep singing, I will keep realizing the end of singing. "Singing" is one of the verbs that fall under the category that Vendler calls "activity terms": roughly, those terms that refer to activities which are complete in themselves and do not have an end outside themselves.[18]

But it now seems that circumstances will abound in which the principle of instrumental reasoning will fail to provide any determinate guidance to an agent. After all, if the agent has conflicting ends, she will have to violate the principle of instrumental reasoning. On this understanding of the end of singing, there is nothing about it that dictates that its pursuit should ever terminate, and thus the pursuit of any end that cannot coexist in time with singing conflicts with my unrestricted end of singing.[19] Moreover, as we know all too well, singing can be done better or worse. Admittedly some shower soloists seem completely oblivious to the quality of their singing, but, in general, having singing as an end, and caring about how it sounds, go hand in hand. If you are among those unfortunate souls who cannot run and sing at the same time, or if you cannot do both just as well concomitantly as in isolation, you cannot, insofar as you are rational, adopt the (unrestricted) end of singing and the end of being a marathon runner. However, the principle of instrumental reasoning says nothing about how you should proceed to revise your ends in such cases.

[18] See Z. Vendler, "Verbs and Times," *Philosophical Review* 66 (2) (1957), 143–60, and see also A. P. Mourelatos, "Events, Processes, and States," *Linguistics and Philosophy* 2 (3) (1978), 415–34. My usage departs slightly from Vendler's. One could take issue with many of the things I say about "singing" and "training for a marathon," but (hopefully) these issues will not matter to the general argument.

[19] One could have as an end singing just for a minute, or from time to time. My only point is that nothing about having singing as an end mandates this structure. However, it is worth noting that for the main purpose of the chapter such ends could also be used; we would only need to fill in more of the story to ensure that there was potential conflict.

Such cases of conflict explain the attraction of moving from a traditional conception of instrumental rationality to a more modern one.[20] The traditional conception of rationality takes the instrumental principle of rationality to be the sole principle of rationality, so it has willing (or pursuing) ends, rather than preferences, as the fundamental attitude to which the principles of instrumental rationality apply. In its primary application, it is not comparative; it simply determines that certain means must be taken (or suffice) for the achievement of a certain end. In this primary instance the only comparative judgments that follow from the principles of instrumental rationality are rather trivial ones; they (nearly) all have the form "it is better to pursue necessary means X to your end Y than not to pursue it." If our ends do have the kind of internal structure I have been suggesting above, they are capable of generating some preferences, and instrumental rationality will be able to make some non-trivial comparative judgments. Typically, when one is building a house as an end, one aims to build an excellent house. So, arguably, commitment to the end already commits one to prefer means that deliver a comfortable house over means that deliver a barely liveable one. The nature of my end in building a house and the instrumental principle suffice to determine a certain partial ordering internal to this pursuit. For instance, *ceteris paribus*, given the empirical facts about construction, insofar as a rational agent aims to build a house, she will prefer to use bricks over papier mâché.

It is worth distinguishing between the claim I am making here and a similar claim made by Korsgaard.[21] Korsgaard says that because a house has constitutive standards, in adopting the end of building a house we are also committed to building a good house. Even a shoddy builder, if he is building a house at all, must be bound by the norms of good house

[20] Of course moving to a theory that favors preference ordering as opposed to ends provides for greater ease in accounting for risk. If what we say here is correct, this is an illusory advantage; if rationality does not mandate anything that approximates a preference ranking in the case in which we have certainty, it will certainly not do it once we introduce risk. However, the view put forward here still allows that an end could determine a preference ordering even with the sufficient precision necessary for a utility measure. Given that we allow that an end does generate a preference ordering internal to itself, there is no reason to think that there is in principle any limit to how precise or fine-grained such ordering would be. Similar things apply to the case of very general means such as money or power. Of course, one would like a more general theory of rationality under risk, but we have to leave this task for another occasion.

[21] C. Korsgaard, *Self-Constitution: Agency, Identity, and Integrity* (New York: Oxford University Press, 2009).

building.[22] I agree with Korsgaard that there is a characteristic function of building a house that determines to some extent that some houses are better than others. Moreover, typically, when one adopts the end of building a house, one adopts the end of building something precisely because it has this function. In such cases, abstracting from competing ends, adopting such an end requires that one choose the better house over the worse house. However, nothing we say here commits us to the view that *everyone* who builds a house must adopt precisely this end. Someone might be building a historically accurate house or a highly profitable house; the fact that a better house is insulated with polyethylene ground cover might be of no practical significance to either builder. There is a broader question of whether any end we adopt will provide grounds for similar comparative judgments relative to the end; again, for our purposes, we need not commit to an answer to this question. But it is important to note that we should not expect that such comparative judgments would always yield anything approximating to a complete ordering: although some houses are clearly better than the others, there are many that are not clearly comparable with respect to the end of house building.

At least in the case of a single end, the comparative judgments needed are, at least in part, readily available. But in exactly these cases we do not need to appeal to an independent preference ranking; the instrumental principle and the ranking generated by the end will fully account for the relevant rational requirements. However, when we come back to different ends, it is not clear what can we avail ourselves of to determine a ranking of options. The two ends, singing and marathon running, conflict, but there is no end of singing-while-marathon-racing that generates an internal ordering (or if there were, we would be looking at an altogether different case).

Since I cannot be fully committed to singing and to running a marathon such that I always choose both the best option from the point of view of running and singing, instrumental rationality requires that I do not pursue both singing and running a marathon in this unrestricted manner. But we cannot appeal to the hyphenated end to determine what would be the sufficient or best means to pursue the end of singing-while-marathon-racing; there is nothing in the nature of either end (or both ends considered together) that determines how the conflict should be

[22] C. Korsgaard, "Acting for a Reason," in Korsgaard (ed.), *The Constitution of Agency* (New York: Oxford University Press 2008), 207–31, and Korsgaard, *Self-Constitution*, 113.

resolved. So, the only unambiguous recommendation in this case for a rational agent is to revise her ends, given that the pursuit of each end in an unrestricted manner is not a coherent possibility.

But nothing so far follows about how they should be revised: that is, how much importance should be accorded to each end such that I know when I should choose to sing and when I should choose to train; when I should rest and when I should take a risk of injury and navigate through treacherous terrain so that I can keep my appointment with my singing coach; etc. One might say that given what has been said so far, any way in which I revise my ends is fine as long as I no longer have conflicting ends. I have much sympathy for this view, but if this is the correct view, we have no reason to appeal to preference ordering. After all, once the ends are no longer in conflict, we can go back to using the traditional conception of instrumental rationality, and let our decisions be guided by the ends themselves. So, for instance, if I revise my ends so that I am just training to complete one marathon and to sing a few hours per week, it seems that I need no further rules of rationality than the instrumental rule: pursue the means to each of these ends. As we will see in a moment, things are a bit more complicated, but so far we have not seen why a preference ordering would be necessary.

Another route to introducing preference ordering would be to argue that (instrumental) practical reason cannot be neutral regarding adjudicating between potentially conflicting ends. In other words, there must be something in the nature of these two ends or the agent's attitudes towards them that determines their relative importance and consequently a preference ordering. There are two basic arguments one can give for such a conclusion. One can argue that there is some feature of the attitude of having an end that will necessarily give rise to a preference ordering. Such an argument might proceed from a general conception of the nature of motivational states, or desires. On this view, desires are not distinguished from each other simply by their content; they are also held with different degrees of intensity. My desire to sing might be very strong, while my desire to run a marathon might be very weak.

We cannot examine such views in detail, but the problems should be quite obvious. If "strong" and "weak" are being used in a non-question-begging way (namely, if we are not identifying "strong" with "there is a strong instrumental reason to pursue it"), it is unclear why instrumental rationality would recommend that preferences track strengths of desire. One could add a principle of rationality that mandates that one pursue one's desires in proportion to strength, or a theory of reasons which implies a requirement of this form, but such principles and theories are not part of a theory of instrumental rationality.

Let us grant that insofar as it is possible to ascribe a complete preference ordering to an agent, then an instrumentally rational agent will maximize utility (when utility is understood as a measure of preference). Suppose, for instance, we can identify a preference ordering for an agent for choices between apples, pears, and bananas. We assume that in such a case the agent will be instrumentally rational insofar as she maximizes utility with respect to her choices among these items. Here a maximizing rule would determine the choices of the agent in a way that goes much beyond any constraints that can be imposed by the principle of instrumental reasoning. I have been suggesting so far that nothing about the nature of practical rationality implies that a rational agent, even an ideally instrumentally rational agent, must have a preference ordering that is determinate enough to imply any constraints beyond those determined by the principle of instrumental reasoning.

But one might now think that it is exceedingly easy to attribute a preference ordering to a rational agent. In fact, we have an effective procedure to determine the preference ordering of any agent to any arbitrary degree of precision: namely, Ramsey's procedure.[23] The procedure asks an agent to make choices between various outcomes in hypothetical choice situations. So a decision theorist with too much time on her hands could ask me a large number of questions about various tradeoffs I would be willing to make between lotteries involving various episodes of singing and various training episodes (and other things that I might be interested in) until she can form a complete preference ordering. But the in-principle availability of such a Ramsey procedure does little to establish the importance of its potential outputs for a theory of rationality. There is no guarantee that my answers are tracking anything significant: there is no reason to think that they are tracking any robust behavioral dispositions, let alone anything that has any relevance to our theory of instrumental rationality.[24]

One might argue that there must be something about the ends that determines the relative importance of each end for the agent, so that in having ends we must be committed to at least some kind of rough preference ordering. After all, we do not take all our ends to be equal.

[23] F. P. Ramsey, "Truth and Probability," in *The Foundations of Mathematics and Other Logical Essays* (New York: Harcourt, Brace, 1931), 156–98.

[24] See Joyce, *The Foundations of Causal Decision Theory*, for a similar point.

We certainly think that some of them should be given very high priority over others: my end of providing a good education for my children takes considerable precedence over my end of growing sunflowers in my garden. It is undeniable that certain ends are more important than others for the agent; the question is, however, whether this fact should supervene simply on the attitudes the agents have in holding each end. In other words, the proposals we are looking at claim that *simply in virtue of having each of these ends* (or at least of having these ends in a certain manner), the agent will also have preferences that express the relative importance of each of these ends to an arbitrary degree of precision. But this is rather implausible. The relative importance of each end should be understood as a further attitude that the agent might or might not have: namely, a second-order end to give priority to one end over another.[25]

A different line of argument in favor of the idea that a theory of instrumental rationality should rely on preference orderings rather than ends is more interesting and important for our purposes. If an agent's ends cannot be each pursued in an unrestricted manner and yet they do not determine a preference ordering, how would a rational agent determine what to do in such situations? Even if all that an agent is required to do is to revise her ends, she must determine how she will adjudicate between the incompatible demands of the original ends. The peace treaty between the warring ends must determine the borders as precisely as possible; it should determine which of my actions will belong to singing and which to training for the marathon. But this means that the revised ends are just a preference ordering determining in which situations I choose singing over training and vice versa.

I do not think that there is any determinate answer to the question of how a merely instrumentally rational agent must proceed in cases in which her ends conflict; in my book, instrumental rationality requires nothing more than that the agent revise her ends so as to end the conflict. The true *substantive* theory of rationality or the good might have something to say about this; perhaps singing is more important than running; perhaps we need to live a balanced life; possibly a human being must do whatever gives her most pleasure in such situations. But these considerations are beyond the scope of a theory of instrumental rationality.

[25] Of course, these attitudes could be grounded on other attitudes or judgments of the agent: perhaps they are grounded on the agent's evaluative belief or the agent's identification with some ends but not others. But this attitude is not rationally required simply by having (or by the manner one has) the ends in question.

However, I will not argue for these claims here. What matters for my purposes is that we can end the conflict without relying on anything as richly detailed as a complete preference ordering. One could also simply adopt instead restricted ends such as "enough singing given that I am also training for a marathon" and "enough training given that I am also a singer." These are vague or indeterminate ends, but, as we said above, there is nothing intrinsically irrational about having ends with this kind of structure. And they need not conflict; one could succeed in the pursuit of each of them. In fact, this is the most natural (and certainly the minimal) way of resolving the conflict: restricting each end in light of the pursuit of the other.

This minimal revision leaves us with two vague or indeterminate ends, and because of this structure there will be no point at which it will be the *maximum* amount of singing I could have done while still being able to train for the marathon. At each point, singing for a millisecond longer would not affect my marathon running, or, at the very least, I would never be in a position to know that it would. If at each millisecond, I had the thought "one millisecond longer will make no difference" and kept on singing, at some point I would realize that it was too late to train for a marathon. Given the possibility of top-down irrationality discussed above, the pursuit of our revised ends to a *maximum*, insofar as we can make sense of the idea, or to pursue our most preferred option at every moment, would be necessarily self-defeating. Thus when evaluating over a period of time whether I was successful in my pursuit of the ends of singing and training for a marathon, the criterion for success could not be whether I reached the greatest amount of singing or training or a maximum point in some function that combines both. I will be successful in my pursuits instead if I have done – well – *enough* singing and training. And since non-accidental success in the achievement of an end should suffice for determining that an agent does not run afoul of any principles of instrumental rationality, we can say that instrumental rationality requires no more than that I satisfice. That is, I should pursue singing until my singing is "good enough" and I should train until my training is good enough; rationality is here judged in terms of whether the agent has passed a certain vague minimal point, not in terms of whether she has reached a maximal point.

This might look like local satisficing, rather than proper satisficing; after all, we are not saying that the agent should choose an action that is good enough *simpliciter* or that has more than a certain minimum amount of utility, but rather that in pursuit of each separate end, she should ensure that she reaches, as it were, a minimum level of each. However, it makes sense to say that a theory should recommend only local satisficing, if local satisficing can be contrasted with global maximizing. But there is no level in the theory in which any kind of maximization is taken to be an ideal.[26] If there is a global measurement of assessment it is also a satisficing one, at least in a natural reading of "satisficing." Global success will be something like "achieve all ends to an acceptable level" or "engage in enough singing, enough training, etc." In either case, global requirements will also be requirements to achieve a certain (vague) minimum threshold.

Notice that we came to the conclusion only by looking at the structure of the ends of a rational agent; we made no assumptions about her computational powers, how much leisure she has to crunch numbers, etc. In sum, a satisficing rule here is the right rule given a perfectly rational set of ends, or a perfectly rational structure of pursuits. If we are right that there is nothing amiss with such ends from the point of view of instrumental rationality, we have shown that satisficing is not just a blunt tool used by limited rational beings operating in a world full of friction. It is, at least in some cases, also the correct rule for a perfectly instrumentally rational agent acting in a frictionless world.

Getting more satisficing

So far we looked only at what we called above "the extended perspective." We saw that in order for an agent to realize ends that are potentially conflicting and indeterminate or vague, the agent will have to use a satisficing criterion of success. But when we look more closely at the structure mandated by ends that introduce the possibility of top-down

[26] Of course, this rules out the possibility that satisficing can be defined in terms of a threshold of utility. H. S. Richardson, "Satisficing: Not Good Enough," in Byron, *Satisficing and Maximizing*, raises this as a more general problem for satisficing. I have tried to avoid relying on a specific satisficing rule, but I should note that, obviously, the views presented here are not compatible with defining satisficing in terms of any kind of precise threshold. To make it fully compatible with the views defended in Tenenbaum, "The Vice of Procrastination," and Tenenbaum and Raffman, "Vague Projects," we should define the basic rule of satisficing relative to an end E something like "Choose an option that is not an unacceptable realization of E and does not prevent the acceptable realization of your other ends." Further refinements are needed, but here I just want to argue for the general plausibility of defending a satisficing rule in this manner. See Tenenbaum, "The Vice of Procrastination," and Tenenbaum and Raffman, "Vague Projects," for further discussion of the notion of "acceptable" employed here.

irrationality, it becomes clear that in the punctate perspective, something like a satisficing standard also plays an essential role in determining what should count as rational action. Let us take, for instance, decisions I make in various circumstances in which I would prefer to do something on each occasion, but for which the cumulative effect of always choosing the most preferred (momentary) option is disastrous. Let us take, for instance, eating. I do not (or at least let us assume I do not) have a long-term vague end or project with respect to gastronomic pleasures. However, at various moments I enjoy eating, especially fatty or sweet foods. If we look at my momentary decisions, I prefer, over a long period of time, to continue eating these foods rather than stop. After all, one more bite of food will not make a difference to my overall health and looks, and it takes quite a bit of time for me to be so sated that I prefer to refrain from having just one more bite of something totally delicious.

Yet this pattern of activity, as we know only too well, has disastrous consequences.[27] If I am right about the possibility of top-down irrationality, this is clearly a pattern of choice situations that allows for this kind of irrationality. At every momentary choice, it might be rational to choose to eat more, but if I always make those choices, my health will certainly suffer in ways that are not compensated by the additional gastronomic pleasures. A rational agent will stop maximizing at some point, even though at this point he could do better (by taking just one more bite). In the view I proposed above, the pursuit of the end of leading a healthy life will generate permissions in the punctate perspective to pursue this end even when it does not maximize utility. In fact, it seems that an agent could exercise this permission whenever confronted with some kind of fatty or sweet food: the agent might simply refuse anything that is not a constitutive item of a healthy diet.

But this would be a sad aspect of one's life, and nothing about the ends of the agent dictates such sadness. The end of having a healthy life, for most of us, is fully compatible with a few indulgences. However, pursuing one's most preferred option (or the best option) at every single momentary choice *is* incompatible with a healthy life. The reasonable agent will indulge here and there while making sure that his indulgences are not unduly jeopardizing his health. But the only way to do this is to stop indulging when one has done it *enough* times. In other words, a rational agent does not exercise a permission to forego a gastronomic pleasure

[27] This pattern is discussed in more detail in Tenenbaum and Raffman, "Vague Projects."

from here on (by, say, letting the server take his plate) until he has enjoyed *enough* gastronomic pleasure, or until he has failed to exercise this permission enough times. Although it is harder to characterize this rational constraint on more traditional satisficing terms, something like the following satisficing rule seems correct:

> In the relevant context, exercise permissions to pursue end E only to the extent that doing so allows you to pursue often enough your momentary preferences.

If I am right, "often enough" cannot be replaced by a precise threshold. But if I am right, postulating precise thresholds is the wrong way to characterize and defend the intuitive idea that, even when better options are available, the rational agent is often satisfied with an outcome or action that is good enough.

Conclusion

If we start with the assumption that expected utility theory is the overall correct theory of rationality, a decided improvement over earlier theories of instrumental rationality, satisficing seems like either a quaint request to be contented with less than we could have, something reminiscent of monkish ideals of self-mortification and abnegation, or at least a resigned recognition of our limited cognitive powers. I have been urging that the mistake is in accepting this assumption without further ado. Pursuing what is just good enough (or some precisification of this idea) is the only possible advice in the context of the extended pursuit of indeterminate ends. When we think of the rationality of *actions* rather than of *decisions* or *preferences*, we wonder how often anything is done that falls outside this context. After all, actions are extended through time, and our actions are particulars, whereas the content of our intentions is general. Perhaps long-term indeterminate ends are not only something that is possible for a rational agent, but are just the kind of ends that rational agents (or at least rational agents that do not have intellectual intuitions) necessarily have. But defending this final claim is a project for another occasion.

3

Interpretation without intentions

HEIDI M. HURD

Not all originalists are intentionalists. But all intentionalists are originalists. And certainly many originalists are intentionalists, for the impulses that lead scholars to embrace originalism in constitutional and statutory interpretation also often incline them to give it an intentionalist turn.[1] Those who defend some form of originalism typically do so because they believe that the rule of law requires the past to rule the present. Some originalists take this thesis to be a conceptual truism: law is not law at all if those who are charged with its application can alter its scope or meaning by bringing to its interpretation things foreign to it at the time of its enactment. Other originalists take the bonds between originalism and the rule of law to be of a moral sort: the values that lie behind the rule of law – liberty, fairness, and equality – are best protected by interpreting laws in a manner that does not permit their meaning to change with time. Finally, some would cast their defence of originalism in political terms, arguing that democracy demands a separation between rule-making and adjudicative powers – a separation that makes it a judicial usurpation of the role of the lawmaker to interpret an enactment in ways that depart from its past meaning.

Special thanks to Larry Alexander and Emily Sherwin for inspiring this piece, and for indulging me in many engaging disputes about its topic. Thanks also to George Pavlakos and Veronica Rodriguez-Blanco for organizing the workshop on "Legal Normativity and the Philosophy of Practical Reason" at the XXV World Congress of Philosophy of Law at Goethe University in Frankfurt, Germany, where workshop participants advanced probing questions and penetrating arguments that helped hone the thesis I here defend.

[1] Indeed, many originalists identify originalism with intentionalism, either because they do not recognize that originalism both conceptually and normatively permits non-intentionalist construals, or because they take intentionalism to be so obvious a theory of interpretation to pair with their originalism as to link the two as though they were one. See, e.g., T. Smith, "Originalism's Misplaced Fidelity: 'Original' Meaning Is Not Objective," *Constitutional Commentary* 26 (2009), 1–57, defining originalism as the thesis "that the meaning of the Constitution should be settled by reference to the original understanding of those who enacted it."

All of these arguments for originalism have been advanced, as well, for intentionalism, and many intentionalists would insist that a theory of interpretation that appeals to authorial intentions best honors the reasons for defending originalism. While they must admit that originalists might appeal, instead, to authorial values, or to the mental states possessed by the original audience to an enactment, they commonly insist that intentionalist interpretation best protects against the sort of "judicial legislation" that threatens the values of liberty, fairness, and equality. Thus, while originalism and intentionalism are distinct, their marriage is so common as to make an inquiry into the one a useful means of gaining the measure of the other.

It is my project in this chapter to examine the ability of intentionalism to make good on its promises to originalism. This is not a novel project for me. I have elsewhere taken on intentionalism (and the versions of originalism that presuppose it) in several other scholarly contexts.[2] In this chapter, I want to examine a fresh defence of intentionalism that reveals both why intentionalism remains persistently attractive, and why it (persistently) fails us as a method of legal interpretation. The defence in question was published by Professors Larry Alexander and Emily Sherwin in their provocative book, *Demystifying Legal Reasoning*.[3] If Alexander and Sherwin succeed in advancing a defensible account of intentionalism, then those who are attracted to originalism can be assured that there is at least one brand of (intentionalist) originalism that is philosophically reliable. If their effort to vindicate intentionalism fails, however, then I take it that originalists must either defend an alternative intentionalist theory from the sorts of criticisms that defeat the theory advanced by Alexander and Sherwin, or retreat to a kind of

[2] H. M. Hurd, *Moral Combat* (Cambridge University Press, 1999), 140–6, 158–68; Hurd, "Living in the Past: Burkean Conservatism and Originalist Interpretation," in Jeffrey Goldsworthy and Tom Campbell (eds.), *Legal Interpretation, Judicial Supremacy, and Democracy* (Aldershot: Ashgate, 2001), 173–206; Hurd, "Interpreting Authorities," in Andrei Marmor (ed.), *Law and Interpretation* (Oxford University Press, 1995), 405–32; Hurd, "Sovereignty in Silence," *Yale Law Journal* 99 (1992), 945–1028.

[3] L. Alexander and E. Sherwin, *Demystifying Legal Reasoning* (Cambridge University Press, 2008), 131–232. Earlier versions of the argument advanced in *Demystifying Legal Reasoning* can be found in L. Alexander and E. Sherwin, *The Rule of Rules: Rules, Principles, and Dilemmas of Law* (Durham, NC: Duke University Press, 2001), ch. 5; L. Alexander and E. Sherwin, "Interpreting Rules: The Nature and Limits of Inchoate Intentions," in Goldsworthy and Campbell, *Legal Interpretation in Democratic States*, 3–28; L. Alexander, "All or Nothing at All: The Intentions of Authorities and the Authority of Intentions," in Marmor, *Law and Interpretation*, 357–404.

originalism that does not place interpretive weight on the intentions with which lawmakers originally crafted their enactments. The first of these prospects seems unpromising, in large part because, as I shall argue, most (if not all) intentionalist options get exhausted in the course of sorting out the merits of Alexander's and Sherwin's particular version of intentionalism, and are thus unavailable as alternatives. And while I will not pursue the matter here, the second means of defending originalism also appears problematic – in large part because efforts to unpack the meaning of laws by appealing to historical facts beyond lawmakers' intentions threaten the clarity, predictability, and democratic pedigree of laws far more than they protect such rule-of-law values. It thus seems to me that the defensibility of Alexander's and Sherwin's intentionalism is a barometer of the defensibility of originalism more generally.

Framing the issues

In addition to articulating a defensible account of the nature of the intentions to which adjudicators should appeal when resolving questions of legal interpretation, intentionalists must protect a number of exposed philosophical flanks against attacks by those who hold non-intentionalist theories of interpretation. First, they must defend their intentionalism against those who would elevate the "plain meaning" of a text over the intentions of its authors when the two are in conflict. Second, they must do battle with those who are prepared to set aside both the plain meaning of a law and its authors' intentions when so doing will better serve "the spirit of the law," construed functionally, rather than intentionally. Third, they must rally against those who would resolve interpretive questions in light of contemporary, conventional values ("the evolving standards of decency that mark the progress of a maturing society,"[4] or "the basic mores of society"[5]), rather than on the basis of the law's plain meaning, authorial intentions, or functional "spirit." And finally, they must defend their intentionalism against the challenges of those who believe that the language of the law ought to be interpreted in light of the best theory available of the natural kinds, natural rights, and natural obligations to which the law refers, so as to ensure that the demands of law

[4] *Trop* v. *Dulles*, 356 US 86, 101 (1958).

[5] *Furman* v. *Georgia*, 408 US 238, 382 (1972); *Kennedy* v. *Louisiana*, 554 US 407, 408 (2008).

approximate as closely as possible the true demands of morality (not just contemporary conventional beliefs about those demands).

There are times when Alexander and Sherwin write as though they can win out against each of these opponents by definition alone.[6] As they repeatedly insist, as if it were an obvious truism, "If one is interpreting, one is seeking the author's intended meaning. When one is constructing a meaning that may not be the meaning intended by the author . . . one is not interpreting but establishing a rule."[7] Were it tautologically true that interpretation amounts to a search for authorial intentions, we would be spared a great deal of philosophical trouble in vindicating originalism, so long as we could sustain the claim that adjudication requires interpretation. But far too much ink has been spilled in contesting the connection between interpretation and intentionalism to permit Alexander and Sherwin a conceptual victory, and they would hardly have dedicated their formidable talents to the project of defending intentionalism if they really thought the matter to be as obvious as claiming that "a rose is a rose."

At the root of their rejection of alternative non-intentionalist theories of interpretation is their conviction that the method of interpretation available to judges follows from law's authority. In their view, if we appreciate why law has authority at all, we will appreciate that it demands an investigation of its authors' intentions in cases in which its meaning is at all in doubt. As they concede, if law were thought to be solely a source of coordination, it could be interpreted in any manner that advanced that goal, without regard to the intentions of its authors. But as they insist, "coordination is not the only benefit we seek from vesting lawmakers with the authority to determine what ought to be done."[8] "We also seek

[6] In his latest addition to his formidable portfolio of works on intentionalism, Alexander is even more explicit in his willingness to claim a conceptual victory. He writes: "when one is interpreting a text, as opposed to doing other things with it, one is necessarily seeking its author's or authors' intended meaning . . . If you derive any meaning from a text other than the authorially-intended one, you are not interpreting that text." L. Alexander, "Telepathic Law," *Constitutional Commentary* 26 (2010), 139–40. For similar insistences that interpretation is synonymous with a search for authorial intentions, see S. Fish, "There Is No Textualist Position," *San Diego Law Review* 42 (2005), 629; Steven Knapp and Walter Benn Michaels, "Not A Matter of Interpretation," *San Diego Law Review* 42 (2005), 651; L. Alexander and S. Prakash, "Is That English You're Speaking?: Why Intention Free Interpretation is an Impossibility," *San Diego Law Review* 41 (2004), 967.

[7] Alexander and Sherwin, *Demystifying Legal Reasoning*, 139. "Interpretation in law as in life is a search for speaker's meaning," ibid., 133.

[8] Ibid., 139.

expertise."[9] "We select legislators, administrators, and judges in large part based on our assessment of their moral expertise, that is, their ability to craft rules that represent moral improvements over the status quo ante."[10] And, as they conclude, if it is the moral expertise of lawmakers that justifies our obedience to the rules they craft, then it must be that we should resolve interpretive questions by seeking their intentions, for to seek their intentions is to seek their expertise.[11]

This claim that an intentionalist theory of interpretation follows from law's authority generates and organizes the questions that will occupy me in this chapter. First, does Alexander's and Sherwin's particular intentionalist theory solve past problems with intentionalism and withstand fresh criticisms so as to vindicate the claim that intentionalism is a viable approach to solving interpretive difficulties? And, second, is it true, as Alexander and Sherwin argue, that there is no viable theory of the authority of the law that does not necessarily commit us to an intentionalist theory of interpretation? Are there any defensible theories of authority that will permit an approach to interpretation that preserves a clean line between interpreting the law and remaking it?

The intentions relevant to intentionalism

What is it for a lawmaker to have an intention with regard to the resolution of a dispute, so that we can say that the law ought to be interpreted in accordance with that intention? In the sections that follow, let me work through a series of possible answers in an effort to isolate the understanding of legal intentions that Alexander and Sherwin defend. My hope is that in so doing, I will exhaust the logical spaces available to them and to other intentionalists so as to provide both a comprehensive menu of the intentional states to which one might reach if undertaking intentionalist interpretation, and a sense of the difficulties that must be overcome by those seeking to invoke any one of these answers.

Adverted-to exemplars

First, one might think that the meaning of a rule-maker's words should be fixed by the objects and circumstances to which the rule-maker in fact adverted when employing those words. Alexander and Sherwin certainly

[9] Ibid. [10] Ibid. [11] Ibid., 141.

believe that "the interpreter is in search of the lawmaker's mental state at the time of the enactment."[12] The most natural understanding of such a claim would be to identify the meaning of the lawmaker's words with the occurrent representations in his mind at the time of utterance – that is, with the exemplars to which the speaker adverted. Thus, if in prohibiting vehicles from the park, the lawmaker pictured automobiles but not farm equipment, then the word "vehicles" within the regulation should be interpreted to be synonymous with "automobiles," and should thus be interpreted to exclude tractors.

Unfortunately, it would seem that the law will quickly run out on us if limited to subjectively contemplated exemplars. If when enacting the prohibition against vehicles in the park, city council members conjured up in their minds images of a white Ford that was recently involved in an incident in the park, it would seem that the prohibition would only exclude white Fords, and not blue Chevys. Or, as Robert Bork argued, precisely because his skepticism about the legitimacy of judicial review motivated him to seek means of emasculating the role of the judiciary in constitutional interpretation, the Equal Protection Clause should be interpreted to apply only to the intended exemplars of its drafters, which were the Black Codes of the Reconstructionist South; it should thus not be thought to render unconstitutional statutes that discriminate between persons on grounds of gender, sexual orientation, or disability.[13] In order to avoid limiting laws to their limited exemplars in ways that would undercut the reasons to have laws at all, it would seem that intentionalists require an understanding of authorial intentions that reaches beyond the mental images that lawmakers entertain as they codify rules of conduct.

Alexander and Sherwin certainly share the view that intentionalist interpretation need not and cannot limit itself to intended exemplars. As they recognize, speakers often have very spare intentions concerning the meanings of the words they use. When one's mother leaves one a note asking that the dog be put out before her visit, she might have written her note while conjuring up a picture of one's past dog, Rover, rather than one's present dog, Plover. Nevertheless, Alexander and Sherwin insist, the note should be read so as to give the word "dog" an extension that reaches beyond one's mother's mental representation. Similarly, a legal prohibition against the keeping of bears within 1,000

[12] Ibid.

[13] Robert Bork, "Neutral Principles and Some First Amendment Problems," *Indiana Law Journal* 47 (1971), 47.

feet of a residential area may have been enacted by those whose occurrent thoughts were to prevent grizzly attacks, and who in no way contemplated the extension of the rule to black bears, let alone Malaysian sun bears and pandas. Still, insist Alexander and Sherwin in a manner that instantly makes their intentionalism more mystifying than demystifying: "we do believe that intended meanings extend well beyond the particular images contained in authors' mental states."[14] "The relevant intent," they argue, "must be something more than intent to govern the particular cases to which the rule-maker adverted."[15]

Conventional word meaning

The second thing that Alexander and Sherwin might say that would make sense of this notion that people's interpretive intentions can extend beyond those exemplars to which they explicitly advert is that people intend to refer to the *class of things* to which the terms they use conventionally extend. Such an interpretation equates a speaker's meaning with the conventional meaning of her words, as best captured by dictionaries that sum up sociological facts about the common usages of those words. On this interpretation, a lawmaker's use of the term "bear" would mean anything that falls within the extension of the word "bear," whether the lawmaker appreciates it or not. Similarly, if a lawmaker's use of the term "vehicles" is interpreted to refer to the class of things captured by the term's "dictionary definition," then it will include any power-driven means of transporting persons or cargo – including a combine, a tank, and an airplane – whether the lawmaker anticipates that extension or not.

But Alexander and Sherwin reject this construal, for they take pains to argue that a speaker's meaning should not be equated with the meaning of her utterance. Speaking directly to their readers, they write: "it is what *we* mean – not what others could have meant by these marks and spaces – that you are presumably seeking to discover when you read this book."[16] To say that what speakers mean by their words is whatever their words mean is to substitute utterance meaning for speaker meaning, and this, they insist, parts ways with intentionalism. It also parts ways with interpretation altogether – or so Alexander and Sherwin argue. If an adjudicator adopts a strategy of interpreting a law in accordance with its

[14] Alexander and Sherwin, *Demystifying Legal Reasoning*, 142.
[15] Ibid., 151. [16] Ibid., 138.

utterance meaning, rather than the intended meaning of its author, "the result is not interpretation of the lawmaker's rule. Rather the interpreter is constructing a rule out of materials provided by the original lawmaker, and in so doing, is acting as a lawmaker in his or her own right."[17]

Alexander and Sherwin have now advanced two claims that are very hard to square: (1) we are not entitled to assume that lawmakers intend to refer to the class of things to which their words conventionally refer; but (2) we must assume that lawmakers may very often intend to refer to things which they have never heard or thought about. Thus, we cannot assume that lawmakers intended their prohibition to include Malaysian sun bears and spectacled bears simply because the dictionary definition of the word "bear" includes such species. Nevertheless, while "the lawmaker may never have seen or even heard of Malaysian sun bears . . . or spectacled bears . . . both he and his audience can be quite certain that he intended to include them within his rule's prohibition."[18] But how are we to determine the things to which a lawmaker refers if we allow ourselves to go beyond the lawmaker's exemplars, but do not invoke, instead, the conventional extensions of his terms? What would it mean to say that a lawmaker intended to prohibit Malaysian sun bears, but not panda bears, when he thought about neither and when the conventional meaning of the word "bear" includes both?

Hypothetical intentions

The third interpretation that might be given to Alexander's and Sherwin's understanding of the intentions relevant to legal interpretation is this: the intentions that fix the meaning of an enactment include whatever intentions lawmakers *would have had* with regard to a given application if they had adverted to it. That is, what lies beyond things actually adverted to are things hypothetically adverted to, and those can be included in the class of things *intended* by the lawmaker. Thus, if lawmakers would have intended to exempt panda bears from their residential prohibition if they had adverted to the question, then the term "bears" within the regulation should not be thought to include panda bears. And if they would have intended to exclude bicycles, but include snowmobiles, within their prohibition against vehicles in the park, then the legal meaning of the term "vehicles" should be fixed accordingly.

[17] Ibid., 138–9. [18] Ibid., 142.

Alexander and Sherwin refuse this interpretation, as well. That is, they reject that the intentions that lie beyond the limits of advertence but that nevertheless count as intentions are merely hypothetical. In their view, it is important not to equate the question "What did you intend regarding unadverted-to situation S?" with the question "What would you have intended regarding S had you adverted to it?" Inasmuch as the latter question has no single answer, the equation of these questions quickly induces doubts about "the facticity of intentions" – doubts which lead to "intention skepticism."[19] In their view, there is a fact about the matter that fixes what a speaker intended with regard to a situation to which he never adverted; and this fact is not given by counterfactual hypotheticals about what he would have intended had he adverted to the situation. As Alexander and Sherwin insist: "We believe that there are real, *not hypothetical,* intentions about matters not specifically adverted to, and that whether or not a rule that bans bears in residential neighborhoods applies to a species of bear of which the rule-makers were unaware is a question of fact."[20]

So the search is still on. Wherein lie *real* intentions about a matter to which a speaker has never adverted? How are we to make sense of Alexander's and Sherwin's claim that we "can be quite certain" that a lawmaker intended to refer to Malaysian sun bears when prohibiting bears within the proximity of a residential area (1) when he did not think about, know of, or imagine that such creatures existed; (2) when we cannot attribute to him the intention to refer to all things conventionally meant by the term "bear"; and (3) when we cannot meaningfully say that he would have included such bears within the meaning of the term "bear" had he adverted to the species when passing the regulation?

Goals/background motivations

A fourth way by which to make sense of Alexander's and Sherwin's quest for real intentions to which lawmakers never adverted is to look to what the lawmakers *meant to achieve* by passing the law – the goals or larger purposes which make moral sense of the passage of legislation to begin with. In determining whether a panda should count as a bear under the terms of the residential prohibition, we should ask: what morally plausible larger motivation accounts for the rule-maker's regulation of bears?

[19] Ibid., 163. [20] Ibid., 165, emphasis added.

If that motivation is well served by including pandas within the meaning of the prohibition's reference to "bears," then a panda should be thought a bear for purposes of the prohibition, but not otherwise.

Such an approach has the virtue of matching what lawmakers mean by the terms employed in legislation to the state of affairs that they intended to achieve. If safety motivated the prohibition of vehicles in the park, the meaning of the term "vehicle" should be construed so as to advance that goal. Thus, while lawmakers never subjectively contemplated the prospect of someone driving a combine through the park, their reference to "vehicles" within the prohibition should be construed to include combines out of deference to the goal that they did, in fact, subjectively intend to advance. Such an interpretive approach would seemingly honor all of the constraints that Alexander and Sherwin have built into their understanding of intentionalism.

While lawmakers may never have thought of Malaysian sun bears when excluding bears from residential areas, the fact that such bears can be shown to be as risky to human life and property as the bears that lawmakers did think about, and the fact that lawmakers can be shown to have been motivated by a desire to reduce such risks, give one a seemingly sound basis for suggesting that lawmakers thus intended the prohibition of Malaysian sun bears.

But once again, Alexander and Sherwin resist our efforts on their behalf. They dismiss the argument that when legislative intentions are under-determined, we should interpret the language of legislation in light of lawmakers' morally plausible background motivations. This is because they are convinced that:

> rules cannot be equated with the more general ends they serve without losing the benefits of their form . . . If the meaning of rules is derived from the moral principles that the rules were designed to serve, there are, in effect, no rules and no means for curbing moral error. Thus, the rule maker's rules must have, and must be intended to have, a meaning that is independent of the rule maker's intent at its highest level of generality.[21]

So we cannot say that what counts as a "bear" under the residential prohibition is anything that meets the goal of keeping residents safe from attacks by temperamental creatures with sharp fangs and teeth (which might include jaguars and exclude pandas). And, inversely, we cannot say that a creature that is as harmless as a guinea pig is not a bear, just because the background reason for the residential prohibition would

[21] Ibid., 151.

dictate its exclusion from the rule's application. As if their rejection of the appeal to intended goals were not puzzling enough, however, Alexander and Sherwin add a caveat. While one may not interpret the term "bear" so as to pick and choose among people's pet bears in light of the lawmaker's background motivation to keep homeowners safe from harm, it is nevertheless the case, according to Alexander and Sherwin, that "to interpret the rule correctly, other aspects of the rule maker's purposes must be grasped."[22]

As they argue, "That is how the interpreter might know that the rule maker did not intend his 'no bears' rule to prohibit escaping a fire with a pet bear by a route less than one thousand feet from a residence."[23] In other words, one can know that legislators intended to allow Malaysian sun bears to be rescued from peril, even though legislators never knew that such bears existed and never contemplated their peril; but one cannot know that legislators intended to exempt pandas from the residential prohibition to begin with, even though pandas are no more threatening than poodles, and legislators explicitly sought to ban bears solely because they were concerned with the disproportionate risks that they posed to human lives and property.

But now it seems to me that to seek intentions that are neither occurrent, nor hypothetical, nor motivational, nor the equivalent of the extension of their terms, is to search for "sakes." Your sake, my sake, his sake, her sake: what is a "sake"? Without being able to equate intentions (1) to the objects of a lawmaker's advertence, or (2) to the referents of his terms, or (3) to counterfactual purposes, or (4) to his background moral motivations, on what principled basis can we conclude, as Alexander and Sherwin do, that legislators *who did not advert to anything other than grizzlies, and who did not contemplate any circumstances in which bears might legitimately be brought within 1,000 feet of a residential development* nevertheless intended their rule to apply to pandas but not jaguars and intended it to be suspended in the event that there was a fire from which a pet bear could not be rescued without violating the 1,000-foot rule?

Retroactive intentions

It would appear that Alexander and Sherwin think that, in principle (time travel permitting!), we could ask rule-makers today what they

[22] Ibid., 152. [23] Ibid.

intended in the past (about things to which they did not advert), and have those answers fix or determine what they in fact intended in the past, rather than simply constituting expressions of what they would now intend, or would now wish they had intended in the past. They write:

> If the rule maker had in mind particular tokens of keeping bears near private residences when he enacted his rule, but would reply affirmatively if asked whether his rule prohibits other tokens that were not in his mind at the time, his intended meaning, and thus the meaning of his rule, is that those latter tokens of keeping bears are prohibited.[24]

Such a passage comes dangerously close to suggesting that Alexander and Sherwin subscribe to a very implausible kind of reverse causation. For it suggests that what lawmakers would say now in fact retroactively fixes the meanings of their past terms. The speaker makes himself intend in the past what he says in the present! Since it seems clear that one cannot make true the fact that one intended something in the past to which one did not advert by adverting to it in the present and declaring it retroactively so, we need to press once again for a conceptually intelligible understanding of Alexander's and Sherwin's intentionalism.

Intentions

Let me make one final effort to understand what it would mean to find intentions in the past that can only be known in the present. If such a claim is to be read to attribute to lawmakers not hypothetical (counterfactual) intentions at the time of enactment, but extant, actual intentions, then we might finally conclude that Alexander and Sherwin believe that legal authors possess unconscious interpretive intentions that can be discovered at a later time as having been governing at the time of enactment. Indeed, once one eliminates all of the above alternative interpretations of their thesis, there seems little left but to credit Alexander and Sherwin with a commitment to the law being a reflection of, and taking its true meaning from, lawmakers' unconscious selves. On this thesis, lawmakers possess semantic intentions about which they are not conscious at the time that they enact given rules (namely, that Malaysian sun bears – of which they have never heard – should count as "bears" under a residential prohibition). These unconscious intentions can, in principle, if not in fact, be reliably evidenced after the fact by

[24] Ibid., 150.

asking lawmakers what they would do about cases to which they never adverted at the time of enactment. In some instances, Alexander and Sherwin argue, lawmakers will confess that their semantic intentions ill-served their background motivations for enacting the rule to begin with. When confronted with the prospect of banning a bear that is old, declawed, defanged, well-trained, gentle, and much beloved by children, the lawmaker might conclude, "I did intend to prohibit all bears, but I was mistaken not to have carved out an exception for bears like this one."[25] And when queried about an emergency situation in which a bear could not be saved without violating the exceptionless 1,000-foot residential restriction, the lawmaker might say, "correctly" according to Alexander and Sherwin, "I didn't intend my prohibition to apply to that case, and it would be absurd for anyone to imagine that I did."[26]

The task of interpretation, then, is apparently a Freudian one. Adjudicators should seek to interpret the meaning of statutory and constitutional enactments by asking about the unconscious semantic, or extensional, intentions that accompanied the conscious exemplars to which rule-makers adverted. To go on such a quest, once again, is not to search for the conventional extensions of the terms used, for presumably speakers can possess unconscious semantic intentions that part ways with conventional utterance meanings. It is also not to search for intentions that they *would have had* if they had adverted to a scenario to which they did not, in fact, advert, for unconscious intentions are actual, not hypothetical. Such intentions were present at the time of enactment; they are not counterfactual constructions of what intentions would have been possessed if facts were other than they were. And it is not to search for the general background motivations that make moral sense of lawmakers having taken legislative action to begin with, for while subjects can "advert in a limited way to the rule maker's purposes in order to grasp what the latter intended to do," Alexander and Sherwin repeat their insistence that one may not "equat[e] the rule's meaning with those purposes."[27]

If legal meaning finally comes to rest in the legal unconscious, one has to confess that the task of intentionalist interpretation is even more practically problematic than it has long appeared. But complaining about the problems of amalgamating a singular legislative intention from dozens of both conscious and unconscious individual intentions is surely

[25] Ibid., 142. [26] Ibid., 143. [27] Ibid., 145.

not to complain about the most glaring problems with this interpretation of Alexander's and Sherwin's intentionalism. One rather should ask, first, whether the notion of unconscious intentions makes any sense at all, for many believe that intentions constitute acts of will – choices – that are made by the conscious, autonomous, rational self. An unconscious intention is, in the view of many who work in the fields of philosophy of mind and the neuroscience of responsibility, an oxymoron: the conceptual equivalent of a married bachelor. And even if there are unconscious intentions – willings or choices that can be made unknowingly by a rational agent – it is hard to imagine that they include the interpretive extension of particular words. One can perhaps imagine vindicating the claim that someone within a dysfunctional relationship might unconsciously intend to harm or antagonize his partner without knowing that he harbors such an intention, but it is very hard to imagine that Alexander and Sherwin can vindicate the claim that someone speaking of bears in the absence of any conscious knowledge of Malaysian bears has had the extension of his reference to "bears" unknowingly altered by commitments unknowingly made by his unconscious self!

What is more, even if such an implausible claim could be supported, one has to wonder why one would think that moral expertise would reside within the unconscious states of lawmakers and, therefore, why one would accord their unconscious intentions any authority. While the fact-finding and deliberative capacities of legislatures might give Alexander and Sherwin some basis for suggesting that legislators have a greater claim to moral expertise than do individual citizens (although I do find it hard to credit many politicians with genuine expertise about the morality of my actions, however great the resources available to them), it strikes me as laughable to imagine that whatever expertise a legislator might acquire would seep into her unconsciousness so as to make her unconscious choices about my actions better for me than my own conscious ones. As such, it strikes me as highly implausible to think that legislative intentions that reside within the unconscious – if such things exist at all – would have a claim to authority that would obligate us to engage in legislative psychoanalysis in order to decipher the meaning of ambiguous statutory language.

If Alexander and Sherwin do not (unconsciously?) intend to embrace the notion that the intentions that govern legal interpretation include unconscious intentions, then it seems to me that their thesis remains mystifying. It is tempting to conclude that Alexander and Sherwin are simply manufacturing mental states that do not exist, and that they are covering up this fact by repeatedly exploiting an ambiguity between internal and external negation. The lawmaker who now says that he did not intend for his bear prohibition to apply in cases of emergency rescue is employing a plausible external negation – namely, it is *not* the case that he *had* an intention in the past concerning the emergency rescue of bears. Alexander and Sherwin are hoping that we mistake this plausible statement of external negation for a far less plausible statement of internal negation – namely, that *without knowing it*, the lawmaker *had* an intention in the past and it was an intention *not to apply* the prohibition to emergencies. But one cannot move from external to internal negation without a sleight of hand.

Interpretation without intentions

I come away from the effort to understand Alexander's and Sherwin's intentionalism fairly convinced of the impossibility of finding a meaningful notion of the authorial intentions that they believe should govern legal interpretation. Inasmuch as I trust in their ability to give intentionalism the best defense that might possibly be mustered on its behalf, I am left, once again, doubting that an intentionalist theory of interpretation best, or even coherently, captures the proper approach to understanding the law's meaning. One is, of course, trapped in what seems to me to be a very unhappy marriage with intentionalism if one is wedded to a theory of legal authority that necessarily requires that one interpret legal texts in light of the beliefs, motivations, or intentions of their authors. And Alexander and Sherwin appear to be so trapped. But it is important to recognize that there is an alternative understanding that vests the authority of law not in lawmakers but in legal texts.

Alexander and Sherwin locate expertise in the mental states of persons – of constitutional framers, legislators, and regulators – and only derivatively in the statements that they use to express those mental states. As such, when words fail to capture those mental states with clarity, it is no surprise that Alexander and Sherwin are convinced that one should seek directly those mental states that the words so imperfectly evidence. But instead of locating the authority of law in the mental states of lawmakers, and only derivatively in the texts they produce, I would suggest that we should locate legal authority in legal texts, and only derivatively (if at all) in the intentions with which those texts were produced. In other words, I would suggest that it is the law, and not lawmakers, that has a claim to authority over our actions. To the extent that detecting the intentions of those who authored the law assists us in fixing the law with a determinate content that promises to guide the actions of citizens and officials in ways that are morally helpful, we have reason to look for authorial intentions. But such intentions are, on this theory, mere heuristics to what is itself a heuristic. The intentions of those who crafted the language of the law are, on this view, heuristics to determining the content of the law, which is itself a heuristic to determining the content of morality. In the end, as I have argued at length elsewhere, only morality obligates. All "secondary principles" by which to determine the content of our moral permissions and obligations, and all interpretive techniques by which to fix the content of such secondary principles, should be judged by their ability to conform our conduct to the demands of morality. In the event that the law is ambiguous, we may find moral guidance by disambiguating its language in light of the intentions with which that language was drafted. But in the event that these intentions are undiscoverable or unreliable, they lose their heuristic value, and we would do well to fix the content of the law by other means, or to seek an alternative guide to moral action altogether. Such is the skeleton of the theory of law's authority and the reason for seeking its meaning that I have developed elsewhere. As a means of making it somewhat more intelligible and defensible here, let me answer a set of challenges that Alexander has recently posed in an article that insists that theories that reject intentionalism are, effectively, theories that reject law itself.[28]

First, the objection will be made that on the theory I have sketched, laws are just like seagull tracks in the sand: without an understanding of their author's intentions, they are mere marks on paper. How can they be interpreted at all when one cannot even know, in the absence of authorial intentions, what language we should read them in?[29] Moreover, given that we do not generally seek to "read" seagull tracks in the sand, why would we want to interpret the marks put on paper by lawmakers, absent a concern for their intentions with regard to those marks? Do we not have to assume that laws are communications by speakers whose intended communications we are interested in understanding in order to make sense of our attention to them at all?

On the contrary, I would argue. If the marks on paper laid down by lawmakers assist us in deciphering the content of our moral responsibilities when we invest them with meaning, then they should be thought

[28] Alexander, "Telepathic Law." [29] Ibid., 139.

to be theoretically authoritative. The same goes for seagull tracks in the sand, the whistling of wind, and the calligraphy carved into Tasmanian eucalyptus trees by the larvae of the "squiggly gum moth," *if* (and this is, of course, a big "if") any of these can be given an interpretation that proves to be morally illuminating. So long as the authorial intentions with which marks on paper were made do not give us reasons for action, we are not bound to determine the content of those intentions as a means of fulfilling our moral obligations. We are free, that is, to invest such marks with a meaning distinct from that contemplated by their authors if so doing better allows us to act on the balance of reasons that determines our moral obligations. It may be that if we know what their authors intended, we can fix the marks with a meaning that is maximally instructive, and if that is the case, we have reason to seek and attend to their authors' intentions. But if such intentions do not exist at all (because the squiggly gum moth lacked intentions altogether) or are unavailable to us (because we lack any reliable evidence of them) or are conflicted (because a multitude of authors in fact possessed a multitude of competing intentions when converging on the terms used in the text), then we would do well to fix the meaning of the marks in other ways or to seek moral help elsewhere.

The second challenge that Alexander anticipates is this: to interpret statutes construed as mere marks on paper, or to interpret squiggles on a gum tree, is not to interpret anything![30] One who "reads" squiggly gum tracks and purports to reason from what one reads is simply engaging in the sort of moral reasoning that one engages in when short on squiggles. One's moral conclusions are phrased in terms of the "symbols" left by the squiggly gum moth, but they are not derived from those symbols. And, similarly, one's moral conclusions may reference statutory enactments, but if those enactments were not interpreted in light of authorial intentions, they were not *interpreted* at all, and as such, one's conclusions are not conclusions *about* those provisions.

My answer is inevitably epistemic. We are constrained in our interpretation of the squiggles on eucalyptus trees by whatever squiggly gum moth semantics maximize our moral insights. Imagine that we find carved in a Tasmanian eucalyptus the following pattern: "Duties of beneficence are not owed to all persons equally, but only to those near and dear." It matters not that the squiggly moth that carved it did not

[30] Ibid., 140.

speak English. We would do well to interpret these marks with English semantics, for by so doing, we may glean insight in a way that we are unlikely to do if we read them in Italian (it being the case that this is pretty lousy Italian) or pass them over altogether. This is so, because for many people, moral insight is more easily obtained if they reason under the guise of interpreting a text than if they reason with Sartrean self-awareness that everything is up for grabs.

The heuristic justification for paying attention to a text (and to things that resemble texts) also gives us a reason to respect and employ certain interpretive restraints, such as looking to conventional semantics or paradigmatic exemplars, or even the intentions of their authors if such intentions are available. The point is that, like all heuristics, the only test of the value of interpretive restraints is their ability to generate insight; and by that test, nothing succeeds like success.

The next move of the critic will be to argue that the reason that legal texts tend to function as sources of moral insight while the squiggles on gum trees do not is that those who draft them themselves possess moral expertise. They pick the marks they do because they expect that we will invest them with conventional meaning, and if we do, we will be led to act in accordance with the demands of morality. We do well to look to the law, as opposed to tree bark squiggles, airline advertisements, shoe box labels, PTA announcements, poetry, or rap music, because lawmakers are better equipped to make moral judgments than are the authors of these other texts. Only the moral expertise of lawmakers can explain the comprehensive theoretical authority of legal texts – a theoretical authority that, unlike every other theoretical authority, has a capacity to influence one's decisions about virtually every aspect of one's life. And if the law's theoretical authority is best explained by recognizing the theoretical authority of lawmakers, it would seem that we should return to the quest for their beliefs and intentions, for those are better evidence of our moral obligations than are the texts that evidence those beliefs and intentions.

I would urge those persuaded by this claim to take seriously Jeremy Waldron's argument that democratic decision procedures yield results that are morally better than those generated by the individual judgments of legislators.[31] Such an argument makes three moves: (1) that democratic decision procedures aggregate individual preferences in a manner required by the applicable social-welfare function; (2) that democratic

[31] Jeremy Waldron, "Legislators' Intentions and Unintentional Legislation," in Andrei Marmor, *Law and Interpretation*, 329.

decision procedures comport with the Condorcet Theorem, which holds that the probability that they are correct is greater than the probability that any one of the views tabulated is correct; and (3) that democratic decision procedures are likely to achieve a "deliberative synthesis" that is superior in content to any view that even the wisest of individual legislators come to possess on his or her own. This set of arguments gives us grounds for according theoretical authority to democratic enactments far more than to the views or intentions of particular legislators considered on their own. It bolsters the claim that one might find epistemic value in something despite it not being produced "by an intentional being ... situated in some enterprise in relation to which he has a purpose or point of view."[32] In short, it remotivates my previous claim that democratic legislation may prove to be theoretically authoritative, even when its authors are not, or even when its authors' beliefs and intentions are unknown and unknowable so as to place their theoretical authority in doubt.

Let me close by returning to Alexander's claim that "to make an argument against following lawmakers' intended norms is to make an argument against law."[33] As he insists, "Even a legal system that lacked legislation and that purported to follow the 'natural law' or the 'moral law,' in order to count as a *legal* system, would require *authorities* to determine what the natural law or moral law required ... their determinations would be authoritative (else they would not be authorities.)"[34] In short, to argue against intentionalism is to argue for anarchy. Well, not exactly. One might think that one has the most essential elements of a legal system when one has a set of secondary principles which function heuristically to simplify morality so as to allow one to act morally more often than one would if one were left to one's own devices; and when one has clear and predictable procedures that ensure that persons honor their moral obligations (except when they have "rights to do wrong" – but that is another essay[35]), in circumstances in which they had fair access to

[32] S. Fish, *Doing What Comes Naturally: Change, Rhetoric and the Practice of Theory in Literary and Legal Studies* (Durham, NC: Duke University Press, 1989), 99–100.

[33] Alexander, "Telepathic Law," 143. [34] Ibid.

[35] There are many sorts of moral "oughts" that the law ought not to enforce – for moral reasons. For an analysis of the circumstances in which morality itself requires persons to be left at liberty to commit moral wrongs, see H. M. Hurd, "Liberty in Law," *Law and Philosophy* 21 (2002), 385–465; Hurd, "Tolerating Wickedness: Moral Reasons for Lawmakers to Permit Immorality," *Philosophia Practica Universalis (Annual Review of Law and Ethics)* (2005), 167–93; Hurd, "When Can We Do What We Want?," *Australian Journal of Legal Philosophy* 29 (2004), 27–69.

those secondary principles so as to be unable to argue that their moral obligations were inaccessible. One might think that the authority of those principles is simply a function of their heuristic value – of the fact that they succeed when one's own judgment, and that of other sources, often fails. Such is not an argument against having law; it is simply an argument for thinking of law as an epistemic handmaiden to morality.

In my view, there are objective moral maxims that bind us. We cannot vest legal texts with any meaning whatsoever without running the risk that such texts will mislead us about our moral obligations. If legal texts are to assist us in acquiring moral beliefs that better cohere with objective moral maxims, we cannot interpret legal texts so that they simply mirror our existing subjective beliefs. We must, instead, employ semantic restraints that generate a proverbial marketplace of ideas. We must adopt interpretive techniques that yield moral conclusions distinct from our own moral beliefs. Only by so doing are we able to test our own beliefs in contrast. Institutionally created laws and principles should thus be thought to have an autonomy all their own. And when they provide reliable insights into the content of our moral responsibilities, they should indeed constrain us.

No doubt there remain many concerns about how such a conception of law is consistent with the ability of law to do all of the action-guiding tasks it is called upon to do – to solve coordination problems and defuse prisoners' dilemmas, for example. Inasmuch as I have devoted a book-length enquiry to this question,[36] I shall resist the temptation to tackle those questions again here. Let me suggest, however, that the challenges that derive from construing and interpreting law as a source of education about antecedently existing moral obligations pale in comparison with the judicial snipe hunts required by theories of legal authority that suggest that we cannot know the law unless we can read the minds of lawmakers.

[36] Hurd, *Moral Combat*.

4

Metasemantics and legal interpretation

ORI SIMCHEN

It can be particularly satisfying when a philosophical dispute is approached from an unexpected direction to fruitful effect. It solidifies the sense that the debate is genuine and affords opportunity for potentially useful connections among disparate areas of theoretical concern. My focus here is on a controversy surrounding the Cruel and Unusual Punishment Clause of the Eighth Amendment to the US Constitution: "Excessive bail shall not be required, nor excessive fines imposed, nor cruel and unusual punishments inflicted."

There is a familiar disagreement between Justice Antonin Scalia of the US Supreme Court and the late Ronald Dworkin over whether the Eighth Amendment could be plausibly interpreted so as to prohibit capital punishment.[1] The dispute gives voice to a deep divergence in approach to statutory interpretation. My aim is to explore this divergence by paying particularly close attention to its metasemantic background. Recasting the Scalia–Dworkin dispute in metasemantic terms will help bring it into sharper focus and point to the general direction in which a resolution lies. To anticipate a little, the metasemantic themes to be explored here favor Dworkin's position over Scalia's. Neither one explicitly attends to the metasemantic underpinnings of their differences, but a metasemantic reconstruction offers a fuller view of the issue that divides them and vindicates the Dworkinian side. Or so I will argue.

The first thing I need to do is introduce the general topic of metasemantics.[2] To understand what the theoretical purview of metasemantics is, it is most useful to contrast it with semantics. We could describe semantics as the study of the significance of linguistic expressions,

[1] See A. Scalia, *A Matter of Interpretation: Federal Courts and the Law* (Princeton University Press, 1997), R. Dworkin, *Justice in Robes* (Cambridge, MA: Harvard University Press, 2006), and Dworkin, *Justice for Hedgehogs* (Cambridge, MA: Harvard University Press, 2011).

[2] Also sometimes referred to as 'foundational semantics'.

but this will not do to distinguish it from metasemantics. Somewhat more helpfully we could say that semantics studies the significance of expressions in an effort to explain how the significance of simple expressions yields significance for complex expressions in which the simple ones partake. More helpfully still, if it is agreed that the significance of whole sentences is adequately captured by the sentences' truth conditions, we could say that semantics studies in the first instance how the significance of simple expressions contributes to the truth conditions of sentences in which the simple expressions partake.[3]

Against this brief characterization of semantics we can now say that metasemantics is concerned with how expressions become endowed with their semantic significance in the first place. While semantics targets the *what* of semantic endowment, metasemantics targets the *how*. Someone says 'He is a spy' pointing at a particular individual. What was said is true just in case the demonstrated individual is indeed a spy. So the demonstrative pronoun 'he' as employed on that occasion apparently contributes the demonstrated individual to truth conditions. Given that a demonstrative pronoun contributes a particular individual to the truth conditions of a sentence in which it partakes on a given occasion of use (semantics), how is it that the pronoun on that occasion of use comes to stand for *that* particular individual as its distinctive contribution to truth conditions (metasemantics)? Or given that the name 'Aristotle' contributes Aristotle to the truth conditions of 'Aristotle was fond of dogs' (semantics), how is it that the name comes to stand for *Aristotle* as opposed to anyone else or no one at all (metasemantics)? Or, given that the term 'gold' contributes gold to the truth conditions of 'Gold is a compound of earth, water, fire, and air' (semantics), how is it that it stands for *gold* as opposed to anything else or nothing (metasemantics)?

My concern is with metasemantics, which is obviously beholden to semantics, as the above examples illustrate, but I will stay clear of semantic details and proceed as if the general framework for semantic theory is more or less settled. I will also stay clear of such pressing metasemantic issues as how to think of the determinants for semantic endowment in light of such metaphysically 'exotic' semantic values as higher-order functions.[4]

3 While this conception of semantics is challenged by information-based approaches such as Discourse Representation Theory, it is still the dominant trend and will be assumed in everything that follows.

4 See O. Simchen, "Token-Reflexivity," *Journal of Philosophy* 110 (2013), 173–93, for some preliminary discussion of such questions.

Finally, I will stay clear of controversies surrounding the semantics–pragmatics distinction.[5]

In recent work I have begun to articulate a contrast between two strands within metasemantics.[6] The first, associated with such figures as Donald Davidson and David Lewis among others, is the interpretationist strand.[7] On this way of looking at things, the fact that an expression has the semantic endowment it has is determined by conditions surrounding the expression's interpretive consumption. Take 'Gold is a compound' as spoken by an ancient Greek. What makes it the case that 'gold' thus spoken applies to whatever it applies to? The interpretationist might say that if we consider 'Gold is a compound' in the worldly circumstances of the speaking, including the speaker's attitudes (themselves shaped by considerations of interpretability) and other sentences the speaker would endorse, the best overall interpretation that balances worldly fit with speaker rationality assigns gold to the speaker's 'gold'. Or the interpretationist might insist that the best interpretation to achieve this balance renders 'gold' a term for anything superficially similar enough to gold. Either way, the expression's semantic endowment on this way of looking at things is *constituted* by the expression's interpretability – by conditions surrounding its post-production assessment. What it is to have such-and-such a significance is to be interpretable as having it, subject to certain constraints.

The second strand within metasemantics is what I call 'productivism'. It is associated with the theoretical efforts of Keith Donnellan, Michael Devitt, Jerry Fodor, David Kaplan, Saul Kripke, and Hilary Putnam, among others. On this way of looking at things the fact that an expression has its semantic endowment is determined by conditions surrounding the expression's production or employment. Consider again the use

[5] But for some recent work on the relevance of pragmatics to matters of statutory interpretation, see A. Marmor, "Can the Law Imply More Than It Says? On Some Pragmatic Aspects of Strategic Speech," in A. Marmor and S. Soames (eds.), *Philosophical Foundations of Language in the Law* (Oxford University Press, 2011), 80–104.

[6] See O. Simchen, *Necessary Intentionality: A Study in the Metaphysics of Aboutness* (Oxford University Press, 2012); Simchen, "Token-Reflexivity"; and Simchen, "Semantic Endowment," available at: http://faculty.acts.ubc.ca/osimchen/publications/SE.pdf.

[7] This nomenclature is rather entrenched in metasemantics but is somewhat unfortunate in the present context due to its unmistakable lexical affinity to 'interpretivism,' the label for the jurisprudential position advocated by Dworkin. As I will argue, Dworkin's position is best construed as not espousing metasemantic interpretationism. I will prefix 'metasemantic' to 'interpretationist' to minimize ambiguity whenever confusion might otherwise ensue.

of 'gold' by the ancient Greek. A productivist would typically claim that what makes it the case that the term stands for whatever it stands for is determined by the term's etiology given the worldly circumstances of its production, which most likely include the presence of gold in the environment together with certain of the speaker's attitudes (themselves understood as mental states or events). Whether or not we are permitted within our overall metasemantic explanation to appeal to speakers' attitudes, in particular to speakers' referential intentions, is an issue that appears to divide the productivist camp, with Devitt and Fodor (together with the early Hartry Field) on the negative side, and Donnellan, Kaplan, Kripke, and Putnam on the positive side.[8] Either way, matters of interpretability are understood here as falling within the epistemology of understanding and do not play a direct constitutive role in the expression becoming endowed with its particular significance. This is in contrast with the interpretationist insistence that such matters do indeed make it the case that an expression is endowed with its significance, and that they do play a direct constitutive role in the facts of semantic endowment.

In other work I offered an analogy from the metaphysics of artifacts to help make vivid the contrast between the two approaches.[9] The parallel to an expression's endowment with semantic significance is an artifact's endowment with a purpose (*telos*). How is it that a given item comes to possess the particular purpose of enabling elevated seating, say? We may contrast two approaches to this metateleological question. Metateleological interpretationism proclaims such endowment to be constituted by the item's interpretability. An overall story that purports to rationalize chair-involving behavior of chair users, given their circumstances and their various mental states and episodes (themselves subject to considerations of interpretability) would assign the purpose of enabling elevated seating to the item in question. It is this that makes it the case that the item has the said purpose on such a view. Metateleological productivism, on the other hand, would make the item's endowment with the purpose of enabling elevated seating determined by conditions surrounding the item's production. Such an approach would typically appeal to the intentions accompanying the production. If we assume that nothing

[8] The typology is somewhat controversial. For example, Devitt vehemently denies that Kripkean metasemantics, at least as it is presented in S. Kripke, *Naming and Necessity* (Cambridge, MA: Harvard University Press, 1980), is intention-based. I will not attempt to settle the issue here.

[9] Simchen, "Token-Reflexivity."

can have the purpose of enabling elevated seating without being regarded as having it by an audience, then the intentions accompanying the item's production might well include the intention that the thing produced be regarded in the relevant way. But such regardability does not enter *directly* into making it the case that the item has the purpose it has, according to metateleological productivism. Rather, being regarded as enabling elevated seating is something intended by the producer or producers in bestowing the said purpose upon the thing produced. Similarly in the case of metasemantic productivism, if we think that an expression cannot have its particular semantic significance without being regarded as having it by an audience, then intentions accompanying the expression's production or employment might well include the intention that the expression be regarded as having the significance in question by an audience. But this regardability is not presumed to enter *directly* into making it the case that the item means what it does. It only enters indirectly via the intention of the expression's producer or employer.

In my other work on the topic I also offered considerations that favor productivism over interpretationism. Most recently I have argued that interpretationism cannot secure singular referential determinacy even under strong Lewisian assumptions about the interpretation of predicates.[10] I argued that for all that the Lewisian can secure metasemantically, if I say 'This is a nice piece of fruit' attending to an apple in my hand in otherwise perfectly mundane circumstances, I might in fact be referring to a number or a planet light years away. I will not rehearse these considerations here and will merely note that productivism does not fall prey to such threats of referential indeterminacy because of the productivist insistence that endowment with significance, and more specifically referential contact with our surroundings, is explanatorily prior to sentential truth or falsity. On the metasemantic interpretationist picture, on the other hand, it is posterior.

Now, it is only to be expected that the aforementioned divide within metasemantics will have implications for matters of interpretation, and more specifically for matters of statutory interpretation. I believe that it certainly has, and that these implications are somewhat underappreciated. I aim to flesh some of them out. The controversy surrounding the proper interpretation of the Eighth Amendment of the US Constitution can be viewed as a test case. Success in bringing metasemantic considerations to bear on statutory interpretation in this

[10] See Simchen, "Semantic Endowment."

particular case will give us reason for cautious optimism regarding the fruitfulness of such an approach in future cases as well.

Textualism regarding statutory interpretation commonly holds that a text produced in the past and presently legally binding has a certain semantic content just in case the said content is assigned to it under an interpretation that the original producers of the text would endorse.[11] Call a text produced in the past and presently legally binding a *legal text*. The right-hand side of the 'just in case' claim contains an elliptical subjunctive – 'had the text's producers interpreted the text, they would endorse an interpretation that assigns said content to it' – so the assumption slightly more perspicuously becomes:

(COMMONLY) For any legal text *T* and content *C*, *T* has *C* if and only if for some interpretation *I*, *I* assigns *C* to *T* and is such that had *T*'s original producers interpreted *T*, they would endorse *I* as *T*'s interpretation.

(COMMONLY) does not allude to how the text's producers *in fact* interpreted the text, and does not take *that* to be the determining factor in the text's semantic endowment, in the interest of generality. While in some cases the producers of a legal text also engage in interpreting the text produced, there is generally no reason to suppose that producers of a text need engage in interpreting it, just as there is generally no reason to suppose that in saying something we need to engage in interpreting the product of our speech. The ground of a legal text having its particular semantic endowment according to (COMMONLY) is how the text's producers *would* interpret it.

There are a couple of things to notice about (COMMONLY) right from the start. The first is a broadly diagnostic point. It is safe to assume that (COMMONLY) figures as part of the textualist effort to discern

[11] Here is but one instance, taken from Scalia's dissent in Board of Ed. of *Kiryas Joel* v. *Grumet*, 512 US 687 (1994):

> [T]he Founding Fathers would be astonished to find that the Establishment Clause – which they designed "to insure that no one powerful sect or combination of sects could use political or governmental power to punish dissenters," *Zorach* v. *Clauson*, 343 US 306, 319 (1952) (Black, J., dissenting) – has been employed to prohibit characteristically and admirably American accommodation of the religious practices (or more precisely, cultural peculiarities) of a tiny minority sect.

The dissent is from the court's endorsement of an interpretation of the First Amendment that by Scalia's lights the text's producers would not endorse.

the overall legal content of a legal text.[12] But if so, the textualist adherence to the principle is best construed as tacitly committing to an interpretationist metasemantics. For why else would the text's interpretability by its producers have any relevance to the text's overall legal content? The textualist aims to recover the semantic significance of a legal text. Surely it is the text's endowment with semantic significance that is for the textualist of primary concern and is determinative of the text's overall legal content. Why else would the textualist even bother qua interpreter to consider how the text's producers would understand it? The most plausible story is that the way in which the text's producers would understand the text is being taken by (COMMONLY)'s adherent as constitutive of the text being endowed with its particular semantic significance. The other option here is to say that the text's interpretability is being taken as a mere sign or marker for the text's endowment with its particular semantic significance. But this seems dubious. The interpretability of a text by its producers is not the sort of thing we would normally appeal to as *evidence* for the text meaning what it does. Epistemologically speaking, the text's interpretability by its original producers is not on a surer footing than the text's endowment with its particular semantic significance. So for the textualist adherent of (COMMONLY) to consider interpretability by the text's producers as a mere sign for semantic endowment is otiose. Much more plausible is the thought that for such a textualist what it is for the text to be endowed with its semantic significance *just is* for it to be interpretable (by its producers) in the relevant way. The relation between the text's interpretability and the text's semantic endowment is thus constitutive rather than evidential according to the most obvious rendering of the textualist endorsement of (COMMONLY).

The point just made is put forward in a diagnostic spirit, which is to say that it is not meant to rule out the sheer possibility of a textualist adherence to (COMMONLY) without a tacit commitment to metasemantic interpretationism. But an interesting question that can be raised about (COMMONLY) is why such a principle of statutory interpretation should be minimally intuitively appealing to the textualist in the first place. And the

[12] Our focus is on the semantic content of a legal text under the assumption that it is a determining factor in the text's overall legal content. No further implication is intended regarding the overall determinants of legal content. For an extended discussion of the relation between semantic content and legal content, see M. Greenberg, "How Facts Make Law," *Legal Theory* 10 (2004), 157–98.

present diagnostic suggestion is that the intuitive appeal of (COMMONLY) dovetails a tacit commitment to metasemantic interpretationism.

A second thing to notice about (COMMONLY) is the inclusion of a subjunctive idiom when alluding to the text's interpretability by its producers, the 'had it been the case that *P*, it would be the case that *Q*' construction. Here we point out that interpretability is a dispositional property. Whether dispositions in general admit of subjunctive analyses is a matter of intense debate and a burgeoning literature in contemporary metaphysics.[13] But setting aside the need to take a stand on the general metaphysical question of the availability of such analyses, it is undeniable that the idea of explaining dispositions subjunctively is prima facie appealing and commonsensically well entrenched. And it is this intuitive appeal that lies behind (COMMONLY)'s inclusion of the schematic subjunctive conditional 'had *T*'s original producers interpreted *T*, they would endorse *I* as *T*'s interpretation'. In short, endorsement of (COMMONLY) is best seen as saddling its textualist adherent with a certain metasemantic baggage – interpretationism – and a certain metaphysical baggage – the subjunctive construal of interpretability. Such commitments are perhaps not inevitable. But at least we can say that without a metasemantic interpretationist background (COMMONLY) seems far less appealing as a principle of statutory interpretation. Moreover, for the textualist adherent of (COMMONLY) to insist that interpretability (by the text's producers) bears only an evidential relation to the text's original semantic endowment seems especially unattractive insofar as the text's interpretability seems no more epistemologically secure than the endowment for which it is claimed to provide evidential support.

Scalia is easily read as committed to some version of (COMMONLY):

> I will consult the writings of some men who happened to be delegates to the Constitutional Convention – Hamilton's and Madison's writings in *The Federalist*, for example ... because their writings, like those of other intelligent and informed people of the time, display *how the text of the Constitution was originally understood.*[14]

> I agree with the distinction that Professor Dworkin draws ... between what he calls 'semantic intention' and the concrete expectations of

[13] See D. Lewis, "Finkish Dispositions," *Philosophical Quarterly* 47 (1997), 143–58, M. Fara, "Dispositions and Habituals," *Noûs* 39 (2005), 43–82, and D. Manley and R. Wasserman, "On Linking Dispositions and Conditionals," *Mind* 117 (2008), 59–84.

[14] Scalia, *A Matter of Interpretation*, 38, emphasis added.

> lawgivers. It is indeed the former rather than the latter that I follow. *I would prefer the term 'import' to 'semantic intention' – because that puts the focus where I believe it should be, upon what the text would reasonably be understood to mean, rather than upon what it was intended to mean.*[15]

The key point in these and related passages is the focus on how the text would be understood – potential semantic uptake. It is this that constitutes for Scalia the text's original meaning. In the background is Scalia's concern to distinguish his version of textualism – originalism – from the position in statutory interpretation known as intentionalism. According to intentionalism, whether or not the Cruel and Unusual Punishment Clause prohibits capital punishment is determined by, among other factors, whether or not the Framers intended that it prohibit capital punishment. As stated, the position does not require that the Framers' intentions be the sole ground for the Eighth Amendment having its legal content, but what else might be needed here need not concern us any further. As a doctrine of statutory interpretation, intentionalism focuses on intentions of a particular kind: the intentions of lawmakers to shape the law in a particular direction. Call these *legal intentions*. According to this doctrine, the goal of interpreting a constitutional provision, let us say, is to recover the Framers' legal intentions. The words employed by the Framers provide a clue, but only a clue, to those legal intentions. Suppose we had direct independent access to those intentions by going back in time and hooking telepathically into the Framers' collective mind without the intermediary of their choice of words. Then it would be the Framers' legal intentions that bind future generations regardless of their eventual choice of words. The question of what the occurrence of 'cruel' in the Eighth Amendment applies to may be considered as well, but only as a means for summoning evidence in establishing the legal intentions of its producers. In short, on the view in question the relation between the semantic significance of 'cruel' and what is a dominant determinant in overall legal content, which is in the first instance the Framers' legal intentions, is itself merely evidential.

Textualism, on the other hand, has it that whether or not the Eighth Amendment prohibits capital punishment is determined by, among other factors, whether or not the occurrence of 'cruel' therein applies, by dint of its semantic significance, to capital punishment. As before in the case of intentionalism, we note that in this case too textualism as

[15] Ibid., 144, emphasis added.

formulated does not require that the semantic content of the relevant occurrence of 'cruel' be the sole factor in determining the legal content of the Cruel and Unusual Punishment Clause. And as before, what else might be needed here lies beyond our present concerns.[16] So Scalia subscribes to a form of textualism in opposition to intentionalism, but also in opposition to what he regards as the undemocratic idea of a Living Constitution whereby non-elected officials – judges – act as legislators. Whatever his differences from Scalia may be, Dworkin subscribes to a form of textualism as well. Here are some relevant passages from Dworkin:

> textual interpretation is nevertheless an essential part of any broader program of constitutional interpretation because what those who made the Constitution actually said is always at least an important ingredient in any genuinely interpretive constitutional argument.[17]

> We have a constitutional text. We do not disagree about which inscriptions comprise that text; nobody argues about which series of letters and spaces make it up. Of course, identifying a canonical series of letters and spaces is only the beginning of interpretation. For there remains the problem of what any particular portion of that series means.[18]

Given their shared broad allegiance to textualism, it might be expected that Dworkin's disagreement with Scalia over the correct interpretation of the Cruel and Unusual Punishment Clause can be reconstructed by considering (COMMONLY) as a point of departure, focusing, in particular, on what should count as a proper instance of (COMMONLY)'s embedded subjunctive conditional.

I will now attempt a reconstruction of the dispute that takes Scalia's allegiance to (COMMONLY) as a starting point. I will proceed in two stages. At first I will consider whether a Dworkinian principle of statutory interpretation can be seen as only a mild departure from (COMMONLY), a departure that still assumes an interpretationist metasemantics in the background. Doing so will pave the way for a superior account of the dispute, one whereby Scalia subscribes to (COMMONLY) with its attendant commitment to metasemantic interpretationism while Dworkin subscribes to a different principle of statutory interpretation altogether, one not accompanied by a tacit commitment to metasemantic interpretationism but accompanied by a tacit commitment to productivism instead.

[16] See n. 12 above. [17] Dworkin, *Justice in Robes*, 118. [18] Ibid., 120.

It can be plausibly maintained that Scalia endorses

> (†) Had the original producers of 'cruel' interpreted it, they would endorse interpretation *Int* that assigns *M* to it,

where *M* is a property that fails to apply to capital punishment. And it might be maintained, correlatively, that Dworkin denies (†) and endorses (‡) instead:

> (‡) Had the original producers of 'cruel' interpreted it, they would endorse interpretation *Int** that assigns *M** to it,

where *M** is a property that applies to capital punishment. And presumably Scalia would deny (‡) in turn. (†) and (‡) are thus understood as instances of the following clause embedded in (COMMONLY):

> (EMBEDDED) For some interpretation *I*, *I* assigns *C* to *T* and is such that had *T*'s original producers interpreted *T*, they would endorse *I* as *T*'s interpretation.

To assess the present construal of the dispute we need to delve deeper into (†) and (‡). We do this against the background of the standard Lewis–Stalnaker semantics for subjunctive conditionals. Finessing irrelevant details, on the standard semantics claims of the form shared by (†) and (‡) – schematized as $P\Box\!\!\rightarrow Q$ or $P>Q$ – are true if and only if at all the worlds closest to the actual one at which the antecedent holds, the consequent holds as well. Let the measure of closeness or similarity among worlds be informed by the Framers' actual moral opinions at the time of drafting the Eighth Amendment.[19] According to Scalia's position, at all such worlds at which the Framers interpret the Cruel and Unusual Punishment Clause, they assign an interpretation to the clause that excludes capital punishment, given the moral opinions they happen to have. (This is under the assumption that the Framers would endorse an interpretation of 'cruel' that is consonant with their actual moral opinions about cruelty – an assumption we will revisit later.) So much for Scalia's endorsement of (†). How about the denial of (‡)? *M* fails to apply to capital punishment while *M** applies to it, so *M* and

[19] In general, the standard of similarity among worlds is something that gets negotiated among participants in the conversation. Here we are assuming that worlds at which the Framers' moral opinions vary from their actual ones are considered irrelevant for the assessment of whether or not (†) is true.

*M** are distinct, and so *Int* and *Int** are distinct. Inasmuch as the Framers would endorse a univocal interpretation of 'cruel', the denial of (‡) follows from the affirmation of (†).

The situation with Dworkin according to the present construal is slightly more complicated. First, Dworkin might not wish to quarrel with Scalia's endorsement of (†). Perhaps the historical facts surrounding the text's actual composition provide ample evidence to ground the determination that at all the closest worlds to the actual one at which the Framers interpret 'cruel', and where closeness is under fixity in the Framers' actual moral beliefs at the time of drafting the text, they endorse an interpretation that assigns *M* to 'cruel'. But if Dworkin does not wish to quarrel with Scalia's endorsement of (†), then he should not quarrel with the rejection of (‡) either, at least insofar as the Framers would not equivocate on the interpretation of 'cruel'. In other words, given the endorsement of (†), there will be at least one such world at which they do not endorse an interpretation that assigns *M** to 'cruel', where *M** includes capital punishment. So on the standard semantics (‡) will turn out to be false. And yet were we not supposed to be mooting the idea of Dworkin endorsing (‡) rather than rejecting it?

The answer is that the Dworkinian position is better construed as treating (‡) as elliptical for:

> (‡′) Had the original producers of 'cruel' interpreted it, *and had they been best informed about being cruel,* they would endorse interpretation *Int** that assigns *M** to it.

And it is (‡′) that Dworkin is better read as endorsing – this against the background of a moral argument to the effect that property *M**, which includes capital punishment, is the property of being cruel. The consequence drawn is that at all the worlds closest to the actual one at which the Framers interpret the Cruel and Unusual Punishment Clause *and are also informed by the best account of cruelty,* they assign an interpretation that renders capital punishment cruel. (This is under the assumption that they would endorse an interpretation of 'cruel' that is consonant with the best account of cruelty, which, as in the case of the parallel assumption behind Scalia's endorsement of (†), we will revisit later.) We also note that endorsement of (‡′) is perfectly compatible with rejection of (‡).[20]

[20] A well-known feature of such conditionals is that, in contrast to material conditionals, strengthening of the antecedent fails for them: $P \wedge R > Q$ is *not* entailed by $P > Q$.

And we note, finally, that (‡′) is not plausibly an instance of (EMBEDDED) but rather an instance of:

(EMBEDDED′) For some interpretation *I*, *I* assigns *C* to *T* and is such that had *T*'s original producers interpreted *T* and were best informed about *C*, they would endorse *I* as *T*'s interpretation.

So on the present construal of the dispute, while Scalia endorses (COMMONLY) as a principle of statutory interpretation, Dworkin endorses a slight variant:

(COMMONLY′) For any legal text *T* and content *C*, *T* has *C* if and only if for some interpretation *I*, *I* assigns *C* to *T* and is such that had *T*'s original producers interpreted *T* and were best informed about *C*, they would endorse *I* as *T*'s interpretation.

Two comments are in order. First, we imagine that what it is to be "best informed about *C*" varies according to the semantic details, but for our purposes we construe this as being best informed about a property. And to be best informed about a property in the relevant sense is to have the best understanding of what it is for something to bear the property in question. Second, the way (‡′) is meant to be an instance of (EMBEDDED′) is against the background of the moral argument alluded to above that identifies *M** with being cruel. It is this moral argument that secures the identification of being best informed about *M** with being best informed about being cruel.

There are at least two grounds on which Scalia could oppose Dworkin's position as outlined here, one concerning cruelty and the other concerning statutory interpretation. As for the first, Scalia might have little sympathy for (‡′) if he supposes as a matter of his considered moral opinion that capital punishment (by lethal injection, say) is not a cruel punishment.[21] So he might deny that under the best theory of cruelty death by lethal injection is cruel. And so, insofar as *M** applies to capital punishment, he would deny (‡′). On other hand, on the side of statutory interpretation, Scalia would most likely consider (COMMONLY′) as not true to the calling of textualism. For (COMMONLY′), with its talk of being best informed about the subject matter of the text, might smack of a future-looking

[21] Such an attitude is manifested, for example, in certain passages in Scalia's concurring opinion in the Supreme Court's decision to deny review in the Texas death penalty case *Callins* v. *Collins*, 510 US 1141 (1994).

orientation, a living constitutionalism whereby each generation will see itself as bound by what it perceives as the final verdict on the relevant subject matter. This would appear to defeat the textualist quest after original meaning in the course of determining overall legal content.

To repeat, the present construal of the dispute over the correct interpretation of the Cruel and Unusual Punishment Clause has Scalia endorse (COMMONLY) as a principle for statutory interpretation while having Dworkin endorse (COMMONLY′). Accordingly, Scalia endorses (†) and rejects (‡), while Dworkin endorses (‡′). Whether or not Dworkin endorses (†) and rejects (‡) as well is uncertain. That Scalia endorses (‡′) is unlikely. What is clear, however, is that endorsing (‡′) is compatible with rejecting (‡). What Scalia and Dworkin disagree about most basically according to this portrayal is which principle of statutory interpretation is correct, (COMMONLY) or (COMMONLY′). The implications for the correct interpretation of 'cruel' can be seen through the following choice: are we to ask how the Framers would interpret the term in light of their actual moral opinions about cruelty, or are we to ask how they would interpret 'cruel' had they been best informed about cruelty? For Scalia it is the first option we should be pursuing. For Dworkin, according to the present reconstruction, it is the second option.

This construal seems to accord well with Scalia's own perception of his disagreement with Dworkin over the proper interpretation of the Cruel and Unusual Punishment Clause:

> ['Cruel'] means not (as Professor Dworkin would have it) "whatever may be considered cruel from one generation to the next," but "what we consider cruel today"; otherwise, it would be no protection against the moral perceptions of a future, more brutal, generation. It is, in other words, rooted in the moral perceptions *of the time*.[22]

Under one reading of this and related passages Scalia appears to be advocating an implausible *semantic* thesis: that the meaning of 'cruel' has the term apply to whatever speakers regard as falling under 'cruel' without any external check provided by the range of phenomena to which the term purportedly applies. As a semantic proposal such phenomenalism about 'cruel' is fanciful, whatever the merits of phenomenalism about moral properties might be within the metaphysics of value. In other words, even if phenomenalism about cruelty is correct, and to be cruel really is to be regarded in a certain way and nothing more, the suggestion that as a matter

[22] Scalia, *A Matter of Interpretation*, 145.

of its meaning the application conditions for 'cruel' are given by 'whatever we now regard as falling under "cruel"' is spurious.

A better reading of this and related passages, however, has Scalia subscribe to (COMMONLY) and its implications, and oppose (COMMONLY′) and *its* implications. On this better reading, Scalia's textualism is committed to the interpretationist metasemantic notion that whatever 'cruel' means in the mouth of the Framers is constituted by how the Framers would interpret it in light of their moral beliefs. Here no appeal need be made to the questionable semantic thesis about 'cruel'. For all the position has to offer, it could still be the case that the significance of 'cruel' in the mouth of Framers turns out to be cruelty pure and simple, simply because the interpretation that the Framers would assign to 'cruel' is just that – cruelty per se – and cruelty does happen to apply to capital punishment. (Here we are imagining that the Framers' interpretation of 'cruel' somehow tracks cruelty per se while bypassing their moral opinions.) Or it might be, as Scalia contends, that the significance of 'cruel' in the mouth of the Framers is some property *M* that excludes capital punishment. A full defense of the latter option would require Scalia to provide some backing for the assumption that the Framers would endorse an interpretation of 'cruel' that coheres with their moral opinions. But there is no further need for Scalia to subscribe to the implausible semantic thesis that the Eighth Amendment's 'cruel' applies as a matter of its semantic significance to whatever the Framers regarded as falling under 'cruel' without any further constraint provided by the phenomena.

It is tempting to oppose Scalia's position on statutory interpretation by pointing out that the semantics of 'cruel' as it occurs in the Eighth Amendment does not bear a descriptive reduction to 'whatever we (the Framers) regard as falling under "cruel"'. As a semantic proposal such a reduction seems questionable at best and runs afoul of well-known difficulties.[23] It might then be said that the significance of 'cruel' is just

[23] There has been a vast literature in the philosophy of language over the past forty years targeting such descriptive reductions in general. Most of the relevant discussion can be traced back to the seminal contributions of K. Donnellan, "Proper Names and Identifying Descriptions," *Synthese* 21 (1970), 335–58. See Kripke, *Naming and Necessity*, and H. Putnam, "The Meaning of 'Meaning,'" in *Mind, Language and Reality: Philosophical Papers*, vol. II (Cambridge University Press, 1975), 215–71. In the case that interests us a proposed distinctly semantic connection between 'cruel' and 'whatever we (the Framers) regard as falling under "cruel"' would have to meet at least the following challenges. In the relevant context the sentence 'To be cruel is not to be whatever we [the Framers] regard as

the property of being cruel, end of story, which puts the lie to Scalia's position on semantic grounds. But a more interesting and nuanced rendering of the Scalia–Dworkin dispute shifts its ground away from such semantic matters. The better account has Scalia endorse an interpretation of 'cruel' that assigns a certain property *M* to it that excludes capital punishment – semantic exotica aside – and has Dworkin endorse another interpretation that assigns a different property *M** to it that includes capital punishment. My present claim is that we can identify a deep source for the disagreement between Scalia and Dworkin over the correct interpretation of the Cruel and Unusual Punishment Clause by attending to the metasemantic backdrop.

In the previous section we attributed to Scalia an endorsement of (COMMONLY) and attributed to Dworkin an endorsement of (COMMONLY′). Both endorsements are best understood under a tacit commitment to an interpretationist metasemantics. Both principles render the text's original endowment as constituted by its interpretability by the text's producers. It is time to make good on the early promise of shifting the ground of the Scalia–Dworkin dispute to metasemantics. On this final construal of the controversy, Scalia is still seen as committed to (COMMONLY) as a principle of statutory interpretation, with the attendant tacit commitment to an interpretationist metasemantics. But Dworkin is now seen as committed to something else entirely, a principle best appreciated through its comparison with (COMMONLY):

(COMMONLY) For any legal text *T* and content *C*, *T* has *C* if and only if for some interpretation *I*, *I* assigns *C* to *T* and is such that had *T*'s original producers interpreted *T*, they would endorse *I* as *T*'s interpretation.

(PREFERABLY) For any legal text *T* and content *C*, *T* has *C* if and only if for some interpretation *I*, *I* assigns *C* to *T* and gets *T*'s original semantic endowment right.

My claim is that Dworkin's opposition to Scalia is most intelligibly rendered as an endorsement of some version of (PREFERABLY). But before turning to establish this claim, let me ponder the alternative principle in more detail.

falling under "cruel"' does not seem (a) necessarily false, (b) a priori false, or (c) contradictory. I believe these challenges cannot be met adequately despite the undeniable ingenuity that has gone into well-known efforts to meet them ever since the original challenges were set. Arguing the point here would take us too far afield.

The most noticeable feature of (PREFERABLY) is that it does not subjunctivize on the text's original producers (the Framers) interpreting the text. It makes a direct and seemingly flat-footed appeal to the recovery of the text's original semantic endowment as a condition of the text's correct interpretation. By not appealing to how the text's original producers would interpret the text as an indirect way of recovering what the text originally meant and thus means, (PREFERABLY) is a much simpler principle. It dispenses with potentially distracting subjunctive 'noise'. When we reconstructed the Scalia–Dworkin dispute under the auspices of (COMMONLY) and (COMMONLY′) above, we noted a background assumption to the effect that the Framers would endorse an interpretation of 'cruel' that is consonant with their moral opinions as to what is cruel. For Scalia the relevant consonance is with the Framers' actual opinions at the time of drafting the Eighth Amendment. For the reconstruction of Dworkin's position under (COMMONLY′) the relevant consonance is with the Framers' opinions as to what is cruel as informed by the best account of cruelty. Let us now reconsider these assumptions, starting with Scalia. His view has it that the following is the case:

> (†) Had the original producers of 'cruel' interpreted it, they would endorse interpretation *Int* that assigns *M* to it,

where *M* is a property that does not apply to capital punishment. (†) is true if and only if at all the closest worlds to the actual one at which the Framers interpret 'cruel', they endorse an interpretation that assigns *M* to it. And we assumed that the intended Scalian measure of closeness or similarity among worlds includes fixity in the Framers' actual moral opinions. But now it seems fair to ask how we are supposed to go about justifying the claim that the Framers would endorse whatever interpretation coheres with their moral opinions at the time of the text's production. Let us grant for a moment the metasemantic interpretationist point that how they would interpret the text is constitutive of the text having meant what it did. And let us grant the originalist point that the text having meant what it did is what it means now. It is still not obvious without further argument that the Framers would endorse an interpretation of 'cruel' that tracks the moral opinions they happened to have. Perhaps they would endorse an interpretation that is more inclusive than what their moral opinions allow, since they were future-looking Enlightenment men of moral progress. Or perhaps they would endorse a more restrictive interpretation than their moral opinions allow due to some shared concern about moral squeamishness. Whatever the case may be – and setting aside the fact that the latter alternative seems far-fetched – it is at least not obvious that consonance with moral opinions is determinative of how the Framers would be inclined to interpret a piece of moral terminology issued from their own pen or mouth. An adherent of (COMMONLY) owes us a defense of the implicated consonance.

Moving on to the Dworkinian position under the reconstruction in terms of (COMMONLY′) above, the following is assumed to be the case:

> (‡′) Had the original producers of 'cruel' interpreted it, *and had they been best informed about being cruel*, they would endorse interpretation *Int** that assigns *M** to it,

where *M** is a property that does apply to capital punishment. (‡′) is true if and only if at all the closest worlds to the actual one at which the Framers interpret 'cruel' and are best informed about cruelty, they endorse an interpretation that assigns *M** to it. But again it seems only fair to ask how we are to go about justifying the claim that at all the relevant worlds the Framers would interpret 'cruel' in a way that is consonant with what is cruel under the best theory of the matter. One can surely be informed by the best theory of cruelty while endorsing an interpretation of 'cruel' that is not compatible with the theory, for a variety of reasons. An argument is needed to convince us that we may safely ignore such possibilities in the present context.

Such challenges are not special to this area and are in fact endemic to subjunctive analyses. They are forced upon us by the tacit commitment incurred by endorsement of (COMMONLY) or (COMMONLY′) to the metasemantic interpretationist idea that interpretability is constitutive of semantic endowment, together with the subjunctive treatment of interpretability. And even if there are workable alternatives to the latter, the move from (COMMONLY) and (COMMONLY′) to (PREFERABLY) dispenses with the need to seek them for the purpose at hand.

(PREFERABLY) makes no reference to interpretability as the route to a legal text's original endowment with significance. It incorporates the text's original semantic endowment directly into the text having the legal content that it has. Of course even the metasemantic interpretationist can endorse the letter of (PREFERABLY) as formulated here – with the understanding that the original semantic endowment of the text is constituted by the text's interpretability. But only the metasemantic productivist can reap the genuine benefits of (PREFERABLY) over the other principles of statutory interpretation we have been considering.

In the context of a recent polemic with legal positivism Dworkin writes: "I have argued for many years that in many circumstances moral facts figure among the basic truth conditions of propositions of law."[24] Armed with (PREFERABLY) we can now appreciate the import of this remark with respect to the Cruel and Unusual Punishment Clause of the Eighth Amendment. In Dworkin we read the following:

> The Eighth Amendment of the Constitution forbids 'cruel' and unusual punishment. Does that mean punishments that the authors thought were cruel or (what probably comes to the same thing) punishments that were cruel by the popular opinion of their day? Or does it mean punishments that are in fact – according to the correct standards for deciding such matters – cruel?[25]

> We have to choose between an abstract, principled, moral reading on the one hand – that the authors meant to prohibit punishments that are in fact cruel as well as unusual... and a concrete, dated reading on the other – that they meant to say that punishments widely thought cruel as well as unusual at the time they spoke . . . are prohibited.[26]

And in a footnote Dworkin adds that the preferred alternative to Scalia's reading is "one that translates the Eighth Amendment as referring to punishments that really are cruel." Dworkin concludes: "If we are trying to make best sense of the Framers speaking as they did in the context in which they spoke, we should conclude that they intended to lay down abstract, not dated, commands and prohibitions."[27] This talk of the Framers' intentions should not be mistaken for the intentionalist idea that the task at hand is to uncover their legal intentions, their intentions to shape the law in a particular direction. Such an intentionalist reading would conflict with the textualist strand in Dworkin's position noted earlier. Rather, the intentions in questions are the intentions that figure in saying what we say: "We must begin, in my view, by asking what – on the best evidence available – the authors of the text in question intended to say."[28] And what they intended to say is to prohibit punishments that are cruel, pure and simple.

As consumers of the text we need not ask ourselves what the text's producers would subsume under 'cruel' given their actual moral opinions. Nor, for that matter, do we need to appeal to what they would subsume under 'cruel' had they been armed with the best theory of cruelty. Both of these options are under the auspices of the metasemantic interpretationist

[24] Dworkin, *Justice in Robes*, 225. [25] Ibid., 120. [26] Ibid., 121. [27] Ibid., 121–2.
[28] Ibid., 120.

idea that what the Framers meant then, and so what their words mean now, is constituted by how they would interpret it. As consumers of the text, what we need to ask ourselves is far more direct. The move from (COMMONLY′) to (PREFERABLY) beckons us to consider directly the semantic endowment that was in fact created when the Eighth Amendment was drafted.

Compare the task of interpreting 'cruel' in the Eighth Amendment to the task of interpreting 'gold' in a hypothetical (albeit fanciful) late eighteenth-century injunction for members of the House to display a gold ring if married. Plausibly in the latter case we would interpret the injunction as requiring members of the House today to display a ring that is really gold. And in determining whether a given ring is gold we would be aided by our best account of the matter. Asking what the producers of the injunction would regard as gold in light of their metallurgical beliefs seems irrelevant. And asking what the producers of the injunction would regard as gold had they been best informed about gold seems gratuitous and circuitous. What we should be asking is what material the producers of the injunction intended to be talking about. They intended to be talking about gold.

Next consider 'fine' or 'punishment' as they actually occur in the Eighth Amendment. Here, too, we ask ourselves, given the original conditions of production of the Bill of Rights, what the Framers intended to be talking about. It is this that is determinative of what those words meant, and so what those words mean. So when considering a given act and whether it falls under 'punishment' as specified in the document, we need to ask ourselves whether the act really does qualify as a punishment – without quotation marks around 'punishment'. Similarly in our case, we should be asking ourselves whether capital punishment really is cruel, because what the Framers intended to talk about was the property of being cruel. We ask ourselves, under the auspices of metasemantic productivism, what semantic endowment the relevant occurrence of 'cruel' from the pen of the Framers possesses. And the most likely answer is that the Eighth Amendment's 'cruel' just meant – and so just means – being cruel.

Let us not pretend that metasemantic productivism does not face its own special challenges. The productivist at the very least owes us an explanation qua metasemanticist of how it is possible to talk about something through a substantial dose of ignorance about it – by no means a trivial task. But the apparent difficulty of such a challenge should not distract us from the natural thing to say about statutory interpretation, which is that correctness of interpretation is measured by whether it gets the original semantic endowment of the text right. And the revisionary rendering of the text's semantic endowment in terms of its interpretability is uncalled for. The legal interpreter does not owe us qua consumer of legal texts a worked out metasemantics. But from a metasemantic perspective, the relative simplicity of (PREFERABLY) over (COMMONLY), coupled with the unmistakable attractiveness of productivism, clearly tips the balance in favor of (PREFERABLY) as a principle of statutory interpretation.[29]

And so, finally, 'cruel' in the Eighth Amendment means the property of being cruel. An interpretation of the Cruel and Unusual Punishment Clause under (PREFERABLY) is correct insofar as it recovers what the Framers meant to be talking about, which is cruelty. But what is cruelty? To answer *this* question plausibly requires direct engagement in moral reasoning, doing the best we can in this regard. We have before us but one instance in which, as Dworkin put it, "moral facts figure among the basic truth conditions of propositions of law."[30] It certainly does fall upon the Dworkinian interpreter of the Bill of Rights to discern what the relevant moral facts are. This should no more occasion concern about the undemocratic nature of unelected officials becoming legislators than does the fact that judges use their powers of reasoning to interpret the terms 'fine' or 'punishment' and determine whether they, too, apply in a given case.

[29] Considerations of space preclude me from entering into a discussion of the distinct metasemantic advantages of productivism over interpretationism. For my own views on the topic, see Simchen, "Token-Reflexivity," and Simchen, "Semantic Endowment."

[30] Dworkin, *Justice in Robes*, 225.

PART II

Normativity of Legal Authority

5

Doing another's bidding

MATTHEW HANSER

By doing another's bidding I mean doing something because another person asked or told you to do it. This is not the same as following advice, which I here understand, rather narrowly, as doing something because another person told you it is what you ought to do. Following advice is a form of epistemic deference – it involves relying on another person's judgment about what you have reason to do. I am interested in a more distinctively practical form of deference – being guided directly by another person's will, so to speak, rather than by (what he represents as) his belief about what you have reason to do independently of his will. You might do another person's bidding for any number of reasons. You might do it because he is your friend, spouse, employer, or commanding officer. You might do it in order to put him in your debt, or because you are in his. You might do it because you fear him, or admire him, or seek his approval. You might even do it because you think you are likely to prosper by doing as he says. This last possibility still differs from taking advice. As I am imagining the case, he does not tell you what he thinks it would be best for you to do; he simply tells you to do it.

Insofar as philosophers have discussed the phenomenon I am interested in, it has usually been in connection with orders or commands (I shall use the terms interchangeably). Commands are an important topic, but there are other ways of bidding another to do something. A single-minded focus upon commands is thus liable to distort our view of the wider phenomenon. Even so, it may be helpful to begin by

Most of the material in this chapter was developed while I was an H. L. A. Hart Visiting Fellow at the Oxford Centre for Ethics and Philosophy of Law. I thank the Master and Fellows of University College for their hospitality during my stay in Oxford. I presented earlier versions of this chapter at the Universities of Oxford, Glasgow, Leeds, and Toronto, and at the St. Louis Annual Conference on Reasons and Rationality. I am grateful for the questions and comments I received on these occasions.

considering what philosophers have had to say about this special case. If nothing else, it will help me identify my topic more clearly.

Commands, requests, and protected reasons

Here is H. L. A. Hart expounding, with approval, what he takes to be a central feature of Hobbes's view about commands:

> the commander characteristically intends his hearer to take the commander's will instead of his own as a guide to action and so to take it in place of any deliberation or reasoning of his own: the expression of a commander's will that an act be done is intended to preclude or cut off any independent deliberation by the hearer of the merits pro and con of doing the act . . . This I think is precisely what is meant by speaking of a command as 'requiring' action and calling a command a 'peremptory' form of address.[1]

This passage begins with an apt characterization of the phenomenon that interests me. When a commander gives an order, he expresses, in a special way, his will that the subject do such and such; and when the subject obeys the command, there is a sense in which he thereby allows himself to be guided by the commander's will, and by the commander's deliberations, rather than his own. There is a sense in which he lets the commander decide for him what he shall do. But this is all rather impressionistic. We need a more precise understanding of the sense in which the subject is guided by his commander's will rather than his own. And in developing this understanding we must be careful not to overstate the case. The commander does not bypass or override the subject's will. The subject *chooses* to act as he does, and presumably has his reasons for so choosing. An adequate account must capture both these aspects of the phenomenon under investigation: the sense in which the subject, in obeying the order, himself wills or decides upon the act; and the sense in which, in obeying, he lets the commander decide for him, and does the commander's will rather than his own.

Hart's account of the phenomenon begins to emerge at the end of the quoted passage, where he links being guided by a commander's will to the requiring force of commands. Hart identifies being required to do

[1] H. L. A. Hart, "Commands and Authoritative Legal Reasons," in his *Essays on Bentham* (Oxford University Press, 1982), 253.

something with having a special sort of reason to do it, and he argues that valid commands generate reasons of this special sort. In his view, the reason generated by a valid command has two important features. First, it is *content-independent*: the reason to perform the action is simply that it was commanded. Had the commander ordered the subject to do something else, the subject would have had reason to do that instead.[2] And, second, it is *peremptory*: the reason generated by a valid command is both a reason for doing the thing commanded *and* a reason for "excluding normal free deliberation about the merits of doing it."[3] Here Hart draws upon, but slightly modifies, Joseph Raz's notion of a *protected* reason.[4] A protected reason for doing something is both a first-order reason for doing it and a second-order "exclusionary" reason for not acting on any of a range of possible contrary first-order reasons.[5] Raz argues that it is a principle of practical reason that exclusionary reasons prevail over the reasons they exclude.[6] The exclusionary component of a protected reason thus "protects" the first-order component from having to compete with a variety of potential contrary reasons. Consider what we might call a "heavily" protected reason: one whose exclusionary component excludes all but the most improbable potential contrary reasons. Typically an agent subject to a heavily protected reason ought, all things considered, to act in conformity with that reason – not because the first-order component, when taken together with other favoring reasons, typically outweighs the contrary reasons, but because the first-order component typically need not compete with contrary reasons at all. The first-order component of a heavily protected reason must compete only with those contrary reasons that are not excluded, and typically there will be no such reasons. Absent extraordinary circumstances, then, the agent ought to act in conformity with the protected reason even if the balance of all reasons (including the excluded ones) favors acting differently. And that, according to Raz, is precisely what it is for an act to be required. A requirement is not a reason so strong that it outweighs most contrary reasons; it is a reason that typically need not outweigh contrary reasons in order to prevail. The exclusionary component of a protected

[2] Ibid., 254. [3] Ibid., 255.

[4] Hart acknowledges his debt to Raz at ibid., 244.

[5] J. Raz, *The Authority of Law* (Oxford University Press, 1979), 17–18. For Raz's fullest discussion of exclusionary reasons, see J. Raz, *Practical Reason and Norms* (London: Hutchinson, 1975; reprinted with a new postscript, Princeton University Press, 1990).

[6] Raz, *Practical Reason and Norms*, 40, 189–90.

reason converts what would otherwise be a mere reason into a *pro tanto* duty or obligation.[7]

Hart's peremptory reasons differ from Raz's protected reasons in two ways. First, while a peremptory reason is, in part, a reason not to *deliberate* about the pros and cons of doing what the reason would have one do, a protected reason is, in part, a reason not to *act* on certain reasons against doing what the reason would have one do. Raz argues that his formulation is superior on the grounds that commanders typically do not mind if their subjects reflect upon the merits of what they have been ordered to do, so long as they do not allow those reflections to influence their conduct.[8] The objection, so stated, is unfair, since Hart's peremptory reasons do not prohibit such idle reflections. The weighing of pros and cons counts as *deliberation* only when the agent engages in it with a view to being guided by the outcome. But Raz's underlying point seems right: commands are meant to rule out contrary *actions*, not (just) the deliberations that might give rise to them. The second difference between peremptory and protected reasons is that Raz explicitly says protected reasons need not exclude *all* competing considerations. Orders are rarely absolute. At a bare minimum, every command is meant to exclude acting on the basis of a mere contrary desire: one cannot justify failing to obey a legitimate order simply by pointing out that one prefers to do something else.[9] The range of additionally excluded reasons depends on the content of the command and the nature of the commander's authority. Hart is less clear on this point. He says peremptory reasons rule out "normal free deliberation" about the merits of the actions in question; he does not say whether deliberation restricted to some subset of the applicable reasons might sometimes be allowed.

For present purposes these differences between Hart and Raz do not matter. Both hold that a subject who regards a command that he Φ as legitimate will take that command to give him a special sort of double-barreled reason, one that (a) counts in favor of Φing, and (b) *bars* him from responding as he otherwise might to certain reasons against Φing. Broadening Raz's use of the term, let us call this second component, whether or not we interpret it as Raz does, the *exclusionary* component. The exclusionary component is meant to capture the sense in which the command places the recipient under a requirement.[10]

[7] J. Raz, *The Morality of Freedom* (Oxford University Press, 1986), 37, 60.

[8] Ibid., 39. [9] Raz, *Practical Reason and Norms*, 22–4.

[10] When Hart and Raz discuss orders, they do so (at least in part) with a view to illuminating the nature of the reasons created by legitimate laws. My focus is entirely upon ordinary interpersonal interactions in which one party asks or tells another to do

Does the view that legitimate commands generate such double-barreled reasons meet the *desiderata* identified above – does it adequately explain both the sense in which the obedient subject wills his own action and the sense in which he is guided by his commander's will rather than his own?

The view clearly yields the result that the subject wills the action himself. When he obeys (what he takes to be) a legitimate order, he does what he thinks he ought to do in light of (what he takes to be) the reasons that apply to him – his action constitutes his rational response to those reasons. It is just that some of the reasons he is responding to were brought into existence by the command. Does the view also explain the sense in which the obedient subject is guided by the commander's will rather than his own? Here there are two possibilities to consider. The explanation might be provided simply by the fact that the command generates (among other things) a first-order reason to perform the commanded act, or it might be provided by the fact that the command generates more specifically a *protected* reason to perform the commanded act. I begin with the second possibility, since this is the explanation that Hart and Raz propose. I shall return to the other possibility.

Here is the explanation in terms of protected reasons. Suppose that a certain command generates a heavily protected reason: it both provides a reason in favor of performing the commanded act and excludes all but the most unlikely reasons against performing it. Absent special circumstances, the commander, by issuing this command, *settles* what the subject must do if he is to respond rationally to the reasons confronting him. The subject must still decide what to do in light of those reasons, but by taking the contrary reasons off the table the commander *in effect* makes the decision for him. The balance of all reasons, pro and con, no longer matters. The commander's expression of will places the subject under a requirement that, barring special circumstances, he can satisfy only by doing what the commander willed him to do. This is the sense in which the obedient subject is *guided* by the commander's will.[11]

something. I make no claim about whether my account of doing another's bidding should be extended to cover acts of obeying the law.

[11] See Raz, *Practical Reason and Norms*, 79; Raz, *The Authority of Law*, 24; and Hart, "Commands and Authoritative Legal Reasons," 253–7. Raz argues that when an agent makes a decision for himself, that decision constitutes a protected reason to perform the act decided upon (Raz, *Practical Reason and Norms*, 66–7). Given this understanding of decision, Raz can hold that commands and decisions leave their subjects in precisely the same practical position. This is a further sense in which the commander "in effect" decides for the subject.

Of course not even a heavily protected reason *automatically* settles what the subject must do. The protected reason's exclusionary component might be outweighed by a competing second-order reason that supports acting on the relevant contrary first-order reasons. And unless the command is absolute, there might yet be unexcluded first-order reasons strong enough to outweigh the reasons in favor of performing the commanded act. Neither eventuality is likely when the reason generated by the command is heavily protected, and so typically, at least, no weighing of reasons will be called for in such cases. These, then, are the cases where, on the present view, it makes most sense to describe the subject as being guided by his commander's will. When a command generates only a weakly protected reason, however, the subject typically *will* need to weigh the first-order component of the protected reason against contrary reasons. And the fewer reasons are excluded, the more similar the subject's actual deliberations will be to what they would have been had the reason in favor of the action not been protected at all. Perhaps, then, Hart and Raz should speak of degrees of being guided by a commander's will. The more unexcluded reasons the subject must weigh against the first-order reason generated by the command, the less the degree to which he will be guided by the commander's will should the reasons in favor of performing the commanded act prevail.

This understanding of what it is to be guided by another person's will, however, will not do. To see why not, consider requests. Raz holds that although a valid request generates a reason to perform the requested act, this reason is not even weakly protected. The fact that you were asked to do something is just one (more) reason in favor of doing it, to be put in the balance with all the other reasons, pro and con. The difference between the reasons created by orders and requests, then, lies in the presence or absence of an exclusionary component.[12] Now Raz is surely right that requests lack the peremptory force of commands. When someone asks you to do something, he does not require you to do it; he merely invites you to do it. Nevertheless, when an agent accedes to a request, he thereby allows himself to be guided by the requester's will, and by the requester's deliberations, rather than his own. The

[12] Raz, *Practical Reason and Norms*, 83; Raz, *The Authority of Law*, 23–4; Raz, *The Morality of Freedom*, 36–7. This contrast is at least implicit in Hart, "Commands and Authoritative Legal Reasons."

phenomenon I am interested in is present in both cases. It consequently cannot be explained by a factor that is present only in the case of commands.

A schematic example will help bring out the way in which the cases are alike. Suppose C calculates that his end would be advanced if another person, S, were to Φ. C wishes to make use of S's agency, to have S serve his end. How might he achieve this result? If he has the right sort of authority, he could command S to Φ. But if he lacks this authority, he could instead ask S to Φ. Indeed, even if he has the authority, he might prefer not to exercise it. Sometimes asking is better than ordering. Whichever option he chooses, however, his aim will be the same: to get S to do his bidding. Now consider the situation from S's point of view. Whether he has been asked or told to Φ, he must decide whether to acquiesce – he must decide whether to accede to the request or obey the command. And in making this decision he must be guided by his own deliberations, by his own assessment of the reasons for and against acquiescing.[13] The considerations bearing on his decision will differ in the two cases, but if he *does* acquiesce, the result will be the same: he will be putting himself at C's service, making himself an instrument of C's will. Neither acceding to a request nor obeying an order is like acting on an ordinary reason. When a subject accedes to a request or obeys an order, he cedes control of his actions to the person making the request or giving the order. He chooses, at least on that occasion and with respect to the matter at hand, to be guided by this other person's deliberations – deliberations to which he was not a party and to whose contents he may not even be privy. He chooses to act as this other person, for whatever reason, would have him act.

We must thus distinguish between: (a) what is involved in one person's doing another's bidding; and (b) the means by which the latter person induces the former to do his bidding. In the case of orders, this means distinguishing between: (a) the sense in which the obedient subject does his commander's will; and (b) the distinctive way in which the commander secures this result, namely by giving an order. Hart begins the passage I quoted earlier with the first point: when a subject obeys a command that he Φ, he allows the commander's will to take the place of his own independent deliberations about the merits of Φing. But Hart immediately goes on to identify the subject's being guided by the

[13] This description is of course idealized. An agent might be disposed to accede to certain requests, or to obey certain orders, without conscious deliberation.

commander's will with his acting as the commander *requires* him to act. Perhaps Hart thinks that only a requirement – only a protected or peremptory reason – can effect this substitution of the commander's will for the subject's. If the subject were allowed to weigh the fact that he was commanded to Φ against all the reasons for not Φing, he would be deliberating, and so the commander's will would not be taking the place of his own independent deliberations. But this reasoning is mistaken, as the case of requests shows. In considering whether to accede to a request, the subject is indeed allowed to balance the fact that he was asked to Φ against reasons for not Φing. But if, as a result of these deliberations, he chooses to accede to the request, he thereby puts himself at the requester's service. He allows himself to be guided by the requester's will, and by the requester's deliberations. Deliberating about *whether* to subordinate one's will to that of another is consistent with being guided by that person's will once one has chosen so to subordinate one's own will. My topic is how best to understand this subordination of the will.

Keeping promises, executing decisions, and doing another's bidding

So far I have argued only that the notion of an exclusionary reason will not figure into a proper understanding of the phenomenon of doing another's bidding. It does not follow that Hart and Raz are mistaken about the nature of the reasons generated by commands and requests. They think that commands and requests both generate first-order reasons to perform the commanded or requested acts; and they think that in the case of commands, but not in the case of requests, these first-order reasons are protected. Since the phenomenon that interests me is present in both cases, perhaps it is explained by the feature that they share. This is the other possibility I mentioned earlier in connection with commands: that perhaps the sense in which an obedient subject is guided by his commander's will is explained simply by the fact that a legitimate command generates (among other things) a first-order reason to perform the commanded act. I turn now to this possibility.

Here is how the explanation would go. When A asks or orders B to Φ, he expresses (in either the asking or the ordering way) his will that B Φ. If A's request or order is legitimate – if he possesses the appropriate sort of standing or authority – then the fact that he has asked or ordered B to Φ gives B a new first-order reason to Φ. And if B in turn accedes to the request or obeys the order, he acts (at least in part) for this new reason.

Since this new reason was brought into existence by A's expression of will, there is a sense in which B thereby does A's will. He acts *as* A willed him to act, and he does so (at least in part) *because* A so willed him to act. Like the account considered above, this account clearly captures the sense in which B does his own will when he acquiesces to A's request or command: his action constitutes his own rational response to the reasons confronting him. But the account does not do justice to the other aspect of doing another's bidding – it does not adequately capture the sense in which B does A's will, and is guided by A's deliberations rather than his own, when he accedes to A's request or obeys his command. The problem is that, according to Raz's view, a subject who Φs because he was asked or ordered to do so acts on what I shall call a *stand-alone, rationally opaque* reason to Φ. But, I shall argue, acting on such a reason is inconsistent with doing another's will. We should consequently reject the view that legitimate requests and commands generate such reasons.

I can most easily explain what I mean by a stand-alone, rationally opaque reason by briefly discussing the reasons generated by promises. When one person promises another that he will do something, he places himself under a *pro tanto* obligation to do that thing, and he bestows upon the recipient of the promise the power to release him from this *pro tanto* obligation. Raz understands the claim that a promise generates a *pro tanto* obligation as the claim that it generates a protected reason: the fact that an agent promised to Φ gives him both a first-order reason to Φ and a second-order exclusionary reason not to act on a variety of possible contrary first-order reasons. And Raz thinks that an agent can obligate himself to Φ simply by communicating his intention to undertake, by that very act of communication, an obligation to Φ. Promises are the conventional expression of such intentions.[14]

Making a promise is something that a person does, and does for a reason. An agent might promise to Φ in order to give the recipient an especially strong assurance that he will Φ. Or he might promise because he believes the recipient will value the normative power that the promise will confer upon him. The agent might promise to Φ in order to give himself an opportunity to demonstrate later that he is the sort of person who keeps his promises. Or, perversely, he might promise so that he can later demonstrate that he is *not* that sort of person. But whatever his

[14] For Raz's views on promising, see Raz, "Promises and Obligations," in P. M. S. Hacker and J. Raz (eds.), *Law, Morality, and Society: Essays in Honor of H. L. A. Hart* (Oxford University Press, 1977), 210–28.

reason for promising to Φ, we may note two important features of the reason to Φ that he thereby acquires. First, neither the force of this reason nor its status as a reason depends upon the soundness of his reason for making the promise in the first place. As long as the promise is valid, it is binding. Not all promises are valid. Arguably coerced promises and promises to perform wrongful acts are not. But an agent's success in placing himself under a promissory obligation does not depend upon the soundness of his reason for so obligating himself. The reason generated by a promise is thus *stand-alone*.

Second, when an agent acts on the reason generated by a promise – when he Φs because he promised to do so – he does not thereby act for the reason for which he made the promise. Suppose that in order to get my son to stop interrupting my work I promise to take him to the beach this weekend. If I then do as I promised, and do so *because* I promised, I do not thereby take him to the beach in order to get him to stop interrupting my work. (It was the *making* of the promise that I thought would put an end to the interruptions, not necessarily the keeping of it.) Of course when an agent promises to Φ, he often takes Φing to be something that he had antecedent reason to do anyway. And when he subsequently Φs, he might do so in part for that antecedent reason. When I take my son to the beach, I might do so in part because of my promise and in part because I think he will enjoy a trip to the beach. The point is that when an agent does something because he promised to do it, he does not *thereby* act for any other reason, or for the sake of any other end. This is the sense in which the reason generated by a promise is *rationally opaque*. If the agent also acts for some other reason, or for the sake of some other end, that is an extra, independent fact. The rational opacity of the promissory reason seems to follow from its being stand-alone. If the fact that I promised to Φ is all by itself a good reason to Φ, quite independently of my reason, good or bad, for making the promise, then why *should* we think that when I act for the promissory reason – when I Φ because I promised to do so – I thereby act for the reason for which I made the promise? The latter reason explains why I brought the promissory reason into existence, but that is all.

On both scores we may usefully contrast keeping a promise with executing a decision. Suppose that an agent is deliberating about whether to Φ. He considers the reasons pro and con and decides to Φ. In so doing he forms an intention to Φ. This intention reflects his judgment that he has sufficient reason to Φ, but it is not itself a reason to Φ. When the agent executes his intention to Φ, he acts for the pro-Φing reasons on the basis of which he formed the intention. If he decided to Φ because he thought that Φing would facilitate a certain end, then in executing the resulting intention he acts for the sake of that end. Because the agent's intention to Φ is not itself a reason to Φ, it follows immediately that it is not a stand-alone reason to Φ. And because in executing that intention the agent thereby acts for the reasons he took to count in favor of Φing when he formed it, it follows that his intention is not rationally opaque. On the contrary, it is rationally *transparent*. Both the intention and its execution constitute the agent's rational response to (what he took to be) reasons for Φing.[15]

Raz would not accept the sharp contrast I have just drawn between keeping a promise and executing a decision. Raz thinks that an intention to Φ *is* a reason to Φ, and that if the intention was produced by a valid decision, then it is a protected reason.[16] (Not every intention is produced by a decision. Decision brings deliberation to a close, and not every intention is a product of deliberation.) On Raz's view, reasons generated by decisions, like reasons generated by valid promises, are stand-alone and rationally opaque. If an agent has decided to Φ, then that decision constitutes a reason for him to Φ even if he erred in making it – even if he was mistaken in thinking, prior to making the decision, that he had sufficient reason to Φ. The reasons generated by decisions are thus stand-alone.[17] And, according to Raz, when an agent executes a decision to Φ, he does not thereby act for the pro-Φing reasons on the basis of which he made the decision. The reasons generated by decisions are thus rationally opaque. Raz acknowledges that if we were to ask an agent why he Φed, he would probably answer by citing the reasons on the basis of which he decided to Φ. If he decided to Φ because he thought Φing would promote a certain end, he would tell us that he Φed in order to promote that end. But Raz thinks we should not interpret this answer

[15] The agent may also have had a reason for settling the question whether to Φ exactly when he did. Perhaps he needed to decide one way or the other by a certain deadline. This reason for bringing deliberation to a close is not a reason *for Φing*, and when the agent executes his intention to Φ he does not thereby act for this reason.

[16] Raz, *Practical Reason and Norms*, 65–71. Not every decision is valid, so not every decision succeeds in producing an exclusionary reason, but Raz thinks that an agent must always regard his decisions as providing him with exclusionary reasons. Raz argues that valid decisions give rise to exclusionary reasons primarily on the grounds that this best explains why agents generally ought not to reconsider their decisions. But we can explain why it is generally unwise to reconsider decisions without assuming that a decision to Φ generates a second-order reason not to act on contrary first-order reasons.

[17] Ibid., 69–70.

literally. The agent would not really be telling us why he Φed. His reason for Φing would simply be that he decided to Φ. Rather, the agent would be telling us the "reason for his reason," i.e. the grounds upon which he brought that reason into existence.[18] Raz does not claim that this is the most natural interpretation of the agent's reply to the "why?" question, only that it is an available interpretation. He directs us elsewhere for his main argument that a decision is a first-order reason for performing the act decided upon.[19] I do not find his argument persuasive, and I think there are good grounds for denying that decisions (or more generally, intentions) are first-order reasons for performing the acts decided upon (or intended), but I cannot go into that here.[20] I shall simply take it for granted that Raz's view is mistaken. We should interpret the agent's reply literally: when he says that he Φed in order to promote a certain end, he means exactly what he says, and he speaks truly. Intentions are not themselves reasons for performing the intended acts, and they are rationally transparent to the reasons that stand behind them.

Promises and decisions, then, present us with two very different paradigms. When an agent Φs because he (validly) promised to do so, he acts for a stand-alone, rationally opaque reason to Φ that he brought into existence by making the promise. When an agent executes a decision to Φ, by contrast, he acts for the preexisting pro-Φing reasons on the basis of which he made the decision. So here's the crucial question: which paradigm, if either, provides the better model for understanding the phenomenon of doing another's bidding?

Raz thinks that doing another's bidding is like keeping a promise: when an agent obeys someone's valid order or accedes to someone's valid request that he Φ, he acts for a stand-alone, rationally opaque reason to Φ that this other person brought into existence by ordering or asking him to Φ. This reason is stand-alone because neither its force nor its status as

[18] Ibid., 71. [19] Ibid., 70, 76–80.

[20] For discussion, see M. Bratman, *Intention, Plans, and Practical Reason* (Cambridge, MA: Harvard University Press, 1987; reprinted Stanford: CSLI Publications, 1999), 23–7; J. Broome, "Are Intentions Reasons? And How Should We Cope with Incommensurable Values?" in C. W. Morris and A. Ripstein (eds.), *Practical Rationality and Preference: Essays for David Gauthier* (Cambridge University Press, 2001), 98–120; T. M. Scanlon "Reasons: A Puzzling Duality?" in R. J. Wallace, P. Petit, S. Scheffler, and M. Smith (eds.), *Reason and Value: Themes from the Moral Philosophy of Joseph Raz* (Oxford University Press, 2004), 231–46; N. Kolodny, "Aims as Reasons," in R. J. Wallace, R. Kumar, and S. Freeman (eds.), *Reasons and Recognition: Essays on the Philosophy of T. M. Scanlon* (Oxford University Press, 2011), 43–78.

a reason depends upon the soundness of the commander's or requester's reason for wishing the agent to Φ. The reason on which the agent acts depends only upon the commander's authority to issue such commands, or the requester's standing to make such requests.[21] And the agent's reason for Φing is rationally opaque because in acting for it he does not thereby act for the reason, good or bad, that prompted the commander or requester to bring this new reason into existence.[22] I think we should reject this assimilation of doing another's bidding to keeping a promise. I agree that orders and requests are like promises in one respect: when an agent is (validly) ordered or requested to Φ, he acquires a stand-alone, rationally opaque reason that he did not have before. I shall say more about the content of this reason below. In another important respect, however, doing another's bidding is much more like executing a decision.[23] When an agent acquiesces to an order or request, he agrees to serve the ends of the person whose bidding he does, and thereby becomes complicit in whatever that person is up to. He acts *for the sake of* the end that the commander or requester intends his action to serve. This does not mean that the acquiescing agent must endorse this end; on the contrary, he may be completely indifferent to whether his action will actually promote it. It would thus be misleading to say that the *agent's* reason for Φing is that doing so will promote the commander's or requester's end. The point is rather that doing another's bidding involves (in a sense that I hope to make clearer shortly) acting for someone else's reasons instead of one's own. The other person's ends play the same role that one's own ends play when one executes one of one's own decisions. Orders and requests are thus, in a sense, transparent to the reasons that stand behind them. When an agent obeys an order or accedes to a request that he Φ, he acts for the sake of the end that the commander or requester meant his act of Φing to serve.

[21] Raz, *The Morality of Freedom*, 47–8.

[22] Raz, "The Problem of Authority: Revisiting the Service Conception," in his *Between Authority and Interpretation* (Oxford University Press, 2009), 144–5. The agent is not barred from acting for the pro-Φing reasons upon which the command or request was based. He may even act for those reasons rather than for the reason created by the command or request. The point is that if he Φs because he was commanded or requested to do so, he does not automatically thereby act for those other, antecedent reasons.

[23] Raz would of course deny that in comparing doing another's bidding to keeping a promise, he thereby contrasts it with executing a decision. As I noted above, Raz thinks that executing a decision is also like keeping a promise. For Raz, commands, requests, decisions, and promises all give rise to stand-alone, rationally opaque reasons. But I have claimed that he is mistaken about decisions, and I shall now argue that he is mistaken about commands and requests as well.

The parallel I have in mind can be illustrated through a series of examples, all of which involve the same basic scenario, loosely based on an incident occurring in the Broadway musical *Guys and Dolls* (made into a movie starring Marlon Brando, Frank Sinatra, and Jean Simmons).[24] Nathan Detroit runs an illegal floating dice game and is desperate to find a location for tonight's game. He would like to hold the game at the Save-a-Soul Mission, which he knows will be unoccupied, but he also knows that Sarah Brown lives across the street from the mission and will call the police if she sees any unusual activity there. Detroit's end of holding his dice game at the mission would be facilitated if Brown were to go out for the night. As it happens, Brown has been working very hard lately and would benefit greatly from a night out. Now for the first pair of examples. In each example the agent executes an ordinary decision.

> **Case 1**. Sky Masterson, a friend of Nathan Detroit's, wishes to facilitate Detroit's dice game and calculates that he can achieve this end by taking Sarah Brown out for the night. So he invites her to have dinner with him in Havana. She accepts and they both have a wonderful time. Masterson realizes that Brown will benefit from a night out, but that is not why he does what he does. He takes her out solely because he believes this will help Detroit achieve his end of holding his dice game at the mission.

> **Case 2**. Sky Masterson believes that Sarah Brown would benefit greatly from a night out, so he invites her to have dinner with him in Havana. She accepts and they both have a wonderful time. Masterson realizes that by taking Brown to Havana he will make it possible for Detroit to hold his dice game at the mission, but that is not why he does what he does. He takes her out solely because he believes she will benefit from such an outing.

In each case, Sky Masterson decides to take Sarah Brown to Havana and then executes that decision. In Case 1, he takes her to Havana in order to facilitate Nathan Detroit's illegal dice game. That is his reason for taking her to Havana, the reason on the basis of which he formed his intention to take her there. In Case 2, Masterson takes Brown to Havana in order to show her a good time. He foresees that by taking her to Havana he will facilitate Detroit's dice game, but he does not take her there in order to facilitate the dice game. I think Masterson acts wrongly in Case 1. His goal in taking Brown to Havana is to help Detroit hold his illegal dice game at the mission; by successfully and effectively acting for the sake of

[24] I have changed some important details to better suit my purposes.

this goal, Masterson becomes complicit in Detroit's illegal enterprise – he makes himself into Detroit's accomplice. But Masterson arguably does not act wrongly in Case 2. Although he foresees that his action will facilitate Detroit's illegal dice game, he does not do what he does in order to help Detroit. He does not make himself into Detroit's accomplice. The fact that taking Brown to Havana would enable Detroit to hold his illegal dice game was admittedly a reason against taking her there. But the fact that she would greatly benefit from a night out was a strong reason in favor of taking her there, and we may assume that in the circumstances this reason in favor outweighed the reason against.

Many moral philosophers would deny that Masterson's reason for taking Brown to Havana affects the permissibility of his conduct. They would say that he acts permissibly if and only if an adequate justification for taking her to Havana is *available* in the circumstances; it does not matter whether that justification provides *his* reason for taking her there.[25] But even these philosophers would agree that Masterson's intentions have a bearing on other sorts of moral evaluation. In Case 1, Masterson acts for a morally inadequate reason. He thus governs himself poorly, and can be faulted for this. In Case 2, Masterson acts for a morally adequate reason and so governs himself well. For my purposes, the important point is that the difference between Masterson's reasons for taking Brown out in the two cases is morally significant. We need not agree upon the precise nature of this significance. Now consider a second pair of cases. In each case the agent does another person's bidding.

> **Case 3.** Nathan Detroit knows that he will not be able to hold his dice game at the mission unless Sarah Brown is gotten out of the way. He explains his predicament to his friend Sky Masterson and asks Masterson to take Brown out for the night. Masterson accedes to Detroit's request. He invites Brown to accompany him to Havana; she accepts and they both have a wonderful time. Masterson realizes that a night out will benefit Brown, but that is not why he does what he does. He takes Brown out solely because Detroit asked him to.

> **Case 4.** Sarah Brown's grandfather, Arvide Abernathy, thinks that she has been working too hard lately and would benefit greatly from a night out. He explains this to his friend Sky Masterson and asks Masterson to take

[25] See, for example, T. M. Scanlon, *Moral Dimensions* (Cambridge, MA: Harvard University Press, 2008), ch. 1. I defend the view that an agent's reason for doing what he does is directly relevant to whether he acts permissibly in M. Hanser, "Permissibility and Practical Inference," *Ethics*, 115 (2005), 443–70.

> her out. Masterson accedes to Abernathy's request. He invites Brown to accompany him to Havana; she accepts and they both have a wonderful time. Masterson realizes that by taking Brown to Havana he will make it possible for Detroit to hold his illegal dice game at the mission, but that is not why he does what he does. He takes Brown out solely because Abernathy asked him to.

Case 3 parallels Case 1. Of course they are not exactly alike. In Case 1, Masterson makes Detroit's end his own and calculates for himself how best to promote that end. By contrast, we need not suppose that Masterson adopts Detroit's end in Case 3. Masterson may remain personally indifferent to whether his taking Brown out for the night will really facilitate the dice game. And it is Detroit who calculates how Masterson can help him achieve his end. Nevertheless, when Masterson accedes to Detroit's request, he makes himself an instrument of Detroit's will: he puts himself at Detroit's service, and so at the service of Detroit's end. As in Case 1, he makes himself into Detroit's accomplice. In both Case 1 and Case 3, Masterson's act of taking Brown out for the night has the purpose of facilitating Detroit's illegal dice game. In Case 1 his action has this purpose because this was the end for the sake of which he decided to take Brown out for the night. In Case 3 his action has this purpose because he is acting at Detroit's behest, and this was the end for the sake of which Detroit asked him to take Brown out for the night. His action inherits its purpose from Detroit's reason for wishing the action to be performed. Detroit's end explains Masterson's act in Case 3 in much the same way that Masterson's own end explains his act in Case 1.

Similarly, Case 4 parallels Case 2. Masterson need not have any personal interest in Brown's welfare in Case 4, but when he accedes to Abernathy's request he puts himself at Abernathy's service, and so at the service of Abernathy's end. In both cases the purpose of Masterson's action is to benefit Brown. In Case 2 his action has this purpose because this was the end for the sake of which he decided to take Brown out for the night. In Case 4 his action has this purpose because he is acting at Abernathy's behest, and this was the end for the sake of which Abernathy asked him to take Brown out for the night. Abernathy's end explains Masterson's act in Case 4 in much the way that Masterson's own end explains his act in Case 2. These parallels in turn explain our parallel moral evaluations of the cases. In Case 3, as in Case 1, I would say that Masterson acts wrongly. He acts as Detroit's accomplice, and Detroit is up to no good. In Case 4, as in Case 2, Masterson acts permissibly. He acts as Abernathy's accomplice, and there is nothing wrong with what

Abernathy is up to.[26] Abernathy's goal is to benefit Brown, and that goal provides an adequate justification for the action that he asks Masterson to perform. The goal of benefiting Brown is sufficient to overcome the *pro tanto* objection created by the fact that taking her out for the night will enable Detroit to hold his illegal dice game at the mission. (As before, even those who deny that ends are directly relevant to permissibility should agree that Masterson governs himself poorly when he agrees to help Detroit but well when he agrees to help Abernathy.)[27]

Requests, then, are rationally transparent in a way that is at least analogous to the way in which decisions are transparent: when an agent accedes to a request that he Φ, he Φs for the sake of the end that the requester meant his act of Φing to serve. And the same is true of orders: when an agent obeys an order to Φ, he Φs for the sake of the end that the commander meant his act of Φing to serve. Had Detroit and Abernathy *told* rather than asked Masterson to take Brown out for the night, Masterson would still have been acting for the sake of their ends when he obeyed. We must thus reject the natural thought that an action is performed for the sake of an end only if that end is the agent's and provides *his* reason for performing the action. No doubt this is the usual source of an action's purpose, but it is not the only possible source. The distinctive feature of doing another's bidding is precisely that it involves giving up this sort of personal control over the purpose of one's actions.[28]

I said earlier that an adequate account of doing another's bidding must capture both the sense in which the acquiescing agent does his own will and the sense in which he does the will of the person at whose behest he acts, and is consequently guided by that person's deliberations rather than his own. We now have a somewhat clearer understanding of the sense in which the agent does this other person's will and is guided by his

[26] In this chapter I am not using the term "accomplice" as the criminal law does. Suppose that A tells B to put poison in C's sugar bowl, and that B obeys. In law, B is the principal and A is the accomplice.

[27] The parallel between decisions and requests can also be illustrated by examples in which the agent's Φing is meant to facilitate a morally worthy enterprise. Suppose that B's Φing would facilitate A's attempt to save another person's life. If B were to Φ at A's behest he would make himself part of the life-saving team, and would thereby earn a share of the credit should the enterprise prove successful (especially if his contribution were costly or risky). B would deserve no credit, however, if he were to Φ for some entirely unrelated reason, with the result that he only incidentally facilitated A's worthy enterprise.

[28] In M. Hanser, "Intention and Teleology," *Mind* 107 (1998), 381–401, I argue that the end the commander meant the subject's act to serve can also help determine what the subject did *intentionally*.

deliberations: the agent acts *for the sake of* the end that this other person meant his action to serve. This is what is not captured by the view that an agent who acquiesces to someone else's valid request or command that he Φ acts on a stand-alone, rationally opaque reason to Φ that was brought into existence by that person's act of issuing the request or command. We need a new account.

Executing another person's intention

Here is my proposal:

(1) A command or request to Φ expresses (or at least purports to express) the issuer's intention that the subject Φ.
(2) If the issuer of the command or request has the appropriate sort of authority or standing, the recipient acquires a reason to execute the intention that the command or request expresses. But note the content of this reason. The reason that the subject acquires as a result of being commanded or requested to Φ is not a reason to Φ. It is a reason *to execute the intention that the command or request expresses.* This reason is stand-alone and rationally opaque: in acting for it the subject does not thereby act for the commander's or requester's reason for bringing it into existence.
(3) When a subject successfully acts for the reason created by a valid command or request that he Φ, he executes the intention expressed by that command or request, namely the issuer's intention that he, the subject, Φ.[29] This intention, which is not itself a reason to Φ, is rationally transparent: in executing it the subject acts for the sake of whatever end the commander or requester meant the commanded or requested act of Φing to serve.

I shall consider some possible objections to Thesis (1) below,[30] but Theses (2) and (3) require more immediate comment. First, it is important to distinguish between (a) the reason in favor of the subject's Φing on the basis of which the commander or requester *formed* his intention that the subject Φ, and (b) the commander's or requester's reason for issuing the order or making the request – i.e. his reason for *expressing* his intention to the subject via an order or request. These two reasons need

[29] A subject may obey a command or accede to a request even when he has no reason to do so. In such cases too he executes the intention that the command or request expresses.
[30] See pp. 117–20.

not coincide. (I shall say more about this below.) The former reason is the one alluded to in the final sentence of Thesis (3). This reason determines the end for the sake of which the subject Φs when he obeys the command or accedes to the request.[31] The latter reason is the one mentioned at the end of Thesis (2). The subject does *not* act for this reason when he obeys the command or accedes to the request.

Second, I must say something about the idea of one person's executing another's intention. When an agent decides to obey a command or accede to a request, he forms a second-order intention to execute the intention expressed by that command or request.[32] I do not assume that the agent would express his intention this way; I mean only that this formulation captures what his intention to obey or accede amounts to. To intend to obey an order or accede to a request is to intend to execute the intention expressed by that order or request. In forming this second-order intention the agent takes on or adopts the intention expressed by the command or request. If the command or request expressed an intention that he Φ, then he takes on or adopts for himself an intention to Φ. But he does not *decide* to Φ. The intention expressed by the command or request was the product of someone else's deliberation and decision, not his own, and he takes the intention directly from this other person.[33] Although the intention is not the product of his own deliberation and decision, he nevertheless allows it to play the same role in guiding his conduct as an intention produced by his own deliberation and decision would ordinarily play. And so he acts *as if* the intention were supported by sound reasons – he treats the reasons lying behind the intention, the reasons that prompted the other party to form it, as if they were sound reasons for him to Φ. He allows himself to be guided by those reasons, even though they are not his. This is so even if he does not

[31] It can happen, of course, that the commander or requester did not mean the subject's act of Φing to serve any further end. In such cases the subject does not Φ for the sake of any further end when he executes the other person's intention, because there is nothing to which that intention is transparent.

[32] An agent can obey an order or accede to a request without *deciding* to execute the intention expressed by that particular order or request. He may have a standing intention, or perhaps merely be disposed, to execute the intentions expressed by the commands or requests of certain people regarding certain topics.

[33] A. Roth, "Shared Agency and Contralateral Commitments," *Philosophical Review* 113 (2004), 359–410, develops a similar picture to explain the "contralateral commitments" that agents engaged in joint enterprises have towards one another. In particular, Roth too holds that one person can adopt and execute another person's intention that he Φ.

himself believe that his act will advance the ends that the commander or requester meant it to advance.[34]

Here is a possible worry about the account I have proposed. I have suggested that a request or order to Φ does not function for the recipient as a reason to Φ. But if he accedes to the request or obeys the order, and if we then ask him why he Φed, he might well reply, "Because A asked/told me to Φ." And does this reply not give his reason for Φing? No, it does not. One can say all sorts of things in answer to a "why?" question, many of which will point only indirectly to what we might think of as a canonical statement of a reason. The answer "Because A asked/told me to Φ" tells us that in Φing the agent was acting for someone else, executing someone else's intention. And having learned this, we can follow up our original question in either of two ways. First, we can ask, "But why did A want you to Φ? What end was your act of Φing meant to serve?" If the agent is privy to A's reasoning, he will be able to answer. If not, he may advise us to address further questions to A. Alternatively, however, we could follow up our original question by asking the agent, "But why did you do what A asked/told you to do? Why did you subordinate yourself to him in this way?" The answer to the first possible follow-up question captures the sense in which the agent was doing someone else's will and serving someone else's ends.[35] The answer to the second possible follow-up question captures the sense in which the agent was doing his own will, acting on reasons that he took to apply to himself, reasons that he himself endorsed. These reasons were not reasons for Φing as such, but rather reasons for executing the other person's intention. They were reasons for subordinating his will to that of the person who gave the order or made the request.[36]

34 Suppose that an agent who was ordered to Φ does so for reasons of his own rather than because he was ordered. This agent does not adopt and execute the commander's intention, but he does do what the commander intended him to do, and (depending on the further details of the case) the commander might be satisfied with this result. If the commander's authority was legitimate, however, then the agent had a reason (perhaps even a duty) *to obey* him. And the agent in this example does not conform to this reason (or fulfill this duty).

35 Because an action's purpose can be determined either by the end that the agent means it to serve or by the end that the person commanding the action means it to serve, there can be cases in which an obedient subject acts for the sake of conflicting ends. For example, an agent might obey a command that he Φ while nevertheless Φing in a manner intended to frustrate or hinder the commander's end. This agent would be *Φing* for the sake of the commander's end but *Φing in such and such a manner* in order to frustrate the commander's end. I cannot explore such complexities here.

36 An analogous bifurcation in the chain of why-questions is possible when an agent executes one of his own decisions. Suppose we ask an agent why he Φed, and he replies, unhelpfully, "Because I decided to." This answer does not state his reason for Φing, but it

Let us return, then, to the two *desiderata* for an adequate account of doing another's bidding: the account must capture both the sense in which the subject himself wills or decides upon the act in question and the sense in which he lets someone else decide for him, and so allows himself to be guided by this other person's deliberations rather than his own. Unlike the accounts considered earlier, my account satisfies the second *desideratum*. The agent who accedes to a request or obeys a command quite literally executes a decision that someone else has made for him, and is thereby guided by that other person's deliberations. But what of the first *desideratum*? On my account the subject himself still chooses to execute the other person's intention, and presumably does so for what he takes to be good reasons. And in executing this other person's intention there may yet be scope for practical reasoning of his own – he may need to work out how best to execute the intention. But it must be admitted that on the Hart/Raz account the subject is more fully the author of his own action than he is on mine. On the Hart/Raz account the subject acts only for what he himself takes to be reasons applicable to himself. This, however, is precisely where Hart and Raz go wrong. When a subject does another's bidding, there is a real sense in which his action is not entirely his own. The other party is the ultimate author of his action. That is what my account captures and what the Hart/Raz account misses.

Dangers of practical deference

In Case 3, Sky Masterson knew why Nathan Detroit wanted him to take Sarah Brown out for the night: Detroit wanted her out of the way so that he could hold his dice game at the mission. And in Case 4, Masterson knew why Arvide Abernathy wanted him to take Brown out: Abernathy wanted her to have some fun for a change. In each case, then, Masterson knew the purpose of the action he was being asked to perform. But in each case, I think, his action would have had the same purpose even if he had not known why he was being asked to perform it. In acceding to the request he would still have been acting for the sake of the requester's

opens the door to two different lines of further inquiry. We could follow up by asking, "But why did you decide to Φ? What end was your act of Φing meant to serve?" Alternatively, we could follow up by asking, "But why do what you decided to do?" And there might be circumstances in which this second line of questioning would be apt.

ends. The sense in which requests and orders are transparent to the reasons standing behind them, then, is not epistemic. It does not presuppose that the subject has privileged epistemic access – or indeed any epistemic access – to the ends that his actions are meant to serve.

Suppose that upon being asked by Detroit to take Brown out for the night, Masterson were to exclaim, "Say no more! You're my friend and you need a favor – that's enough for me. Of course I'll do as you ask. I don't need to know why you want me to do it." In acceding to Detroit's request Masterson would still be making himself into Detroit's accomplice. He would still be putting himself at the service of Detroit's ends, whatever those ends might be, and so he would still be acting wrongly. In short, doing another's bidding is morally risky. When you put yourself at another's service, when you allow him to guide your actions, you place the moral quality of your actions (at least partially) in his hands. You take it on faith that he will not lead you astray, that the ends he will have you serve will be sufficient to justify the actions he will have you perform. If it turns out that he has used you to advance a morally unacceptable end, you will turn out to have acted wrongly. The most you can hope for is an excuse.[37] If your misplaced faith in him was reasonable, your culpability will be lessened, perhaps eliminated entirely, but you will still have done wrong.

The phenomenon of acting for an unknown end is not unique to cases of doing another's bidding. An agent can be unaware of the end for the sake of which he is acting even when he is executing one of his own decisions. Here is an example. Today I must make travel reservations for an upcoming trip. I remember that yesterday I decided to book an early morning return flight, but I cannot now remember why I decided this. Would a later flight not make more sense? That way I could sleep in. But I am sure I must have had a good reason for my decision, so I execute it anyway – I book an early morning flight. Later I remember: I decided to book an early flight so that I could arrive home in time for my son's school concert. If I were then asked why I booked an early morning flight, I could reply, surely correctly, that I did so in order to arrive home in time for my son's concert. My inability to remember my reason at the

[37] This may be too strong. Some would argue that when a subject obeys the command of a legitimate authority, he acts permissibly no matter what end his action is meant to serve. His duty to obey insulates him morally from the commander's ends. I cannot here investigate whether this view is defensible.

time of action does not undermine the correctness of this answer.[38] And the same sort of thing can happen when the reason for which one acts is a bad one. Perhaps yesterday I decided to Φ for a petty and vengeful reason. Today I remember that I decided to Φ but cannot remember why. Confident that I must have had a good reason, I execute my decision. Later, to my shame, I remember why I decided to Φ. In this case I have Φed for a shameful reason, and although my blameworthiness for performing the action is perhaps somewhat mitigated by the fact that I was not then aware of why I was performing it, I cannot avoid blame entirely. Nor am I to blame only for my decision. My *action* was petty and vengeful. Intentions preserved in memory remain rationally transparent to the reasons standing behind them – in executing such intentions one acts for those reasons, whether or not one is aware of them at the time of action. Trusting one's earlier self, like trusting others, is morally risky.

Objections and replies

I shall close by briefly discussing some possible objections to my account's first thesis: that a command or request to Φ expresses (or at least purports to express) the issuer's intention that the recipient Φ.

Objection 1: It is impossible for one person to intend another to do something. This is one of the chief respects in which intentions differ from desires. There is no barrier to desiring another person to do something, but one can intend only what one shall do oneself.

Reply. Why should we think that it is possible to desire, but not to intend, another person to do something? Here is one possibility. Intending is a *practical* attitude, so I can intend something only if I believe its occurrence is (in some appropriate sense) up to me. Desires are subject to no such restriction. I may want it to be sunny tomorrow, but I cannot intend it to be sunny because I do not believe that tomorrow's weather is up to me. I may want the President to sign a certain bill into law, but I cannot intend him to do so because I do not

[38] It is often unwise to execute a decision when you cannot remember why you made it. Perhaps you need to know the reason in order to perform the action in the right manner, or in order to know when to stop. But even in such cases you might begin the action, hoping to remember the reason before it is too late. It does not follow that you would then be performing the action only in order to jog your memory, and not for the original, unremembered reason.

believe that his actions are up to me. If someone is disposed to do my bidding, however, then in a perfectly good sense it *is* up to me what he shall do. Within limits, it is up to a commander what his subordinates shall do, and up to an employer what his employees shall do. The "up to the intender" restriction consequently does not rule out the possibility of one person's intending another to do something.

Of course I cannot perform other people's actions. My intention that another person Φ is consequently not one that I can execute. But in the present context it would surely be question-begging to assume that every intention must be executable by the person who forms it. It would be question-begging to assume that the actualization of an intention's content cannot depend upon that intention's first being communicated to, and then adopted by, another person.[39]

Objection 2: Even if it is possible for one person to intend another to do something, orders do not express such intentions. A commander seeking grounds to punish a disliked subordinate might order him to Φ, intending thereby to provoke him into disobedience. This commander would not intend the subordinate to Φ, and the subordinate might know this. The order would nonetheless be genuine and sincere. Orders, then, do not even purport to express intentions that their recipients perform the commanded acts.[40]

Reply. We must first distinguish between the intention that an order expresses (or purports to express) and the intention with which it is issued. The intention with which an order is issued reflects the end that the commander hopes to achieve by means of issuing it. Typically, a commander who orders someone to Φ does so with the intention of thereby inducing that person to Φ. But as the above example illustrates, an order to Φ need not be issued with such an intention. If the recipient is the sort of person who can be counted on to do the opposite of what he has been told to do, a commander might even order him to Φ, intending (and not merely hoping) thereby to ensure that he *does not* Φ. But the intention with which an order is issued is not the same as the intention that the order expresses. My first thesis concerns the intention

[39] Obviously there is much more to be said on this topic. For a recent discussion, see L. Ferrero, "Can I Only Intend My Own Actions? Intentions and the Own Action Condition," in D. Shoemaker (ed.), *Oxford Studies in Agency and Responsibility*, vol. I (Oxford University Press, 2013), 70–94.

[40] For a version of this argument see D. Owens, "Promising Without Intending," *Journal of Philosophy* 105 (2008), 742.

(purportedly) expressed by the order, not the intention with which it is issued. Second, we must remember that a commander need not actually have the intention that his order purports to express. Consider an analogy. Not every assertion that p expresses the speaker's belief that p – speakers sometimes assert things they do not believe. But every assertion *purports* to express something believed. An assertion that does not express a genuine belief is insincere, but it is an assertion nonetheless.

With these points in mind, let us return to the objection. If a commander issues an order with the intention of provoking the recipient into disobedience, his intention in issuing the order does indeed seem inconsistent with his genuinely intending the recipient to perform the commanded act. And so his command cannot actually express such an intention. But it does not yet follow that his order does not *purport* to express such an intention. On my account, if a commander lacks the intention that his order purports to express, then his order is insincere. So the crucial question is whether the order in the example is fully sincere. I think that it is not. It is of course sincere in one respect: the commander really does mean to be ordering his subordinate to Φ, and to be thereby placing that subordinate under an obligation to Φ. (Likewise, someone who asserts that p without believing that p really does mean to be making an assertion.) But the order is nonetheless *insincere* insofar as the commander does not really mean his subordinate to do what he is telling him to do. I see nothing counterintuitive in the claim that this is a species of insincerity, so I see nothing in the example inconsistent with the thesis that every order purports to express an intention that the recipient perform the commanded act.

Objection 3: Even if a command to Φ purports to express the issuer's intention that the recipient Φ, a request to Φ does not. When I command someone to Φ, I communicate a decision I have made regarding what he shall do – I represent what he shall do as having been settled. But when I merely ask someone to Φ, I do not represent what he shall do as having been settled. Requests consequently do not express intentions.

Reply. I agree that requests do not express "flat-out" intentions. It would be more accurate to say that they express "provisional" intentions.

Suppose I am planning a vacation. And now consider two different ways my deliberations might go. First, I might begin by deciding that I shall take a three-week trip to France. In deciding this I form a flat-out intention to take a three-week trip to France. But further deliberation is still required to settle the details. What part of France should I visit? Should I move around, staying in hotels, or should I stay in one place for the entire period, perhaps renting an apartment? As my deliberations progress I make further decisions, each resulting in a new intention (or, perhaps better, each decision adding more structure and complexity to my original intention). That is one way my deliberations might go. But here is another. I might begin by *provisionally* deciding to take to a three-week trip to France. I do not yet regard this as settled, because I am not yet sure that a trip to France will be feasible. Can I afford it? Will the dates fit into my schedule? In order to answer these questions I must work out more of the details of the proposed trip. So, having provisionally decided upon a trip to France, I continue deliberating in order to construct a more complete plan. This plan will remain provisional until I can satisfy myself that it is feasible. Only then will I form a flat-out intention. I will adopt the entire complex plan in one go, so to speak, rather than piecemeal.

Now suppose that I am devising a complex plan for how to achieve one of my goals, and that one part of this plan involves A's Φing. Because I am unable or unwilling to command A to Φ, I instead ask him to do so. Until he agrees, this part of my plan must remain provisional, unsettled (and if the entire plan depends upon his acceding – if there is no one else whom I could ask should he turn me down – then the entire plan must remain provisional). My request to A expresses a provisional intention or plan regarding what he shall do. When he agrees, my intention that he Φ becomes a flat-out intention, and he likewise adopts a flat-out intention to Φ. We might understand a provisional intention as a conditional intention – that is, as an ordinary, flat-out intention having a conditional content. When I provisionally decide to visit France next summer, I form an intention to visit France *if it should prove feasible*. When I ask another person to Φ, I express an intention that he Φ *if he is willing*. Another possibility, however, is that provisionally intending to Φ and flat-out intending to Φ are distinct attitudes with the same content. I cannot here pursue the question of which understanding is preferable.

6

Legal authority and the paradox of intention in action

VERONICA RODRIGUEZ-BLANCO

Introduction

We face the conflict of changing our actions and personal plans, modifying our interests, values, and preferences because the law requires or demands us to do so. This situation presents us with an antagonism between the way we conceive ourselves as rational, self-governed, and autonomous individuals, on the one hand, and as individuals bound by an external force called law, on the other. Nevertheless it can be maintained that when we follow legal rules or authoritative directives, we follow them, in paradigmatic cases, in full agency, i.e. intentionally. We sign mortgage contracts, pay taxes, stop at traffic lights, park our vehicles in permissible areas, compensate victims for our negligent behaviour, and we perform these and other legal acts intentionally.

Our practical reason and practical capacities show themselves in our intentional actions. The standard view about intentions is that they are mental states. This view, however, confronts insurmountable difficulties in explaining how the agent is the source of change in the world, able to control her or his actions, and able to adjust her or his conduct according to the contingencies and obstacles that are presented when an action is performed. When we act intentionally, we know the reasons why we are doing this or that, and this knowledge enables us to achieve the end of our action in a controlled manner. The standard view of intentional action cannot provide a satisfactory explanation for this feature. The solution to the antagonism between our autonomous character and law as an external force that changes our actions must lie in the idea that law in general, and

I would like to thank William Edmundson, Ken Ehrenberg, Kevin Falvey, Matthew Hanser, Ben Laurence, Brian Leiter, George Pavlakos, Michael Sevel, and Candace Vogler for comments on previous drafts. I have presented this material at the University of Chicago and the University of Frankfurt (IVR Workshop on 'Legal Normativity and the Philosophy of Practical Reason') and am grateful for comments I received from the audiences.

legal rules specifically, must show themselves, so to speak, in our practical reasoning. In this way, we gain control and governance over our own actions in spite of this external force called law. It is the agent who acts and follows legal rules intentionally and not blindly, and in doing so the agent needs to 'tap into' the grounding reasons of legal rules.

Legal rules show themselves in the form of the rules' grounding reasons as good-making characteristics. In other words, the rules need to be grounded in reasons as good-making characteristics to be able to make their appearance in our practical reasoning. The agent, in following legal rules, is able to grasp, in the exercise of his practical knowledge and practical capacities, the reason-giving character of the legal rules. This is necessarily so because legal rules are the result of the exercise of practical knowledge and practical capacities by legislators, judges, and other legal officials. Consequently, in order to follow legal rules we also need to engage and exercise our practical knowledge and practical capacities. However, this view on the authoritative and normative character of law is not the common understanding among legal philosophers. For example, Joseph Raz has argued that the exclusionary character of legal rules is essential in order to explain the authority of law. Raz advances a model of legal legitimate authority that connects legal rules and reasons and at the same time adumbrates the view that there is no need to evaluate the grounding reasons of legal rules to determine how they bind us.[1] Raz tells us that you can conform to the norm without evaluating the content of the norms or legal rules. This is the way that authoritative legal rules operate and influence our practical reasoning.

In my work,[2] I have defended the 'guise of the good' model for legal rules. It is argued there that when we follow legal rules the rule itself is not the primary reason for action; instead the grounding reasons as good-making characteristics[3] of the rule are the primary explanation and these grounding reasons need to be transparent to the agent. If it is the case that the 'guise of

[1] In its paradigmatic case, legal rules are binding because they fulfil the 'dependence' and the 'normal justification theses'. See J. Raz, *The Morality of Freedom* (Oxford: Clarendon Press, 1986), 47–57.

[2] V. Rodriguez-Blanco, 'The Moral Puzzle of Legal Authority', in G. Pavlakos and S. Bertea (eds.), *New Essays on the Normativity of Law* (Oxford: Hart Publications, 2011), 87–106, and *Law and Authority under the Guise of the Good* (Oxford: Hart Publications, 2014).

[3] Rodriguez-Blanco, 'The Moral Puzzle of Legal Authority', 87–106, and *Law and Authority Under the Guise of the Good*; Aristotle, *Nichomachean Ethics*, trans. H. Rackham (Cambridge, MA: Harvard University Press, 1934), I.i.2, III.V.18–21. See also T. Aquinas, *Summa Theologiae*, trans. Thomas Gilby, Latin and English text (Cambridge University Press, 2006), Ia2ae.12.I.

the good' model as applicable to the legal rule-following phenomenon holds true, this contradicts the 'exclusionary reasons' view on legal rules. Raz has defended the 'guise of the good' model of reasons for actions in general, but thinks that it does not apply to authoritative legal rules.[4] Hence Raz advances two different conceptions of reasons for actions. In law, legal rules are exclusionary reasons for action[5] whereas actions in general follow the 'guise of the good' model.[6] In the latter case intentional action plays a key role in showing what our reasons for action are.

Contra Raz, I propose a unified account of reasons for action for both ethics and law. Raz advocates the idea that when we follow legal rules, we follow them unintentionally: the action is a voluntary one. However, the will of the agent as pursuing reasons as good-making characteristics is not engaged. Consequently, says Raz, the 'guise of the good' model does not apply to authoritative legal directives and rules. From these considerations, a paradox arises which I shall call 'the legal paradox of intention in action'. If it is truly the case that we follow legal rules unintentionally, then, for example, when I sign a mortgage contract, stop at the traffic lights, follow the fire and safety regulations of my office building, pay my taxes, and so on, all these actions are done unintentionally. Are these voluntary but unintended actions? Since they are unintended, are they also irrational or a-rational actions? Raz tell us that they are not irrational or a-rational because, in the normal case, if we follow legal rules, then we can conform to the reasons that apply to us and we have a better chance of succeeding in complying to the reasons that apply to us than if we try to follow such reasons independently. Consequently, legal directives as exclusionary reasons help us to comply with the reasons that apply to us. However, the idea that we follow legal rules unintentionally is certainly counter-intuitive.

In search of a unified account of reasons for actions, a reconstruction of Raz's view on legal rules in the light of the 'guise of the good' model might be as follows. I follow legal rules because authority is a good sort of thing. This interpretation is in line with the teleological justification

[4] Arguably, there are traces of the 'guise of the good' model in his early work. Thus, the idea of a complete reason in J. Raz, *Practical Reason and Norms* (Oxford University Press, 1999; first published by Hutchinson, 1975), 23, and the idea of the normal justification thesis can be seen as seeds of the 'guise of the good' model.

[5] Ibid., 73–84.

[6] J. Raz, *Engaging Reason* (Oxford University Press, 1999), 22–45, and Raz, 'On the Guise of the Good', in S. Tenenbaum (ed.), *Desire, Practical Reason and the Good* (Oxford University Press, 2010).

provided by Raz and the normal justification thesis.[7] But the question that arises is how can the goodness of legal rules exclude the goodness of my other intentional actions? The answer is this. Authoritative legal rules express an intention: they intend you, for example, to stop at the traffic light and follow health and safety regulations, and, in order that you do this, you need to have as the end of your action a central description of a good-making characteristic, i.e. avoiding collisions with other vehicles, and staying healthy and alive. In the ideal or paradigmatic case, the authorities and law-abiding citizens are able to avow the good-making characteristics and they constitute the *logos* or grounding reasons of legal rules. These can be found through applying the why-question methodology. Imagine a dialogue with a road traffic officer:

> *Citizen*: Why do you intend that I press the brake pedal?
> *Road traffic officer*: Because there is a red light.
> *Citizen*: Why do you intend that I stop at the red light?
> *Road traffic officer*: Because doing so will protect your life and the lives of others.
> *Citizen*: Why do we have to protect my life and the lives of others?
> *Road traffic officer*: Because life is valuable.

Does this mean that, according to the 'guise of the good' model, I need to have transparent grounding reasons for following rules? The answer is positive. However, Raz would argue, this reconstruction contradicts the idea that rules are authoritative and hence undermines their function, i.e. they perform a mediating role between reasons and persons. In other words, we act not because of the rule, but because of the grounding reasons as good-making characteristics of the legal rules, which we can decide not to avow. Consequently, rules will be redundant since they will play no role in our practical reasoning. Raz would strengthen his position that in order for rules to be part of our practical reasoning, they cannot be transparent to us.

The argumentative strategy of the chapter will be as follows. First, I will advance a criticism of the idea of second-order reasons and show that the 'guise of the good' model can compete with the 'exclusionary reasons' model. Then I will discuss what I call the paradox of intention in action, and show that if we apply the 'guise of the good' model to authoritative directives and legal rules, then the paradox vanishes.

[7] J. Raz, 'The Problem of Authority: Revisiting the Service Conception', in *Between Authority and Interpretation* (Oxford University Press, 2009), 1003–44.

The result is an indirect defence of a weak version of Raz's service conception of authority in which the idea of reasons as exclusionary is abandoned.

Reasons for actions in Raz's legal and moral philosophies

In the early work *Practical Reason and Norms*, Raz established that only reasons understood as facts are normatively relevant. Beliefs can help us to determine reasons for actions because they make us aware of the facts in the world.[8] The premise for this conclusion is the idea that reasons guide us in our actions and, consequently, in order to decide what we should do we need to look at what the world looks like.[9] Reasons as mental states, i.e. beliefs and desires, are merely theoretically explanatory. They do not help us to understand why the agent has acted as he or she did; they play a secondary role in understanding action.[10]

Some key distinctions for understanding exclusionary reasons

Raz distinguishes between (a) complete and operative reasons and (b) first-order and second-order reasons. A complete reason is, Raz tells us, not always explicitly stated and has different parts which are also reasons. For example, let us suppose that I tell you that I am going to the station; however, I do not tell you why I am going to the station. If I am asked why, I might reply:

> *Enquirer*: Why are you going to the station?
> (a) 'Because James will be arriving at the station'; (b) 'James will be pleased if I meet him at the station'; and (c) 'I would like to please James.'
> *Enquirer*: But why would you like to please James?
> 'Because (d) I have promised that I will meet James at the station; (e) One ought to please one's friends.'

For Raz, a complete reason is a set of complex reasons: something similar to what one obtains as a result of the why-question methodology.[11] However, in *Practical Reason and Norms*, Raz does not endorse the view that the chain of successive steps of action can be unified in an intelligible form by a reason as a good-making characteristic. On the contrary, in his early work, Raz asserts that (d) and (e) are not reasons for going

[8] See Raz, *Practical Reason and Norms*, 18–20. [9] Ibid., 18. [10] Ibid., 22.
[11] For a use of the 'why-question' methodology see G. E. M. Anscombe, *Intention*, 2nd edn (Cambridge, MA: Harvard University Press, 2000; first published 1957).

to the station, but rather reasons for reasons for going to the station.[12] The idea of reasons for reasons and that reasons have a relative strength, as some reasons can override other reasons,[13] entails the view that there are second-order reasons in addition to first-order reasons. According to Raz, every complete reason includes an operative reason.[14] Operative reasons are either values or desires or interests.[15] One should not interpret operative reasons as subjective motivational reasons, since operative reasons might include values.[16]

A criticism of second-order reasons

Raz argues that exclusionary reasons are a sub-species of second-order reasons. However, when we look closely at the examples provided by Raz, we see that there is truly only *one* layer of reasons, which are connected by the successive steps of the actions and the result is a connected chain of reasons for actions, or so I will argue.

In previous work I have explained the structure of agency that is obtained when one engages in the why-question methodology. Thus, reasons for actions can be elucidated when one asks the agent why such and such an action was performed. Actions are explained in terms of other actions, and the inquiry stops when a reason as a good-making characteristic is provided. This reason is the end of the action that unifies all the successive actions. Applying the 'guise of the good' model of intentional action to the example of collecting James from the station, the series of actions, i.e. taking a vehicle, driving to the station, parking at the station, getting out of the vehicle, entering the station and meeting James, is explained in virtue of the two reasons, namely the promise that I have made to James and the fact that to please friends is a reason as a good-making characteristic for the action. If I am asked why I have fulfilled my promise to James, the answer might be 'because fulfilling promises to friends shows our respect for them'. Thus (d) and (e) are not second-order reasons or another layer of reasons, but they are the reasons for action for going to the station. Following the structure of the Aristotelian practical syllogism, a reformulation of (d) or (e) as the premises of the good-making characteristics of the action are as follows: (e′) it is good to please one's friends and (d′) it is good to fulfil one's promises.

[12] Raz, *Practical Reason and Norms*, 23. [13] Ibid., 25–8. [14] Ibid., 33.
[15] Ibid., 33–4. [16] Ibid., 34.

> (c) James is my friend and I would like to please James, and (c′) I have promised that I will meet James at the station. (b) James will be pleased if I meet him at the station.
> (a) James will be arriving at the station.

I will go to the station!

Raz denies this explanation. He asserts, 'there are reasons for the reasons for going to the station'. However, if I am going to the station because James will be arriving there, this does not necessarily make the action intelligible. It might be that James will arrive there, he is my enemy, and wishes to kill me. Obviously, I have no intelligible reason for going to the station. The answers 'I have promised that I will be there' or 'One ought to please one's friends' are the reasons as good-making characteristics that illuminate the other parts of the intentional action. The explanation that there is another layer of reasons contradicts the way we think about reasons for actions within the classical tradition also advocated by Raz in his later work.[17] Does this argument show that there is no such thing as second-order reasons and that, therefore, the status of exclusionary reasons as second-order reasons can at the very least be put in doubt? The argument only shows that we need a better characterization of second-order reasons.

The 'guise of the good' model as competing with the 'exclusionary reasons' model

There are three independent arguments advanced by Raz that aim to show that there is another layer of reasons, as opposed to first-order reasons or a continuum of reasons and successive steps towards an action. These arguments are: the phenomenological argument, the teleological argument, and the analogy argument. I will argue that the 'guise of the good' model can satisfactorily explain the phenomenological and teleological arguments and I will offer some criticisms of the analogical argument.

The phenomenological argument

Raz gives three different examples to show the plausibility of exclusionary reasons.[18] In the first example Ann wishes to make a good financial investment. Late in the evening, a friend tells her about a possible investment opportunity. The drawback of the offer is that Anne needs to decide

[17] Raz, *Engaging Reason*, 22–3. [18] Raz, *Practical Reason and Norms*, 35–9.

that evening about the investment, otherwise the offer will be withdrawn. Due to her fatigue she decides not to accept the offer. She rejects the offer not because she has considered the merits of the case and takes it that there are good reasons to reject the offer, but because she cannot trust her own judgment due to her fatigue. Anne, consequently, has not acted on the balance of reasons, but her first-order reasons are excluded by an undefeated exclusionary reason, i.e. the fact that she cannot trust her own judgment. In the second example, Jeremy, a soldier, is ordered by his commanding officer to appropriate a van. His friend urges him to disobey the order; however, Jeremy believes that he should obey and that it is not up to him to decide whether or not to obey an order. The order of the commanding officer excludes Jeremy's first-order reasons for action. In the third example, Colin promises his wife that in all decisions affecting the education of his son he will act only according to the son's best interests. He now needs to consider whether to send his son to a private school; doing so will mean that he will be unable to quit his job to write his book. Colin's promise does not affect his first-order reason, i.e. the fact that he has reasons to pursue a career as a writer; rather it excludes his first-order reason.

We can criticize the examples and question whether they are cases of acting according to reasons for actions. In the case of Anne, following the 'guise of the good' model, we can say that there is only one action: she goes to bed because she is tired and she needs to sleep. On the other hand, before this action she takes a decision 'not to act and not to invest her money' and as there is no action involved, there is no execution of any action. Alternatively, we can say that she intends an inaction, i.e. not to invest her money, and her reason for such inaction is that she does not intend to lose money because avoiding ill-considered investments has, in her view, good-making characteristics. In the case of Jeremy, we could say that he obeys the authority because authority is a good sort of thing (there are cases in which citizens follow legal authorities because authorities are a good sort of thing, without avowing the grounding reasons as good-making characteristics of an action). In the case of Colin, we have seen from the example of 'I am going to the station to collect James' that a promise can be a reason for action as a good-making characteristic. The action is 'Colin takes his son to a private school' and the reason for action as a good-making characteristic is that 'he has promised his wife that he will act only according to the best interests of his son' and Colin believes that 'one should fulfil one's promises'. These two reasons are the reasons for actions as good-making characteristics that unify all of Colin's actions, i.e. completing the application form for the school, accepting the offer of a place on behalf of his son, and paying the school fees.

Let us, for the sake of argument, accept that Anne, Jeremy, and Colin are acting for exclusionary reasons. Raz tells us that when we disregard exclusionary reasons and act following our first-order reasons, we feel torn and uneasy in a way that we do not feel when we decide not to act for overriding reasons and act according to weaker reasons. The phenomenological argument aims to show that the strength of exclusionary reasons is different from the strength of overriding first-order reasons. Let us suppose that Jeremy decides to disobey and not to follow the order of his commanding officer. He has good reasons not to obey the authority's reasons and knows that he has done the right thing by disobeying. Nevertheless, he still feels torn and uneasy in a way that is different from occasions when he acts according to weaker reasons. To account for this phenomenological experience, Raz tells us, we need to postulate that there are different layers of reasons. Exclusionary reasons, consequently, explain the phenomenon in a satisfactory manner.

However, the 'guise of the good' model can explain the phenomenon of uneasiness as follows. If we consider that authority is a good sort of thing, then we feel that we have sacrificed one good, most likely a good that is impartial and that affects many people in the community, for another good which is more personal, and this might produce feelings of loss, i.e. the loss of the good that the authority could have delivered not just to me, but to many people if I had followed the authority's rule or directive. It seems natural to feel that the goodness that the authority could have delivered is more important than the goodness of my act and that, therefore, the feelings of being torn are stronger than when I decide between two different personal goods. In Jeremy's case, he might feel that by disobeying the order of the commanding officer he had risked or lost the goodness of the coordinating actions that the authority provides. However, he knows that he has acted well in not appropriating the van. He feels torn because the authority of the commanding officer seems to him key to succeeding in the military operation that they are involved in.

The teleological argument

Like many other legal philosophers, Raz has argued that authoritative legal rules are a good sort of thing.[19] They help us to avoid personal

[19] Ibid., 58–9, 195.

errors and reduce the risk of such errors. They are labour-saving devices and we can rely on the fact that others will follow them, and consequently they provide certainty in our interactions with others. Authoritative legal rules provide a service for us and they cannot serve their purpose unless they are treated as exclusionary reasons for actions.[20] Authorities can secure coordination only if legal norms are considered exclusionary reasons. Citizens must defer to the authority and put their first-order reasons to one side.

I take it that it is obvious that the teleological argument can equally be explained by the 'guise of the good' model.[21] However, there is some ambiguity in the notion of 'service' and I use this ambiguity to make apparent the idea that authoritative legal rules serve us in an 'ethical-political' manner.

It should be emphasized that Raz's phenomenological and teleological arguments are not used to support the idea of rules under the 'guise of the good' model. Rather, Raz's arguments are used to show that they favour rules as exclusionary reasons, but also rules as construed by the 'guise of the good' model. What so far has been shown, at least, is that the idea of rules conceived under the 'guise of the good' model competes with the idea of rules as exclusionary reasons.

There is a third argument against Raz's view on legal rules as exclusionary reasons that will be advanced. It is, in my view, the most compelling argument and to its examination I now turn.

The analogical argument

Raz argues that there is an analogy between decisions and legal rules;[22] in both cases, once they have been formed, you do not submit them for revision.[23] Arguably, however, decisions are acts of the will. They do not merely involve a mental state because if they are merely mental states the question that arises is how they can cause our actions in the right sort of way. Furthermore, the mentalist or inward interpretation of the notion of decisions is not compatible with Raz's views on beliefs and reasons.

[20] Ibid., 72.

[21] See L. Green, 'Law as Means', in R. Cane (ed.), *The Hart–Fuller Debate in the 21st Century* (Oxford: Hart Publications, 2010), 169–88.

[22] The analogy argument aims to show the role that rules and decisions play in our practical reasoning (Raz, *Practical Reason and Norms*, 74).

[23] Ibid., 67.

For Raz neither beliefs nor reasons are merely mental states. Beliefs are relevant for actions to the extent that they make us aware of facts in the world and enable us to act according to such facts. No obvious arguments support the mentalist interpretation of decisions in conjunction with the rejection of the mentalist interpretation of beliefs and reasons. If no such distinction is made, then decisions are more than merely mental states. Decisions, in the classical tradition, are acts of will.[24]

Raz argues that rules are like decisions or *electiones*. He makes a distinction between a deliberative and an executive stage of decision-making. In the former stage we make choices, and in the latter stage we just follow rules and neither make choices nor deliberate. Rules, like decisions, always seem to work, Raz tells us, at the executive stage.[25] This view seems to contradict the perspective advocated by the classical tradition on the matter. In Aristotle, for example, not all deliberation is with the view to making a choice; there is also deliberation when one executes a choice. Choices or decisions (*prohairesis*) require not only virtue in selecting the end, but also 'cleverness' in executing the choice.[26] We can only deliberate on the things that are within our powers. True, we do not deliberate on the blind following of rules.[27]

Thus, the doctor needs to deliberate about the best treatment and other means to cure his patient in just the same way that the legislator, judge, and citizen need to deliberate about the way to proceed according to the grounding reasons as good-making characteristics of legal rules. Legal rules are not determined and specified as are the rules of orthography. Nevertheless, knowledge of the rules of orthography is not sufficient to write an essay. Analogically, nor it is sufficient to know the meaning of words and legal concepts to create and follow legal rules. Thus, to create and follow legal rules, because law is a purposive activity, one needs to deliberate on how to achieve the grounding reasons as good-making characteristics of rules. They might be presented in a complex way or unfold as we follow and create them. The phenomenology of following legal rules shows that we do not follow legal rules blindly: we engage with legal rules and believe that we do so as autonomous and active agents, controlling the steps or successive actions necessary to follow and create rules, and thus we conceive ourselves as exercising deliberation and practical reasoning.

24 Aquinas, *Summa Theologiae*, Ia2ae.13.I, n. 3.

25 J. Raz, *Ethics in the Public Domain* (Oxford University Press, 1995), 205–6.

26 Aristotle, *Nicomachean Ethics*, 1144a20. 27 Ibid., 1112b3–12.

Let us think about my decision to go to the station to collect James. I go to the station because he will be there, I wish to please him, and in my view it is good to please one's friends. According to Raz, you do not need to deliberate any further on your reasons for going to the station. I execute the decision, which cannot be submitted to revision. True, it might be that the decided act, i.e. going to the station, is not submitted to revision; however, according to the classical tradition, in executing my choice or decision I need to engage in deliberation. This engagement is necessary in order to deliberate about how to execute the choice or decision. Consequently I need to understand the end of my decided act in order to assess the means to achieve it. I know that I am going to the station to collect James in order to please him. I need to deliberate on whether I should take the car, the bus, or two bikes, one for me and one for James. I know that James does not like to cycle, and because my grounding reason is to please James, it then seems obvious that I should choose between the bus or the car. I also know that James has just completed a very long journey and therefore may not be able to walk to the bus station and sit on a crowded bus. Therefore it seems better to bring the car. Let us suppose that you order me to collect James at the station, but the grounding reasons of your order are not transparent to me, i.e., the good-making characteristics that you are pursuing. I collect James but I bring a bike for him to cycle, not knowing that he hates to cycle. You will obviously not achieve the end of your action, i.e. pleasing James.

The argument so far has attempted to undermine the idea that there is always a clear line between the decision/deliberative stage and the executive stage in both decisions and legal rules. In many cases there is instead a continuous spectrum between the two stages. Consequently the argument indirectly aims to undermine the idea of rules as exclusionary reasons where engagement with deliberation is absent and mere execution is required. True, there will be legal rules where engagement with deliberation at the executive stage is not necessary due to the fact that in some cases they involve a single or non-complex action. But if there are cases in which the continuity of the stages is shown, then this will suffice to throw doubt on the soundness of the analogy argument as construed by Raz. If it is true that decisions are like legal rules, then due to the fact that the execution of decisions requires deliberation, we might say that execution of legal rules also requires engagement with deliberation. The argument also shows that in the normal cases the grounding reasons as good-making characteristics need to be somehow transparent to the agent. By contrast, exclusionary reasons are opaque to the agent.

Exclusionary reasons and the legal paradox of intention in action

Let me summarize the core arguments that support the idea of legal rules as presented in the 'guise of the good' model: (a) the 'guise of the good' model is the primary explanation of how we act intentionally; (b) the claims of authorities should be interpreted as expressions of an intention about how authorities will perform their legal actions;[28] (c) when we follow legal rules, paradigmatically, we follow them intentionally. Therefore, following from (a), we can say that the 'guise of the good' model is the primary explanation of following legal rules.

The core arguments of Raz's *Practical Reason and Norms* are the following:

(a) Authority can serve us, i.e. it can coordinate our activities, but only if individuals defer their judgments to it.
(b) Therefore, in the circumstances of authority, individuals cannot act according to their reasons for action, even if they are right.
(c) We, however, act rationally when we follow legal authorities in spite of the fact that we do not act according to our own reasons.
(d) Consequently, legal rules issued by legitimate legal authorities ought to be exclusionary reasons.[29] This means that the idea that legal rules provide exclusionary reasons is the best possible explanation of (a), (b), and (c).

I will qualify (a), (b), and (c) and reject (d) below.

What is the conception of reasons in Raz's later work[30] and how is it compatible with the idea of exclusionary reasons as a sub-class of first-order reasons? I have explained that to act for reasons is to act intentionally. This notion of intentional action is characterized by Raz as 'the intention with which I perform an action'.[31] Raz's later conception of reasons for actions, except for the cases of legal authoritative directives, does not differ much from the one defended here.[32] Intentional action is taken as the paradigmatic case of action.

[28] Rodriguez-Blanco, 'Claims of Legal Authorities and "Expressions of Intentions": The Limits of the Philosophy of Language', in M. Freeman and F. Smith (eds.), *Law and Language* (Oxford University Press, 2013).

[29] See a later formulation by Raz of his own notion of authority in terms of protected reasons in J. Raz, *The Authority of Law* (Oxford: Clarendon Press, 1979), 17–18.

[30] Raz, *Engaging Reason,* n. 6.

[31] Raz, *On the Guise of the Good*, 117.

[32] Ibid., 16.

In his early work,[33] however, Raz did not examine the legal agents' explanations of their own actions, which reveal the reasons for their actions as good-making characteristics. If we follow legal rules intentionally, should not the 'guise of the good' model be the best possible explanation of legal rule-following phenomena? By contrast, if we follow legal rules according to the 'exclusionary reasons' model, then we do not follow legal rules intentionally. Consequently, it seems that to follow legal rules under the model of exclusionary reasons is a case of peripheral agency and not of full agency. However, what would justify conceiving reasons for actions under the 'guise of the good' model, while conceiving exclusionary reasons as a different kind of reason? In the latter case, contrary to Raz's view on his later work and the predominant view,[34] we would have reasons for actions, but not an intentional action. We might find some answers to this puzzle in Raz's texts. Raz, for example, asserts that intentional action should be considered as a matter of degree.[35]

Anscombe's work on intentions also seems to support this interpretation.[36] There are cases, she tells us, in which the answer to the question 'why did you do so and so?' is clearly a reason as a good-making characteristic as perceived by the agent. There are, however, other occasions when we answer as if we have only discovered that we are doing *x* because it has been observed that we are doing it. For example, you ask me why I have put a hot pan on your hand, and I reply, 'Oops, sorry, I didn't realize!' I was obviously not aware of my action and my action was unintentional. There are other occasions when I act involuntarily and unintentionally: for example, I jump when I hear a loud bang. On other occasions I act voluntarily but for no reason.[37] Can we say that when we follow exclusionary reasons we act within a wide range of actions? We have learned that if there are reasons for action, then there is an intentional action. The application of the question 'Why?' enables us to distinguish actions that are intentional from the ones that are non-intentional or unintentional, but we have learned that because of the wide application of the question 'Why?' there is an equally wide spectrum between intentional and unintentional actions, and possibly a wide spectrum within the category of intentional actions; arguably,

[33] Raz, *The Authority of Law*, and Raz, *The Morality of Freedom*.

[34] Anscombe, *Intention*. [35] Raz, *On the Guise of the Good*, 123.

[36] Anscombe, *Intention*, §§17–18.

[37] Ibid., §25; cf. S. Tenenbaum, *Appearances of the Good* (Cambridge University Press, 2007), 90–9.

if we characterized intentional action in terms of reasons for actions, it is a matter of degrees, but the action is identified as intentional. If we follow legal rules as exclusionary reasons, then we follow them intentionally, and the question that arises is how exclusionary reasons can be reasons as good-making characteristics for the agent who follows legal rules without assessing the content of the reasons. In other words, *how do such reasons become transparent to the agent?* The problem that arises, Raz would tell us, is that if such reasons become transparent to the agent, then the rule cannot perform its function of serving us. The pre-emptive thesis explains how rules provide a service for us. According to the pre-emptive thesis, the requirement of performance by an authority is a reason for its performance. This reason should not be added to all the relevant reasons (for actions) when assessing what to do. Therefore, because rules or authoritative directives reflect the reasons, which apply to the subjects, then they replace people's own judgments on the merits of the case.[38] If the rules remain opaque, then they can preserve their function of serving us in our decisions, but then our actions are not because of the rule as a reason. We cannot characterize our actions as intentional and therefore say that we are acting for reasons. We can only characterize them using the terminology introduced by Raz; the agent merely conforms with (exclusionary) reasons for actions.[39]

When we follow legal rules, we know how to continue with the action despite the fact that something might have gone wrong during the action and this is the case because we are able to grasp the grounding reasons as good-making characteristics of the legal rules. Therefore, contra Raz, I argue that, in the normal cases, we follow legal rules intentionally. For example, let us suppose that the traffic lights at a certain junction in my town have stopped working. I stop carefully and wait until there are no vehicles, cyclists, or pedestrians. I am able to follow the legal rules of road traffic, even though something has gone wrong, i.e. the traffic lights are faulty, because I understand that the grounding reasons of the rules of road traffic are the safety and protection of the lives of pedestrians, drivers, and other road users.

An objector might reply that we are able to continue with the road traffic rules because we follow what others are doing and we have learned

[38] Raz, *The Morality of Freedom*, 59.

[39] Raz, *Practical Reason and Norms*, 178–82, 190, 194; Raz, *The Morality of Freedom*, 41; Raz, 'The Problem of Authority: Revisiting the Service Conception', 1014, 1017–19, 1022; and Raz, *The Authority of Law*, 29.

this by convention. My response is that this is a mistake. If, while I am driving, I look at what others are doing and see that they are stopping at the red traffic lights and I also observe that they stop at the traffic light even when it is not working, I could conclude, in line with the objector, that they have learned about these contingencies through mere conventions. Following the convention, I will also stop. However, it is a mystery how I am supposed to continue driving. Should I stop when I see pedestrians or cyclists, or only pedestrians? Should I stop when I see someone on a scooter? What about a tricycle or a carriage? How can I learn all these contingencies just by convention now at the moment of acting? How can I learn all these contingencies on the rule and apply them at the same time as I am acting? How can I look and interpret the behaviour of others when in order to act I need to look at the road, the pedestrians, my own vehicle, and the broken traffic light? Furthermore, how can I do all these things while 'remembering' my mental state of 'acceptance'?

These reflections enforce the view that in the normal cases when we follow legal rules we do so intentionally. The majority of contemporary scholars agree that law guides us.[40] We are now able to understand the legal paradox of intention in action that emerges from the notion of exclusionary reasons.

The legal paradox of intention in action: If we follow legal rules intentionally, then legal rules cannot be exclusionary reasons. If we do not follow legal rules intentionally, then legal rules do not have a reason-giving character. Therefore, either legal rules cannot be exclusionary reasons or legal rules do not have a reason-giving character.

From a textual analysis of Raz's works we can infer that he accepts the antecedent of the second horn of the paradox, i.e. we do not follow legal rules intentionally (in full agency), and that he rejects the consequent: namely, he argues that we have exclusionary reasons for action. Let us analyse Raz's position. For Raz, compliance with reasons for actions is relevant only to the extent that it is a secure route to conformity with

[40] J. Finnis, 'Foundations of Practical Reason Revisited', *American Journal of Jurisprudence* 50 (2005), 109–31. H. L. A Hart, *The Concept of Law*, 3rd edn (Oxford University Press, 2012); Raz, *Practical Reason and Norms*, 15; G. Postema, 'Implicit Law', *Law and Philosophy* 13 (1994), 369; and G. Postema, 'Positivism, I Presume? . . . Comments on Schauer's "Rules and the Rule of Law"', *Harvard Journal of Law and Public Policy* 14 (1991), 799–800.

reasons for actions.[41] Paradoxically, however, conformity with reasons does not require the exercise of our practical capacities as we can act unintentionally.[42] Raz argues that in cases of nonfeasance, overdetermination, and unintended action conformity with reasons does not require being aware of the reasons which apply to one and reacting directly to them. He asserts that there is good reason to think that we cannot reliably conform to reason unless much of the time we do so automatically and unthinkingly.[43] We act, therefore, without deliberation and in the absence of our practical capacities. Raz also points out that in cases of authoritative directives there ought to be some reliable beliefs that the conditions for legitimate authority are met.[44]

The problem with this view is that if one can conform to reasons without assessing the merits or grounding reasons of authoritative directives or legal rules merely because one has reliable beliefs about the legitimacy of the authority, then the grounding or underlying reasons (in Raz's terminology) play no role in guiding our behaviour. But, Raz tells us, the authoritative directive or the rules are themselves reasons for actions (exclusionary ones). We have raised doubts about the possibility of layers of reasons and therefore the plausibility of second-order or exclusionary reasons for actions. Furthermore, in later work Raz asserts that we can respond to reasons because we have a will and are capable of having intentions, and engaging in intentional actions.[45] We need an explanation of why the same characterization does not apply to secondary reasons and exclusionary reasons to the extent that they are also reasons.[46]

In previous work, I have shown that in paradigmatic cases one cannot follow rules unless one either avows the grounding reasons of rules or the goodness of the authority. This means that one can avow or understand the grounding reasons of rules if one follows legal rules intentionally. Let us analyse the example provided by Raz. He tells us that at the scene of an accident, coordination is required to recognize that one particular person is in charge of the rescue, and this is essential if lives are to be saved.[47]

41 Raz, *Practical Reason and Norms*, 190, and Raz, 'The Problem of Authority: Revisiting the Service Conception', 138.

42 Raz, *Engaging Reason*, 95.

43 *Raz Practical Reason and Norms*, 94, and Raz, *The Authority of Law*, 24–5.

44 Raz, 'The Problem of Authority: Revisiting the Service Conception', 1025–6.

45 Raz, *Engaging Reason*, 115.

46 Raz provides a partial explanation: norms are ontologically different from reasons (*Practical Reason and Norms*, 79–80).

47 Raz, 'The Problem of Authority: Revisiting the Service Conception', 101.

Let us call the coordinating authority at the scene of the accident 'Beatus'. According to the model of exclusionary reasons, I followed Beatus's instructions regardless of my reasons for actions (Beatus's reasons are exclusionary reasons). I do not need to be aware of or know the merits of the grounding reasons of the directives and rules issued by Beatus. However, my argument is that the grounding reason of the rule unifies the required series of actions such as phoning for an ambulance, providing reassurance to the injured parties, helping to make them comfortable, and so on. The grounding reason as a good-making characteristic of all the different directives issued by Beatus at the scene of the accident is 'to save as many lives as possible'. Without engaging with the grounding reasons, the addressee will not be able to follow the instructions of the coordinating authority – Beatus – and adjust his or her conduct accordingly. Let us suppose that at the scene of the accident Beatus orders that wounded persons should be moved carefully if there are exceptional circumstances only. Imagine that I find myself in the position of needing to move the first wounded person in order to make room for another wounded victim, as there are no other suitable safe places. I must understand that the aim is to preserve life and that if I must move any injured person it must be with extreme care, avoiding bending any limbs. I cannot carry out these actions unless I do so intentionally, bearing in mind the grounding reason as a good-making characteristic of the authoritative directive, i.e. to preserve as many lives as possible. To merely follow the authority's order unintentionally, though conforming to reason, is not to exercise our practical reasoning.

According to Raz, authoritative legal directives and legal rules facilitate compliance with reasons for action as objectively good or right and make a difference in the practical reasoning of the addressees.[48] There is, however, some ambiguity in the notion of 'service'. A strong reading advocates the view that the authority provides the service of mediating between reasons and the addressees. Thus, the addressees of a legal directive or legal rule accept they should obey it even if they believe there is no merit in performing the required actions.[49] This is the view advocated by Raz. However, there is a weaker reading of the service conception. According to this reading, the authority provides the service of showing, through the rules and authoritative directives, the good-making characteristics that apply to the case. These reasons for actions

48 Raz, *The Morality of Freedom*, 58–62, and *Practical Reason and Norms*, 194.

49 Raz, *The Morality of Freedom*, 40.

as good-making characteristics are the grounding reasons of the rules and unify the successive series of actions that are required in order to follow the legal rules.

Conclusion

I have argued in favour of the weak reading of the service conception. However, it is not true that we always need to avow the grounding reasons of legal rules as good-making characteristics in order to follow legal rules. Authorities' claims and compliance with the rule of law can create a presumption of the goodness of authority and its legitimacy. But I have not discussed this possibility in this chapter.

Why has the strong reading of the service conception been so persuasive among legal philosophers? The moral puzzle of legal authority[50] is formulated from the deliberative viewpoint,[51] but the answer that Raz gives, i.e. rules are exclusionary reasons for actions, is from the theoretical perspective. Thus, the answer seems unsatisfactory from the deliberative viewpoint. One view is that there is an asymmetry between the authority's perspective, which is theoretical, and the deliberative point of view.[52] Raz's view on the strong service conception seems appealing if we only consider the theoretical perspective or the third-person point of view, i.e. the point of view of the person who describes what following an authoritative directive means. However, from the deliberative point of view the agent, due to his own self-understanding as a full agent in the following of legal rules, needs to be engaged with the merits, in Raz's terminology, or the grounding reasons of rules.

[50] Raz, 'The Problem of Authority: Revisiting the Service Conception'.

[51] For an explanation of the 'deliberative point of view' see J. Finnis, 'Law and What I Truly Should Decide', *American Journal of Jurisprudence* 48 (2003), 107–29, and J. Finnis, 'On Hart's Ways: Law as Reason and as Fact', in *The Legacy of H. L. A. Hart* (Oxford University Press, 2008).

[52] F. Schauer, 'Rules and the Rule of Law', *Harvard Journal of Law and Public Policy* 14 (1991), 692–3.

7

The deliberative and epistemic dimension of legitimate authoritative directives

ANTONY HATZISTAVROU

What reasons do legitimate authoritative directives generate in their subjects? Raz identifies two relevant reasons: (a) a first-order reason to do as directed; and (b) a second-order, exclusionary reason not to be motivated by at least some of the first-order reasons which conflict with the corresponding legitimate directive. In this chapter, I put forward two claims. The first claim, which I develop in the first section of the chapter, introduces a revision to the Razian framework: I argue that legitimate authoritative directives also exclude a particular type of reasoning about the balance of first-order reasons which is similar to the type of reasoning involved in the reconsideration of decisions. This captures the deliberative dimension of legitimate authoritative directives. The second claim, which I develop in the second section, is that the reasoning-excluding reasons legitimate authoritative directives generate have important epistemic value. This captures their epistemic dimension.

My revisionism does not affect Raz's account of legitimate authority, and more specifically his normal justification thesis. Rather I presuppose it in developing my arguments.

Reconsideration and reasoning-excluding reasons

What exclusionary reasons exclude has been a matter of debate.[1] We can take them to exclude motivation by, consideration of, or reasoning about a certain range of first-order reasons.

Earlier drafts of this chapter were presented at the IVR Workshop on 'Legal Normativity and the Philosophy of Practical Reason' and a seminar of the Philosophy Department of the University of Stirling. I am grateful for comments received on both occasions.

[1] See, for example, M. Moore, 'Authority, Law and Razian Reasons', *Southern California Law Review* 62 (3–4) (1989), 854–6; C. Gans, 'Mandatory Norms and Exclusionary Reasons', *Philosophy* 15 (1986), 383–4; H. M. Hurd, *Moral Combat* (Cambridge University

(1) *Motivation-excluding reasons.* Raz takes exclusionary reasons to be normative reasons which favour 'not being motivated in one's actions by certain (valid) considerations' and 'exclude reasons from being one's motivation for action'.[2] For example, Leonidas' command to the 300 Spartans that they hold Thermopylae is a reason for the latter not to be motivated by a desire to save their own lives. 'Motivation' is ambiguous in this context. On the one hand, we may take Leonidas' command to demand a lot of his soldiers: they should not even be tempted by considerations of the sweetness of life and experience a pull or an inclination towards throwing down their shields and running away. On the other hand, Leonidas' command may be less demanding: we may understand Leonidas' command to exclude only that considerations about survival will not be the motive that gets his soldiers to act. I have argued elsewhere that the second, less stringent reading of motivation-excluding reasons is more plausible.[3] Given that motivation-excluding reasons are not the focus of this chapter I will not dwell further on this distinction.

(2) *Consideration-excluding reasons.* Alternatively, we may understand exclusionary reasons to rule out that the agent consider certain reasons. Consideration of reasons may take two forms. First, it may mean entertaining certain thoughts in one's mind or preoccupying oneself with elements of one's mental imagery. For example, one may think of or mentally visualize a romantic dinner with one's sweetheart. In some cases there may be good reasons not to entertain such thoughts or mental visualizations. For example, if one has decided to become a monk (and let us assume for the sake of the argument that this is a good decision), one may have good reasons not to think of romantic dinners. Similarly, if one has dedicated oneself to the pursuit of certain ends which require single-minded devotion (climbing Everest or trying to prove a mathematical conjecture), the achievement of these ends may be threatened by thoughts or mental representations of various forms of *joie de vivre*.

Press, 1999), 76–80; cf. A. Hatzistavrou, 'Reconsideration, Motivation and Exclusionary Reasons', *Ratio Juris* 25 (2012), 318–42.

[2] J. Raz, *Practical Reason and Norms*, 2nd edn (Oxford University Press, 1999; first published London: Hutchinson, 1975), 185.

[3] Hatzistavrou, 'Reconsideration, Motivation and Exclusionary Reasons'; cf. A. Hatzistavrou, 'Instrumental Rules and Motivation', *Legal Theory* 12 (2006), 315–45.

Second, we may understand consideration as equivalent to taking certain factors into account when one is deliberating. In this case, consideration-excluding reasons exclude taking into account certain factors. For example, once Leonidas has issued his command to hold Thermopylae, in deciding how to position themselves in the battlefield the Spartans should not take into account the possibility of leaving open a route for escape. The point is not that the thought of an escape route should not cross their minds or that they should not mentally visualize running away from the field or mentally replicate the feeling of relief from the stress of the battle correlated with their imaginary escape. The second understanding of consideration-excluding reasons does not require guarding against thoughts that crop up in one's mind or mental quasi-perceptions. It only requires that these thoughts are treated as irrelevant in the context of one's deliberations.

Consideration-excluding reasons are not equivalent to motivation-excluding reasons. First, thoughts which crop up in one's mind or mental quasi-perceptions need not have motivational clout. The monks or the dedicated mathematicians who think of romantic dinners need not be tempted by them to change course in life (one's sweetheart may be far away, one may be too old or too shy to seriously consider amorous relationships a real option). One's thoughts or mental images may be nothing more than a distraction from the normal activities of the life one has dedicated oneself to (fingering the prayer beads while one counts the repetitions of prayers, or going through the steps of an elusive proof).

Second, the mental action of taking something into account is conceptually distinct from the condition of being motivated by something. More importantly, factors one may register in one's deliberations may turn out to be motivationally inert. We often take into account certain factors in our deliberations while being sceptical about whether they are actually going to play a role in our decisions or even while being convinced that they will not. For example, I may initially take into account the torque power of a certain model of car in the process of deciding which car to buy, even though I may not have made up my mind about whether it is an important consideration for me (i.e. a consideration which may incline me towards buying the car), or even about whether it would be the decisive reason for selecting a car (i.e. a consideration which may get me to buy the car). Or I may take it into account even though I know it is not important for me simply because I want to have a clear picture of the engine capacity of the car. So, in one sense consideration-excluding reasons exclude more than motivation-excluding reasons: they exclude taking into account certain considerations even though the latter might turn out to lack motivational clout.

Third, in another sense motivation-excluding reasons exclude more than taking into account certain factors. Psychological elements other than factors we register in our deliberations may motivate us. For example, we may be moved by unreflective desires for some good.

(3) *Reasoning-excluding reasons.* Finally, we may understand exclusionary reasons to exclude not simply taking into account certain factors while deliberating but engaging in certain types of reasoning. We may distinguish types of reasoning by reference to their ends: that is, what they are about. For example, if I have adopted a personal rule or policy, say, to never smoke cigars, I may reason about whether in certain cases I should block the application of this rule. In this case I reason about the defeasibility conditions of my rule. Or I may question whether smoking cigarillos is excluded by my rule against smoking cigars. In this case I reason about the applicability conditions of my rule. But we may also differentiate between types of reasoning by reference to what I will call their 'modality'. The modality of the reasoning is determined by the intentions of the agent who engages in the reasoning. For example, I may go through the steps of my decision to adopt a rule of abstaining from smoking cigars as part of an idle exercise: that is, while having no intention of changing my decision if I find my reasoning faulty. Alternatively, I may reconsider my decision which means, as I will explain shortly, that I am willing to change my mind if I find my original reasoning faulty. Though in both cases my reasoning is about the same thing, namely whether my original decision is valid, the modality of my reasoning differs, since my intentions with respect to the conclusion of my reasoning are different.

Some valid exclusionary reasons exclude a particular type of reasoning: namely, reasoning about a particular end and of a particular modality. This type of reasoning is paradigmatically involved in the reconsideration of decisions or personal rules. It is also similar in kind to the reasoning involved when one questions the legitimacy of authoritative directives. For convenience I will call the exclusionary reasons valid decisions, and legitimate authoritative directives generate 'reconsideration-excluding reasons' and 'reconsideration-like reasoning-excluding reasons' respectively.

Though Raz insists that exclusionary reasons exclude only being motivated to act by certain considerations, he provides an analysis of the exclusionary function of decisions which implies that they (also) provide reconsideration-excluding reasons. Raz claims that 'decisions are exclusionary reasons in the sense that it is logically true that if x has decided to do A then x *believes* that his decision is a reason for him to disregard further reasons for or against doing A'.[4] Disregarding further reasons for or against doing A is treated as equivalent to a refusal to 'go on looking for more information and arguments and to decline to listen to them when they crop up in one's mind or are suggested by other people'.[5] Raz suggests that only decisions the agent is justified in making are valid exclusionary reasons.[6] This account of the exclusionary function of decisions captures a defining feature of valid decisions. Valid decisions exclude reconsideration, i.e. they exclude deliberation about the first-order reasons that the decision is meant to reflect with a view to reassessing the decision.

This normative relation between valid decisions and non-reconsideration is explanatorily more basic than the logical relation between decision and non-reconsideration. I mean the following: it is necessary that the person who has made a decision believes (at least implicitly) that she has normative reasons not to reconsider her decision – in the absence of this belief the person cannot be considered to have made a decision. The emphasis on the normative relation between decisions and reconsideration is probably motivated by a desire to avoid bootstrapping. My belief that I have exclusionary reasons not to reconsider a decision does not create a reason not to reconsider it. The decision must be valid.

I will distinguish three criteria for the validity of decisions.

(a) *Evidential validity*. Decision d of X is valid if and only if the content of d is supported by the balance of the reasons available to X or the reasons X can reasonably access.

(b) *Validity as (action-based) practical truth tracking*. Decision d of X is valid if and only if the content of d is supported by the balance of the reasons reflecting the practical value of the options available to the agent.

[4] Raz, *Practical Reason and Norms*, 68 (italics in original). An alternative way of explicating the logical relation between decisions and reconsideration is by relying on Broome's concept of normative requirement. J. Broome, 'Normative Requirements', in J. Dancy (ed.), *Normativity* (Malden, MA: Blackwell, 2000), 78–99. According to Broome, the agent must believe that she is normatively required not to reconsider and not that the decision is a reason for her not to reconsider. To avoid complicating the exposition of my argument in the main text I simply follow Raz's account of the logical relation between decisions and reconsideration.

[5] Raz, *Practical Reason and Norms*, 67. [6] Ibid., 68.

(c) *Systemic validity*. Decision d of X is valid if and only if the content of d is supported by the balance of the reasons reflecting the systemic value of the options available to the agent, i.e. d improves (non-accidentally) the quality of the agent's ability to make decisions which are evidentially valid or track action-based practical truths or both.[7]

The content of the decision may be a specific action (do A at t), or a conditional action (do A if p occurs), or a general policy or personal rule (do A whenever circumstances C obtain). These criteria may yield different results when applied to the same decision. Though a decision may satisfy the first criterion it may fail to satisfy the other two. For example, though it may have been rational for me to decide to buy bonds from a specific bank in August, given the information I possessed and the information I could have been reasonably expected to collect at the time of my decision, it may still both be a disastrous financial investment and fail to improve my decision-making ability. Similarly a decision may satisfy the second criterion but fail to satisfy the first. For example, if the suggestions of the university's quality office turn out to have adverse effects on the educational experience of the students then it is not rational for me to decide to accept them (even though I did not have any evidence that there were problems with them). Finally, a decision may satisfy the first two criteria but not the third. For example, my opposing the introduction of a certain set of academic regulations at the senate may have satisfied the first two criteria. However, I may have paid a great price for my decision. The intellectual labour I have spent in coordinating the opposition and the stress involved may simply have drained me emotionally and left me unable to face some tougher personal or academic decisions. My decision turned out to lack systemic validity.[8] Alternatively, if I had decided to avoid opposing the academic regulations

[7] Instead of my pluralist approach to the validity of decisions one may wish to adopt a stringent view according to which a decision is valid only if it satisfies all three criteria of validity I distinguish in the main text. This stringent view does not affect my main contention that valid decisions generate reconsideration-excluding reasons. It simply stipulates a very high benchmark of rationality (indeed too high when compared to the standards we ordinarily employ in speaking about rational decisions).

[8] An extreme form of this predicament (that is, the predicament of making decisions which are both evidentially valid and track practical truths but lack systemic validity) is captured beautifully by Cavafy in the last lines of his poem 'Che fece … il gran rifiuto': 'He who refuses does not repent. Asked again, / he'd still say no. Yet that no – the right no – / drags him down all his life'. In C. P. Cavafy, *Collected Poems*, trans. Edmund Keeley and Philip Sherrard, ed. George Savidis (London: Chatto and Windus, 1990), 12.

my decision would lack both evidential and practical truth-tracking validity but be systemically valid.

These criteria capture different aspects of our ordinary understanding of the validity of decisions. Sometimes we are interested in the evidence the agent had for the decision and assess it from that perspective. At other times we are interested in whether the reasoning of the agent successfully captured the relevant practical reality. Finally, sometimes we are interested in the effect of a single decision on the overall decision-making capacity of the agent. On all these criteria of validity valid decisions may be considered to generate reconsideration-excluding reasons. But first we need to understand what reconsideration involves. It involves reasoning about a specific end which is characterized by a specific modality. When the agent reconsiders her previous decision she reasons about the balance of reasons that support her decision. That is, she weights up afresh the reasons for and against her previous decision and comes up with a new judgement on the balance of reasons. This judgement may reaffirm the original decision, or modify or reject it. Furthermore, when the agent reconsiders she has a particular mental attitude towards her reasoning about the balance of reasons of her previous decision: she is willing to change her mind about her decision on the basis of her new judgement on the balance of reasons and be guided by her new judgement in her deliberations. Thus, valid reconsideration-excluding reasons exclude reasoning about the balance of reasons of her previous decision which is accompanied by her willingness to change her mind about that decision and be guided by her new judgement in her deliberations. But the exclusion of reconsideration cannot be absolute. Sometimes one may have reasons to reconsider one's valid decision. For example, sometimes one cannot execute or act in accordance with one's decisions because the external circumstances have changed. In these cases it is mandatory that one reconsiders. Or sometimes one may have good reasons to adopt as a general policy that one reconsiders one's decisions from time to time if only to reassure oneself of the validity of one's decisions. It seems prudent to treat valid decisions not as reasons which always exclude reconsideration but as reasons for treating non-reconsideration as the *default* position of the agent. If one has made a valid decision one has normative reasons to have as one's default position that one does not reason about the balance of reasons of one's previous decision while being willing to change one's mind about the balance of reasons and be guided by one's new judgement on the balance of reasons in one's deliberations.

I do not understand valid decisions as prima facie reasons for non-reconsideration. Rather I take them to be conclusive reasons for non-reconsideration being the default position of the agent. The notion of prima facie reason does not correctly capture the normative cum logical connection between valid decisions and non-reconsideration. This intrinsic connection indicates that valid decisions do not simply offer some support for non-reconsideration which may be defeated by other reasons. It is not as if when I have made a valid decision I have one reason not to reconsider which I can weigh up against others and make up my mind about how to proceed. An essential part of the function of decisions is that they guide the agent through being the starting points of relevant further deliberations. Non-reconsideration should then be considered the default option of the decision-maker: one should not reconsider unless one has significant reasons to the contrary.

The reasoning guidance that the decisions provide relates to another intrinsic feature of theirs. Decisions are not simply time- and labour-saving mental devices but also assurance conditions. They furnish the agent with a significant degree of epistemic assurance that she will not deviate from her plans because of a change of mind and that she will continue building on and expanding them. For it is not only external conditions or bad luck that may frustrate one's plans but also the tricks that one's mind plays. Doubts may lurk in one's mind and may lead to continuous retraction or hesitation. For example, it does not make sense for me to make plans about how to organize my holidays on Santorini next summer if I believe that my decision to spend my holidays there is open to constant reconsideration. Furthermore, this epistemic assurance enables the coordination of joint plans and social interaction. For example, it does not make sense for my partner to plan to join me on Santorini if she believes that I am not committed to going there.

On each of the three criteria of validity which I distinguished earlier it is rational for the agent to treat non-reconsideration as her default position. On the criterion of evidential validity the relevant norm of rationality prescribes that the agent's default position should be not to reconsider decisions reached by proper evaluation of the information which it was reasonable to expect her to be able to gather at the time of making her decision. On the criterion of practical truth-tracking validity the relevant norm prescribes that the agent's default position should be to exclude reconsideration of decisions which correctly track practical reality. Finally, when the criterion of systemic validity is employed, it is deemed to be rational for the agent to treat as her default position abstention from reconsideration of those decisions which improve her decision-making ability.[9]

When I treat my decisions as reconsideration-excluding reasons I conform de facto to the authority of my previous self (namely, the self which took the decision). I may or may not remember the reasoning behind my past decision. In either case I follow the judgement of my previous self and not my current self (namely, the self which has to act on the basis of the past decision). (Even if I remember the reasoning behind my past decision, I do not proceed on the basis of my current evaluation of my past reasoning. If I do, I have reconsidered my past decision.) If my decisions are valid, then I have normative reasons to follow the judgement of my previous self, and my previous self has legitimate authority over my current self.

This link between non-reconsideration and acceptance of the authority of my past self provides useful insight into the nature of exclusionary reasons legitimate authoritative directives generate. I will argue that on a particular understanding of legitimate authority it provides normative reasons for the deferring parties not to engage in reasoning whose end and modality are similar in kind to the end and modality of the reasoning involved in the reconsideration of decisions. The understanding of legitimate authority I have in mind is expressed by Raz's normal justification thesis. According to it, authoritative directives are legitimate with respect to a deferring party if the latter is more likely to conform to the balance of reasons which apply to her independently of the authoritative directives by following the authoritative directives rather than her own judgement about the balance of reasons.[10]

Raz does not clarify how we should understand the balance of reasons which applies to the deferring party and which the legitimate authoritative directives reflect. I suggest that we understand it on the model of the three criteria of the validity of decisions I distinguished earlier. First, it may be the balance of reasons assessed evidentially. In this case the point of the normal justification thesis is that the deferring party is more likely to conform to the balance of reasons which is evidentially

[9] One may wish to take a stringent view according to which only if a decision is evidentially and systemically valid and also tracks practical truths is it rational for the agent to treat non-reconsideration as her default position. As I explain in note 7, this may create a high benchmark for the rationality of decisions but does not affect my main point that valid decisions generate reconsideration-excluding reasons.

[10] J. Raz, *The Morality of Freedom* (Oxford University Press, 1986), 53.

valid by following the judgement of the ruling party rather than relying on her own collection and assessment of the relevant evidence. Alternatively, the balance of reasons may be understood to be assessed by reference to whether it corresponds to the relevant practical reality. In this case the normal justification thesis claims that the deferring party has normative reasons to conform to the judgement of the ruling party which is more likely than her own judgement to possess practical truth-tracking validity. Finally, the judgement of the ruling party may be more likely to be systemically justified since it may be more likely than the judgement of the deferring party to enhance the overall decision-making ability of the latter. In this case the deferring party has normative reasons to conform to a judgement reliance on which in future deliberations is more likely to improve her overall decision-making ability than reliance on her own judgement.

Raz's account of legitimate authority captures an essential feature of authority relations. Being the deferring party in an authority relation involves following not one's own judgement but the judgement of the person or institution in authority. This is similar to the situation in which I submit to the authority of my previous self. As I have argued, I challenge the authority of my previous self not only when I am motivated by considerations which conflict with my decision but when I reconsider it: that is, when I reason about the balance of reasons of my decision while being willing to change my mind and be guided in my future deliberations by the judgement of my current self on the balance of these reasons. I suggest that in a similar manner I challenge the authority of the ruling party not only when I am motivated to act by considerations which conflict with her authoritative directive but when I reason about the balance of reasons of the authoritative directive while being willing to be guided in my deliberations by my own judgement on the balance of reasons. If the authoritative directives are legitimate, I have reasons not to engage in this type of reasoning with respect to the authoritative directives.

There are two arguments in favour of the thesis that the deferring party has normative reasons not to engage in this type of reasoning. The first is that the link between legitimate authoritative directives and the exclusion of this type of reasoning is, like the link between valid decisions and non-reconsideration, normative cum logical. Unless the deferring party believes (at least implicitly) that the directives of the ruling party provide her with normative reasons not to reason about the balance of reasons of the authoritative directive, while being willing to be guided in her deliberations by her own judgement on the balance of reasons, she has not accepted the authority of the corresponding ruling party. For example, if the 300 Spartans believed that they were free to reason about the pros and cons of Leonidas' command to hold on to Thermopylae while being willing to be guided in their deliberations about what to do by their own judgement on the balance of reasons, then they would not have accepted the Spartan king as their leader. In a similar manner, a judge who believes that she is free to weigh up the pros and cons of a certain statute and follow her own judgement about the relevant balance of reasons in deciding a legal case does not accept the authority of the statute. Thus, legitimate authoritative directives provide reasoning guidance similar to the one provided by one's valid decisions.

The second argument is that the deferring party is better off accepting this reasoning guidance of legitimate authoritative directives. If I am more likely to get it right about the balance of reasons by following the authoritative directive rather than my own judgement, then I had better not reason about the balance of reasons while being willing to be guided in my deliberations by my judgement. I minimize the risk of getting it wrong and save time and intellectual labour. Furthermore, the reasoning guidance legitimate authoritative directives provide has significant value as an epistemic assurance device that facilitates further planning, coordination of activities, and joint action. Unless each Spartan believed that Leonidas' command constrained his own and his fellow soldiers' deliberations about the battle with the Persians, it would not make sense for him to plan to sharpen the blade of his sword or get into formation. Similarly, if the judge does not believe that a certain statute constrains her judicial reasoning she has no reason to make plans about checking its correct formulation and the lawyers of the defendant have no reason to base their defence on the statute.

There is a complexity concerning the exclusionary function of legitimate authoritative directives which does not normally arise in the case of decisions.[11] The deferring party may often come up with a judgement

[11] It sometimes arises though. Think, for example, of a case in which I form a judgement about what to do in the circumstances and then I recall a relevant earlier decision I have taken. In this case I might be at fault for having forgotten my original decision. By contrast the colonel in the example I mention is not at fault for forming a judgement about what is best for his regiment to do before he receives an order from the general. He may indeed be under a duty to form such a judgement.

about what is the best course of action in the circumstances before receiving a command. For example, the colonel may have reasoned that the best thing for his soldiers is to retreat from the hill they occupy before he receives an order from the general to hold onto the hill. If the command is legitimate (that is, it satisfies the normal justification thesis) then the deferring party should not weigh up her original view against the command while being willing to be guided in her deliberations by her new judgement about the comparison between the command and her original view. For example, the colonel should not weigh up his judgement that his troops should retreat against the command while being willing to be guided in his deliberations by his new judgement about which of the two best reflects the balance of the relevant military reasons.

The exclusionary force of legitimate authoritative directives is not absolute. Rather it should be understood in the same manner as the exclusionary force of decisions. The deferring party should treat not reasoning about the balance of reasons against the command while being willing to be guided in her deliberations by her judgement on the balance of reasons as her default position. In some cases the deferring party may be justified in challenging the authority of legitimate directives and reason about the balance of reasons as in some cases one is justified in reconsidering one's valid decisions.

The reconsideration-like reasoning-excluding reasons that legitimate authoritative directives generate are not equivalent to motivation-excluding reasons. The latter exclude only the mental condition of being motivated by certain considerations which conflict with the authoritative directives and not the mental action involved in reasoning about the balance of reasons which the authoritative directives reflect. Furthermore, as I have already mentioned, agents may be motivated to act by sudden urges or thoughts which may crop up in their mind and are not conclusions of deliberation. Even though the reasoning-excluding reasons may *a fortiori* exclude that one be motivated by one's judgement about the balance of reasons their exclusionary scope does not cover motivating factors which are not reached as a result of a process of reasoning.

Similarly, the reconsideration-like reasoning-excluding reasons which legitimate authoritative directives generate are not equivalent to consideration-excluding reasons. On the one hand, like reconsideration-excluding reasons they exclude only a type of reasoning and not mental visualizations or thoughts. On the other hand, the reconsideration-like reasoning excluded by legitimate authoritative directives has a specific end: that is, it is about the balance of reasons which support the authoritative directives and a specific modality: in other words, it is accompanied by willingness to rely on one's own judgement in one's deliberations. There are types of reasoning about legitimate authoritative directives which involve taking into account reasons that conflict with legitimate authoritative directives but are not excluded by reconsideration-like reasoning-excluding reasons:

(1) reasoning about the defeasibility conditions of general authoritative directives;
(2) reasoning about the applicability conditions of general authoritative directives;
(3) reasoning about the execution of occasion-flexible authoritative directives;[12]
(4) reasoning about the relevance of conditional authoritative directives;
(5) reasoning as part of an idle exercise about the considerations supporting or contravening authoritative directives.

Insofar as reconsideration-like reasoning-excluding reasons are concerned, one is free to engage in all five types of reasoning. For example, the colonel is free to reason about whether the application of the general's command that the colonel's regiment should go for training to the nearby forest every Thursday is defeated by the consideration that a severe storm is forecast for the following Thursday. He is also free to reason about whether the fact that the forest has been destroyed in a fire renders the rule inapplicable. Similarly if the general has issued an occasion-flexible command that the regiment should go for training to the nearby forest once a month, the colonel would be free to reason about which day of the month to send his troops for training. And the conditional command of the general that the regiment should retreat to the forest if the enemy's main offensive is on the regiment's right flank allows that the colonel may reason about whether the enemy's attacks on the regiment's right flank are a mere diversion. In none of these cases does the colonel reason about the balance of reasons of the general's command, though he may take into account certain reasons which contravene the command. Finally, the colonel is permitted to reason

[12] I borrow the phrase 'occasion-flexible' from M. Bratman, 'Intention and Personal Policies', *Philosophical Perspectives* 3 (1989), 443–69 (Bratman speaks of occasion-flexible intentions).

about the balance of reasons of the general's command as an idle exercise. For in the latter case, though he reasons about the balance of reasons, he is not willing to be guided in his deliberations by his own judgement on the balance of reasons.

To sum up, in this section I have argued that valid decisions generate reconsideration-excluding reasons and legitimate authoritative directives (at least on a particular account of legitimate authority) generate reconsideration-like reasoning-excluding reasons.[13] In the next section I turn to the issue of the epistemic value of legitimate authoritative directives.

Legitimate authoritative directives and epistemic agency

I have argued that the deferring party has conclusive reasons to treat refraining from challenging the legitimate authoritative directives as her default position in her deliberations. I explained the value of this refraining attitude by reference to the importance it has for practical agency.[14] The agent is better off not challenging the legitimate authoritative directives since she is more likely to act in accordance with the balance of reasons by following the authoritative directives rather than by following her own reasoning and is thus more likely to promote her practical goals. The contribution of this refraining attitude to the attainment of one's practical goals is indirect. By this I mean that it has negative causal influence: that is, it contributes to the attainment of one's practical goals in the way in which the absence of an impediment may causally influence an outcome. Other things being equal, refraining from challenging a legitimate authoritative directive significantly raises the probability that the agent will act on the directive and thus attain her practical goals; while, other things being equal, challenging a legitimate authoritative directive raises the probability that the agent may not act

[13] I am a pluralist about the types of exclusionary reasons valid decisions and legitimate authoritative directives generate. That is, I accept that valid decisions and legitimate authoritative directives may normally also generate motivation-excluding and in some cases even consideration-excluding reasons.

[14] For an elaborate account of the value of non-reconsideration from the perspective of practical agency, see M. Bratman, *Intention, Plans and Practical Reason* (Cambridge, MA: Harvard University Press; reprinted Stanford: CSLI Publications, 1999); cf. M. Bratman, 'Temptation Revisited', in his *Structures of Agency* (Oxford University Press, 2007), 257–82.

on the directive, since she might follow her own judgement after examining the balance of reasons, and thus fail to attain her practical goals.

This suggests that the value of reconsideration-like reasoning-excluding reasons depends in an important sense on the value of motivation-excluding reasons. Refraining from challenging legitimate authoritative directives is a means of preventing acting on certain conflicting considerations. One has reason to refrain to the extent that one has reason not to be motivated to act by certain considerations. This does not entail that reconsideration-like reasoning-excluding reasons are equivalent to motivation-excluding reasons for reasons I explained in the previous section. But it makes motivation-excluding reasons the primary reasons legitimate authoritative directives generate.

However, the perspective of practical agency does not fully capture the value of refraining from challenging legitimate authoritative directives. There is another perspective from which to assess its value: the perspective of epistemic agency. We have not only practical but also epistemic goals. We aim not only to fulfil our practical plans but also to attain knowledge or at least a comprehensive body of true beliefs. This refraining attitude contributes to the attainment of our epistemic goals. On the one hand, it has instrumental epistemic value. When one follows an authoritative directive, then, absent cases of akrasia, one forms a corresponding judgement about what is best for one to do. For example, the colonel who follows the general's order to capture the hill forms the belief that he should act so as to lead the regiment's attack on the hill. If the directive has legitimate authority, then one has epistemic reasons to be unwilling to challenge it. For by challenging it, one enhances the probability that one may lose an epistemically good state. If the legitimacy of the relevant authoritative directive depends on how the corresponding balance of reasons which it reflects is assessed *ex ante*, this state consists in the preservation of a belief which is justified by the available evidence at the time the directive is issued. In this case the agent has epistemic reasons to treat the relevant justified practical belief as the default position of her deliberations. For one should give precedence to beliefs justified by the available evidence. If the legitimacy of the relevant authoritative directive depends on whether the corresponding balance of reasons that it reflects correctly represents practical reality, this state consists in a belief which tracks a practical truth. In this case again the agent has normative reasons to be unwilling to challenge the authoritative directive. For one should retain beliefs which track truths. Finally, if the authoritative directive is systemically justified, then the relevant refraining attitude should remain the default position of the agent. One's decision-making capacity clearly has an epistemic dimension, since it enables one to reach practical truths in the future. So it is rational for one to retain a relevant practical belief which corresponds to the authoritative directive and has systemic value for one's epistemic agency because it raises the probability that one will track a large number of important practical truths in the future. In all these cases refraining from challenging legitimate authoritative directives is valuable because it is an instrumental means to the preservation of a state which is epistemically good.

On the other hand, this refraining attitude has value in itself as a constituent of good epistemic agency. Unwillingness to challenge legitimate authoritative directives is constitutive of intellectual trust in others since it exhibits respect for the epistemic authority of others and in particular those who in an important sense deserve to be treated as epistemic authorities. Trusting others in general is a prerequisite of my epistemic agency and my ability to reach accurate and comprehensive beliefs. Epistemic agency is impossible without epistemic trust in my current self, my current opinions and decisions.[15] But epistemic trust in my current self is inextricably linked with intellectual trust in others. Given the social construction of our system of beliefs there is an intellectual pressure to trust the opinions and testimony of others. In order for us to be able to form our own judgements we need to rely on information provided by others which we either have no means or no time to check and assess. We have to take them on trust. More importantly we cannot plausibly trust our own reasoning capacities unless we, at least implicitly, have trust in the beliefs of others. Foley puts this point succinctly:

> our most fundamental concepts and assumptions, the material out of which our opinions are built, are not self-generated but rather are passed down to us from previous generations as part of our intellectual inheritance. We are not intellectual atoms, unaffected by one another. Our views are continuously and thoroughly shaped by others. But, then, if we have intellectual trust in ourselves, we are pressured also to have prima facie intellectual trust in others. For, insofar as the opinions of others have shaped our opinions, we would not be reliable unless they were.[16]

[15] For the importance of self-trust, see R. Foley, *Intellectual Trust in Oneself and Others* (Cambridge University Press, 2001), and K. Lehrer, *Self-Trust: A Study of Reason, Knowledge and Autonomy* (Oxford University Press, 1997).

[16] Foley, *Intellectual Trust in Oneself and Others*, 102.

Foley speaks of prima facie intellectual trust. I think that the prima facie jargon fails to capture correctly the intrinsic link between intellectual trust in others and intellectual self-trust. First, the link is best understood as being normative cum logical in a way familiar from my discussion in the previous section. That is, unless I at least implicitly believe that I have normative reasons to intellectually trust others, I cannot be thought to intellectually trust myself. Intellectual self-trust involves trust in my beliefs: that is, beliefs that are born out of concepts and assumptions shaped by the beliefs of others. Talk of self-trust becomes vacuous unless the agent at least implicitly believes she has normative reasons to trust the beliefs of others who have shaped the concepts and assumptions of her own beliefs. Now, mere belief in the existence of normative reasons for trusting the beliefs of others does not entail that the relevant normative reasons exist and are binding. One has normative reasons to trust the belief of others only if their beliefs are valid. (The validity of their beliefs can be analysed along the lines of evidential, practical, or theoretical truth-tracking and systemic validity, as I explained in the previous section.) Second, the requirement that one trusts the valid beliefs of others is not absolute. One may occasionally have reasons to examine the foundations of the valid beliefs of others as one may occasionally have reasons to reconsider one's own valid decisions. So it is best to understand that the epistemic agent has normative reasons to treat trusting the valid beliefs of others as her default epistemic position. She should question them only if she has good reasons to examine their epistemic foundations.[17]

[17] This view, which is in essence a modified version of Foley's modest epistemic universalism, is contrasted to what Foley labels as 'epistemic egotism' and 'epistemic egoism' (Foley, *Intellectual Trust in Oneself and Others*, 83–92). The first claims that I have no normative reasons to trust the views of others and thus my default position should always be to determine for myself the validity of their views. The second claims that I have normative reasons to trust the beliefs of others only if I believe in their reliability: that is, the fact that their views are valid is not a reason for me to trust them unless it is backed by the fact that I believe that they are reliable. I do not have the space here to argue against these two theories. I will only note that they both appear to rest on the view that only beliefs the agent has can be reasons for her to adopt the epistemic attitude of trusting the beliefs of others. By contrast, I hold that only facts (like the fact that the beliefs of others are valid or that they are more likely than the agent's beliefs to be valid) are reasons for adopting the aforementioned epistemic attitude. For a defence of the view that reasons are facts and not beliefs, see J. Gardner and T. Macklem, 'Reasons', in Jules L. Coleman and Scott Shapiro (eds.), *The Oxford Handbook of Jurisprudence and Philosophy of Law* (Oxford University Press, 2002).

If I have normative reasons to trust by default the valid beliefs of others, then I have a fortiori normative reasons to trust by default the judgement of those who are more likely than I am to get it right about the balance of reasons. These people may possess a higher level of intellectual expertise or competence than I do. But they need not. Their judgement about the balance of reasons may be more trustworthy than mine because it is less likely to be blurred by contravening factors (stress, fear, emotional attachment) than my judgement, even though we share the same level of intellectual expertise or competence.

The mental attitude of refraining from challenging legitimate authoritative directives (understood along the lines of the normal justification thesis) may be reasonably considered an aspect of or a way of expressing default intellectual trust in the valid beliefs of others. Furthermore, since self-trust shapes my epistemic agency and is in itself shaped by default intellectual trust in others, default intellectual trust in the valid beliefs of others may be considered a constituent of good epistemic agency. It is thus reasonable to regard the mental attitude of refraining from challenging legitimate authoritative directives as having value as a constituent of good epistemic agency.

I have argued so far that this refraining mental attitude has both instrumental epistemic value and value as a constituent of good epistemic agency. I believe that these considerations provide us with adequate reason to identify default intellectual trust of legitimate authorities as an intellectual virtue. I do not mean that whenever one intellectually trusts legitimate authorities one exhibits an intellectual virtue. For one could do this unreflectively or by accident. Rather I mean that one can through habituation and training develop an ability to identify legitimate authorities (which includes an ability to identify their jurisdiction) and treat their directives as providing deliberative guidance. I will not provide a detailed account of the form and function of this intellectual virtue. I will simply offer a sketch of it which I hope will make its existence at least plausible.

A contrast between epistemic and practical agency is a good starting point. A good practical agent is not simply someone who consistently does the right thing. It is also someone who has a specific character: that is, certain mental attitudes towards her actions. For example, a courageous person is not simply someone who holds her position in the battlefield and does not run away to save her life. It is someone who performs a certain range of actions or refrains from others out of a certain motive – say, out of a desire to defend her country as opposed to a desire to accumulate wealth or overcome a childhood trauma; who engages in certain mental actions – for example, resisting fears or the temptation of daring actions; and who appreciates certain pleasures – for example, she enjoys the confidence generated by her not succumbing to fear or the temptation of daring actions. In a similar manner, a good epistemic agent is not someone who accumulates true beliefs and acquires pieces of knowledge in a consistent manner. It is someone who has in addition the right mental attitude towards her belief-formation processes: she approaches a cognitive field out of a certain cognitive motive, such as a desire for knowledge; engages in particular types of mental actions, such as resisting quick conclusions or the temptation of elaborating on trivial issues; and appreciates certain cognitive pleasures, like the pleasure of doubting an unclear argument and the confidence associated with the firm grasp of a truth or the development of her own cognitive abilities.

These mental attitudes may be considered intellectual virtues. And the attitude of showing default intellectual trust in legitimate authorities may be among them. By refraining from challenging legitimate authorities the agent treats her cognitive resources in a prudent manner (since she avoids engaging in unnecessary and potentially faulty reasoning), exhibits relevant epistemic humility, and cultivates an attitude of epistemic respect for the beliefs of others which is essential for the advancement of knowledge. These intellectual qualities may become, after a process of habituation and training, more or less stable features of her epistemic agency. The initial focus of habituation and training may be certain relevant intellectual tendencies human beings have which one may regard as intellectual proto-virtues. As one may regard certain tendencies human beings have towards their emotions – for example, the tendency to disregard fear when angry – as practical proto-virtues which can be properly calibrated, one may equally regard a tendency to rely on other people's views as a relevant intellectual proto-virtue. Once this proto-virtue is properly calibrated and related to other intellectual proto-virtues – for example, a tendency for creativity and independence of thought – it may become a proper intellectual virtue.

To sum up, in this chapter I have explored two dimensions of legitimate authoritative directives. On the one hand, they have a deliberative dimension, since they exclude a particular type of reasoning which is similar to the type of reasoning involved in the reconsideration of valid decisions. On the other hand, they have an epistemic dimension, since their relevant exclusionary function has both instrumental epistemic value and value as a constituent of epistemic agency.

8

Public transit

A. J. JULIUS

Reasons

The old man, when we stop to pick him up, is going slow and leaning on his cane. To keep his balance will be a struggle if he is still in the aisle when the bus pulls away from the curb. If I were to stand up, he could sit down. It seems to me that I should stand up and that this is because my standing up will make the seat available to this person who needs it more than I do. His need for the seat gives me reason to get up out of the seat.

This reason for standing exemplifies a wider normative pattern. Where I have reason to perform some action, the fact that I have reason to do it is typically explained by its possession of independently valuable features: features that make the action valuable, I mean to say, independently of any conative, evaluative, or normative attitude that I take toward them; and independently of any fact as to whether I am going to perform this action, whether I have decided to do it, whether I am disposed to do its like.

Standing up makes the seat available to a person who needs it more than I do. That is what is good about standing up, and that is what gives me reason to surrender the seat. Maybe I also approve of standing up, maybe I want to do it, maybe I am tending to do it, maybe I have decided to do it. In that case my motives are correct, and my tendencies of action are good. But if I stand up my action will not owe its value or its support by reasons to any such fact of my actual motivation or tendency toward doing it. Better to say that my motivation is correct and my tendencies good because I have reason to stand.

Law

I am about to get up when the driver points to a sign over my head:

> Priority seating for the elderly and disabled.

For their comments on earlier drafts of this chapter I thank Sarah Bittman, Arudra Burra, Laura Gillespie, Jonathan Gingerich, Mark Greenberg, Barbara Herman, Véronique Munoz-Dardé, Alexi Patsaouras, George Pavlakos, Seana Shiffrin, and Steve White.

I have never noticed this before. But I see now that in pointing to this sign she is pointing toward an important further element of the situation. That I should stand is true because this would yield the seat to someone who needs it more than I do. But apparently also because the action is required of me under the law. The prelegal reason for standing that arises from the elderly passenger's need to sit down is apparently doubled or shadowed by a second reason of law.

In some of my moods I will find this annoying or even bizarre. *Do they think I do not know* that this man needs the seat more than I do? Don't they *trust* me to do the right thing? Those are the reactions that surface when I am lazily thinking of my legal obligation as something that other persons have created by deciding that I will stand or by ordering me to rise with the purpose of getting me to do it. Fearing that my grasp of mass transit ethics is unreliable, the legislature has stepped in with a failsafe. It has fitted me out with a further legal reason for standing that can be expected to bring me to my feet even when I am having "an off day" and failing to appreciate prelegal reasons. I cannot accept this picture, and not because I do not have off days. (My grasp of mass transit ethics is firm but not infallible.)

Suppose for a moment that a person L's telling a person C to do x can directly ground the fact that C should do x. It is a remarkable power. She who has it should use it carefully. It seems to me that L should not use it for the envisioned purpose of bringing C to do x despite C's failure to pick up on independent reasons for x-ing. I have argued elsewhere that L should *not* try to get C to do a thing unless L is thereby facilitating C's performing the action for reasons that C has independently of the activity through which L is trying to bring C's action about.

But I also doubt that a legislator enjoys any such power. That anyone does. I do not see what could make it true of a person that her order or decision makes it the case that I should stand. Let me say a few words about one attempted explanation.

Algorithm

A promising defense of the supposedly direct reason-giving power of legislators exploits an *algorithmic* understanding of the determinants of what I should do.[1]

[1] The "algorithmic" proposal criticized in the text is roughly inspired by Joseph Raz's "service conception" of authority. See, for example, Joseph Raz, *The Morality of Freedom*

Suppose it is the case that, if I do everything that the legislature tells me to do and nothing that the legislature tells me not to do, my action is better supported overall by the reasons I have independently of the legislature's commands, than if I do everything that I take to be sufficiently supported by those reasons and nothing that I take to be sufficiently opposed by them. The account I have in mind urges that in that case the legislature's telling me to get up makes it true of me that I should get up.

To take this on is to renounce a familiar, perhaps even commonsensical principle holding that I should perform an action only if it is sufficiently supported by the independent reasons. For that trusty formula the algorithmic theorist must substitute some more sophisticated general principle relating the facts as to what I should do and the independent reasons that bear on what I might do.[2] Maybe this one:

> Suppose that I have epistemic access to the assignments of actions to me by the algorithm A. Suppose that if I do every action A tells me to do and omit every action A tells me not to do, then my action is better supported overall, by reasons I have independently of A's assignments, than if I do the actions and omissions assigned to me by any other algorithm to which I have epistemic access. Then the fact that A tells me to do (or omit) some action makes it the case that I should do it (or omit it).

This roots a requirement to do what someone is telling me to do in reasons that govern my action independently of her say-so. I am glad that the connection to independent reasons is made. But I doubt that this is the right connection.

Error

Imagine that I am a terrible judge of reasons. As bad luck would have it, so are all the other people with whom I am in contact. Some others are a bit better but still quite bad. I am the village idiot in a village of nothing but idiots.

(New York: Oxford University Press, 1986), part I. I am not confident enough in my reading of Raz to ascribe the proposal to him. Please take it to be made of straw.

2 Let us be clear that what is needed is a theory of the determinants of what you should do and not just a theory of how you might bring yourself to do the things you should do however those are determined. Maybe you will do more of what you should if you take a pill of the kind beloved of philosophers of self-manipulation. It *might* follow that you should take the pill as a way of bringing yourself to do more of what you should. To say so is not to claim that the actions you do, on the pill, are ones that you should do because they are the ones the pill disposes you to do. Cf. Derek Parfit, *Reasons and Persons* (Oxford University Press, New York, 1986), 12–13. The current claim is that an action of standing is made to be something that I should do by the fact of a legal requirement to do it.

Every algorithm at hand in the village is just some fool's assignment of actions to me. Let Terrance be, by a thin margin, the wisest of the fools. Then the algorithm [do what Terrance tells me to do] can satisfy the supposition of the algorithmic proposal – it can outperform my own judgment and the action assignments of all other accessible algorithms – even as all but one of the actions that Terrance orders are violently opposed by the Terrance-independent reasons. Then it is true of every action recommended by Terrance that I should do it. But that is incredible. It is incredible that all but one of the things I should do over the course of my life are fiercely opposed by the Terrance-independent reasons. I should not do those worthless things; I should do better.

Maybe the authority whose commands I am to obey must meet some threshold of *absolute* reliability with respect to the independent reasons. Then I need not do what Terrance tells me to do. He is not nearly reliable enough. However, this leaves the question of what I should do where no accessible authority is over the threshold. The alternative that comes to mind is that I should do what I have adequate independent reason for doing. Does the determination of what I should do revert, in such abject cases, to this standard of independently correct actions? That would have the absurd consequence that, as the least idiotic accessible algorithm improves enough so as to pass through that threshold and acquire authority over my action, the action that I should perform suddenly gets much worse.

And this is no joke. If the community were benighted enough, its least unreliable assigner of actions might be the legislator, public official, or bus driver who orders black passengers to yield their seats to whites. I would guess that, if you are black, and if the driver points to a sign that says:

> Priority seating for white people

you might do well to stay where you are. Not because your tired back or sore arches give you a reason for sitting that somehow outweighs a reason to stand that you have in virtue of the order to stand, but because the command does not speak in favor of standing.

When they arrested Rosa Parks for keeping her seat they charged her with disobeying an order to stand. We are in her debt because she declined to treat as a reason what was not.

Discussion

How does a bill become a law? In a democracy it would happen at least partly through discussion. Someone thinks of something that she thinks we should do. To make a law of it she tries to convince activists, voters, legislators, and judges that it is worth doing. Now she has got to cough up reasons why it is the thing to do. The courses of action that become the objects of legal obligation are ones that many different persons have come to believe are worthwhile. Many have come to believe this as the outcome of a discussion through which they were exposed to others' views about what is to be done and the reasons for doing it. Through this discussion some people acquire new warrants for believing that the legally obligated courses of action are worthwhile. That is partly because, during the discussion, others have said that the action is worthwhile in a way that directly entitles someone who hears this to take it as true. It is partly because others have mentioned reasons for performing these actions that had never before occurred to the listener but that, after some thought, she accepts in her own right. But perhaps it is also because the very fact that some course of action has emerged with substantial support from this discussion is evidence that it is worth doing.

If you take an algorithmic view you might also regard these epistemic virtues of legislation-as-discussion as evidence that the algorithm [obey the law] outperforms your own judgment. You might conclude that an action's being assigned to you by that algorithm makes it the case that you should do it. I have argued that this last step goes too far.

A bill's becoming a law can be a reason to *believe* that I have a reason to do the actions it calls for. It fails to follow that legislation gives me a reason to *do* those actions. And yet it is pretty credible that the discursive and deliberative character of democratic lawmaking makes a practical and not just an epistemic difference for me. How it does that remains to be explained.

Coordination

After discussion, a second mainstay of algorithmic authority is coordination. Each person should do what some person L tells us all to do. And this is true where and partly because: L tends to tell each person to cooperate in situations that have the structure of prisoners' dilemmas; L tends to tell each person to do her part of the best of several coordination equilibria; or L tends to pick one of several equally decent coordination equilibria and to tell each person to do her part of that one.

Consider the prisoner's dilemma. The algorithmic theorist presumably thinks that I have most reason to defect. That is why she expects that, unbound by any authority and consulting only my own judgments about reasons, I will defect. So what is the respect in which, when I cooperate rather than defect, I better conform to the reasons that apply to me? It may be that I live better, or that I have fulfilled more of my independent obligations when we all follow the rule than when we each defect. But by hypothesis those considerations, brought to bear only on the question of what I am to do, call for defection.

Apart from the reasons I have to choose one or another action within this situation, I also have reasons to transform it if I can. Maybe those transformative reasons are served by my submission to the authority. If I could do something that would result in most persons cooperating rather than all defecting, then my underlying self-concerned or moral reasons might favor my doing it. But I do not myself transform the situation in this way just by following the algorithm of obedience to L. The situation changes only if many or most or all of us submit. If the others submit, my adherence to independent judgment cannot reverse the transformation. And my adherence to independent judgment, because it would have me defect while the others cooperate, would better serve my non-transformative reasons even as the transformative one looks on indifferently.

Now consider pure coordination, in everyone's favorite example of traffic. The algorithm tells me to drive on the right or the left side according as L tells me and all the others to drive on the right or on the left. If the others follow this rule, then my following it qualifies me as conforming to reasons that apply to my action. But the rule does not outperform the presumptive outcome of independent judgment. Where I should believe that the others will follow this rule, where L has decreed the right side, and where I believe as I should, I will judge that driving on the right is supported by the independent reason that I have to do that where most others are going to do it.

Where it is false, on the other hand, that some other person will follow this rule, it is false that my following it qualifies me as better conforming to reasons. On the contrary it could get us both killed. So I do better, overall, to go on performing the action that seems best to me given what the others are going to do.

If I were disposed to do what the authority orders, that might be good for the others because it would give them a firmer basis for predicting that I will do my part and so for deciding themselves to do their parts. But this value in the disposition cannot make it the case that I should perform the action assigned by the authority. The fact that a disposition to do what has the property f is good, in some way apart from my having reason to do what has f, cannot make it the case that the action's having f gives me reason to do it.

It is looking unlikely that my individual obedience of authority makes it the case that my action better conforms to the independent reasons. You may wish to enter a different rationale for obedience. You might offer that all persons' obedience of some authority can make it the case that all persons' action better conforms to reasons. And you might take this fact as giving me good reason myself to obey. This is a new idea. The proposal I have been considering says that I should obey the authority as a way of bringing myself to do more of what *I* have reason to do. Perhaps it is time to change the subject, from my reasons to ours.

Publicity

The elderly passenger is a person, a subject of reasons. I can ask not only what I have reason to do around him but also what he has reason to do around me. One answer is that he has good reason to take a seat. If he does not sit down, he might fall, hurt himself, upset a second traveler, or spread disequilibrium up and down the bus. On his feet he will not enjoy the repose he needs for remembering his younger days or for planning his golden years.

I claim that, if I have good reason to stand up, that is partly because the old man has good reason to sit down. My standing makes available to this other passenger an action for which he has good reason. That he has reason to sit gives me reason to stand. The thesis is that reasons are *public* in the following respect.[3] Your subjection to reasons for your actions is the source of further reasons for me. That you have good reason to perform some action can give me a reason-given reason to facilitate this action of yours, to abstain from hindering it, or to abstain from doing what would make it not worthwhile.

I believe that this reason-given reason to facilitate the action for which you have good reason is grounded on the reason that I have to act consistently with your acting for the reasons you have. It is for its own sake good that a person act for the reasons she has. It is up to her, in the end, to achieve this value. But the value also reaches across the practical

[3] I follow T. Nagel, *The Possibility of Altruism* (Oxford University Press, 1970), part 3. See also C. Korsgaard, *Self-Constitution: Agency, Identity, and Integrity* (Oxford University Press, 2009), 188–202; and R. J. Wallace, "The Publicity of Reasons," *Philosophical Perspectives* 23 (2009), 471–97.

challenges of different persons, giving each person reason to act for the sake of the other's acting for the reasons she has.

I do not have room to defend this thesis of publicity here. I will try to show some advantages of taking it on. I will argue that it helps to make sense of the predicament that I share with my fellow passenger and that it helps to explain law's capacity to spring us from that predicament.

Independence

I should stand so that the other passenger can act for the reason he has to sit. The proposal draws many objections, some good and some bad. Ignoring the good ones, let us consider a *terrible* objection. You might object that, if I will go on sitting in the seat, then the other passenger cannot by sitting there ride comfortably or safely. You might conclude that the old man does not have good reason to sit in this seat if I will not give it up. He does not have good reason to do what he cannot do or what is not valuable given my own tendencies of action. If I will go on sitting there, this fact helps to give him good reason to look for some other seat or to try his luck swinging in the aisle. When I stay seated and so hinder his taking the seat I afford him an action for which he has good reason after all. My retention of the seat does not stop him from acting for the reasons he has. It upholds the public value of persons acting for the reasons they have.

I hope you share my sense that this apology for keeping my seat is ridiculous. But it is a little hard to say where it goes wrong. A person who is surrounded by other people can only perform the actions that are causally afforded her by the activity and the practical dispositions of the others. And her available actions depend for many of their good or bad features on the facts as to what the others will do.

The problem is that I am a person myself. There is still the question of what I have reason to do. I need to work out whether my possible action of keeping the seat is consistent with the other passenger's doing what he has reason to do. On the current telling I am to answer that question by taking as given my own tendency to retain the seat. The fact that I will be sitting here gives the old man good reason to move on. So it makes it the case that my sitting is consistent with his acting for the reasons he has. I think that I should not take the fact that I will be sitting here as helping to make it okay. Actions do not secure their own justifications in this bootstrapping fashion. If an action is one that I may or should do or that I have good reason to do, that is because of facts that hold independently of the fact that I will be doing it.

If there is anything to the idea of publicity, publicity must insist on a reason-given reason to yield the seat. We should rethink the assumption that the old man's reasons are simply determined by the physical affordances of a causal environment that includes my own activity and practical dispositions. My fellow passenger has good reason to sit even if I am going to make this action unavailable to him. It is because he has reason to sit that I have reason against making it unavailable. This suggests a different test for a person's having good reason to perform some action. If some valuable feature of A's x-ing gives the person A good reason to do x, then it must be that an x-ing will be available to A, and that it will bear the relevant values, *if persons act in the ways for which they are given reason by the fact that A has good reason to do x.* The old man's reason for sitting passes this test on the hypothesis that his reason for sitting gives me reason to stand. He can sit down, and his sitting down will be good, provided that I will do what his having reason to sit calls for me to do: give up the seat.

The simpler view with which mine competes holds that my reason for standing up is given by the fact that by emptying the seat my standing up will help to bring it about that the new passenger sits down. Like a shaky and very slow-moving pinball he will either come to rest in my seat, if I am out of it, or be deflected from it, if I am still there. The physics is hard to quarrel with, but I doubt that it settles what I should do. The disabled person will sit or stand as he sees fit. If he is not going to sit, standing so that he can sit is not so sensible. Maybe what I need is an extended physics – physics plus psychology and sociology – capable of predicting what he will do according as I sit or stand. I have argued that this is not the right approach to the many-body problem when the bodies belong to persons. Instead of asking what I am to do given the difference in our physical capacities and given his predicted responses to my possible courses of action, I should ask what he and I are to do given only the difference in our physical capacities. Only that difference is given to us in the sense of being determined independently of his and my deliberation about what to do.

Imagine that I stand up because he has reason to sit down. Imagine that he sits down because he has reason to sit down. I am standing up. He is sitting down. At one level of description we are acting differently in a way that is explained by the difference between our bodies. But he and I are each also making-a-move-because-the-man-needs-to-sit-down.

At this second important level of description we are each doing the same thing in a way that is explained by the fact that the same reason applies to each of us. On his way down and on my way up we might trade a look that says "I am doing what you are doing." It is a nice look, nicer than others to be had on the bus.

Jointness

The old man's having reason to sit is not in virtue of the fact that I will stand. His reason to sit calls for me to stand, and he succeeds in doing what this reason calls for me to do in virtue of his sitting and my standing. His practical success is our joint product. I think that his action and mine are related by a second interdependence of a similar nature. I have good reason to travel safely and comfortably on my feet. If the bus is crowded enough, then I cannot stand up, or stand safely and comfortably, unless the other passenger sits. There is no room in the aisle for the two of us among all the others who are struggling there to stay upright. It seems to me that he has reason to sit partly because I have reason to ride comfortably and safely on my feet. The fact that he will not sit down cannot deprive me of this reason for standing. When I succeed in acting for the reason I have to ride comfortably and safely on my feet, I succeed in virtue of his sitting as well as of my standing.

Each person is in her own right the subject of an underlying reason to travel safely and comfortably on this bus. That one person has the reason gives the other good reason to facilitate the other person's action by staying out of the other person's way. Each person succeeds in virtue of both reasons and does this in virtue of both individual actions. You cannot characterize a *person*'s normative practical success without mentioning both passengers' reasons to ride safely. And you cannot characterize the fact of compliance with any one such *reason* without mentioning both individual sitting or standing actions.

I think that this double, cross-cutting interdependence is well marked by saying that the elderly passenger's reason for travelling comfortably and safely in the seat and my reason for travelling comfortably and safely on my feet give *me and him* good reason for the pattern of his and my actions that has him sitting down and me standing up. Each of the two persons is the subject of a standard set by both underlying reasons that calls for the performance of both individual actions of sitting down or standing up. Each person is the subject because each is accountable to both underlying reasons and because each succeeds in doing what is called for by the two underlying reasons in virtue of the two individual actions.

When I stand up and he sits down, my standing up does not give him reason to sit down, and his sitting down does not give me reason to stand up. The pair of these actions through which we trade places is already one for which we share good reason independently of whether we are going to do it.

Coordination on the bus

If you have traveled on crowded trains or buses where seating for the elderly and disabled is not designated by law, you know that often enough there is a further issue. Many people are now sitting, any one of whom could easily ride on her feet. Who will be the one to get up?

There exist several distinct patterns of individuals' sitting and standing through which we might all act for the reasons each has to ride comfortably and safely. I could get up as the disabled passenger and the others sit. Or you could, or she could, or he could. You and I and she and the elderly passenger have sufficient reason to fall into any one such pattern. And we have good reason against the pattern in which all the physically robust riders keep their seats, leaving the disabled passenger to struggle for stability on her own.

We will need to pick. But interpersonal picking is not always easy. It is not easy even to say what interpersonal picking is. Let me describe one form that it might take.

Each person might bring to this domain of her action what I will call a *democratic intention*. Let C(S, A, x) be a circumstance in which some person has proposed to each of many persons a pattern S in all their actions that includes A's x-ing; no one has rejected that proposal by pointing out good reasons against it; and A has judged that if we all do our parts of S then each does what is called for by the independent reasons she has and by the reason-given reasons she has to facilitate the others' doing what they have reason to do. A's democratic intention is then her intention to perform an action of x-ing in C(S, A, x).

I suspect that some of my fellow riders are carrying intentions of this kind. As the disabled newcomer approaches the area where we are sitting, we exchange mildly embarrassed glances. Finally one of us indicates by a slight shift in her body language that she is on her way up. She is proposing that she stand up so that the others may keep their seats as the disabled passenger takes a seat. No one rejects the proposal by speaking against it or by making as though to stand up herself. We return our attention to our headphones or daydreams. Each then carries out her intention to sit or stand in the pattern that is proposed and on the basis of her judgment that it is a fine pattern.

Maybe you will regard this as an idealized description of actual coordination on the bus. Maybe you think it is a fantasy. Never mind. Whether or not this is how we really get along, I want to argue that it is a good way of getting along.

If we all have these intentions, each ends up intending to perform one part of the same good pattern of our sitting and standing, and we end up sitting or standing in that pattern. This is good partly because we succeed in acting for the reasons we already have to realize the pattern. We sit or stand in a good pattern, and each person sits or stands in execution of an intention that arises from her judgment that we have good reason for sitting or standing in the pattern. We do not make the pattern to be good by proposing or accepting a plan that prescribes it to us or by forming and exercising the democratic intentions that bring us to carry it out.

It can seem that our motivations and dispositions, though they do not make the pattern good, make a person's individual action of sitting or standing something that a person should do. Our dispositions cause all of the others to play their parts of the picked pattern. So they make it the case that I have reason to play my part. This is what I have denied. When things go well with our action and deliberation, the facts as to what the others are going to do, do not settle the question of what I should do. I should do my part because it is part of a good possible pattern. In standing now I join the others in satisfying a standard that, before we began to think about it, has already called for us to perform one or other of the several good patterns.

Unfreedom and cooperation

If I keep my seat when a pattern that calls for me to stand has been proposed and not rejected, I am going wrong. The simplest explanation of my failure is that I have good reason to stand, a reason that went into force when it was decided that I would be the one to stand. My action of keeping my seat would be fine in other circumstances, such as when it is proposed that I keep it. This suggests that our decision gives me a reason for standing that I would otherwise lack. I have just argued against this explanation of my failure. But I owe you an alternative account.

Suppose that I keep my seat because I simply want to sit. I want to sit even if some other passenger shows a greater need for the seat. I want to sit even if it has been proposed that I stand as you and the old man sit and even if no good objection to that plan has come to light.

Now you and the old man are faced with my disposition to sit no matter what. The elderly passenger fails to sit, or he fails to ride comfortably, if he tries to sit where I am sitting. You fail to facilitate his riding comfortably if you keep your seat. You are each bound to take my disposition to sit as calling for the old man not to sit where I am sitting and as calling for you to surrender your seat. In deciding what to do, it would be rash of you to overlook the fact that, whatever you decide, I will not budge from the seat I call mine.

Suppose that these actions of yours constitute your acting for the reasons you have. I give you reasons to perform them by being disposed to keep my seat no matter what. Then I may take the fact that I want to sit no matter what as making my sitting consistent with your acting for the reasons you have. My disposition to sit no matter what makes itself okay by making it okay me for to stay seated. I have argued that this will not do. My disposition to sit does not bootstrap a permission of my sitting.

I conclude that the actions I compel you to take are not ones that you can perform and thereby act for the reasons you have. My proclivity for sitting leaves you with certain options. You do the best you can given my immobility. It makes you unfree, in doing the best you can, to act for the reasons you have. I go wrong in being disposed to sit in a way that makes unavailable to the rest of you an action of acting for the reasons you have.

You might think it follows that I should give up the seat partly so that it is false that I have this disposition that makes the rest of you unfree. This would take back my earlier insistence that reasons for a person's action are not grounded on the values or disvalues of the dispositions that she manifests insofar as she is motivated by those reasons.

But this last step is not necessary. It is not needed for practical guidance. I can decide to give up the seat, not so as to avoid the bad disposition that would make you unfree, but simply because it forms part of a pattern for which we have good reason. When I carry out my intention to sit or stand according to a pattern that has been proposed, I can take my action as one for which I have reason because it forms part of a pattern through which no one hinders a comfortable ride by anyone else.

Legislation

Here is a story about how it might have come to pass that a sign reading

> Priority seating for the elderly and disabled

hangs over the front few seats on the bus. People who ride buses have a number of problems in common. From time to time we manage to talk our problems through together. At first this happens just between two or three passengers riding the same bus and griping because it is running behind schedule, one of the windows broken, the air conditioner stuck. Eventually someone suggests we get together to talk about fares, routes, and larger systemic matters. We rent a hall and advertise for a Tuesday night meeting open to all riders.

At one point in the discussion someone raises the question of physical disability. She argues that a disabled person has a greater need to sit, and that this counts in favor of able-bodied riders' standing so that disabled riders may sit. Many other people come up to the microphone to agree.

Complications arise. What counts as disability? Which forms of disability make for which degrees of difference in the need to sit down? Which distribution of passengers over the seats and standing areas is favored by these facts?

Someone writes down an explicit definition of physical disability. Objections are raised, and the definition adjusted. Another rider draws a seating chart indicating, as an area of priority for the disabled, the three frontmost side-facing seats to the left of the aisle. It is pointed out that because a disabled passenger who boards the bus from the right would have to cross the aisle in order to reach the designated seats, this designation makes for more congestion than if we were to set aside the three frontmost side-facing seats to the right of the aisle. The chart is redrawn. After a few more hours of give and take, a resolution is read out to the effect that no person who fails to meet the explicit definition of disabled will sit in that area if someone who meets the definition has yet to find a seat. The motion carries. A few activists volunteer to hang the familiar signs over the front seats tomorrow. Before going to bed someone posts online the resolved definition of disability.

Tomorrow if I keep my seat under the newly hung sign I am going wrong. My failure is not my failure to perform a standing action for which I am given reason by the fact of our decision. If I keep my seat, that will be because I am disposed to keep sitting there no matter what. My disposition to sit no matter what makes the rest of you unfree, in exercising your own dispositions to do what the sign says, to act for the reasons you have. Someone else will have to stand because I am keeping the rest of you out of the seat I occupy.

As before, it does not follow that I should vacate the seat so that I will lack this disposition that makes you unfree. But the badness of my undemocratic disposition is in any case redundant to a good decision. It is open to me to decide to rise for the reason I already have to make way for the other passenger.

That my action is required under democratic law, I propose, is the fact that by doing it through the exercise of a democratic intention I could join the others in acting for the reasons we share for patterns of action through which each person facilitates or abstains from hindering the actions of others for which those others have reasons. That my action is required under the law does not give me reason to do it. It bears an important relation to my reasons for action all the same. We could act for the reasons we have by doing what is legally required of us in exercise of our democratic intentions.

I see no reason to confine this conception of the law and its value to bus problems or the competition of bodies for space. Here is another social problem. Each person has good reason to employ material resources in her valuable projects. She has good reason to facilitate other persons' acting for such reasons. She can do this by keeping her hands off certain things that the others might use or even by making things for the others to use. But if I am disposed to enclose what I need for my projects and to exclude you from the things you need for yours, I compel you to make do with what I leave for you. You will have to reckon with the accomplished fact of my appropriation. It makes you unfree, in carrying out the projects this affords you, to act for the reasons you have.

But we could yet act for these reasons. Each person might intend to play her part in schemes for the general use of external resources that are proposed in an open discussion about reasons for sharing them out through those schemes.

Public notice

I have been talking about coordination. I would now like to reconsider discussion. The independent reasons that call for us to interact in one or another of the good patterns also give each person reason to try to persuade the others that we should act in the patterns they recommend.

Suppose that we were disposed to follow a pattern that is picked for us, not after a discussion, but by a fairly reliable lottery. Then I could not act for the reasons I have to persuade the others to do what is required by the independent reasons. I would know that they will be doing whatever is put out by the lottery. A similar point tells against dispositions to follow patterns selected through a discussion that excludes some person from proposing or criticizing patterns or that puts certain considerations of value off-limits. Our dispositions to act in the patterns selected on this basis would keep the excluded persons from acting for the reasons they have to argue for worthwhile courses of action. Or they would keep us from acting for the reasons we have to defend or criticize patterns on the grounds of the excluded considerations.

These are not incidental flaws. I have argued that the value of our deciding to perform our parts of proposed plans consists in the fact that this allows us all to act for the reasons we have for carrying those plans out. No procedure of coordination can have this value if it prevents persons from acting for those same reasons by arguing for action on grounds of those reasons.

Open discussion is necessary for the democratic legal project to have the value I have claimed for it. So is common knowledge of the plans that are taken up. Each person needs to know that all persons know which patterns are being picked. This is not because each needs to be assured that the others will do their parts. It is because each needs to know that her own action will not be taken by some other person as directly determining what the other must do. Suppose that I am the disabled passenger. If I were not to know that you know that the front right-hand seats are reserved for disabled riders, I would have to worry that you will regard my own action of keeping my seat as compelling you to stand in the aisle.

But if we have talked about a plan for reserving seats for the disabled, and if the plan is marked in a place where everyone can see it, then I can know that you know that in keeping my seat I am not just compelling you to go along with what I am doing but am rather leaving you free to act for reasons you have to stand. I see that you see the sign I see. I know that you know that in yielding your seat you are yielding it not to me but to the law. That is the value of a sign.

A democratic direction

Democracy is not "the worst form of government except for all the others."[4] Democracy is wonderful. Can philosophy say what is so wonderful about democracy? Or is that asking too much?

[4] As if you were going to take Winston Churchill's word for it.

People were excited in 1994 because it seemed that the new government of South Africa would start improving South African social life in "substantive" ways that could be characterized independently of the legal "procedures" by which that government arrived in power or exercised it. Where people were once packed onto the rickety private minibuses that carried them from townships to workplaces along extremely indirect routes, the new government would build a system of public transportation and run it so that everyone might enjoy the same possibility of mutually unobstructed motion over the territory.[5] But we were also happy because we expected those buses to be built by a government that the people had lined up to vote for, and administered through laws the riders had proposed and criticized.

I think that there is no need to choose between substance and procedure so understood. The destination is important. It also matters how the people get where they are going.

[5] This seems to be happening, twenty years later, with the institution in some South African cities of Bus Rapid Transit. But it has been a struggle. Those who would keep the new buses from transporting people across the old lines cannot stop this from happening, but they have retained the power to slow it down. Celia W. Dugger, "A Bus System Reopens Rifts in South Africa," *New York Times*, February 21, 2010.

9

Ought we to do what we ought to be made to do? Cohen and Nagel on the personal and the political

WILLIAM A. EDMUNDSON

> In warming himself at French social theories he had brought away no smell of scorching. We may handle even extreme opinions with impunity while our furniture, our dinner-giving, and preference for armorial bearings in our own case link us indissolubly with the established order. And Lydgate's tendency was not toward extreme opinions: he would have liked no barefooted doctrines, being particular about his boots.[1]

In the tradition of criticism/self-criticism, Jerry Cohen interrogated his own way of living. He was a "red diaper baby" by birth, an egalitarian by conviction, and yet by vocation a long-time Fellow of All Souls College, Oxford, by some measures the least egalitarian institution in Western history. He was vexed by the difficulty of reconciling three propositions that had become true, as applied to him.

I am grateful to Brian Bix, Saul Smilansky, David Enoch, Irit Samet, Jeremy Farris, and commentators on earlier drafts, including those noted throughout. I owe thanks to the participants in the IVR Workshop on "Legal Normativity and the Philosophy of Practical Reason," Goethe Universität, Frankfurt, August 14–18, 2011, especially Veronica Rodriguez-Blanco and George Pavlakos, its organizers; and to participants in the MANCEPT workshop on "Legitimacy, Authority, and Political Obligation," University of Manchester, September 5–7, 2012, especially Massimo Renzo and Chris Mills, its organizers, and to Bas van der Vossen, Annie Stilz, Chris Bennett, Kimberley Brownlee, and Matt Smith. At an annual meeting of the Analytical Legal Philosophy Conference, March 1–2, 2013, at the University of Miami School of Law, I benefited from suggestions by Stefan Sciaraffa and Seana Shiffrin, as well as by other commentators too numerous to name. Finally, I thank Russ Covey and my colleagues at Georgia State for the recommendations they offered at a Faculty Workshop on March 11, 2013.

[1] George Eliot, *Middlemarch* (1874). Cohen quoted a different passage from *Middlemarch* as the epigraph to his essay "Political Philosophy and Personal Behavior," in G. A. Cohen, *If You're an Egalitarian, How Come You're So Rich?* (Cambridge, MA: Harvard University Press, 2000), 148–79. In it, Eliot acquits the damned, self-righteous but self-deceived Bulstrode of "gross hypocrisy."

> [T]he triad which formulates ... the problem that exercises me:
>
> (1) (*A* believes that) *A*'s behavior is not out of line with his own principles.
> (2) *A* believes in equality.
> (3) *A* is rich (which means that *A* does not give a relevant amount of his money away).
>
> It is an interesting question whether the behavior reported in 3 is congruent with the belief reported in 2.[2]

The question is whether (1), which asserts that congruence, is consistent with the conjunction of (2) and (3). Leave out the parenthetical "*A* believes that" in (1), and – under plausible interpretations of the remaining language – there is an inconsistent triad. Consistency is restored by putting the parenthetical back in, but "logical consistency is a very thin thing."[3] What we have is "an inconsistency in *A* herself."[4]

The triad can be generalized.

Cohen's Triad in general form

(1) (*A* believes that) *A*'s behavior is not out of line with *A*'s own principles.
(2*) *A* believes in principle *P*, a principle of distributive justice.
(3*) *A* is rich (which means only that *A* does not give away the difference between the amount of money *P* requires a just state to extract from *A* for the purpose of distributive justice, and the smaller amount that the state in fact extracts).

The "difference" might be the product of regressive marginal tax rates, of unwarranted shelters, credits, and deductions, of the tax basis itself (income, sales, property, etc.), or of some combination of these. Although phrased in terms of an "amount of money," the incongruity extends to other goods. Paid work, for example. There are few fields in which there is not a supply of younger, under- or unemployed people who may be at least as qualified as their elders. An older, well-provisioned employee might think it a shame that she is not made to retire in order to make way for one of the younger people who have had to postpone or pass up a career in a field (such as academia) where jobs are scarce. Such an older worker, even if well provisioned for retirement, and persuaded

2 Cohen, "Political Philosophy and Personal Behavior," 156–7. 3 Ibid., 158.
4 Ibid., 156.

of the justice of mandatory retirement, is unlikely to retire merely because she thinks it her duty.[5]

The triad formulates an incongruity in the lives of egalitarians of all types, as Cohen notes, including Rawlsians. On Rawls's view, distributive justice makes no direct demands upon us, but we do have a duty to "support and comply with just institutions that exist and apply" to us, and to endeavor to "further just arrangements not yet established . . . when this can be done without too much cost" to ourselves.[6] How much is too much? Presumably, if a Rawlsian believes she is under-taxed by some amount, then parting with that amount would not be "too great" a cost to her, were she to spend that much to reform her political system. Thus, there is an analogue of Cohen's problem that ought to trouble even those egalitarians who take the Rawlsian view that distributive justice makes no unmediated demands of us, but requires that we direct our individual efforts to institution-building and reform. The only Rawlsian who remains outside its reach is one who insists (implausibly) that the amount she ought to be taxed is a matter of pure procedural justice, measurable by no independent criterion, and thus entirely divorced from the question of what sacrifices natural justice requires she make to support just institutions. In short, Cohen's Triad poses a challenge to egalitarians, non-egalitarian prioritarians, utilitarians, sufficientarians, most Rawlsians and, in fact, anybody who believes in a principle of distributive justice that warrants redistributive taxation.

The Cohen Triad in general form does not express an incongruity in the lives of those who are not rich (in the relevant sense), or who deny the existence of any principle of distributive justice. Nor does it capture any incongruity in the lives of the well-to-do believers whose principles do not warrant redistributive taxation.[7] Believers in laissez-faire, for example, may give away nothing in good conscience, because on their principles the state cannot justly tax them at all for redistributive purposes. Similarly, those whose distributive principle *P* merely permits, but does not require, redistributive taxation have nothing to have to justify.[8]

[5] Cf. S. Smilansky, "The Paradox of Beneficial Retirement," *Ratio* 18 (2005), 332–7. P. Van Parijs, "The Disfranchisement of the Elderly, and other Attempts to Secure Intergenerational Justice," *Philosophy and Public Affairs* 27 (1998), 292–333.

[6] J. Rawls, *A Theory of Justice* (Cambridge, MA: Belknap Press, 1971).

[7] Cohen's worry might arise for an anti-redistributivist who believes that, for the provision of a public good, she is being unfairly under-taxed. See L. Murphy and T. Nagel, "Taxes, Redistribution, and Public Provision," *Philosophy and Public Affairs* 30 (2001), 62.

[8] Elizabeth Anderson, "What Is the Point of Equality?" *Ethics* 109 (1999), 287–337, underlines the distinction between justice and compassion. The redistributarians at issue here

There is thus a prima facie difficulty facing anyone who does believe that justice requires the state to tax her at a rate higher than that at which she is currently being taxed. That takes in a lot of people, including me. But it is worth taking another step back. There may be a quick way to dispel this uneasiness. Thomas Nagel was the first to allude to it (as far as I know).

> Admittedly there are cases in which a person should do something although it would not be right to force him to do it. But . . . I believe the reverse is true. Sometimes it is proper to force people to do something even though it is not true that they should do it without being forced.[9]

Nagel made the more general point in the context of taxation, too. In his view, "It is acceptable to compel people to contribute to the support of the indigent by automatic taxation, but unreasonable to insist that in the absence of such a system they ought to contribute voluntarily."[10] Cohen's worry arose because many existing systems of "automatic" taxation ask less of the rich than what those systems could and ought to demand of them.

The absence of compulsion both Nagel and Cohen had in their immediate sights is not a pre-political vacuum, but a failure of modern states to do what they could readily do and ought, in justice, to be doing. Nagel suggested that the individual's predicament in the midst of this kind of political failure should be assimilated to a more general pattern. Nagel's more general point can be stated with reference to this abstract form:

Nagel Triad

N1 There is a moral principle *P* and actors *A* and *B* such that *B* ought to make *A* Φ.
N2 *A* is not made to Φ.
N3 *A* has no duty to Φ.

Nagel's general point is that a triad of propositions of this form can be true together. For simplicity, I will let "principle *P*" encompass both the abstract principle and the circumstances that, coupled with the abstract

are concerned with a "perfect" duty of justice rather than an "imperfect" duty of compassionate charity, which a tax system might reduce to a conveniently dischargeable quantity.

9 T. Nagel, "Libertarianism without Foundations," in Jeffrey Paul (ed.), *Reading Nozick* (Totowa, NJ: Rowman & Littlefield, 1981), 199–200.

10 Ibid., 200.

principle, trigger the requirement that *A* be made to Φ. Wherever necessary, I elaborate what circumstances *C* obtain, such that, given *P* and *C*, *A* ought to be compelled to Φ.

Also for simplicity, I will stipulate that Φ is to be interpreted flexibly enough to encompass both an institutional act, whose description implies institutional facts, and an extra-institutional act that could count as a substitute performance. For example, if *A* is not required to pay a tax, then nothing *A* could possibly do could count, strictly speaking, as paying that tax.[11] What *A* might do as a substitute performance would be a donation or voluntary transfer, to some suitable recipient, in an amount equal to what *A* ought to be taxed.[12] There is always a possibility that there will be no good enough second-best to serve as a needed substitute. This could happen if, for example, the only available recipients were so corrupt that a voluntary transfer would have pernicious consequences. But it would be a world much worse than our own in which no recipient agency could be trusted.

So, if the Nagel Triad is satisfied with respect to *A*'s principle of distributive justice, P, then *A* can rightly be easy of mind in not Φing. *A* awaits the call to Φ, but the duty to Φ does not arise until the call issues. It just happens that the call is not going to come. Because the call is not going to come, if *A* Φs anyway, *A*'s Φing is an act of supererogation, not one of discharging a duty. The task is thus to collect cases that satisfy the Nagel Triad, and to determine whether any of them is similar enough to Cohen's worry to relieve it.

Making it the case versus making someone

The reasons that make it true I ought to be made to do something seem capable of differing from the reasons that have to do with what I ought to do. The reasons for the maker and the reasons for me can be different. Hospitality requires hosts to make it the case that their guests relax, but guests have no duty to relax if their hosts otherwise fail to get them to. The reasons that obligate *B* to make it the case that *A* Φs need not "leak" over to *A* in a way that would obligate *A* to Φ.[13]

[11] Luis Duarte d'Almeida forced me to acknowledge the need for this simplification.

[12] Cf. S. Smilansky, "On Practicing What We Preach," *American Philosophical Quarterly* 31 (1994), 73–9.

[13] Paul McNamara, "Deontic Logic," in Dov Gabbay and John Woods (eds.), *The Handbook of the History of Logic*, vol. VII: *Logic and the Modalities in the Twentieth Century*

Our focus, however, is not the logic of "making it the case that *A* Φs," but the logic of "making *A* Φ." Leakage is unlikely to be objectionable here: the reasons that favor *A*'s Φing have to be much stronger because they have to overcome a strong commonsense presumption of liberty. I can make it the case that you read this paragraph, for example, by writing it and publishing it in a journal you follow. But how would I make you read it, as distinct from making it the case that you do? Hold a gun to your head? There had better be some very powerful reasons at work to justify my doing that. Moreover, those reasons would have to be ones equally available to you, if it is you who are to be made to read the paragraph. "Leakage" looks not to be a problem, but a justificatory requirement.

Making someone do something versus getting someone to do it

Getting someone to do something and making someone do something are also crucially different. They both differ from making it the case that someone does something. Getting someone to do something normally involves requesting and persuading, but making it the case that someone does something need not. Making someone do something normally involves a manifest readiness to go beyond persuasion to compel action if necessary. Typically, making others do something begins when getting them to do it has failed or would fail. These differences have a bearing on what is needed to justify making someone do something as opposed to merely getting her do it. A significantly stronger principle is needed to justify making someone do something than to justify getting her to do it.

It is easy to devise examples in which a moral principle makes it the case that *A* ought to be gotten to Φ that are not cases in which *A* has a duty to Φ; so, if the Nagel Triad were stated in terms of "gotten to" rather than "made to," it would be easy to satisfy. Suppose that the parents of Little Ricky, a very small child, have a parental obligation to get him to pick up his clothes from the floor. But suppose they do not do that. It ought to be the case that Little Ricky picks up his clothes, but it does not follow that Little Ricky has a duty to do it – not yet anyway.

But now add a few years to Little Ricky's age – enough to make it the case that he has a duty to do as he is told. If Little Ricky is old enough

(Amsterdam: Elsevier, 2006), 256, calls it the "Leakage Problem." It arises under the so-called Meinong–Chisholm reduction of the idiom "*A* ought to Φ" to "*A* ought to make it the case that *A* Φs."

to have a duty to pick up his clothes from the floor when his mother tells him to, how can he not also have a duty to pick them up without being told? The answer here seems easy: Little Ricky's mother has authority, which, when exercised, imposes on him a duty he would not otherwise have. But the case is not yet an instance of the Nagel Triad. To make it so, we must appeal to the duty Little Ricky's mother has to make him pick up his clothes, which she (for whatever reason) neglects. Little Ricky's mother has a duty to make him pick up his clothes; but she does not make him pick up his clothes. And Little Ricky has no duty to pick up his clothes? His duty is conditional upon being made to do it? It would seem that the reasons that are sufficiently important to impose on his mother a duty to make him pick up his clothes, and to impose on him a duty to pick up his clothes when told to, ought to be sufficiently important to impose upon him a duty to pick up his clothes whether or not his mother fulfills her duty. And if the underlying reasons are sufficient to do that, it looks as though they are sufficiently important to make it Little Ricky's duty to pick up his clothes, full stop.

The puzzle

Here, once again, is the puzzle that is at the root of Cohen's problem. How can a sane, competent adult believe that others – parents and officials, principally – have a moral duty (and permission) to compel him to do something, see that those others are failing in their duty, and yet believe he has no duty to go ahead and do that something? Nagel alluded to the existence of a class of objective possibilities that, allegedly, satisfy what I have been calling the Nagel Triad, and I will call that class the Nagel Class. The Nagel Class is a class of cases, to repeat, such that someone *B* has a duty to compel someone *A* to Φ, *B* will not compel *A* to Φ, and yet *A* has no duty to Φ. With respect to the members of that class, it will of course be coherent for *A* to adopt the corresponding subjective view, namely, that things are so.

In what follows, I will further inquire whether the Nagel Class is populated or empty. If I am unable to show that it is empty, I will then ask whether the case of redistributive taxation is relevantly similar to the kinds of members that I conclude do belong. If I am able to show that redistributive taxation is not relevantly similar, then I will press the question whether a person *A*, believing in a principle *P*, can coherently (though erroneously) believe that it is. I think I can make it plausible that the Nagel Class is a null set. Even if I fail in that, I believe I can make a plausible case that redistributive taxation, from the perspective of the rich redistributivist, is not relevantly similar to putative members of the Nagel Class. I conclude that, unless the rich redistributivist adopts an extreme form of the view that distributive justice is an institutional, not a personal virtue, or that it is a matter exclusively of communal rather than several obligation, she ought to be uneasy. Her life betrays her principles, exactly as Cohen worried.

"Excessive demand" cases

One might, with Nagel, say that there is no duty where acting without compulsion would require "excessive demands on the will."[14] If "excessive" means "impossible," then the triad can indeed be satisfied –assuming Kant's principle: "ought" only if "can." But if the Nagel Class is made up only of cases of this kind, there is no solace for those troubled by Cohen's problem, for there is nothing impossible about giving away one's money. So, "excessive" has to mean "possible but too difficult to be morally required."

Here is a possible case. Pooh and dozens of children go spelunking. In the dark windings of a cave, they become lost.[15] But, at last, they are led by a slight current of air to the mouth of a narrow crawl-space. It is the only plausible way out. Unfortunately, Pooh, going first, gets stuck; and, even with everyone pulling and pushing, he cannot be unstuck. It so happens that one of the children has found a blasting cap, and Pooh, as all know, has matches. If the fuse of the cap is lit and it is wedged between Pooh and the passage wall, an explosion will clear the passage, allowing the dozens of children to escape to safety. But the explosion will be fatal to Pooh; and the children cannot bring themselves to hurt Pooh.

Even if we assume for argument's sake that there is a true "choice of evils" principle that permits and even requires Pooh's being blasted out of the way, some will say it is too demanding of Pooh to say that it is his duty to give up the matches and submit to being blown up. I do not say that I would find it easy to do the right thing if I were Pooh; but it seems clear to me that Pooh's duty is to tell the children where to find the matches and to submit to being blown out of the way. Those who would insist that this would be merely supererogatory on Pooh's part are, I suspect, resisting the choice of evils principle. That they may do, but

14 Nagel, *Libertarianism without Foundations*, 199–200.

15 This is a variation of P. Foot, "The Problem of Abortion and the Doctrine of the Double Effect," *Oxford Review* 5 (1967), 5–15.

then they cannot say that the Pooh case is one that belongs in the Nagel Class: N3 is made true, N2 remains true, but N1 is no longer true without the support of something like the choice of evils principle. What set of reasons could require and permit the children to sacrifice Pooh without simultaneously requiring Pooh to submit to the sacrifice? And any that could be strong enough to require Pooh to submit to being sacrificed, and require the children to carry it out, would have to be strong enough to require Pooh to do the deed if they cannot.

I think Pooh's duty is clear, but some will not, and will count Pooh's case as one belonging in the Nagel Class. But even if it does, as Cohen pointed out, there is a world of difference between difficulty and cost: writing a check is costly but not difficult. Pooh's taking part in blowing himself up or even maiming himself is costly and difficult in a way that a rich woman's writing a check is not.

Sacrifices can be demanding in different ways. Suppose Aubrey and his best friend Clive are on the battlefield and it becomes obvious that Clive is a traitor. Their commanding officer, Bertram, orders Aubrey to execute Clive on the spot, as Clive poses an immediate risk to the entire unit. (Assume for the moment that in the circumstances Aubrey would have had standing authority to shoot Clive as a traitor anyway, without being ordered; and that neither Bertram nor anyone else other than Aubrey is able to do the deed.) Suppose now though that Bertram (for whatever reason) will not give the order. Surely Aubrey is not under a duty to shoot Clive on his own initiative because, without the insulation provided by Bertram's order, Aubrey would not be able to shoot his best friend without undoing his very integrity as a person. "The order from above is what enables the agent to take shelter from his very self," is how Irit Samet puts it in correspondence. If the circumstances of the battlefield are sufficiently exigent, Aubrey ought to be made to shoot Clive. But it would be contrary to Aubrey's integrity for him to be obligated to shoot Clive, his best friend, without being made to.

My response here is to insist that, if Aubrey ought to be made to shoot his best friend, then he ought to shoot his best friend if he is not made to. Suppose Commander Bertram gravely places his hand upon Aubrey's shoulder, preparing to discuss the needful thing. A shell bursts, killing Bertram, and leaving Aubrey in command. Hard as it is, Aubrey's duty is clear. If Aubrey ought to have been made to kill Clive before, Aubrey ought to kill Clive now. And if Aubrey ought to kill Clive now, he ought to have killed Clive before, while Bertram still lived but negligently failed to issue the command.

But this response maybe misses the point. The point may be that it cannot be true that Aubrey ought to kill his friend Clive, in a personal or deliberative "ought" sense, even though it is true that it ought to be the case that Aubrey kills his friend, if Aubrey can be decently sheltered from his very self in doing so. It is not that Aubrey should take the order as a factor in calculating what to do. The order functions differently: it makes the killing in some sense not fully Aubrey's act. It would be better if the commanding officer could hypnotize Aubrey or drug Aubrey and have Aubrey do the killing at an even more vivid remove from Aubrey's very self. But the command structure and the order, under the circumstances, suffice: it is still true that Aubrey ought to be made to kill Clive; and still not true that Aubrey ought to kill Clive if not made to. It is a Nagel case.

A rich redistributivist is far removed from the predicament of the unfortunate Aubrey. Writing a check in whatever amount is a sacrifice not quite of the order of shooting a best friend. This distance noted, I would still not admit the case as a member of the Nagel Class. For N1 and N3 to be true together, it ought to be the case that Aubrey is made to kill Clive while it is not the case that Aubrey ought to kill Clive absent the order. What is the magic of the order? The order is supposed to spare Aubrey's integrity in a way that Aubrey's acting in direct response to Clive's treachery and the necessity of saving the unit cannot. Aubrey, after the deed is done, can tell himself that he killed his best friend because he was ordered to. I cannot agree that Aubrey's integrity is better preserved this way.

I assumed that Aubrey was independently authorized to shoot Clive. Suppose, though, that Aubrey was not authorized to shoot unless ordered to do so, and Bertram, as before, does not and will not give the order. In this variation, it seems plausible that the Nagel Triad is satisfied. Aubrey ought to be made to kill Clive; Aubrey will not be made to kill Clive; and Aubrey has no duty to kill Clive. But now the case is no longer an excessive-demand case, but an "authority" case –nothing turns on the fact that Clive is Aubrey's best friend. I postpone treatment of that category of cases to a later section.

Futility cases

Here is another kind of possibility.[16] Pooh is not stuck in the mouth of the cave, but a boulder is. Fortunately, a sturdy rope is tied around the

[16] Matthew Hanser pointed out to me that I have to deal with this possibility.

boulder, and it can be moved away if all pull together. The children ought to make Pooh pull with them if he will not voluntarily; but the children are too dejected to do any pulling themselves, much less to make Pooh do anything. So, N2 is satisfied, and N3 is too because Pooh's pulling will not accomplish anything (except maybe make the children even more despondent, seeing that the bear's efforts are for naught). But if matters are as dire as this, N1 is no longer satisfied. Unless there is a common effort in prospect, it is not true that Pooh ought to be made to pull on the rope.

Another example.[17] Suppose a river is badly polluted and everyone ought to be made to stop dumping things into it. But nothing is being done to stop it, and Jonathan is tired of carrying the bag of orange peels he happens to be holding. Jonathan ought to be made not to throw the bag into the river, but why ought he not to toss it in, if it makes no difference whether he does or not? N1, N2, and N3 are all satisfied – no? Well, no. If N1 is satisfied by some relevant principle *P* that – for some reason – singles Jonathan out, then Jonathan ought not to toss the bag; but then that falsifies N3. If, on the other hand, N1 is satisfied by a principle *P* that applies to Jonathan and a wider class to which he belongs, in order to achieve a good that requires universal or near-universal cooperation, that too appears to falsify N3. In a later section I will consider some embellishments that might tug intuition in a different direction: but as yet there is no Nagel case.

The futility cases tend generally to involve some cooperative solution to a collective action problem, which is important enough that everyone ought to be made to perform some cooperative act Φ. Then a lack of cooperation is assumed, which is supposed to leave untouched the obligation to make agent A Φ, i.e. do what would be an act of cooperation, while simultaneously relieving A of any duty of A's own to Φ, i.e. to perform the cooperative act. Call the relevant threshold level of cooperation level L. If cooperation is below L, N3 is satisfied. Why ought A to Φ if Φing is futile? But, by the same token, why make A do what is futile? If A's performing cooperative act Φ is futile, then N1 is not satisfied. There is no Nagel case. Of course, if cooperation is above L, N1 is satisfied, but then N3 is not. Unless there is an argument to show that L is relevant to N1 but some different level L^* is relevant to N3, there is no reason to assume that any futility case is a Nagel case.

[17] Brian Bix suggested this example.

Here is another example of this type of case, from Walter Sinnott-Armstrong:

> the fact that your government morally ought to do something does not prove that "you" ought to do it, even if your government fails. Suppose that a bridge is dangerous because so much traffic has gone over it and continues to go over it. The government has a moral obligation to make the bridge safe. If the government fails to do its duty, it does not follow that I personally have a moral obligation to fix the bridge. It does not even follow that I have a moral obligation to fill in one crack in the bridge, even if the bridge would be fixed if everyone filled in one crack, even if I drove over the bridge many times, and even if I still drive over it every day. Fixing the bridge is the government's job, not mine. While I ought to encourage the government to fulfill its obligations, I do not have to take on those obligations myself.[18]

This example seems to need only one embellishment to count as a Nagel case: that is, the feature that the government ought to make "you" fill in a crack in the bridge. (That is what is needed to satisfy N1.) But why ought the government make you do that, if your filling in the crack contributes only negligibly to the bridge's being made safe for whatever reason, perhaps because the government cannot or will not get sufficiently many others to pitch in? It ought not to. But, again, suppose that there is a critical level *L* of crack-patching that can be achieved by making you pitch in. N1 is satisfied, but now N3 is not – that is, unless your patching a crack, because made to, has some crucial moral feature that your patching, without being made to, lacks. Conceivably, a being-made-to might have an ought-making value that a doing-without-being-made-to lacks, and a case of that kind is taken up later. But this is not such a case, absent further embellishments.

It is true that the government ought to make you and everyone else in relevantly similar circumstances pitch in to patch the bridge. Think of this group as the duty-bearer in N1, making it true. Then, it also seems to be the case that N3 is now false. The group ought to pitch in and patch up the bridge. The Nagel Class still seems empty. But here an objection comes in. From the fact that a group to which you belong has a duty to do something – call it a collective duty – it does not follow that anyone in the group has a severable duty to do it. One might take the

[18] W. Sinnott-Armstrong, "'It's Not My Fault': Global Warming and Individual Moral Obligation," in Walter Sinnott-Armstrong and Richard Howarth (eds.), *Perspectives on Climate Change: Science, Economics, Politics, Ethics* (Amsterdam: Elsevier, 2005), 295.

position that duties of distributive justice are all of this collective type. This position is available whatever one thinks of the Nagel Class. But it was not Cohen's view, nor was it even Rawls's.

Even if there were any futility cases in the Nagel Class, they would not offer any consolation to the rich redistributivist unless they are combined with some powerful futilitarian argumentation. Giving money to relieve inequality is not like not tossing a bag of orange peels into a polluted river, or smearing concrete on a crumbling bridge. Unlike Pooh's solitary yanks on the rope, giving to others can go a small but significant way toward mitigating inequality.

Assurance-problem cases

These cases differ from the futility cases in that they accent unfairness rather than drastic underachievement of an underlying aim, such as repairing a bridge. Nagel's discussion suggests that the three components of the Nagel Triad might be true together in cases instancing what Rawls called "the assurance problem," namely:

> The sense of justice leads us to promote just schemes and to do our share in them when we believe that others, or sufficiently many of them, will do theirs. But in normal circumstances a reasonable assurance in this regard can only be given if there is a binding rule effectively enforced.[19]

The truth of N2 could be symptomatic of a general failure of assurance. If the reason *A* will not be compelled to Φ is that no one will be made to, or only a few will be (or will Φ anyway), then, insofar as Φing represents *A*'s share in a just scheme governed by *P*, *A* will not be led by the sense of justice to Φ "off his own bat," in Cohen's phrase. And, if *A*'s sense of justice will not lead *A* to Φ, then it is safe to conclude that *A* has no *P*-derived duty to Φ.

So, here is a type of case in which N2 and N3 are true, and there is a principle *P* in the neighborhood. But it is not a type of case that can go into the Nagel Class unless N1 is satisfied too. But how could it be? How could *P* permit *A* to be compelled to Φ if there is a general failure of an assurance that is a condition of *P*'s applicability? It cannot. But suppose assurance is not a problem for *A*, because there is a failure of enforcement only in *A*'s and perhaps a few other cases. N1 is satisfied; but now it is difficult to understand why N3 is not, by that very token, falsified.

[19] Rawls, *A Theory of Justice*, 267.

One might insist that all relevant duties of distributive justice are of conditional form. Never, "*A* ought to part with *n*," but "*A* ought to part with *n* if but only if made to." But this move runs afoul of the fact that duties of distributive justice do not seem to be of this form, and surely are not generally. If a chunk of manna that would feed both starving *A* and *C* falls into *A*'s lap, *A* has a duty to part with enough to feed *C* whether or not anyone *B* is in a position to make *A* share.

Relative-disadvantage cases

Nagel's remarks also suggest that N1, N2, and N3 might be true together in case it might reasonably be thought that *A*'s uncompelled performance would leave her at a significant "relative disadvantage" vis-à-vis others. Cohen suggested that this might point to the most eligible solution to the Cohen Triad problem. The emphasis here is not so much on unfairness but on sheer burdensomeness; but unfairness hovers in the background as well.

The fact that the performance of a duty will leave one worse off than others who do not perform their similar duty cannot, as a general matter, relieve anyone of doing what there is decisive moral reason to do.[20] Suppose Oliver has grown to adulthood making his way in the world by picking pockets. He lives with his family in a neighborhood where most residents are prosperous thieves. Oliver comes to believe that stealing is wrong and, moreover, that the constabulary and courts ought to put an end to theft. Oliver would gladly find another occupation if the police showed any serious interest in apprehending thieves, but they do not. If Oliver stopped stealing, however, his income would drop dramatically and his family would suffer. Their financial suffering would be aggravated by the fact that their friends, neighbors, and

[20] Liam Murphy advocates a "cooperative principle" according to which the demands of beneficence cannot exceed one's fair share, as that is calculated with an assumption of compliance by others with what beneficence demands of them. L. Murphy, "The Demands of Beneficence," *Philosophy and Public Affairs* 22 (1993), 280. Call this the Murphy share. Cohen's worry is not that our principles might demand more of us than our Murphy share if others fail to contribute theirs. The worry is whether we ought to contribute our Murphy share even if the state fails to demand it in full. My claim is that we have a duty to give our full Murphy share even if the state does not demand it, and even if others are not giving theirs. Cf. L. B. Murphy, "Institutions and the Demands of Justice," *Philosophy and Public Affairs* 27 (1998), 251–91.

relations would remain at the level of affluence the Oliver family had grown accustomed to.

Despite all this, Oliver surely has a duty to stop stealing. The fact that doing so will leave him and his family worse off is neither here nor there, unless his ability to discharge other duties will be seriously impaired. If that is so, then Oliver has landed himself in a dilemma. But that dilemma presupposes, and does not cancel, his duty not to steal. On Nagel's behalf, one might respond that if indeed the enforcement of property rights is at such a low ebb, there is an assurance problem. But that type of case was examined in an earlier section, and the conclusion reached there was that assurance problems cannot supply examples in which N1, N2, and N3 are jointly satisfied.

Here is another possible case.[21] Kelly attends a rough, inner-city middle school. The principal ought to make students leave their pocketknives at home. But the principal is negligent, and pocketknives are commonplace. During intervals between classes, kids like Kelly are likely to be bullied and possibly even assaulted by tough kids wielding pocketknives. Not having a pocketknife might be seen as an invitation to be bullied. Complaining to the principal will only make matters worse. And assume that the armed guards at the school are under the school board's instructions only to intervene in cases involving firearms (I jest). Surely, Kelly has no duty to go to school without a pocketknife.

It is important to be precise about the kind of wrong involved (if any) in bringing a pocketknife to school. Lawyers distinguish *malum in se* (acts wrong in themselves) and *malum prohibitum* (acts not wrong in themselves, but made wrongful by prohibition). Is there a rule against students having pocketknives at school? If there is not, there is a question how N1 is satisfied. If N1 is satisfied because taking pocketknives to school is wrong in itself, then the case is like Oliver's but with the additional suggestion that very dire harm will result by doing what duty would require if a duty is recognized. But the fact that very dire harm will likely be suffered by one who does as duty requires normally invites the further distinction between *pro tanto* and all-things-considered duties. If Φing is *malum in se* but, in the circumstances, *A* would suffer great harm by Φing, the usual thought is that *A* has a *pro tanto* duty to Φ. But then N3 is falsified. Unless, that is, the Nagel Triad is only of interest if the duty in N3 is an all-things-considered duty.

[21] I owe Annie Stilz for this one. Matt Smith suggested how I should handle it.

But that apparently was not Nagel's thought, or Cohen's. And the rich redistributivist will find no comfort in the whimsical possibility that a catastrophe might occur were she to give what she ought to be made to be giving. How could it be that some catastrophe relieves her of any all-things-considered duty to give off her own bat but does not simultaneously defeat the supposed duty to make her give?

So, taking pocketknives to school has to be understood as *malum prohibitum*, if we are to have a Nagel case that does not reduce to one of the types already treated. Which means that it has to be understood that there is a rule against pocketknives that the principal is failing to enforce. If the rule were generally enforced, then presumably Kelly would have a duty to obey it. Of course, even given generally effective enforcement, Kelly might one morning realize that a dire, emergency threat made it prudentially imperative to have a pocketknife at school that day. If that is the case, then Kelly's *pro tanto* duty is in conflict with a competing duty of self-preservation (or with countervailing, morally admissible reasons), and may have to yield. But that is not to deny that Kelly had a *pro tanto* duty not to take a pocketknife to school. What is the relevant difference between this case and the case of general but illegitimate non-enforcement of a valid rule? Why would Kelly not have a *pro tanto* duty in the non-enforcement case as well? If Kelly does have a *pro tanto* duty, N3 is falsified, and there is no Nagel case.

A rule had to be stipulated to move the pocketknife example along, but let us not make too much of that. To say that there ought to be a rule that makes students leave their pocketknives at home is not yet to say that students ought to be *made now* to leave their pocketknives at home. It certainly is not generally true that if there ought to be a rule that makes students Φ then students ought to be *made now* to Φ. Maybe there ought to be a dress code that requires students to wear uniforms. There is evidence to support this: uniforms discourage cliques and bullying. But it would be absurd to send a kid home *now* for not being in uniform, in the absence of a rule. Whether the reasons for a rule are compelling enough to dispense with the usual process for making a rule depends on the kind of rule it is and the kind and weight of the reasons that are the backing for the rule. But if those reasons are such that students ought to be *made now* to leave their pocketknives at home, then they ought *now* to leave their pocketknives at home, rule or no rule.

But suppose the relevant duty is a conditional duty, in the following sense. Certain duties arise, or are triggered, only when sufficient assurance is given that others will do likewise. The principal ought to make everyone leave his or her pocketknives at home, not because he ought to make Sam leave his, and Kelly leave hers, and so on, severally. Rather, it works the other way. The principal ought to make Kelly leave hers at home because he ought to make everyone do that. The principal's duty is not an aggregate of several duties. So, the principal ought to trigger a general duty to leave pocketknives at home by making everyone leave pocketknives at home (N1); the principal fails to pull the trigger (N2), and therefore Kelly has no several duty to leave her pocketknife at home (N3). It is a Nagel case.

Or is it? If Kelly were the schoolyard terror, then the principal perhaps ought to make Kelly leave her pocketknife at home and – as a separable matter of fairness – make others do so as well. If this is how things stand, N3 does not look very solid. But if Kelly is not a problem by herself, and the situation in the schoolyard will not be improved unless the rule is generally enforced, then "Kelly ought to be made to leave her pocketknife at home" does not simply fall out of "The principal ought to make everyone leave his or her pocketknives at home." What does follow is "Kelly ought to be made to along-with-everyone-else-leave-her-pocketknife-at-home."

If the predicate that satisfies N1 is "ought-to-make-*A*-along-with-everyone-else-leave-pocketknives-at-home," then N3 is falsified, because Kelly ought to along-with-everyone-else-leave-her-pocketknife-at-home. Not a Nagel case. Of course, "Kelly ought to leave her pocketknife at home" does not follow from "Kelly ought to along-with-everyone-else-leave-her-pocketknife-at-home." The "individual" duty is not detachable from the "solidary," or collective duty. Does this reveal a different but better source of comfort for the rich redistributivist? Earlier on, I dismissed the suggestion that duties of distributive justice are conditional duties, conditioned upon coercive enforcement. But is there not a better case that can be made that duties of distributive justice are collective duties? That would mean that they are conditional, where the relevant condition is sufficient if not universal compliance by others. Enforcement serves merely as an assurance of that compliance.

This tack could work if duties of distributive justice were a species of fair-play duties. A compliance condition (among others) does have to be satisfied before anyone can be accused of unfairly free-riding on the efforts of others. But distributive justice is not a solution to a coordination problem (even if achieving it involves solving some of them). The distinctive "unfairness" of inequality does not consist in the well-off not doing their share to contribute to a cooperative scheme whose aim is to achieve distributive justice. If it did, then there would be no problem of distributive justice in the absence of an up-and-running scheme to address it – which is absurd. And if the only worry an individual need have about her own conduct is whether she is or is not doing what is in fact being asked of her, then Cohen, Nagel, and the rich redistributivists generally have been fretting about nothing. Cohen, for one, expressly denies that the only duties of distributive justice are communal ones[22] and the manna example I gave above confirms that view.

At the center of any concern at all about distributive justice is the perception that there is something wrong – structural, genetic, or otherwise – with the existing pattern of holdings. And at the center of any concern that one might, oneself, be in a wrongly advantaged position in that pattern is the perception that – maybe, just maybe – one ought to alter one's position in that pattern, vis-à-vis those less advantaged. Of course, one cannot all by oneself fix the whole pattern, and of course one ought to support efforts toward a general fix. The question is whether one can justly restrict one's efforts to the general, when the general effort is not doing its job. The candidate Nagel cases looked at so far have not answered it.

A rich but not super-rich redistributivist might reason this way: maybe Kelly alone ought to be made to leave her pocketknife at home – full stop – *if* she is the schoolyard terror. Maybe mighty Samson ought to be made to repair the bridge all by himself, even if it would be fairer if others were made to help. It may even be that the Richest of All ought to be made to share even if nobody else is made to do likewise. Maybe, possibly, this is true of anyone arbitrarily picked out from the richest 1 percent. But surely that does not go all the way down. Even if it is plausible that singling out the Richest of All to be made to give to improve the pattern is permissible, even required, it is implausible that the *n*th richest ought to be singly made to give, where *n* corresponds to any arbitrarily picked person who is better off than she ought to be. The fact that making this change would improve the pattern is not reason enough. Not everything that lessens injustice is demanded as a matter of justice.

This line of reasoning should not be dismissed as a *sorites* tending toward the false conclusion that all duties of distributive justice are collective ones. At the outset, I stipulated that "the rich" includes any person

[22] G. A. Cohen, On *the Currency of Egalitarian Justice and Other Essays in Political Philosophy*, ed. Michael Otsuka (Princeton University Press, 2011), 247–50.

possessing more wealth than what a distributively just state would allow her. That opens a way to the consoling thought, "Well, I'm not rich in *that* sense," much as the balding man staring into the mirror may say to himself, "Well, so-and-so is *really* bald (and therefore I am not)." This kind of consolation, however, is not of the kind that Nagel suggested. And, again, there is reason to doubt that the only duties of distributive justice that are enforceable against individuals are collective. If a citizen has an enforceable duty to Φ-along-with-all-others-of-a-description, then she has no duty absent perfect compliance by others. That seems absurd. On the other hand, if a citizen has an enforceable duty to Φ, it is not easy to understand how that can be unless she is independently morally required to Φ.[23]

Here is another kind of relative-disadvantage case. In Luke's community there is an epidemic. Luckily, there is an effective vaccine that is almost universally safe. Luke knows, however, that he has a rare genetic susceptibility to having a serious adverse reaction to the vaccine. Mandating universal vaccination will save many lives, but it is not feasible to make allowances for individuals with Luke's condition. The condition is too rare and if exceptions start to be allowed there is a significant risk that the vaccination process will be slowed down enough to cost lives. Although Luke's condition is rare, the risk of death from the vaccine for anyone with the condition is high. On the day the vaccinations are given, however, Luke discovers that his name has been left off the list by mistake. Sufficiently many others will be vaccinated to stop the spread of the disease anyway. Here is a case in which Luke ought to be made to submit to vaccination, Luke will not be made to submit to vaccination, but it seems not to be the case that Luke ought to submit to vaccination without being made to.

Isn't this a Nagel case? N2 and N3 are satisfied, but is N1? For N1 to be satisfied, it must be the case that it was wrong not to make Luke be vaccinated. The discussion assumes, however, that the "ought" involved here and throughout is an objective "ought," determined by what there is most reason to do, rather than by what people happen to think there is most reason to do. Understood this way, Luke ought not to have been made to submit to vaccination. Doing so would unnecessarily risk a life.[24]

[23] L. B. Murphy, *Moral Demands in Nonideal Theory* (New York: Oxford University Press, 2000), 83–4, refers to this as a "constraint against unrequired sacrifice."

[24] One might say it was unfair, and thus wrong, not to make Luke submit to vaccination. But if under a principle of fairness it is wrongful not to make Luke submit to vaccination, how would it not also be wrongful of Luke to fail to present himself to be vaccinated?

Arguments can be made against the objective "ought," and they will be discussed in a later section; but, understanding "ought" objectively, this is no Nagel case.[25]

Vary it. Luke is a small child and it is Luke's parents who would be made to have Luke vaccinated. The worries about integrity that came up in the best-friend-battlefield-traitor case could have greater traction here, where an innocent child's life is in the balance. The parents ought not to vaccinate the child because the child might rightly feel betrayed if the parents decide to take the risk without being made to. The compelled performance lacks, in this particular, a crucial vice that the uncompelled performance happens to possess. And, in general, the circumstances that attend an uncompelled performance can vary from those attending a compelled one. But, to constitute a Nagel case, the difference has to supply a reason not merely to think that the duty to perform without compulsion is defeated, but that it was no duty at all, not even *pro tanto*. The vaccination case and variants do not supply this.

"It's the making-do and not the doing" cases

One can imagine cases in which making someone do something – or being made by someone to do something – has a value that is detachable from the value of the doing. Suppose that aliens threaten to destroy the Machiguenga, an Amazonian tribe, unless Bobby makes Allie break Corky's eyeglasses.[26] To avoid this catastrophe, Bobby ought to make Allie break Corky's eyeglasses, and thus Allie ought to be made to break Corky's eyeglasses. Otherwise, the Machiguenga will be exterminated one and all. But Bobby is unshakably convinced that the aliens are bluffing, and so will not make Allie break Corky's eyeglasses. Allie therefore has no duty to break Corky's eyeglasses.

Why not? Because the aliens are not interested in what Allie does per se or in what happens to Corky's eyeglasses. The aliens are only interested in what they can get Bobby to do just by making a credible threat. Allie's breaking Corky's eyeglasses will save the Machiguenga only if Bobby *makes* Allie do it. The Machiguenga will die anyway if Allie breaks Corky's eyeglasses without Bobby having made her. If Allie breaks Corky's eyeglasses without having been made to, the world is out one South American tribe and one pair of eyeglasses, which is a worse

[25] Saul Smilansky suggested this case, but in the form of the variation that follows.
[26] I thank Uwe Steinhoff for giving me this case to think about.

outcome than the loss of the tribe coupled with the preservation of Corky's eyeglasses. Therefore, Allie ought not to break Corky's eye-glasses, unmade to, even though she ought to be made to. (Assume that Allie cannot fool the aliens into thinking she has broken Corky's glasses because Bobby made her – they are not that stupid and it might make them angry.)

The Nagel Triad is satisfied. Allie ought to be made to do something, she is not going to be made to do it, and she ought not to do it without being made to. Two responses occur to me. The first is that the rich redistributivist's situation is not at all similar to Allie's. The second is to note how it works. Suppose Bobby were not skeptical and tried to make Allie break Corky's glasses. Bobby's success would depend upon Allie's breaking Corky's glasses. Allie would then have a duty to break Corky's glasses, but it is a contingent duty, in the sense that she has it only because she is made to perform it. So, Allie's duty, properly stated, is not to break Corky's glasses, but to break Corky's glasses if, but only if, she is made to.[27]

It could be consoling to think that certain grownup duties are such that having them is conditioned upon being made to perform them. Duties of this kind need not satisfy the Nagel Triad the way they do in this example, which is due to the peculiar fact that the performance has a negative value if it occurs in the absence of the making. In the aliens case, the making and the doing have a value together that they lack in isolation. But what of the vastly more common cases of performances that independently have positive value, such as giving or spending money to mitigate distributive injustice? Is it possible that the (net) positive value of some doing is not great enough, on its own, to trigger a duty to do, while at the same time the combined value of the doing and the being-made-to-do suffices to render the making-to-do obligatory for someone other than the doer, namely, the maker? I would assume that the value of a making-to-do is a function of the value of the thing done, and normally has no independent value.[28] So, I restate my puzzlement:

[27] Stated precisely, there is no Nagel case unless Bobby's duty is to make Allie break Corky's glasses because she is made to. Otherwise, N1 and N3 do not line up.

[28] Others may disagree. Suggesting an analogy to the value of being able to bind oneself by promising, Stephen Perry writes: "the capacity intentionally to impose obligations on others can also have intrinsic value." S. R. Perry, "Political Authority and Political Obligation," in Leslie Green and Brian Leiter (eds.), *Oxford Studies in the Philosophy of Law* (Oxford University Press, 2013), 36, n. 50. Perhaps successful exercises of that capacity have value greater than the value of the obligor's uncompelled performance.

how can a performance be valuable enough to support a duty to compel it, and at the same time not be valuable enough to support a duty to perform without the compulsion? This seems to me to be possible only if acting under compulsion either had some independent value or contributed to a certain Moorean organic whole (namely, the performance + the acting under compulsion to perform) whose value is enough to trigger the duty to compel. Could legitimate political authority instantiate this possibility?

Legal authority cases

Legal authority is typically thought to consist not only in the possession of a moral permission to compel, but also in the possession of a moral power to impose moral duties upon citizens.[29] Obversely, to be subject to such an authority simply consists in being morally liable to have moral duties thrust upon one, willy-nilly, by the relevant legal authority's say-so, and it being permissibly compellable to perform them. This being the nature of authority, why is there any problem in holding that *B*, an authority, can have the moral power and duty to compel *A* to Φ, where Φ is something *A* has no duty to do absent the exercise of *B*'s moral power? Is that not, in a nutshell, what legal authorities (if any there be) do? Does this not supply a huge reserve of cases satisfying the Nagel Triad?[30] Not surprisingly, that reserve will almost certainly encompass matters of redistributive taxation.

This class of cases is unlike the older Little Ricky case considered above. In that case, the duty to pick up after oneself stands on its own legs. Legal authorities (and perhaps also parents) are not restricted to enforcing freestanding rules that penalize *malum in se*. Suppose that

In a similar spirit, David Owens writes that "human beings have an interest in the possession of authority for its own sake, regardless of any further purpose this authority might serve." D. Owens, *The Shaping of the Normative Landscape* (Oxford University Press, 2012), 146. Possibly this interest imparts additional value to effective exercises of authority, endowing the compelled performance with a "duty-grade" value that the uncompelled performance would lack. Both suggestions are problematic, especially when brought to bear on the kinds of cases relevant here, in which an authority fails to do as it ought. Even if one believed that something's merely being compliant with an authoritative directive adds value to it, it is a further question whether it generally, or ever, adds decisive value.

29 See Perry, "Political Authority and Political Obligation."

30 Bob Goodin prodded me to address this case. I do not know that he would approve my treatment of it.

circumstances are such that uniform traffic rules are desperately needed. The content of some of these rules will be arbitrary, in the sense that an opposite rule might have done equally well. The stock example is dividing roadways to avoid head-on collisions. It matters little whether the rule is "Stay to the right" or "Stay to the left." If the rule laid down by law is "Stay to the left," then (assume) a duty arises to drive on the left. But only then. Isn't this a kind of case satisfying the Nagel Triad?

It is not. Prior to the decree, N3 is satisfied – i.e. *A* has no duty to drive on the left. N2 is satisfied – i.e. *A* will not be compelled to drive on the left. But N1 is not satisfied. N1 is not satisfied because there is no principle *P* applicable to *A* that requires and permits *A*, prior to the decree, to be compelled to drive on the left. Of course, N1 is satisfied with respect to a more abstractly specified Φ – i.e. it is required and permitted to compel *A* to drive on the side of the road *to be stipulated* by general decree. But, with Φ so specified, N3 ceases to be satisfied, for *A does* have a duty to drive on the to-be-stipulated side of the road once the stipulation is made. The same alternative attaches, I suspect, to any other proposed satisfier of the Nagel Triad: state Φ concretely enough to make N3 true, at the cost of falsifying N1, or state Φ abstractly enough to make N1 true, at the cost of falsifying N3. To have a name for it, this phenomenon could be called a "foregrounding effect."

Acknowledging the foregrounding effect does not mean giving up on the possibility of locating an intermediate level of abstraction in which Nagel cases can be found. Suppose that the choice between side-of-the-road rules is not entirely arbitrary. Suppose that there is a significant advantage to driving, say, on the right. Most people are right-handed and it is better that the stronger hand be closer to the midline of the vehicle, perhaps better to manage manual controls. Right is better than left. Suppose that right is so much better than left that drivers ought to be made to drive on the right. But, as it may happen, they are not. Either there is no rule, or the rule is "Drive on the left." In either circumstance, all of N1, N2, and N3 are satisfied. Driver *A* ought to be made to drive on the right; driver *A* is not made to drive on the right; and driver *A* has no duty to drive on the right. Nagel case.[31]

This example finesses the foregrounding effect by having just the right degree of what one could call *institutional proximity*. The term refers to the huge distance that separates what people in a rough state of nature

[31] I owe the outline of this example to David Enoch.

would have to be made to do in order to realize any political ideal, and what people ought to be made to do in the actual or a near-actual world. If we imagine a state of nature in which there is no property-rights regime, it would be fanciful to suggest that anyone there ought to observe the rules that would be laid down in a civil society – even if he (along with everyone else) ought in some slightly less fanciful sense to be made to observe them.[32] But if instead we imagine a property-rights regime that is up-and-running, but unjust in some serious regard, it does not seem fanciful at all to think that one ought to act, compelled or not, in a way that mitigates that very injustice. So, the rich redistributivist stands to derive greater reassurance the more an otherwise plausible Nagel example possesses institutional proximity. The rule-of-the-road example, as amended, exhibits institutional proximity, because its background has been enriched by supposing additional, morally relevant facts that are not merely fanciful.

What it does not exhibit, however, is an institutional failure of justice. Rather, the failure is a policy failure. What makes the example work is that it supposes that a superior policy is one that ought to be mandatory, in the strong sense that it would be wrong not to mandate it, that is, wrong not to make people comply with precisely *that* policy. I doubt that reasons of mere policy rise to that level in the context of rules of the road, but never mind that. Surely, *some* policy reasons are so weighty that it would be wrongful not to make people do what the policy requires. For example, suppose it is wrong for an authority not to forbid airlines to transport certain flammable items. Anyone injured as a result of a failure to regulate will have been wronged. But, in such a case, it is not easy to agree that the regulated party would not also have wronged those injured. If the airlines ought – and here, for emphasis, I will add ought *morally* – to have been forbidden to carry the items, they ought not to have carried the items, period. Under examination, then, rules-of-the-road cases are not Nagel cases; and I hazard the claim that no other legislative example will survive scrutiny as a Nagel case.

"Objective" versus "subjective" ought

The discussion so far has assumed an "objective" notion of duty and "ought." The terminology can easily mislead, but I will not clarify it any more than the present topic demands. Doubt has been cast upon the

[32] Matt Smith suggested this example to me.

objective "ought" in discussions of an example first put forward by Frank Jackson.[33] A variation on it may turn out to be a Nagel case.

First, Jackson's "Jill" case as originally put: Jill is a doctor whose patient suffers from a serious health impairment that will become permanent and incurable unless quickly treated. Jill has only three treatments at her disposal: drug *A*, which she knows will safely effect an only partial cure; drug *B*, which will safely effect a complete cure; and drug *C*, which will be fatal. Unfortunately, although Jill knows that one of the two, *B* and *C*, is a safe and complete cure, and the other is deadly, she does not know which is which. In these circumstances, there is a powerful intuition that Jill ought not to administer drug *B*, even though it will bring about the best outcome. Moreover, there is a powerful intuition that she ought to administer drug *A*, rather than do nothing. Poignantly, she concludes that she must do what she knows will not bring about the best outcome. Should we not agree? Let us assume, then, that this is a case in which Jill ought to administer drug *A* and not drug *B*, which, for all she knows, could be the fatal one. (Assume for the argument's sake that there are no complications arising from the need to get the patient's consent.)

Now, the variation.[34] Jack is a brilliant colleague of Jill's. Jack knows (for reasons he is unable to communicate in time) that drug *B* will safely cure the patient. Jack has a disability (think "House") and cannot administer treatment himself. Jill's esteem for Jack is such that he can make Jill administer drug *B*; yet he (for whatever reason) does not. Jack ought to make Jill administer drug *B*, but Jill – as intuition told us – ought not to administer drug *B* but drug *A*. Here, then, is a case satisfying the Nagel Triad: moral principle requires that Jill be made to administer drug *B*; Jill is not made to administer drug *B*; and it is not the case that Jill ought to administer drug *B* (in fact, Jill ought *not* to administer drug *B*).

An interesting feature of this example is that it is not only a possible Nagel case, it suggests certain relevant similarities to Cohen's predicament. If distributive justice is as much a matter of uncertainty as Rawls believed[35] and if democratic authority has epistemic credentials as solid as David Estlund[36] has argued they can be, then an under-taxed

[33] F. Jackson, "Decision-Theoretic Consequentialism and the Nearest and Dearest Objection," *Ethics* 101 (1991), 462–3.

[34] I owe the variation to Bas van der Vossen.

[35] J. Rawls, *Political Liberalism* (New York: Columbia University Press, 1996), 229–30.

[36] D. M. Estlund, *Democratic Authority: A Philosophical Framework* (Princeton University Press, 2009).

redistributivist could be positioned as Jill is, with respect to a greater epistemic authority, such as Jack. Jack might be falling down on the job, and Jill might even *know* that Jack is falling down on the job, while Jill has no duty to do what she ought to be made to do – not even if she has a hunch about what that is. Jill ought to do the safe thing and not follow her hunch.

But the analogy falls apart the moment we recall that it is not going to kill anyone if the rich redistributivist takes a chance that her duty of distributive justice is more exacting than what the state will enforce. Furthermore, thoughtful redistributivists are unlikely to concede that their epistemic situation, relative to the state's, is relevantly similar to Jill's with respect to Jack's. It is unnecessary to contest the analogy, however, if further reflection undermines the intuition that Jill ought not to give drug *B*. Certainly, Jill could not be blamed for giving drug *A* and not *B*. Indeed, Jill could be reproved if she gave drug *B*, for she would thereby have taken a huge, unjustifiable chance with the patient's life. But wrongness and blameworthiness are distinct moral properties, each capable of attaching where the other is absent.

It may indeed be "appalling" and "unconscionable" (as Michael Zimmerman[37] has argued) of Jill to administer drug *B* – but if in a set of circumstances we ought to be made to do what it would be unconscionable for us to do without having been made to, my intuition is that we must say that we sometimes ought to do what is unconscionable, just as we quite readily recognize that sometimes (albeit rarely) we ought to do what we are blamable for doing (particularly where we ought to be made to do it by one who may blamelessly make us do so).

Jackson rightly says "we would be horrified" if Jill gave drug *B* or drug *C*;[38] but that reaction will yield, sooner or later, to one of relief if Jill administers drug *B* rather than *C*. Jackson and Zimmerman are correct about what intuition we ought to have at the moment drug *B* or drug *C* is given, if we know no more than Jill does at that moment; but much more is needed to nourish the separate intuition that it would not only be safer but "ought-er" that the patient be given drug *A*. It is more likely an instance of what Liam Murphy has called "blameworthy right-doing."[39] Of course, if it is *very* wrong to take risks of this sort involved in ignoring

[37] M. J. Zimmerman, "Is Moral Obligation Objective or Subjective?" *Utilitas* 18 (4) (2006), 342.

[38] Jackson, "Decision-Theoretic Consequentialism," 466.

[39] Murphy, *Moral Demands in Nonideal Theory*, 132.

the safer alternative drug *A*, then a proper adjustment of the relevant value function could easily unravel the hypothesis that the "objectively" best outcome is to be had by means of Jill's giving drug *B*. Suppose that, in giving drug *B* and effecting a complete cure, Jill had ignored the patient's express refusal of treatment with drug *B*. It would be wooden in the extreme not to discount the value of the outcome in some measure to reflect the rights violation by means of which the complete cure was effected. But the Jill case serves Jackson's and Zimmerman's purpose of undermining the "objective" view only if the drug *B* treatment involves the highest-valued outcome.

Pace Zimmerman, I conclude that Jackson's "Jill" case is insufficient to overthrow the dominant view[40] that duty and "ought" are to be understood objectively rather than "decision-theoretically"; and, even if it were sufficient, the "Jack" variant of Jackson's "Jill" is too far removed from the situation of the rich redistributivist to furnish her any comfort. Moreover, if it were correct to insist that "ought" be understood in some subjectivized way, the Jack variant of the Jill case would still fail as a Nagel case. Jackson's decision-theoretic "ought," for example – like subjective "oughts" as a class – is tacitly subscripted to the epistemic situation of the duty-bearer. So, Jack $\text{ought}_{\text{Jack}}$ to make Jill give drug *B*, Jack fails to make Jill give drug *B*, and it is not the case that Jill $\text{ought}_{\text{Jill}}$ to give drug *B*. But this is not a Nagel case: the subscripted oughts differ in N1 and N3.[41]

Conclusion

I have surveyed excessive-demand cases, futility cases, assurance-problem cases, relative-disadvantage cases, "It's-the-making-do-and-not-the-doing" cases, legal-authority cases, and – finally – cases meant to call the "objective" ought into question. I am persuaded that any other putative Nagel case will be fairly assimilable to one or more of these categories and will yield to the same types of treatment. Anyway, genuine Nagel cases – though perhaps not metaphysically impossible – are too recherché to console the rich redistributivist.

Cohen concluded his desultory look at the problem by acknowledging that "a rich egalitarian may have good reasons for not giving

[40] Jackson, unlike Zimmerman, is willing to let a hundred "oughts" bloom. Jackson, "Decision-Theoretic Consequentialism," 471–2.

[41] David Enoch suggested that I emphasize this.

extravagantly [*sic*] in an unequal society."[42] If by this he was adverting to some safe haven among the Nagel cases, I have shown those reasons to be specious at best. The inescapable consequence for persons of integrity is that they accept that they have a duty to do whatever the regime they inhabit – if decently just – would compel them, as a matter of substantive justice, to do. And substantive justice encompasses distributive justice. Doing these things is what *justice* compels.

Some rich redistributivists will shrug off Cohen's predicament by insisting that the demands of distributive justice are exclusively collective, or institutionally mediated. Theirs are not "barefooted doctrines" that would deprive them of designer footwear. Cohen's doctrine, however, *should*, unless the "personal prerogative" (the heavy-footed *deus ex machina* whose tracks mark crucial pages of *Rescuing Justice and Equality*) can decently be invoked. The personal prerogative – deriving from Scheffler[43]– is a moral permission to do other than what morality would otherwise require. Normally, the personal prerogative constrains the demands not only of morality but also of the state, and on the same rationale: the importance of liberty to live autonomously, by one's own lights. How then could a personal prerogative dissolve a personal duty to Φ and not, in the same stroke, render unjust the imposition of any political duty to Φ? If a personal prerogative indeed sheltered the sum one ought to have paid if properly taxed, it would seem also to condone avoiding any tax increase of that same amount – obviously not a consequence a redistributivist can welcome. Nor is it open to the rich redistributivist to take comfort in the thought that her inertia is a case of blameless wrongdoing – where one's wrong act is motivated by a disposition that would be wrong to lose.[44] On the contrary, normally one ought to be disposed to do what one ought to be made to do *without* being made to do it.[45]

The fundamental issue is not hypocrisy: keeping one's thoughts to oneself does not render those thoughts any more coherent or accurate. The issue is rather one of integrity and justice. If justice is a personal virtue, and encompasses matter classified under the heading "distributive

[42] Cohen, "Political Philosophy and Personal Behavior," 179.
[43] S. Scheffler, *The Rejection of Consequentialism* (Oxford University Press 1982).
[44] Murphy, *Moral Demands in Nonideal Theory,* 24.
[45] Malte Willer's "Dynamic Thoughts on Ifs and Oughts," *Philosophers' Imprint* 14 (2014), 1–30, appeared too late for me to take into account. His proposal for a "dynamic" non-monotonic deontic logic is, I hope, consistent with the argument presented here.

justice," it will make demands of us independently of, even in advance of, institutional sanctions. Eliot's lesson was: choose theories and principles wisely, for if we do not, and sit by them for long, we are liable to get "scorched," in the sense that we may feel a sharpening sense of discomfort in maintaining what we thought was an agreeably righteous posture. But of course it would be craven to choose our principles mainly to suit our comfort and convenience. In deliberating, we sometimes wish that our better angels would be more forceful with us if they mean to be so strict; and, by imagining them to be *making* us do what they propose we do, we are sometimes able to fortify ourselves. Are they not telling us that what we have decided we ought to be made to do is what we ought to be doing anyway?

10

Juridical laws as moral laws in Kant's *The Doctrine of Right*

BEN LAURENCE

Introduction

According to *The Metaphysics of Morals*, the crown jewel of Kant's practical philosophy, the doctrine of morality (*philosophia moralis*) is properly divided into two parts: the doctrine of right (*Ius*), and the doctrine of virtue (*Ethica*). Kant associates each of the subdivisions of morality with a distinct form of lawgiving and law: juridical, on the one hand, and ethical, on the other. Kant thus divides *The Metaphysics of Morals* into two parts, *The Doctrine of Right* and *The Doctrine of Virtue*, and the work contains three separate introductions. The introduction to *The Metaphysics of Morals* presents an initial characterization of juridical and ethical law, and locates them both under the common genus of moral law. The introduction to *The Doctrine of Right* then further develops the idea of juridical law from an initial characterization of the concept of right. The introduction to *The Doctrine of Virtue* does the same for ethical law, beginning this time from the concept of an end that is also a duty.

The ambition that is embodied in this architectonic structure is part of the great appeal of Kant's mature practical philosophy. Following the tradition of the natural lawyers, Kant divides juridical law into natural law, on the one hand, and positive law, on the other.[1] He calls knowledge

Thanks to my co-teacher Anton Ford and the outstanding graduate students in our spring 2013 seminar on *The Doctrine of Right* at the University of Chicago, and to the participants of two workshops, one on *The Doctrine of Right* at Universität Leipzig, and the other the Legal Theory Workshop at Northwestern University Law School, where I presented earlier versions of this chapter.

[1] I. Kant, *Metaphysics of Morals*, 6:224. All references to Kant's works follow *Kants gesammelte Schriften*, Deutsche Akademie der Wissenschaften (formerly Königlich Preußische Akademie der Wissenschaften) (Berlin: Walter de Gruyter, 1968). References list volume and page number of the Prussian Academy edition of Kant's works. All English translations are taken from Immanuel Kant, *Practical Philosophy*, trans. M. Gregor (Cambridge

of the system of natural law "juridical science" (*juriscientia*).[2] Once juridical science has been expanded by empirical knowledge of a system of positive law, juridical science becomes jurisprudence (*jurisprudencia*).[3] By locating right, along with ethics, under a common genus of moral law, Kant promises to bring jurisprudence, including an understanding of private, public, and international law, within the purview of his powerful moral philosophy. For the general concept of a moral law is developed in his celebrated ethical writings, first in the *Groundwork to the Metaphysics of Morals*, and then more systematically in the *Critique of Practical Reason*. Kant thus promises to treat jurisprudence as one distinct department of a single morality of reason and freedom.

At the same time, Kant's architectonics marks the profound difference between right and ethics. All morality involves our relations to others, but right (*Ius*) is relational, institutional, and public in some distinct and special sense that sets it apart from the rest of morality. For those moved by the thought that the phenomena treated by jurisprudence are categorically distinct from ethics, this embodies a real insight. The unity-within-difference of Kant's architectonics thus holds great appeal for answering a central question of jurisprudence: how is law related to morality?

However, *The Metaphysics of Morals* has made it difficult for commentators to understand how Kant's claim that juridical law is moral law is consistent with what he says about the specific difference between juridical and ethical law. In particular, it has seemed hard to see how juridical laws could be moral laws at all. For juridical laws, according to Kant, do not require an agent to act from the incentive of duty, but moral laws do. Furthermore, there are passages in *The Metaphysics of Morals* that seem to treat juridical laws not as requirements to be taken up by the reason of those subject to them at all, but rather as licenses for one agent to externally coerce another agent into compliance. This has understandably conveyed the impression that – emphatic protestations to the contrary notwithstanding – Kant does not really intend to subsume the phenomena of jurisprudence under his morality of reason and freedom after all.[4]

University Press, 1996). The following abbreviations are used to refer to Kant's texts: *CPR* (*Critique of Practical Reason*); *G* (*Groundwork for the Metaphysics of Morals*); *MM* (*Metaphysics of Morals*); *OCS* (*On the Common Saying: That May Be Correct in Theory, But it Is No Use in Practice*); *TPP* (*Towards Perpetual Peace*); *V* (*Vigilantius Lecture Notes*).

[2] Kant, *MM* 6:239. [3] Ibid.

[4] For reasons of space, I have been forced to omit detailed discussion of the relevant passages, especially §E of the introduction to *The Doctrine of Right*. My interpretation of

The clearest attribution of this incoherence to Kant's text can be found in the work of Marcus Willaschek. In a series of papers stretching over several decades, he has argued that Kant's official position is impossible to reconcile with his account of right. At various times he has asserted that *The Doctrine of Right* does not belong in *The Metaphysics of Morals*,[5] that juridical laws as characterized by Kant cannot be categorical imperatives,[6] and that juridical laws possess features incompatible with those attributed to moral laws, as these are discussed in *The Groundwork to the Metaphysics of Morals* and *The Critique of Practical Reason*.[7] Other commentators who are less willing to attribute confusion to Kant, such as Allen Wood and Katrin Flikschuh, are moved by the same features of the text to downplay the generic unity of ethics and right in Kant's practical philosophy. They thus embrace many of Willaschek's conclusions, while simultaneously arguing that these conclusions are not in tension with Kant's understanding of his own position.[8] In this chapter I wish to resist such readings, and argue that we should take Kant's claims that juridical laws are moral laws at face value. My hope is that by seeing where these commentators go wrong we can remove one obstacle to understand how *The Metaphysics of Morals* might deliver on the appealing unity-within-difference promised by its architectonics.[9]

this passage, and critique of alternative readings are available at philosophy.uchicago.edu/faculty/laurence.html.

5 M. Willaschek, "Why the Doctrine of Right Does Not Belong in *The Metaphysics of Morals*," in Arthur Ripstein (ed.), *Immanuel Kant* (Aldershot: Ashgate, 2008). Willaschek has walked this rhetoric back in his later writings, while leaving the substance of his criticism intact.

6 M. Willaschek, "Which Imperatives for Right? On the Non-Prescriptive Character of Juridical Law in Kant's *Metaphysics of Morals*," in Mark Timmons (ed.), *Kant's Metaphysics of Morals: Interpretative Essays* (New York: Oxford University Press, 2002).

7 M. Willaschek, "Right and Coercion: Can Kant's Conception of Right be Derived from his Moral Theory?" *International Journal of Philosophical Studies* 17 (1) (2009), 49–70.

8 See Katrin Flikschuh, "Justice Without Virtue," in Lara Denis (ed.), *Kant's Metaphysics of Morals: A Critical Guide* (New York: Cambridge University Press, 2010), 51–71, and Allen Wood, "The Final Form of Kant's Practical Philosophy," in Denis, *Kant's Metaphysics of Morals: Interpretative Essays,* 1–23, at 9. Indeed, Willaschek himself, as we will see, tries to argue that Kant recognized the tensions Willaschek attributes to *The Metaphysics of Morals*, and that he was working to resolve them within the text at the time it was published.

9 For reasons of space, in this chapter I focus on the arguments of Willaschek and Wood. I believe the critique I offer could also be used to undercut Katrin Flikschuh's claim that juridical laws involve freedom but not autonomy, and that being just does not involve acting from the incentive of duty. But apart from a few remarks in closing, I do not undertake to show this here. See Flikschuh, "Justice Without Virtue."

The unity of right and ethics

For Kant, all of nature works according to principles (laws), including rational nature.[10] When a stone falls, to be sure, it does so in accordance with the principle of gravitation, but it does not know this principle. Rational nature is distinct, Kant thinks, in that it acts according to principles through the representation of these principles.[11] Reason is law-governed because it governs itself.[12]

If we are speaking about practical reason, the principles through which reason governs itself represent actions falling under them as in some way good, and so necessary to perform.[13] Kant draws a distinction between conditional and unconditional practical principles. A conditional practical principle represents actions falling under it as necessary relative to the pursuit of some end that the action furthers.[14] The necessity in question is thus conditional on pursuit of the end, and the action required is instrumentally good as a means to this end. When a rational being eats as a way of satisfying her hunger, she acts on a general knowledge that consuming food is good in relation to her end of satisfying hunger.

By contrast with such instrumental principles, an unconditional practical principle represents an action as necessary regardless of one's ends. The necessity of actions falling under the principle is thus not conditional on the pursuit of some antecedently given end, and the action required is good intrinsically rather than instrumentally. As Kant colorfully puts it at one point, in this case the action itself contains a law.[15] Moral laws, on his conception, are unconditional practical principles in this sense: they represent an action as intrinsically necessary and so good to perform in a non-instrumental sense.[16] When a rational being returns your book because she promised she would, she acts on a general representation of returning the book as something that is morally good, and so necessary to do, in light of the fact that she committed herself to it.

For beings who are exposed to non-rational inclination, and so do not conform to practical principles by an inner necessity of their nature, all

[10] Kant, *GW* 4:412. [11] Ibid. [12] Ibid., 4:433, 4:440.

[13] Ibid., 4:414; Kant, *MM* 6:222. [14] Kant, *MM* 6:222; *GW* 4:414–15.

[15] Kant, *GW* 4:402. It is one of Kant's central ideas that unconditional practical principles make an action necessary directly through the representation of the action's form. For a profound treatment, see Stephen Engstrom, *The Form of Practical Knowledge* (Cambridge, MA: Harvard University Press, 2009).

[16] Kant, *MM* 6:221.

practical principles show up as imperatives telling them what they *ought to* or *must* do.[17] Imperatives for Kant thus represent the subject of the imperative as one who must, at least potentially, constrain herself to conform to the principles they express in the face of inclinations to the contrary.[18] The practical *necessity* of actions that fall under the law thus shows up in imperatives as the *necessitation* of the subject to perform the actions the law requires.[19] For imperfect beings, conditional practical principles are what Kant calls "hypothetical" or "technical" imperatives, necessitating agents to perform actions that are necessary as means to their ends.[20] Unconditional practical principles are "categorical imperatives," necessitating agents to perform actions that are intrinsically necessary.[21] All moral laws are categorical imperatives for human beings.[22]

Obligation, as Kant defines it, is the necessity of a free action under a categorical imperative of reason.[23] When we represent ourselves as obliged to perform an action, we thus represent an action as necessary to do in light of a moral law. Obligation thus relates an action to a moral law as the ground of its necessity. Furthermore, it represents that grounding relation as holding for a subject who must be necessitated or constrained to perform the action in the face of the contrary inclinations to which she may be exposed. For human beings, all moral laws give rise to obligations.

Kant calls a "duty" the action that we are obligated to perform by a moral law.[24] He tells us that we can be bound to perform the same duty in different ways. For this reason, he refers to duty as the "matter" of obligation, with the implication that the same duty can serve as the matter informed by different kinds of obligation.[25] To represent an action as a duty is thus to represent it as the object of some obligation; it is to represent the action as necessary, and intrinsically good, in relation to some moral law. For human beings, all moral laws give rise to the duties that are the object of the corresponding obligations.

[17] Kant, *GW* 4:413; *MM* 6:222. [18] Ibid. [19] Kant, *MM* 6:223.
[20] Kant, *GW* 4:414–16; *MM* 6:222. [21] Kant, *GW* 4:414. [22] Kant, *MM* 6:227.
[23] Ibid. [24] Ibid., 6:222.
[25] We will return to this point later on pp. 222 ff.; it requires some care to be interpreted properly. It will turn out that the "different ways we may be being bound" to perform a single duty cannot be based on different objective grounds, and so different laws. Rather, Kant has in mind the same law binding us to a single duty in more than one way simultaneously, and so giving rise to more than one form of obligation.

According to Kant, both juridical and ethical laws are moral laws.[26] Since human beings are exposed to inclinations, for us both sorts of laws are categorical imperatives.[27] As a result, they both lay obligations on us to perform duties.[28] Kant is explicit that these concepts of moral law, categorical imperative, obligation, and duty are common to both right and ethics, and can be used to characterize both ethical and juridical laws.[29] Juridical and ethical laws thus share a generic unity as moral laws. Willaschek aptly dubs this "Kant's official position" on the relation of right and ethics to morality in general.[30] It is this official position that Willaschek is concerned to argue fails to cohere with the specific distinction between juridical and ethical laws. I now turn to this difference.

The difference between right and ethics

Kant distinguishes between two species of lawgiving, and two associated species of law, juridical and ethical. In architectonic comments scattered throughout the three introductions, Kant represents both juridical and ethical laws as having their basis in different aspects of a unitary concept of freedom, understood as a power of reason.[31] According to Kant, freedom is the power to act from moral laws.[32] Kant suggests at several places that the division of moral law into ethical and juridical law flows from the fact that the operation of the power of human freedom is exposed to two sorts of hindrances or obstacles lying in our nature, one internal and one external.[33] The doctrine of virtue, which deals primarily with ethical laws, is concerned with the internal hindrances to the exercise of freedom from the sensible inclinations to which we are exposed that can influence reason's operation.[34] The doctrine of right,

[26] Kant, *MM* 6:213. For a characterization of practical philosophy as structured by the genus of morals, and the species of right and ethics, see also Kant, *CPR* 6:379.

[27] Kant, *MM* 6:222. [28] Ibid., 6:220–1, 6:222.

[29] The section where these definitions are found is in the first introduction to *The Metaphysics of Morals* that precedes both *The Doctrine of Right* and *The Doctrine of Virtue*. Kant precedes the definitions of categorical imperative and obligation with the sentence, "The following concepts are common to both parts of *The Metaphysics of Morals*." See also Kant's explicit assertion that the concept of moral law and categorical imperative apply to duties of right at *MM* 6:396, and his ubiquitous use of the terms "obligation" and "duty" in connection with juridical laws.

[30] See Willaschek, "Why the Doctrine of Right," 7 ff. [31] Kant, *MM* 6:220–1.

[32] Ibid., 6:221–2. [33] Ibid., 6:396.

[34] Ibid., 6:380. For an illuminating discussion, see Stephen Engstrom, "The Inner Freedom of Virtue," in Timmons, *Kant's Metaphysics of Morals: Interpretative Essays*, 288–317.

which deals with juridical laws, is concerned with external hindrances to the exercise of our freedom arising from the choices of others.[35]

Starting with the ethical side, the hindrance to our ability to act from the moral law lies in our non-rational inclinations and passions. Since such inclinations bear only a contingent relation to acting morally, the subject must be capable of setting them aside and constraining herself to act rightly through respect for the moral law.[36] Virtue is Kant's term for the standing inner strength required to set aside contrary inclinations and act from the moral law.[37] Such virtuous self-constraint is a hindering of the influence on reason of sensible inclinations that are themselves obstacles to our freedom. As a result, subjection to such discipline is properly conceived as strengthening the power of freedom and not diminishing it.[38] Famously, for Kant, to be free is not to be lawless, but rather to be bound by a law that one gives oneself.[39] Kant views this variety of internal hindrance in the hearts of individual ethical subjects as giving rise for human agents to a distinctive form of law – ethical law – that articulates duties of virtue – the requirements of inner self-constraint on an ethical subject.

Let us see how Kant conceptualizes this form of law. According to Kant, all lawgiving involves two elements:

> **first**, a law, which represents an action that is to be done as *objectively* necessary, that is, which makes the action a duty; and **second**, an incentive, which connects a ground for determining choice to this action *subjectively* with the representation of the law.[40]

The first element is the moral law that represents the action as necessary, and so serves as the objective ground making the action a duty. The second element is an incentive that connects the representation of the law with a subjective ground for choosing to do the action required by the law. The subjective ground is what explains the choice of the subject to

[35] Kant, *MM* 6:396. [36] Kant, *CPR* 5:79; *MM* 6:379. [37] Kant, *MM* 6:380.

[38] This is in part what explains Kant's opposition to the liberty of indifference account of our freedom at *MM* 6:227. Freedom is a rational power; moral laws are the principles of the proper exercise of this power. The inclinations that make possible deviation from moral law are thus hindrances or impediments to the proper exercise of our freedom. As a result, exposure to them cannot be rightly said to constitute that freedom; for freedom is a power and they are properly speaking indicative of inability rather than ability. For an illuminating discussion of the philosophical issues involved, and the failure of neo-Kantians to absorb them, see Douglas Lavin, "Practical Reason and the Possibility of Error," *Ethics* 114 (3) (2004), 424–57.

[39] Kant, *MM* 6:213–14. [40] Ibid., 6:218.

do the action. "Connects" here is, I believe, an intentionally abstract term that needs to be interpreted with care and may amount to different things in different cases.

Of these two elements, Kant locates the specific difference in forms of lawgiving with the second. He writes,

> That lawgiving which makes an action a duty and also makes this duty the incentive is *ethical*. But that lawgiving which does not include the incentive of duty in the law and so admits an incentive other than the idea of duty itself is *juridical*.[41]

The subjective ground or incentive in ethical lawgiving is duty. A duty, as we have seen, is the matter of an obligation: it is an action that is represented as necessary under a categorical imperative. For duty to serve as the subjective ground of choice is thus for an agent to act from the recognition that the action she performs is necessary under a moral law. In this case, the subjective ground of the agent's action will be the same as the objective ground making the action a duty, namely the law itself.[42] When this identity holds, the agent can be said to derive the action directly from the law, as its sufficient ground.[43]

Let us now attend to the locutions Kant employs to describe the "connection" forged in ethical lawgiving between this incentive and the representation of the law. In the passages quoted above, he discusses the "connection" in terms of what the lawgiving "makes" the incentive, and he further glosses this by saying that ethical lawgiving "includes" the incentive "in the law." Thus the connection between the representation of the law and the subjective ground of choice in ethical lawgiving appears to be that the subjective ground is contained in the representation of the law. At various points, he speaks of this containment in terms of what the law "requires" or "demands" of the subject.[44] In ethical lawgiving the subjective ground of duty is thus represented as part of the requirement specified by the law.[45]

41 Ibid., 6:218–19.

42 Kant thus moves freely between saying that ethical lawgiving makes duty, obligation, and the law itself the incentive, e.g. at *MM* 6:231. For talk of the law as incentive, see also *CPR* 5:71–2.

43 Kant, *GW* 4:412; *CPR* 5:71–2.

44 Kant, *MM* 6:214, 6:231.

45 I think, strictly speaking, we would have to say that the subjective ground is represented as part of the content of the categorical imperative that expresses the law. The concepts of duty and obligation do not apply to holy wills. For them, there are no obligations and duties, and so no distinction between ethical and juridical obligations. See Kant, *GW* 4:397. (How we are to conceive of right as it might apply to beings with a holy will is a difficult topic.)

In ethical lawgiving, the law itself is represented as requiring that one perform an action falling under the law *from the recognition that the action is required by this very law*. Therefore, ethical lawgiving represents a law as requiring an identity between the maxim that expresses the subjective ground of my choice and the practical law that is the objective ground of the necessity of the action to be performed. The implication is that I can only satisfy the relevant ethical obligations when this identity obtains, and I derive my action from the law that makes the action a duty. Ethical laws thus articulate duties of virtue: requirements that an agent constrain herself through respect from the moral law by acting from that law even in the face of opposing inclinations.

This conception of acting from the incentive of duty should be familiar to students of Kant's practical philosophy, since it is the same idea that figures in his account of morally worthy action from *Groundwork* I and II. Famously, Kant argues there that morally worthy action is action done from duty, where this entails acting from respect for the moral law.[46] Kant contrasts this with acting merely in accordance with duty, where I perform an action that is a duty, but not *because* it is a duty, and so do not derive the action from a moral law but rather from some sensible inclination to do what happens to be the right thing.[47] The incentive that ethical lawgiving "connects" with the law is the same as the incentive that Kant argued was necessary for morally worthy action. His account of ethical lawgiving is thus that ethical obligations can be fulfilled only by morally worthy action. When it comes to ethical principles, we only satisfy the relevant obligation by doing the right thing because it is right.

If we now turn to juridical lawgiving, we see that things are quite different. Here the obstacles to the operation of freedom arise from an external source in the choices of other agents. Thus, in the introduction to *The Doctrine of Right*, Kant tells us that the concept of right underlying juridical lawgiving concerns the external relation between agents, insofar as their actions can have influence on one another.[48] In particular, the relevant form of influence is the possibility of hindering the freedom of

[46] Kant, *GW* 4:400–1, 4:403; *CPR* 5:71; etc.

[47] The examples discussed at *GW* 4:397 ff. are meant to bring this contrast out. See also, for example, *CPR* 5:71, where Kant writes, "What is essential to any moral worth of actions is that the moral law determine the will immediately."

[48] Kant, *MM* 6:230.

others by constraining them through our choice.[49] Right is the sum of conditions under which it is possible to connect the choice of each with the freedom of each other.[50] Right thus pertains to a distinctive sphere of morality that concerns the threat to freedom that comes not from within our hearts, but from the external relations of domination that can arise when one agent is constrained by the choice of other agents.[51]

From this explication of the concept of right, Kant immediately produces the Universal Principle of Right (UPR). It reads,

> Any action is right if it can coexist with everyone's freedom in accordance with a universal law, or if on its maxim the freedom of choice of each can coexist with everyone's freedom in accordance with a universal law.[52]

The UPR is the first natural law principle defended by Kant in *The Doctrine of Right*. On its own it specifies our one intrinsic right: the freedom of the person that is "internally ours."[53] It serves as the basis for the rich unfolding of juridical laws in the remainder of the work. The UPR tells us that an action that is compatible with the freedom of others is right. In the text accompanying this principle, Kant argues that if an action is right, hindering it is incompatible with freedom, and so is wrong.[54] He goes on to argue, however, that not all hindrances to action are on a par. For, since a wrongful action is itself an obstacle to freedom, to hinder that action is to hinder a hindrance to freedom.[55] In parallel with his argument concerning ethical self-constraint, Kant argues here that the rightful constraint of others furthers rather than diminishes the power of freedom by removing the external obstacles to its operation.[56] Once again, the idea that lawlessness is not freedom plays a crucial role.

Let us see how Kant develops these ideas in his account of the specific character of juridical law. By contrast with ethical laws, Kant tells us that in juridical laws the representation of the law does *not* include the incentive of duty.[57] We might expect Kant to say that it "includes" other incentives "in" the law in the place of duty. But this is not what he says. Kant instead glosses the claim about the incentive of duty by saying that juridical lawgiving "admits" other incentives. About these other incentives that juridical lawgiving "admits" but does not "include," he says

[49] Ibid. [50] Ibid.

[51] For an excellent discussion of these conceptual marks of the concept of right, and the theme of freedom as non-domination, see Arthur Ripstein, *Force and Freedom* (Cambridge, MA: Harvard University Press; 2010), 30–56.

[52] Kant, *MM* 6:320. [53] Ibid., 6:237. [54] Ibid. [55] Ibid., 6:231, 6:396.

[56] Ibid., 6:231. [57] Ibid., 6:218–19.

only that they must be drawn from pathological (sensible) determining grounds of choice, and from aversions in particular.[58]

Whatever connection is forged between incentives and the representation of the law in juridical lawgiving, the connection is not one of inclusion within the represented content of the law. This is confirmed by passages where Kant describes juridical lawgiving as requiring the legality of an action, which he defines as "the mere conformity or nonconformity of an action with law, irrespective of the incentive to it."[59] As a result, juridical obligations, unlike ethical obligations, can be fulfilled by action that is not done from the incentive of duty. They can thus be fulfilled by action that is not morally worthy, action that possesses legality but not morality.

This characterization of juridical lawgiving is apt given that the domain of right arises from the confrontation of freedom with external hindrances. Kant writes, concerning the UPR, the first and ultimate juridical law:

> it cannot be required that this principle [the UPR] of all maxims be in turn my maxim, that is, it cannot be required that *I make it the maxim* of my action; for anyone can be free so long as I do not impair his freedom by my *external action*, even though I am quite indifferent to his freedom or would like in my heart to infringe it. That I make it my maxim to act rightly is a demand that ethics makes on me.[60]

Kant reasons here in the following way. Right is concerned with the practical relation between free choosers insofar as they can impair one another's freedom through their external action. If I do not choose to influence the power of choice of another agent so as to hinder or constrain it, I have not impaired her freedom through my external action. This is true even if I am morally indifferent to her freedom, and make the choice on some other ground: for example, out of fear of the long arm of the law or of her righteous wrath. It is thus possible for my external action to be united with the freedom of choice of another in accordance with a universal law, without my having performed that action because of this fact.

Since juridical laws concern precisely such external relations between the choices of agents, they do not include the incentive of duty. It is thus possible to fulfill juridical obligations without acting out of respect for the relevant juridical law, including through action induced by anticipation

[58] Ibid. [59] Ibid., 6:213, 6:219; *CPR* 5:71. [60] Kant, *MM* 6:231. Emphasis in original.

of coercion. It is the flipside of the same point that I cannot coerce someone on the grounds that her action, although right, is not morally worthy. For juridically right action done for the wrong reason is not a hindrance to anyone's freedom, and rightful coercion is not necessary to overcome it.[61]

The paradox of juridical imperatives

Willaschek thinks Kant's account of moral laws as categorical imperatives, and his claim that juridical laws do not require acting from the incentive of duty, are in conflict.

By insisting that imperatives are meant to "necessitate" the will of those who may possibly be tempted to violate the laws,[62] Kant makes it clear that the whole *point* of imperatives, as opposed to their corresponding practical laws, is to be *obeyed*. Hence, the point of *categorical* imperatives is to be obeyed unconditionally, not (merely) because of some end one may have, but (also and in any case) because that is what the imperative demands. Put differently: the only way to obey a categorical imperative, as such, is to obey it for its own sake.[63]

The point Willaschek makes is a genuine insight. As we have seen, Kant holds that moral laws are principles that govern rational nature by serving as the grounds from which rational agents derive actions.[64] "The whole point" of unconditional practical principles is for their subjects to derive actions from them; this is precisely what distinguishes laws of freedom from laws of nature. To respond to an unconditional practical principle *as an unconditional practical principle* just is to derive actions from it. Categorical imperatives are the way these principles of reason show up for a rational agent, who is exposed to subjective hindrances to the operation of these principles. "Their whole point" is thus for those subject to them to obey them by deriving actions from them in the face of countervailing temptations from inclination. One thus treats a categorical imperative as a categorical imperative by constraining the opposing

[61] Indeed, it is not even possible for external coercion to overcome this problem. It is one of Kant's central points that coercion could never succeed in bringing agents to act from the motive of duty, since it induces action by connecting it with aversive inclination rather than respect for the moral law. See *MM* 6:381, 6:383.

[62] Cf. Kant, *MM* 6: 222; *G* 4:413–14.

[63] Willaschek, "Which Imperatives?" 70.

[64] Kant, *GW* 4:412–13.

inclinations, and deriving actions from the practical law it expresses, as the ground of those actions.

However, Kant's account of juridical laws seems in tension with this conception of the point of moral laws. Willaschek writes:

> But then, it seems, juridical laws cannot find expression in categorical imperatives, after all, because juridical laws do *not* require obedience for their own sake ... the juridical rightness of an act does not depend on whether it has been done out of respect for the law or some other reason. Thus it seems that, on Kant's view, juridical laws, as such, cannot give rise to imperatives at all, since these would have to be categorical imperatives in order to prescribe unconditionally, but they cannot be categorical imperatives if they respect the externality of Right.[65]

The specific nature of juridical law, as opposed to ethical law, is constituted by the fact that juridical laws do not require that one satisfy them with action that is done from the incentive of duty. "The whole point" of juridical laws is that they can be satisfied without acting from duty.

So, on the one hand, Kant advances a conception of a moral law according to which to respond to something as a moral law is to act from the incentive of duty. Furthermore, he claims that juridical laws are a species of moral law; moral law is the common genus that juridical laws share with ethical laws as laws. On the other hand, Kant holds that juridical laws do not require action done from the incentive of duty. This is the differentia that marks them as juridical rather than ethical. The problem is that the features of the species seem to conflict with those of the genus. To respond to juridical law as *law* I **must** act from the incentive of duty. By contrast, to respond to juridical law as *juridical* I **need not** act from the incentive of duty. The paradox then emerges when we ask what it would be to respond to juridical law as *juridical law*, for it would seem that it both **does** and **does not** require that I act from the incentive of duty. Willaschek calls this "the paradox of juridical imperatives."[66]

According to Willaschek, Kant could have avoided this paradox if he had abandoned the claim that juridical laws are moral laws and so issue in categorical imperatives.[67] This is a more dramatic divergence of juridical from ethical principles than Kant's official position countenances.

[65] Willaschek, "Which Imperatives?" 73.

[66] The particular formulation of the paradox in terms of species and genus is mine. I do not know if Willaschek would accept all the details of my presentation of it.

[67] Willaschek, "Which Imperatives?" 72–3, 75 ff.

If juridical principles are not moral laws, then their "whole point" is not to be acted from by agents who are subject to them. And if, as a result, they are not categorical imperatives, then although they may be normative in some broader sense, they do not lay obligations on those subjects who are exposed to contrary inclinations.

Willaschek softens the force of this proposed revision to the "official view" by noting that Kant speaks of an "indirect" ethical obligation to perform juridical duties. It is possible to take an ethical perspective on juridical laws, and from this perspective one may view juridical laws as categorical imperatives. But this, he claims, is a perspective foreign to right.[68] Allen Wood concurs with Willaschek on this point. What Wood says is instructive.

> Both parts [right and ethics] involve categorical imperatives, because Kant holds that juridical duties *as such* are also ethical duties (*MM* 6:219). In so far as juridical duties are regarded as ethical duties, they can be brought under the principles of ethics, which can also be used to show that we have good reasons for valuing external freedom (or right) and respecting the institutions that protect right through external coercion.[69]

The picture of what it would be to "have good reasons" for valuing external freedom is on display in the following quotation:

> Even if we do not question Kant's analysis of the concept of right, however, we may think that his principle has to go beyond that concept if it is to provide us with a *reason* (a moral one) for respecting the external freedom of others. Now there is no question that Kant believes the dignity of humanity provides us with a *moral incentive* for respecting people's rights . . . But these moral incentives have nothing to do with the *principle* of juridical duties.[70]

Wood draws the conclusion that juridical laws are, after all, categorical imperatives, but only because they can be supported by independent moral reasons for respecting rights (e.g. human dignity) that fall under "the principles of ethics," and "have nothing to do with" the principles of right.

In similar reflections, Willaschek says that "strict right" is an idealization that abstracts from the "ethical considerations" with which it is always "mingled" in real life. Once these ethical considerations are taken into account, we may after all view principles of right as categorical imperatives.[71] What Willaschek and Wood take away from the realm

[68] Ibid., 86–7. [69] Wood, "The Final Form," 9. [70] Ibid., 7–8.
[71] Willaschek, "Which Imperatives?" 86.

of right with one hand, they return with the other in the form of an indirect ethical obligation to do what is right.

The paradox resolved

I think the paradox of juridical imperatives can be resolved without abandoning either the claim that juridical laws are categorical imperatives, or the claim that they do not require action from the incentive of duty. The key is to see that one can respond wrongly to a principle without failing to fulfill the requirement it articulates. In the case relevant to the paradox, one may fail to respond to a categorical imperative as a categorical imperative, without failing to fulfill the obligations it specifies. For help in seeing how this is possible, I will present an analogous claim about a set of norms that are clearly not categorical imperatives.

Consider an arbitrary and highly artificial system of etiquette prevailing in some society. To the extent that this system of principles makes actions practically necessary in some way, and so good in Kant's exacting sense, it does so either through an occasional overlap with moral considerations, or by enabling one to pursue ends of a social kind. In short, a few nice points of convergence with morality aside, the system has normative bite only by giving rise to hypothetical imperatives. Nevertheless, these rules do require, or permit, or forbid actions. In this respect they may be rather like the rules of games, but with much greater social importance and consequence.

Now let us imagine a fanatical devotee of this system of etiquette who makes a religion – or perhaps better, a *morality* – out of the norms of etiquette. She treats them not as a set of artificial social practices that it is often necessary to follow as means to achieve various sociable ends, but rather as principles that make action good in itself. She thus accords the requirements of etiquette the status of categorical imperatives. Some signs of this pathology include her tendency to view the politeness of someone's behavior as direct indication of her moral worth; to uphold the finer points of etiquette in contexts where they ought to be let go; to feel guilt and remorse about any failures of etiquette on her part; and to move freely between moral principles and social mores without marking any difference between the two.

Now, there will no doubt be many things going wrong with this agent from a moral point of view. For example, she will fail to fulfill some moral duties when doing so would involve breaking the rules of etiquette, and will treat as moral duties many things that are not. No doubt this will result in some shabby treatment of others. But I would like to set aside her moral failings, and focus solely on how we are to describe her relation to the norms of etiquette alone. As I am imagining the case, she hews closely to the rules of etiquette. In terms of the content of the requirements they articulate, she is as sterling as someone exposed to inclinations can be. The problem with her action thus does not come into view if we restrict ourselves to the content of the requirements put on her by the norms of etiquette. It is tempting to say that, as far as etiquette goes, there is no problem with the agent.

In a sense this is true, since she almost never knowingly violates any of the relevant social niceties. But, in another sense, it is not. Consider, would we rightly say of her that she is responding to the norms of etiquette *as the norms of etiquette*? I have stipulated that the norms of this highly artificial system render action practically necessary only either through contingent overlap with moral considerations, or instrumentally in relation to social ends. The nature of the norms in question is thus that they are an arbitrary social construction that gives rise in intelligible ways to various hypothetical imperatives conditional on the pursuit of social ends. But this is not how our envisioned agent responds to them. In fetishizing them, she treats them as laws for a kingdom of ends.

Given the nature of the norms in question, our agent at once fulfills the letter of their requirements, while failing to respond to them in a way that is appropriate to their nature. This rational failure is explained precisely by the character of the relevant norms: since they are arbitrary social fiats, to respond to them as though they are categorical imperatives is to make a rational mistake. However, this mistake cannot be captured in terms of the *content* of the requirements they put agents under. We are not imagining that etiquette requires agents to fulfill the norms in the consciousness of their arbitrariness; by failing to place the norms correctly the fanatical agent is not rude to anyone, and does not, for example, accidentally send inappropriate signals about whom she intends to marry, or do any of the other things that the code forbids. It follows that to respond to a norm of etiquette as the norm it is, more is required than merely fulfilling the content of the norm. For one can do *that,* while responding in a way that is wildly inappropriate given its nature.

Let us return to moral laws and categorical imperatives. These differ from the norms of etiquette in being unconditional practical principles. But the lesson I would like to draw is that it is also sometimes possible to respond wrongly to such principles without failing to fulfill the content of the obligations they put us under. Now, of course, this will *not* be the case where the content of the obligation includes responding to the principle as the principle that it is. According to Kant, this is precisely how it is with ethical laws and ethical lawgiving. To fulfill these obligations, I must act from the recognition that the action in question is required under a categorical imperative of reason. But, were there a category of moral law where the requirement the law specifies does not include responding to the law as law, it would then be possible to draw the same distinction we drew with respect to the norms of etiquette between the narrow requirements for fulfilling the relevant obligation, and the broader requirements for responding to the law as law. For it would then be possible to fulfill the relevant obligation, while nonetheless failing to respond to the law appropriately.

But this is just how it is with juridical laws, according to Kant. Suppose then the agent fulfills the letter of the requirements of a juridical law, while failing to act from the recognition that the action is required by a categorical imperative of reason. In that case, the agent will have fulfilled the requisite obligation, but nonetheless gone wrong. Gone wrong how? Well, the principle in question is, after all, a moral law, a categorical imperative of reason. To respond to it as a categorical imperative is to act from the recognition of the practical law in question by deriving actions from it; as Willaschek says, rightly, *that is the whole point of a categorical imperative.* So the mistake is failing to respond to a principle of reason as a principle of reason. Although this mistake does not consist in failing to fulfill the content of the obligation the principle specifies, it is nonetheless explained precisely by the nature of the principle as a moral law.

We could thus diagnose the paradox of juridical imperatives as arising from an ambiguity in speaking about what one "must" do in regard to juridical law. For we could mean two things by such talk. Speaking narrowly, we signify the actions that would be required to fulfill the obligation a juridical law lays on us. In that sense, with respect to juridical laws, it is false that one must act from duty; one may fulfill a juridical obligation with less than that. Speaking of "must" broadly, we signify not only what would be required to fulfill the obligation in question, but also what would be required to respond to the law as a law. In the broad sense, with respect to juridical laws, it is false that one need not act from duty. A contradiction only seems to result when we equivocate between these broader and narrower senses of 'must'.

Indeed, there is textual evidence that Kant himself affirms the two senses of "must" distinguished in just this way. Speaking of juridical laws, he writes:

> whether freedom in external or in the internal use of choice is considered, its laws, as pure practical laws of reason for free choice generally, must also be internal determining grounds of choice, although they should not always be considered in this respect.[72]

Here he acknowledges that given the nature of juridical laws as laws of reason, one *must* take the law as the subjective determining ground of choice. Here we have an appearance of the broad sense of "must" that arises from the nature of practical laws. However, Kant also adds, "they [juridical laws] should not always be considered in this respect." This suggests that there will be some way of considering juridical laws in which it is not appropriate to say that one must make juridical laws the subjective ground of one's choice.

Later Kant writes, about the relevant respect, "When one's aim is not to teach virtue but only to set forth what is *right*, one need not and should not represent that law of right as itself the incentive of action."[73] A natural gloss on "setting forth what is right" would be "specifying the content of the obligations that juridical laws lay on us." If this is correct, then Kant himself distinguishes two expository purposes, and two corresponding senses of "must." When one wishes to describe how an agent responds rightly to a juridical law as a law of reason, one legitimately says that the agent must make the law her subjective ground of choice. On the other hand, when one wishes to describe the actual content of the obligations that the law lays on an agent, one "need not and should not" represent the law as requiring that agents make it the subjective determining ground of their choice. This is exactly the distinction between the broad and narrow sense of "must." There is no paradox of juridical imperatives.

Indirectly ethical duties

Those sympathetic to the Willaschek–Wood interpretation will likely be frustrated by my attempted dissolution of the paradox of juridical imperatives. For the very passages in Kant to which I have just appealed to dissolve the paradox appear in the context of his discussion of the

[72] Kant, *MM* 6:213. [73] Ibid., 6:231.

ethical obligations to perform duties of right. It is thus open to them to reply that these passages do not distinguish between broader and narrower ways in which we might consider a subject responding wrongly to a juridical law, but rather discuss the "moral reasons" or "ethical considerations" that support making juridical laws the subjective ground of our choice.

We have already discussed Kant's account of the difference between ethical and juridical lawgiving. These two lawgivings give rise to two respective forms of obligation: one that involves the necessity of action from the incentive of duty, and the other that does not. We have also seen that Kant treats duty as the matter of obligation, and says that we may be bound in more than one way to perform a single duty. In particular, Kant holds that "all duties, just because they are duties, belong to ethics."[74] We are thus bound to the duties of right in two ways: one juridical and one ethical. Kant thus says at one point that all duties of right are thus "indirectly ethical" duties.[75]

This may seem to support the Willaschek–Wood line, since it is very natural to take these passages to be asserting that there are ethical grounds for performing all duties of right. But a more careful inspection shows that this is not what Kant intends. In the introduction to the *Doctrine of Virtue*, Kant writes:

> For any one duty only *one* ground of obligation can be found; and if someone produces two or more proofs for a duty, this is a sure sign either that he has not yet found a valid proof or that he has mistaken two or more different duties for one . . . If, for example, someone wants to draw a proof for the duty of truthfulness first from the *harm* a lie does to other human beings and then also from the *worthlessness* of a liar and his violation of respect for himself, what he has proved in the first case is a duty of benevolence, not of truthfulness, and so a duty other than the one for which proof was required.[76]

Although his example involves two duties of virtue, Kant clearly asserts the more general point that any one duty can have at most one objective ground of obligation. If there are two different grounds of obligation for performing the same action, one thereby specifies *two different duties* that this action fulfills. The explanation of this fact is that duty is that to which we are bound by obligation, and obligation is necessity under a categorical imperative of reason. Duty is thus a relational concept: to view something as a duty is

[74] Ibid., 6:219. [75] Ibid., 6:221. [76] Kant, *GW* 4:403.

always to relate it to some definite moral law as its objective ground. In Kant's example, the moralist is confused when he sloppily provides two separate grounds in support of the duty of truthfulness. Properly speaking, Kant thinks, when we consider two grounds for refraining from lying, we are considering two different duties – truthfulness and benevolence – that a single action might fulfill in a given case.

We can see the problem this poses for the Willaschek–Wood view, if we switch examples to consider an alleged ethical ground for performing a juridical duty. For example, perhaps we think that we ought not to falsely represent ourselves as having fulfilled a contractual obligation for two reasons: ethically speaking, because doing so would involve a violation of the respect for the worth of our own person, and juridically speaking, because it would violate the bilateral commitment involved in contract right. If we are right about both these grounds, then the action of refraining from falsely representing ourselves as having fulfilled our contractual obligations has two different grounds of obligation: it would be *lying* and it would be *fraud*. Kant's analysis in keeping with the passage above is clear: this action then satisfies two *different* duties: one duty of right not to defraud others, and the other duty of virtue not to lie. The idea that there might be ethical grounds for performing juridical duties thus rests on confusion about the concept of duty. So this cannot be the proper interpretation of the idea that we are bound to perform duties of right in two ways.

Indeed, this is a point that Kant himself makes in the most emphatic terms. Kant writes, intending to forestall exactly this confusion:

> It can be seen from this that all duties, just because they are duties, belong to ethics; but it does not follow that the *lawgiving* for them is contained in ethics: for many of them it is outside ethics. Thus ethics commands that I still fulfill a contract I have entered into, even though the other party could not coerce me to do so; but it takes the law (*pacta sunt servanda*) and the duty corresponding to it from the doctrine of right, as already given there. Accordingly, the giving of the law that promises agreed to must be kept lies not in ethics but in *Ius* . . . For if this were not the case, and if the lawgiving itself were not juridical so that the duty arising from it was not really a duty of right (as distinguished from a duty of virtue), then faithful performance (in keeping promises made in a contract) would be put in the same class with actions of benevolence and the obligation to them, and this must not happen.[77]

[77] Kant, *MM* 6:219–20.

In this passage, Kant tells us that ethics does not provide a new objective ground for performing juridical duties. It rather takes these duties as *already given* from the doctrine of right. Thus the only objective grounds for performing these duties are those specified by the relevant juridical laws. If a moralist tried to introduce ethical considerations as objective grounds for performing juridical duties, as Wood seems to envision, he would inadvertently substitute an ethical duty for a juridical one.[78]

How then are we to understand the claim that there are ethical obligations to perform juridical duties? Kant tells us that all ethics teaches about duties of right is that we are to perform them *because* they are duties of right.[79] In other words, all ethics adds is that we are to respond to juridical laws as the laws of reason they are.[80] Viewing duties of right as indirectly ethical thus does nothing more than explicitly thematize the sense in which an agent responds to a juridical law inappropriately when she fails to act from the incentive of duty. In other words, talk of indirect ethical duty is a way of marking the broad sense of "must." Since ethical lawgiving involves a form of obligation that requires acting from the incentive of duty, and since one must act from the incentive of duty to respond to a juridical law properly as a law of reason, Kant thinks it is fruitful to class this broader sense of requirement together with other directly ethical obligations. However, he clearly marks the distinction within this class between *indirectly* ethical duties that rest solely on juridical laws as their objective ground, and *directly* ethical duties that rest on ethical laws.[81]

It follows that the fact that duties of right are also indirectly ethical duties does not make juridical laws categorical imperatives. Were juridical laws not *already* laws of reason, serving as categorical imperatives for us, then no ethical grounds could make them so. In fact, the reverse is true: juridical duties are indirectly ethical precisely *because* juridical laws

[78] In unpublished work that he has kindly shared with me, Allen Wood's position has evolved. He no longer claims that ethical principles provide moral grounds for juridical principles. (He does not explain what has occasioned this change, but it could be an appreciation of the passages I quote above.) However, he continues to maintain that juridical laws are categorical imperatives only because they give rise to indirectly ethical duties. I argue below that this is a mistake. Were he to give up this claim, I am happy to say that we would be in agreement.

[79] Kant, *MM* 6:220. [80] Ibid., 6:213.

[81] What about Kant's claim that representing duty as the incentive to perform duties of right is appropriate only when teaching virtue (*MM* 6:231)? Is not virtue an ethical ground for performing juridical duties? No. For virtue is the moral strength of the will to act from the incentive of duty, whatever its objective ground. *MM* 6:394, 6:406.

are already categorical imperatives of reason. What Willaschek and Wood take with one hand they are left holding in the other.

Conclusion

I would like now, very briefly, to indicate the consequences of our discussion for Kant's attempt to bring jurisprudence under his morality of reason and freedom. The UPR that has served as our sole example of a juridical law is the thin wedge through which Kant introduces his system of ever-richer juridical principles. The story in rough outline is the following.[82] In Part I of *The Doctrine of Right* on private right, Kant argues that, having accepted the right of the individual to the freedom of her own person, we must acknowledge – on pain of contradiction of this freedom with itself – the right of individuals to acquire and have objects external to the self.[83] Kant calls this second juridical principle the "Postulate of Practical Reason with Respect to Right." This postulate confers the right to acquire things (property), the performances of others (contracts), and even persons, as one may acquire a husband, or wife, through marriage, or children through childbirth or adoption.[84]

However, it is the next part of Kant's story that these domains of acquired right are in a certain sense unintelligible outside the context of the public institutions of a political community.[85] On this basis, Kant argues once again that freedom will be in contradiction with itself if the abstract natural law principles he has defended are not embodied in a contingent system of institutionalized and enforced positive law under a duly constituted public authority.[86] This is the basis for Kant's defense of his third natural law principle, the Postulate of Public Right, putting agents under a categorical imperative to exit the state of nature and enter into the civil condition, the condition of public right.[87] If freedom of the person legitimates private right, private right in turn legitimates public right, including the right of political authorities to settle and enforce necessarily contingent matters involved in concrete positive law.

Unlike natural law that Kant argues is both necessary and knowable a priori, positive law is contingent, and can be known only through promulgation of the law by the relevant authorities.[88] But the relevant

[82] I follow here the illuminating outline sketched by E. Weinrib, "Poverty and Property in Kant's System of Rights," in *Corrective Justice* (Oxford University Press, 2012), 263–97.
[83] Kant, *MM* 6:246. [84] Ibid., 6:247–8. [85] Ibid., 6:245–55, 6:264.
[86] Ibid., 6:307. [87] Ibid. [88] Kant, *V* 27:511; *MM* 6:311.

authorities are authorities – if they are – only because they are authorized to make contingent law by the a priori natural law principles Kant discusses.[89] If positive law has been made by duly constituted authorities, and is not in conflict with natural law principles, the postulate of public right confers on it the force of a categorical imperative for the citizens subject to it.[90]

Action required by categorical imperatives is morally rather than instrumentally good. Therefore, if I follow positive law merely out of fear of punishment or social disapproval, then, although I may satisfy my juridical obligations, I instrumentalize what is intrinsically good, making its pursuit conditional on my inclination to avoid trouble. I thereby alienate myself from the legitimate moral principles that govern my community.[91] If, on the other hand, I respond to rightful positive law appropriately, recognizing its moral authority, then I derive my actions from a categorical imperative of reason. By acting from a principle of reason, I recognize juridically right action as a manifestation of freedom, the power of reason to be practical. Jurisprudence is thus a part of moral philosophy, the science of human freedom.

These are wildly ambitious and heady claims. My aim here has been to remove one obstacle to accepting Kant's own characterization of the architectonics of his mature practical philosophy. I have argued that Kant's account of juridical laws as moral laws is consistent. Whether it is true is another question.

[89] Kant, *V* 27:529; *MM* 6:230.

[90] Kant, *V* 27:529. It is important to note that for Kant the natural law includes many elements of political justice, including the form of a Republic, equality of citizens, support for the poor, and so on.

[91] Indeed, on Kant's view, legitimate positive laws of my political community are principles of my will as a citizen of the political community, since I give positive law alongside others, as sharing in the general will under a Republican constitution. When I act from the threat of coercion I am alienated from the general will, which is also mine. See *MM* 6:223, 6:313–14; *OCS* 8:294–5.

11

The relation between moral and legal obligation: an alternative Kantian reading

GEORGE PAVLAKOS

Outline

In this chapter I shall scrutinize the claim – attributed by many to Kant – that law and morality give rise to separate kinds of obligation and I shall, for the purposes of this essay, understand this claim as one that concerns the grounds of the respective obligations.[1] Accordingly, while a moral obligation exists when the agent is in some appropriate intentional state,[2] a legal obligation is premised on totally different grounds: here the intentional state of the agent is irrelevant for the existence of the obligation. For legal obligation concerns the external behaviour of agents, not their intentionality. Conversely, what grounds legal obligations are facts of institutional coercion.

After spelling out the traditional picture in detail, I shall proceed to argue that separating the grounds of moral and legal obligation threatens to fragment the meaning of our normative concepts (such as 'ought', 'obligation', and so on). This conclusion need not be compulsory for Kantians, however, since I will maintain that Kantian meta-ethics has always resisted any move that purports to locate the grounds of obligations in the intentional states of the agent. Having disproved the relevance of intentional states, I will turn to the role of coercion (or

I would like to thank for valuable comments the participants of the IVR Workshop on 'Legal Normativity and the Philosophy of Practical Reason' which was held in Frankfurt on 15–18 August 2011. Barbara Herman, Arthur Ripstein and Marcus Willaschek have offered valuable comments on antecedent versions of this chapter. The paper has benefited from the long-term strategic development financing of the Institute of State and Law of the Academy of Sciences of the Czech Republic (RVO: 68378122).

1 'Obligation' for the purpose of this chapter will mean 'categorical obligation' as opposed to any other normative requirements, such as the standards of rationality or prudential reason.

2 Kant talks about 'incentives'. However, I will take incentives to range over to intentional states for the purposes of this chapter. The modification should not be significant with regard to questions of grounding, which I take to be central to my approach.

enforcement) as a self-standing source of the separation of law and morality. Having dispelled the myth of the relevance of intentional states to the grounds of obligations, the function of coercion emerges in a new light. In this new light, coercion/enforcement is no longer a separate ground for obligations in the realm of law; rather it works *in tandem* with the moral law in preventing instances of heteronomy from interfering with the grounding of obligations. Finally I will discuss some potential difficulties with and objections to the unified account of obligations I offer.

The traditional picture

How is it that law and morality can generate different grounds for the respective obligations they impose? The answer requires a brief excursion into Kantian moral psychology and an understanding of the arguments adduced by proponents of Kantian moral psychology for the manner in which the domains of law and morality engage the intentionality of the agent. According to these arguments, while morality requires that the content of the obligation be simultaneously the content of the incentive of the agent, legal obligation is premised on totally different grounds; there the incentive of the agent is irrelevant for the existence of the obligation. Legal obligation, goes the argument, concerns the external behaviour of agents, not their motivational reasons. Thus moral obligation, on the one hand, requires that the agent makes the moral law (or, perhaps more accurately, the maxims that pass the reflective endorsement test of the moral law) the content of her motivation. On the other hand, individual willing plays no role at all in legal obligation; the agent need not endorse what counts as obligatory, for legal obligations concern entirely and purely the external behaviour of agents. Law does not care about the motivation of the agents it addresses, nor does it try to elicit the appropriate states of the will ('appropriate' in the sense that they aim to match the relevant legal obligations). Instead, it uses coercive means to bring the behaviour of agents into line with the conduct it prescribes.[3] Accordingly the content of legal obligations analytically entails an authorization to coerce those who infringe them.[4] As a consequence,

[3] Cf. A. Ripstein's recent reconstruction in his 'Reply to Flikschuh and Pavlakos', *Jurisprudence* 1 (2) (2010), 317.

[4] I. Kant, *Practical Philosophy*, trans. M. Gregor (Cambridge University Press, 1995), 6:231 (pagination follows the Edition of the Prussian Academy).

the determinants of legal obligation display two key differences from those of morality: they do not involve the motivation of the agent; they do involve the external imposition of behaviour.

This reconstruction has led to the claim that Kant is a positivist when it comes to legal obligation: in other words, he endorses some version of the separation thesis, i.e. the claim that there exists no necessary connection between legal and moral obligations.[5] (It may be noted, as an aside, that within stricter versions of the claim, legal obligations are grounded on coercive social institutions, whereas moral obligations are grounded on facts about agents' intentional states.[6])

The paradox of many meanings

I shall turn next to outline some undesirable consequences of the claim that legal and moral obligations rest on separate grounds. In a nutshell the claim threatens to fragment the meaning of the normative concepts we employ in our argumentative practices (I call this the *paradox of many meanings*). Take the normative sentence (NS) 'you should not steal'. If the thesis about the separation of the grounds of legal and moral obligations holds good, I shall argue, the meaning of NS will shift depending on whether it is uttered in a legal or a moral context. Thus the meaning of the *legal sentence* (LS) 'you ought not to steal' will be different from the meaning of the *moral sentence* (MS) 'you ought not to steal', despite them sharing the same linguistic form. Were this to happen, I will maintain, our normative discourse would be threatened with a loss of meaning and understanding. Let me unpack the argument a little.

Sentences express propositions. Propositions are abstract contents (or meanings) which remain invariant across different configurations of the same sentence. Cases of shifting between languages are a standard way to illustrate this point: 'der Schnee ist weiss' and 'the snow is white' express the same proposition, even though they differ phonetically and syntactically. On a standard truth-conditional semantic account, what

[5] See, instead of others, M. Willaschek, 'Which Imperatives for Right? On the Non-Prescriptive Character of Juridical Laws in Kant's *Metaphysics of Morals*', in M. Timmons (ed.), *Kant's Metaphysics of Morals: Interpretive Essays* (Oxford University Press, 2002), 65–87.

[6] These are facts about agents' attitudes concerning maxims that have been validated by the moral law.

individuates the relevant proposition is whatever makes it true/false: for short its *grounds*. Constancy of grounds secures stability of the proposition, which in turn guarantees the possibility of translation between sentences of different languages that express the same meaning. Conversely, any shift of the grounds will amount to a shift of the proposition and, concomitantly, the meaning of the sentence that expresses it.

It is notable that such propositional shifts occur in sentences containing indexical terms:[7] what makes true the sentence 'I am a woman', when Mary utters it, is a different ground from that which makes it false when John utters 'I am a woman'. It follows that the same sentence expresses different propositions when embedded in a different context. As remarked earlier, this shift of proposition entails a shift of meaning: Mary's utterance has *a different meaning* from John's. This should not come as a surprise in the case of indexical expressions. Indeed it is consistent with the very function of indexical terms that they be understood in a way that allows their grounds (hence, the relevant proposition) to shift, depending on the context. This is illustrated by the fact that in reporting the speech of the other, John and Mary would not disquote on 'I', even though they would when reporting their own speech.[8]

Things become murkier when we move to normative language. We saw that the same sentence will shift its meaning if a shift of the grounds of the relevant proposition occurs. According to the traditional picture of the relationship between legal and moral obligation, the grounds of moral obligation consist in facts about the intentional states of agents, while legal obligation is grounded on coercive institutional facts, which are external to the agents' intentionality. Let us label the former type of fact *moral grounds* (mG) and reserve the label *legal grounds* (lG) for institutional coercive facts. If we combine this information with the earlier remarks on the meaning of sentences we get:

(MS) 'you ought not to steal' (expresses proposition p on grounds mG)
(LS) 'you ought not to steal' (expresses proposition q on grounds lG)

Along these lines LS $\neq$ MS because p $\neq$ q, which in turn is explained through the grounds that in each case individuate the relevant proposition. The proposition expressed by MS is one that is grounded on facts

[7] See T. Williamson, 'Knowledge, Context and the Agent's Point of View', in G. Preyer and G. Peter, *Contextualism in Philosophy: Knowledge, Meaning and Truth* (Oxford University Press, 2005), 91–114.

[8] Ibid.

about the intentional states of the agent (facts about how his or her incentive relates to the moral law). The proposition expressed by LS is one that is grounded on facts about institutional enforcement.

An interesting result of this reconstruction is that it is possible to explain away apparent contradictions between law and morality: take, for instance, the prohibition of the death penalty. The same sentence expressing this prohibition can be simultaneously affirmed and denied without contradiction:[9] 'S and not-S' (where S stands for the prohibition of the death penalty). What allows this move is precisely the fact that S expresses a different proposition when uttered 'in law' and when uttered 'in morality'. It follows that affirming and denying *different* propositions does not amount to any contradiction.[10] To put it differently, the apparent contradiction that manifests itself at the level of sentences does not translate to a contradiction at the level of propositions; hence, there is no violation of the law of the excluded middle, as might have appeared at first glance.[11]

However, this outcome comes at a relatively high price: a sentence and its negation can consistently co-exist only if they exemplify distinct propositions, i.e. only if they express different meanings. Yet there is danger that those who utter the same sentence in different contexts are simply talking past each other.[12] In the case of indexical expressions the problem is not as acute because indexicals contain as part of their meaning a reference to the context – they give an early 'warning' to the speaker that what they mean cannot be determined independently of the context in which they are uttered. However, this is not the case with normative/evaluative language; when we use terms like 'ought',

9 The relevant contradiction is expressed as a violation of the law of the excluded middle, a logical standard that says that one ought not affirm and deny the same proposition ("You should not: 'p and not-p'").

10 For the contradiction to occur one needs to affirm and deny the *same* proposition; see Williamson, 'Knowledge, Context and the Agent's Point of View'.

11 This claim derives from the semantic programme of contextualism which gives the contextualist view its great advantage over relativism. While the relativist answer is that different speakers hold different claims to be true *relative* to them, the contextualist solution is compatible with the possibility of objectivity: even if the same sentence may be evaluated differently in different contexts, propositions are as absolute as you like. Thus, the negation of 'Mary knows . . .' in the epistemological context amounts to the negation of proposition P; however non-P is not the negation of Q, or the proposition expressed by 'Mary knows . . .' in the ordinary context – in other words the apparent contradiction withers away. See Williamson, 'Knowledge, Context and the Agent's Point of View', 92, 94.

12 The same applies when the same speaker utters the same sentence in different contexts: the same utterance shifts its meaning with the context.

'obligation', 'just', or 'good' in prescriptive speech there is nothing to indicate how and if those expressions relate to the context of uttering them. While indexical expressions have a transparent relationship to the context of utterance, normative terms are opaque with respect to the context of utterance. In the latter case we are threatened with confusion, misunderstanding, and, ultimately, loss of normative meaning. What is more, these predicaments amount to much more than mere linguistic shortcomings: considering that normative language is the vehicle for conveying standards for human action (so-called 'reasons for action'), conceptual confusion with respect to it is bound to have grave consequences for individual and collective agency.

To illustrate this point let me assume separation between two given contexts – the moral and the legal – and let us consider the normative sentence 'No one should profit from his or her own wrongdoing' as it is affirmed and negated in those contexts. When it is *affirmed* in the moral context it expresses the proposition (Pm): *Morally speaking it is wrong to profit from one's own wrongdoing*; when *negated* in the legal context, however, it expresses the proposition (Pl): *Legally speaking it is right to profit from one's own wrongdoing.* Those who take this view about the semantics of normative terms want to argue that despite the fact that the two sentences contradict each other, as uttered in each context respectively, the contradiction is only apparent, for in actual fact the sentences individuate two distinct propositions. Thus the negation of Pm will not amount to the negation of Pl. What is more, while the evaluation of the same sentence varies with the context, the proposition that corresponds to each context is *absolutely* true (or false).

Whereupon the following question arises: 'How can a normative proposition generate reasons for action if its meaning shifts with the context?' The question aims to capture an additional constraint that is imposed on normative language, one that is not readily present in non-normative speech (including indexical terms), that is, the constraint that normative language should provide continuous guidance for the actions of the agent. This constraint is generated as part of a key feature of normativity and one which in the past has been addressed under the *normative question.* This feature submits that no normative standard can be construed independently of the agent's point of view, on pain of losing its normative status.[13] For something acquires the status of a reason for

[13] C. Korsgaard, *The Sources of Normativity* (Cambridge University Press, 1996), ch. 1.

action by remaining relevant to the practical problem of the agent.[14] Further, 'remaining relevant' means being capable of offering a justified solution to the practical problem in question where justification is a notion that is agent-relevant in a deep sense: in other words, it depends on the reflective capacity of the agent to assess reasons from the first-person perspective. It follows that normative propositions *from a point of view* (i.e. those that are context-dependent) are no longer focused on the relevant practical problem for the agent and hence fall short of generating sound normative reasons.[15]

In conclusion, the plurality of grounds, and the paradox of many meanings which is generated by the plurality of grounds, force upon us a perplexing dilemma: either our use of normative language is contradictory, or normative sentences express different propositions when uttered in different contexts. There is much to say in favour of trying to escape this dilemma, not least the fact that our practice of normative communication functions in a manner that does not appear to be caught on either of its two horns.

Intentional states are irrelevant for grounding

Why should we worry if our normative language succumbs to the above dilemma? Perhaps it can be argued that we would only face the worry in circumstances of a compulsory dualism of legal and moral grounds as would occur if the grounds of obligation shifted following a movement between the moral and legal realms. There is nothing, however, in Kant's philosophy to support the inevitability of such a shift.[16] Rather the contrary seems to be true. Kant's own meta-ethical considerations – mostly laid down in the *Groundwork* and the *Critique of Practical Reason* – seem to speak against any such shift that would be premised on the role of intentional states of agents.

[14] Williamson, 'Knowledge, Context and the Agent's Point of View', 102–6.

[15] Contrast with Raz's theory of legal obligation. For Raz the content of legal obligation can be specified in isolation from its capacity to obligate, as a consequence of the service conception of authority. J. Raz, *The Morality of Freedom* (Oxford University Press, 1986); J. Raz, 'The Problem of Authority: Revisiting the Service Conception', *Minnesota Law Review* 90 (2006), 1003, reprinted in J. Raz, *Between Authority and Interpretation: On the Theory of Law and Practical Reason* (Oxford University Press, 2009), 126–65.

[16] I believe that the shift is unjustified *simpliciter*. However, I am limiting my exposition to Kantian philosophy. For a more general formulation of the argument see G. Pavlakos, 'Practice, Reasons and the Agent's Point of View', *Ratio Juris* 22 (2009), 74.

It would appear that what is at work in the traditional picture, discussed above,[17] are two argumentative paths that purport to work *in tandem*: the first one claims that the grounds of legal and moral obligation are distinct owing to the difference pertaining, on each occasion, to the intentional environment of the agent. The second adds that all legal obligation contains something that is not found in moral obligation at all, i.e. external imposition (or coercion) through social institutions; hence, one must account for a specific difference in the grounds of legal obligation.

It follows that in order to question this reading one must level a twofold attack: first to take on the thesis that intentional states matter to the grounding of (legal and moral) obligation; second, to argue that coercion does not concern the grounds of legal obligation, but is merely akin to an enabler for legal obligation. In what remains of this chapter I shall attempt primarily to deliver the first prong of the attack while offering some implicit suggestions for delivering the second. I argue in favour of a distinction between grounds and motivation that can easily be accommodated by Kantian meta-ethics. This distinction takes one a considerable distance along the way towards the conclusion that motivational reasons qua intentional states are irrelevant to the grounds of both moral and legal obligation. Conversely, it is reasons qua normative facts which in both cases can ground an obligation. Resting on this finding I proceed to argue that coercive institutions – those considered by some to be bearers of a separate ground for legal obligation[18] – are merely *enablers* of legal obligations. What this boils down to is that institutions complement those reasons that morality grounds in two ways and develop them further into more particular reasons which deal with the concrete problem that the institution is called upon to solve.

I begin now with the question of motivation which, it is proposed, ought to be kept distinct from questions of grounding not just in law but, first and foremost, in morality. I think that one of the great qualities of Kant's meta-ethical account of duties, and a quality that has been ground-breaking within the history of ideas, is the contention that duties are grounded not on the intentional states of agents but on a universal test of reflective endorsement. Thus the intentional states of agents, regarded not only in isolation but also in the aggregate when they act

[17] See pp. 229–30.

[18] See, instead of others, A. Ripstein, *Force and Freedom: Kant's Legal and Political Philosophy* (Cambridge, MA: Harvard University Press, 2009).

in concert, are irrelevant to the grounding of obligation. Let this stand as an early suggestion that when it comes to the grounding of obligations, moral reasons and reasons from right might share more than is commonly assumed.

On a plausible interpretation Kant's key meta-ethical contention is that motivation is irrelevant to the grounding of practical obligation[19] if motivation is conceived of as an operation that is in addition to or is distinct from the universal test of reflective endorsement, which is prescribed by the moral law.[20] To put this in simpler language, what makes it the case that I ought, say, to repay my debts is not my *desire* to repay my debts but the (normative) *fact* that I ought to repay my debts.[21] My desire to repay my debts is not antecedent to that fact but consequent to it, at least to the extent that I do not suffer any additional pathology in my moral psychology. Along these lines the Kantian idea of moral obligation entails that I am acting morally when I make the (normative) fact that I ought to pay my debts the content of my motivational state. This is significantly different, however, from saying that the one or the other intentional state grounds the truth of the fact that I ought to repay my debts. Even though the operation of reflective endorsement involves as its starting point subjective states of the will, which are eventually scrutinized in the light of the requirements of the moral law, the final stage of the reflective endorsement test is a state of the will only in name, for it coincides with that which would have been willed by an ideal agent. The content of such idealized or counterfactual states of the will is given by propositions that are truth-evaluable, as opposed to actual states of the

[19] My interpretation seems to be in line with a growing body of literature in Kantian ethical theory that argues for a distinction between moral obligation/permissibility and moral praiseworthiness. The argument, to the extent to which I can distil it in a generic form, is that moral obligation, as a property pertaining to acts, ought to be individuated independently of praiseworthiness, as a property pertaining to acts with respect to agents' motivation. While obligation is determined on the grounds of what constitutes a right reason, praiseworthiness requires us to look into the psychology of agents. Some authors (e.g. Markovits) go so far as to claim that praiseworthiness also needs to be worked out in accordance with what is deemed obligatory. For the relevant literature, see T. Scanlon, *Moral Dimensions* (Cambridge, MA: Harvard University Press, 2008); J. Markovits, 'Acting for the Right Reasons', *Philosophical Review* 119 (2010), 201; U. Heuer, Chapter 1 of this volume.

[20] Admittedly, this requirement concerns primarily moral reasons. However, to the extent at least that the moral law is placed at the foundation of practical reason in its entirety, the way that moral reasons work is decisive for all other kinds of reasons.

[21] Talk of facts is perfectly compatible with Kantian philosophy to the extent that we take facts to be constituted through the test of the moral law.

will, which do not admit of truth-values. To speak with Michael Smith, such idealized or counterfactual states are no longer psychological states but (normative) facts.[22]

This reconstruction allows us to remove facts about intentional states from the grounds of moral obligation and replace them with normative facts. It does not, however, offer us yet a way out of the dilemma which arose from attributing different grounds to legal and moral obligation. For even if one argued that intentional states do not ground moral obligations (and, instead, argued that normative facts ground moral obligations), legal obligations would continue to be subject to a separate kind of grounding (that is, through facts of institutional coercion). That would still leave us with the puzzling occurrence of attributing different meanings to the same normative sentence, depending on whether it was uttered in a legal or a moral context (what we called earlier 'the paradox of many meanings').

The persistence of the paradox notwithstanding, one important step will have been accomplished: when facts about intentional states featured in the grounds of moral obligation they were in open conflict with the grounds of legal obligation, the latter being precisely configured in such a manner as to exclude that type of fact. With the removal of intentional facts some progress has been achieved, for now the grounds of moral and legal obligation need not stand against one another in a manner of definitional opposition. Further progress would be gained if it could be shown that facts of institutional coercion – now the only remaining grounds for arguing for the separation of legal obligation – in fact stand in a complementary relation to the grounds of moral obligation.

The next section will, therefore, endeavour to demonstrate that they do and to show that facts of institutional coercion are not a new or separate type of ground, but are merely *an extension of the grounds of moral obligation.*

The unity of obligation

I shall now begin the argument for a unified account of the grounds of legal and moral obligation. Such unity dissolves the paradox of many meanings and restores continuity between legal and moral obligation.

22 M. Smith, 'Internal Reasons', *Philosophy and Phenomenological Research* 55 (1995), 109–31 (at 122–3).

Before we move on, however, we should pause to ponder a little on the relevance of autonomy – one of the central notions of Kantian ethics – to the grounding of (any) obligation. It would seem that Kant's grounding strategies respond to a key requirement to ensure that obligation is autonomy-preserving (in his case even autonomy-enhancing). Kant understands obligation as the outcome of a (self-)legislating process that is premised on our capacity to set our ends free from interference, solely on the basis of what reason prescribes. Obligations can bind us only if they are based on reason because autonomy is grounded on reason. In contrast, any deviation from reason would count as a violation of autonomy, or to use the antonym, as heteronomous. Heteronomy, in this sense, does not depict just a single type of interference with autonomy but, rather, a wide range of deviations from reason. Accordingly, either the infiltration of our moral agency through subjective mental states, or the brute force of nature, or the intentional intervention of another who literally twists my arm to perform an action, would count as instances of heteronomy. To that extent the notion of heteronomy is a unifying concept which depicts a common function across the various contexts of agency: for anything to count as a valid obligation it cannot be grounded on anything that will interfere with autonomy (for if interference occurs, so will heteronomy).

I shall claim next that the task of blocking heteronomy underpins any domain where obligations are generated. This task has two key consequences: first, since avoidance of heteronomy is what drives choice of right grounds, and since the content of heteronomy remains invariable across the various domains of practical reason, nothing that counts as interference with autonomy in one domain can function as a ground in some other domain. While this formulation is not intended as a rigorous definition, it is sufficient for illustrating the need for continuity among the grounds of obligations across domains. Thus, the second consequence is that what may appear as separate (or even opposite) grounding strategies in law and morality, ought to be interpreted as complementary in their task to preserve unity of grounds for legal and moral obligation (overcoming the paradox of many meanings). More precisely, I shall argue that coercive imposition is merely the flip-side of the moral law when one moves from the moral to the legal realm. While the moral law undertakes the primary task of grounding obligation *simpliciter*, coercive imposition complements the task of the moral law by blocking additional instances of heteronomy, such as those that arise through the actual interaction of agents in contexts of joint agency. To that extent coercive imposition complements and elaborates further (I shall use the term 'enables') those obligations that arise from the moral law.

Let me begin with a brief survey of how the moral law performs its grounding function. We have previously seen that nothing that interferes with autonomy can constitute a sound ground of obligation. Here interference is the property that divides all possible grounds into those that succeed in grounding obligation and those that fail; it is rendered a litmus test for what may count as a valid ground for generating a binding obligation. But what counts as interference with autonomy? Which grounds succeed in obligating us and which do not? The answer to that question is tied up with Kant's conception of autonomy as it is advanced through the discussion of the moral law in his two major works of practical philosophy (*Groundwork of the Metaphysics of Morals* and *Critique of Practical Reason*). There autonomy is fleshed out as the ability to choose one's own reasons for action unhindered by anything that would constitute heteronomous interference with the ability of agents to choose under conditions of freedom.

Along these lines Kant's account of the moral law as the condition of autonomy spells out conditions of 'purity' for what may count as genuine practical reason: nothing that is imposed by sources external to the agent's own reflective endorsement can constitute genuine practical reason for that agent. The upshot of this argument is that reasons for action, in line with the commands of the moral law, ought to assume the form of general propositions whose validity does not depend on particular circumstances or the substantive aims of the agent, but remain valid *simpliciter*. Such propositions are laws (norms) not unlike the laws of physics and can provide a complete answer to the question of whether any 'p' is a genuine reason for action. Thus, on this account, it is not possible that 'p' be a reason to Φ for agent A and that there still be room left for A to wonder: 'is "p" a valid reason to Φ?' Resting on this formal conception of practical reasons we arrive at a rather abstract understanding of the structure of what counts as interference with an agent's autonomous choice.

Now let us attempt to relate the grounding function of the moral law to that of institutional coercion in law. It is clear that if one takes the grounding function of the moral law to somehow involve the intentional states of the agent, it will be rather difficult to find any point of contact with the grounding function of institutional coercion in law. For, as we have seen, in law the internal psychology of the agent does not matter at all for the content and validity of legal obligations. That should not worry us, however, for such a misunderstanding is contrary to Kant's own strategy of grounding moral obligation and ought to be removed.[23]

Once we remove psychological facts about agents' intentional states the role of institutional coercion can be seen in a new light: coercion is no longer an alternative ground that competes, at the level of law, with agents' intentions. Rather it aims to affirm the grounds of our moral obligations and preserve their content throughout various domains (morality, law). Strictly speaking, coercion does not perform a self-standing grounding function as has previously, and misleadingly, been assumed. It works, from a perspective that is complementary to morality, with an eye to extending the validity of the grounds of our obligations into interpersonal relations covered by law. If this supposition is correct then it would resolve the paradox of many meanings and preserve the invariance of obligations across contexts.

At this point in the chapter a closer look at the elements that make institutional coercion complementary to moral obligation would be beneficial. While in morality one must start from subjective intentional states and work one's way through a test of reason to non-subjective normative facts, in the case of law the process is the reverse: here the Kantian philosopher is not interested in the question of how to elevate subjective intentional states to (objective) obligations, but is instead interested in how to put obligations – those arrived at by way of sound moral reasoning – into the business of guiding the behaviour of actual agents. As an answer to the latter question, coercion (or enforcement) assumes simply the role of an *enabler* for pre-existing obligations. In this sense coercion in law is the flip-side of the test of reason in morality; where, in the case of morality, the subjective mental states of agents cannot be relied upon to *ground* sound obligations so it is in the case of law that the subjective motives of agents cannot be relied upon to *pursue* sound obligations. Whereas in morality a test of 'pure reason' takes the role of 'purging' subjective intentions, coercion in law has the role of aligning subjective intentions with a view to acting on sound obligations. In either case what grounds obligations are normative truths (facts). However, these facts need to be linked to an agent's capacity for action: internally in morality (by considering the raw psychological set of agents); externally in law by eliciting a uniform

[23] See pp. 234 ff.

response of actual agents to right reasons through coercion (enforcement).[24]

The role of coercive institutions

Where, then, should we look for an explanation of the role of institutional arrangements? Arthur Ripstein in an important recent work[25] has argued that coercive public institutions go further than the picture of autonomy that I have sketched allows. In his view an understanding of interference which flows exclusively from autonomous agency and the moral law fails to capture the richness of the obligations that fall upon us under conditions of social co-existence.

Ripstein argues that a complete account of interference in Kant's legal philosophy requires the inclusion of a further dimension, a collective dimension as it were, which extends beyond the confines of the agent's reflective endorsement. It is the aspect of public authorization or, in his words, 'omnilateral authorization' (I would be reluctant to call it endorsement even though this actually is the role it purports to play) that is exclusively rooted in the public institutions of a legal system (the 'rightful condition').[26] It is true enough, and Ripstein would agree, that the structure of interference can be determined through the elements of autonomous agency that render it in the first place ill-suited to obligation. However, a comprehensive account of interference and the requirements for legitimate obligation that originates in some other person's sayings and/or doings call for institutional arrangements that ensure a public form of authorization, for otherwise any act backed by the moral law but that remains unilateral would constitute illegitimate interference in the agency of others.

It seems to me that Ripstein wishes to argue that the notion of interference (which is key to specifying the grounds and content of legal obligation) becomes richer when we move from the agent's point of view to conditions of interaction between plural agents, who of course are symmetrically endowed with reflective capacities for autonomy.[27]

[24] A note of caution is called for: on the reconstruction I propose the 'normative work' is not done by coercion but by the reasons which can be legitimately enforced. It is not the case that the state can enforce whatever it can coerce upon its citizens but, conversely, it may use coercion to enforce obligations that count as genuine from the point of view of practical agency.

[25] See Ripstein, *Force and Freedom*.

[26] Ibid., 190 ff.

[27] Ibid., chs. 3 and 4.

The enriched notion of interference circumscribes an array of new possibilities for the content of obligation which we would miss out on if we were to restrict our query only to Kant's account of individual autonomy (even though the latter suffices for outlining the structure of interference).

It is a moot point whether in contributing to the content of legal obligation coercive institutions form a self-standing ground or whether they merely undertake a concretization of pre-existing obligations.[28] To be sure, if the former were the case it would instil new energy into the paradox of many meanings and its devastating consequences, as spelled out earlier.[29] To that extent it would be better to steer away from any premise that supports the conclusion for separate grounds, which I think Ripstein's idea of omnilateral authorization does.[30] Pending a more definitive answer to the matter, I would like to sketch out an alternative picture of the role performed by coercive legal institutions.

Painting with a broad brush, institutions seem to play the role of bridging the gap between obligations that are valid *simpliciter* and their instantiations in particular contexts of interactions between agents.[31] A principal effect of this interplay between the universal and the particular is the fact that the same obligation may admit of distinct instantiations in different institutional contexts. However, and importantly in my opinion, difference or diversity in context does not necessarily entail difference in the grounds of obligation. As a consequence, the same obligation may find different institutional expressions without any need to suppose that its grounds change too. To that extent institutions may be regarded as *enablers* rather than as providing *grounds* of obligations.

[28] In other work I have distinguished between the grounding and the application of valid obligations. Whereas at the level of grounding coercive arrangements seem to play little or no role, their existence is important for implementing what we deem a valid obligation: thus even if there is an obligation on A to respect some aspect of B's life, irrespective of any institutional arrangement, it would be illegitimate for B to enforce the obligation unilaterally. See G. Pavlakos, 'Legal Obligation in a Global Context', in *EUI Working Papers*, Robert Schuman Centre for Advanced Studies 2012/16, available at: hdl.handle.net/1814/21758. Even so, the existence of the relevant obligation would not depend on the existence of the enforcing institution.

[29] See pp. 230 ff.

[30] For a more detailed discussion of Ripstein's account, see G. Pavlakos, 'Coercion and the Grounds of Legal Obligation: Arthur Ripstein's *Force and Freedom*', *Jurisprudence* 1 (2) (2010), 305; and Ripstein, 'Reply to Flikschuh and Pavlakos'.

[31] For a more thoroughgoing discussion of the distinction between *reasons simpliciter* and *reasons in a domain*, see Pavlakos, 'Practice, Reasons and the Agent's Point of View', 74–94.

Enablers behave toward grounds differently than intentional states. Different enablers may correspond to the same ground even if they lead to obligations that are distinguishable in their content. The ground remains the same because the function of the ground does not compete with that of the enabler on the same level: the ground continues to determine the normative or practical force of the obligation even though its 'direction' might take a different turn depending on the enabler that is in play. However – and this is crucial – it is the ground that still has the last word even on the question of which enablers are relevant (and to which extent) on each occasion.[32]

But if the function of the enabler is all that the alleged difference between moral and legal obligation boils down to, then Kant's account of obligations of right is seen to be only a special case of his general account of moral obligation. For want of a more thorough argument, which would demonstrate that institutional authorization is capable of generating distinct grounds for obligation, it is sufficient to say that there exist obligations *simpliciter* which in spite of, or rather because of, their interaction with the various enablers that come their way, determine the grounds of every other obligation that arises within the various domains of what we together do.

The present analysis leaves a number of questions unanswered, especially with regard to the role and function of coercive institutions in respect of legal obligation. The scope of the analysis is, however, modest. In the main it has endeavoured to displace the received view that the different foci of law and morality (external behaviour in the first case, internal incentive in the second) entail a difference in kind between obligations of law and obligations of morality. Successfully displacing this view demonstrates the unsatisfactory nature of: (i) the standard view of the role of coercion; and concomitantly (ii) Ripstein's suggestion that omnilateral willing deserves the status of a special ground for legal obligation.

[32] Things are different when we move to intentional states. If psychological states of the will are assumed to play a distinct role in the grounding of obligations, then they compete with anything else that purports to be a ground – in fact they carry the grounding role. Now, if a case could be made successfully that there existed collective states of the will, or states of the will that exist over and above their individual constituents, then a genuine difference in terms of grounds could be introduced between moral and legal obligation. If, however, no such case is likely to succeed, as I think among others Ripstein would also agree, then all states of the will can do is to function anew as enablers.

PART III

The Social Dimension of Normativity

12

Law's artifactual nature: how legal institutions generate normativity

KENNETH M. EHRENBERG

There can be no doubt that law presents itself as a system of norms. The doubts arise when we start to ask how and to whom those norms apply, if ever. In recent decades much of the discussion in attempts to answer those doubts has focused on notions of validity. Sometimes the discussions of validity have centered on a kind of contextual, practice-centered sort of validity we know as legal validity. While some people have tried to show a direct relationship between that practice-centered validity and a wider sort of moral normativity, a consensus has formed (between legal positivists and modern natural lawyers) that legal validity itself need not be directly dependent upon that wider validity. Sometimes the discussions have been more directly about that wider validity – what makes it the case, if ever, that one has a good reason to obey (or at least conform one's behavior to) the law. Those discussions are about what might give law (at least some of) the authority it claims for itself. If that authority is legitimate, then the law's norms (where legitimate) are valid in a broader way. That is, where it is legitimate, we have good reason to obey the law, where that reason applies to us as human beings or members of a given community and not merely as legal addressees.

The difficulties arise in the space between the two validities: how to get from a merely practice-dependent normativity to the wider normativity to which the law aspires.

Some have tried to deflate this problem altogether, arguing it is not really one for legal philosophers to concern themselves with, or that the way in which the law activates our wider norms is unproblematic since it cannot really create any new norms in that wider sphere. I want to explore the idea that it is for legal philosophers to investigate and that there is a possibility for the law's creation of new practice-centered norms to imply the "robust" creation of new reasons applicable in the wider sphere. I contend this possibility is to be found not so much in an investigation of the validity conditions or the legitimization of legal authority by themselves, but in the relation between these facets and law's ontology. A better understanding of law's nature will answer questions about how its normativity arises and connects to us as human beings or community members, rather than only as legal addressees.

The basic idea is that law is an institution and that a deeper understanding of institutions will allow us to see how they can create new non-prudential reasons for those subject to the institution. The focus on non-prudential reasons is justified because they are clearly more difficult to create anew and also because we are used to seeing the law create prudential reasons when it threatens us with coercion. In this latter case, "trigger" is more apt than "create" precisely because our basic prudential reasons are mostly already present.[1] It is merely by altering empirical and contingent facts that those prudential reasons are triggered. The focus on non-prudential reasons is also appropriate precisely because attempts to issue authoritative directives are attempts to create a duty,[2] and duties are a usual form that non-prudential reasons take.[3]

The question of who is subject to an institution is ultimately a question of what legitimates its authority. But seeing precisely where the questions of its authority arise can allow us to understand how its claims to impose reasons might be valid more broadly. To say that law is an institution is to say that it is intentionally created by human beings to serve a purpose, which is to say that institutions are (generally) special kinds of artifacts,[4]

[1] This is true in the sense that the paths we take to happiness or wellbeing can change throughout our lives, as our characters and abilities change, interests wax and wane, and new relationships are formed and lost. In distinguishing between the triggering and creation of reasons I am borrowing some ideas of David Enoch. See "Authority and Reason-Giving," *Philosophy and Phenomenological Research* (forthcoming: http://onlinelibrary.wiley.com/doi/10.1111/j.1933-1592.2012.00610.x/abstract), and "Reason-Giving and the Law," in Leslie Green and Brian Leiter (eds.), *Oxford Studies in Philosophy of Law*, vol. I (Oxford University Press, 2011), although I do not follow his precise understanding of the nature of this distinction, as will become apparent.

[2] "[T]he distinctive feature of authorities is that the reasons they can give robustly are reasons of a special kind, *duties*." Enoch, "Authority and Reason-Giving," 11, emphasis in original.

[3] Aesthetic reasons (insofar as they are still reasons for action as opposed to belief) are arguably another form in which we see non-prudential reasons, but they need not concern us here.

[4] Amie L. Thomasson, "Realism and Human Kinds," *Philosophy and Phenomenological Research* 67 (2003), 580–699, at 592. Hart claimed "that legal obligations are very often (though not always) human artifacts." H. L. A. Hart, "Legal and Moral Obligation," in Richard E. Flathman (ed.), *Concepts in Social and Political Philosophy* (New York: Macmillan, 1973), 188 (immediately extending this to include "rights, powers, immunities and disabilities"), the caveat likely reserved for customary laws: understanding artifacts to

albeit often abstract ones. Artifacts themselves are special kinds of tools. Tools are things created or adapted to perform a function. Artifacts are special in that they are created in order to be a specifically recognizable kind of tool.[5] Institutions are special in that their ability to perform their function is dependent upon some kind of collective recognition, and not merely on their structural features.[6] Hence institutions are understood in terms of their functionality, generally involving the conferral of a status that implies deontic powers. A deeper exploration of the relation of the institutionality of law to its normativity will answer questions about what lends potentially wider robust validity to the norms it claims to impose.

The challenge of reasons and normative theory

When we talk about the way in which the law creates or manipulates our reasons, there are two different kinds of reasons we might be talking about.[7] There are reasons of which an agent is psychologically aware and which form the agent's beliefs about her justifications for her action or inaction, sometimes called "motivating reasons." When an agent is weighing the pros and cons of an action and resolves the decision-making process in favor of a specific option, the considerations weighed by the agent in favor of the option chosen and against the options rejected can be said to be the motivating reasons.

require deliberate creation. See also Brian Leiter, "The Demarcation Problem in Jurisprudence: A New Case for Scepticism," *Oxford Journal of Legal Studies* 31 (2011), 663–77, at 666. John Gardner follows Hart in noting that law, as a generality, is a "genre" of artifacts, while individual laws and legal systems are the actual artifacts. John Gardner, "The Legality of Law," *Ratio Juris* 17 (2004), 168–81, at 171. Elsewhere the word "kind" is used instead of "genre" (as in "artifactual kind"). Amie L. Thomasson, "Artifacts in Metaphysics," in Anthonie Meijers (ed.), *Philosophy of Technology and Engineering Sciences* (Amsterdam: Elsevier, 2009).

5 On the relation between tools and artifacts, see Randall R. Dipert, *Artifacts, Art Works, and Agency* (Philadelphia, PA: Temple University Press, 1993), 27–30. Thomasson argues that artifacts do not have to be understood or identified in terms of their functions in order to provide for artworks, but that many kinds still are best understood in terms of the functions they are to perform. Amie L. Thomasson, "Public Artifacts, Intentions and Norms," in Maarten Franssen *et al.* (eds.), *Artefact Kinds: Ontology and the Human-Made World* (Heidelberg: Springer, 2013). In conversation, Thomasson agreed that institutions are a kind of artifact understood in terms of their functions.

6 Thomasson, "Realism and Human Kinds," 585, citing John R. Searle, *The Construction of Social Reality* (New York: Free Press, 1995), 124.

7 My discussion here parallels that of Enoch, "Reason-Giving and the Law," 15. See also Ulrike Heuer, "Reasons and Actions and Desires," *Philosophical Studies* 121 (2004), 43–63, making the same distinction between "justificatory" and "explanatory" reasons.

The other kind of reason that we might be talking about is a normative reason, which serves as a justification for an action. Sometimes this is called an "objective reason," although that locution seems to carry more metaphysical baggage.[8] One important facet, however, of such reasons is that the agent can have them without being aware of it. This is the kind of reason one has to step aside when there is an anvil about to fall on one's head, even though one may be unaware of the anvil. As one type of such reasons, one can be under an obligation without acknowledging or being aware of the obligation. If we believe in the existence of a critical morality in some form, then we are implying that the critical morality entails normative reasons. Even beyond morality, if there are goals that are valuable to everyone regardless of whether one has personally adopted that goal, then we would say that everyone has a normative reason to pursue that goal. An example here might be happiness, understood as the ultimate source of all prudential reasons.

Non-prudential reasons can be motivational or normative. If one's belief that one has a reason to make a sacrifice motivates one to do so, then that belief is serving as a motivating reason. Generally, however, our interest here in non-prudential reasons is in their normative flavor since the main question is the relation between the institution of law and its putative creation of non-prudential reasons.

It might initially be supposed that there is no problem with the law creating objective normative reasons in the sense that there is no doubt that the law exists in some form (yet to be explained) and hence there is some "reality" to the reasons it creates. If a given law is valid by the standards of validity in place for the jurisdiction in question, then it is "real" law and therefore provides a kind of objective reason, although it is then a separate question whether anyone should ever follow that law upon weighing all reasons in play. There is some merit to this way of seeing things, especially as it seems to reflect an understanding of institutional reality. But our question is whether and how a particular legal reason might break through to be a newly created objective normative reason for anyone to whom the law is addressed. To say that it is an objective reason in the way that it is addressed is to imply that it has a

[8] If one does not wish to be an externalist about reasons, one could believe that all of one's practical reasons are dependent upon one's "subjective motivational set" but that one could be unaware of all of the implications of the elements of that set. Bernard Williams, "Internal and External Reasons," in T. R. Harrison (ed.), *Rational Action* (Cambridge University Press, 1979), 18.

moral character of trumping at least some other reasons held by those to whom it is addressed. That is, it may preempt at least some of those other reasons. This it may do by being a reason to exclude those other reasons.[9]

If the law can create or manipulate objective normative reasons at all, it must be only in virtue of its legitimate (i.e. justified) authority and hence limited to those cases in which it is legitimate. So it might initially appear that natural law has a point in its favor: the law is deficient if it is not legitimately manipulating objective reasons, which it can only do when it is legitimately authoritative. That requires the legal directives to be morally acceptable. Hence, the only way for the law to impose objective reasons would be if they are reflecting objective reasons we already have, since it is these preexisting objective reasons that determine what is morally acceptable.

This is where Joseph Raz comes in to explain how the law could be manipulating objective reasons even where the law itself is only what humans have made it and subject only to the validity conditions that they make for it. On his view, legal validity is a kind of limit on law's claim to authority in that the claim only covers what is legally valid. However, what legitimates law's claim to authority is independent of that legal validity. What generally determines whether the law's claim to authority is legitimate according to Raz is whether the law's directive helps the subject to conform better to the right balance of reasons that already apply to her than she could do on her own.[10] (Hence it is piecemeal, in that legal authority is only legitimate for certain laws, applied to certain people, at certain times.) So it is possible for there to be a putative legal directive that would reflect the right balance of reasons but for it not to be legally valid (e.g. a valuable piece of legislation that is unconstitutional),

[9] Here I follow Joseph Raz, *Practical Reason and Norms*, 2nd edn (Princeton University Press 1990; first published London: Hutchinson, 1975), 39. I also follow Raz in believing that these reasons, where normative, operate to exclude counter-indicating reasons from being acted upon, rather than deliberated about. Joseph Raz, "Authority and Justification," *Philosophy and Public Affairs* 14 (1985), 3–29, at 7; J. Raz, *The Morality of Freedom* (Oxford: Clarendon Press, 1986), 39. The opposing view can be seen in H. L. A. Hart, *Essays on Bentham* (Oxford: Clarendon Press, 1982), 253; Scott J. Shapiro, "Authority," in Jules L. Coleman and Scott Shapiro (eds.), *The Oxford Handbook of Jurisprudence and Philosophy of Law* (Oxford University Press, 2002), 406–7.

[10] Raz, *Morality of Freedom*, 55–6; J. Raz, "The Problem of Authority: Revisiting the Service Conception," *Minnesota Law Review* 90 (2006), 1018. The notion of the "right balance of reasons" reflects the idea that there is possibly a correct answer in many situations where we are weighing reasons in deciding how to act, which we would arrive at if we were giving all of the applicable normative reasons their appropriate weight.

and of course for there to be a legally valid directive that does not reflect the right balance of reasons (for that person, under those circumstances). Legal validity therefore serves as the determinant for the practice-dependent normativity operative within the context of law. But authoritative legitimacy is the determinant for whether those practice-dependent norms succeed in having a wider "robust" normativity and whether the law can therefore impart non-prudential reasons.[11]

Another way to approach this distinction is to consider the difference between an engaged and detached perspective from which to approach any normative system. Raz's example is of the meat-eater saying, "You ought not to eat that; it has meat," to his vegetarian friend.[12] The meat-eater speaks to the friend from inside the normative system that the friend has embraced without thereby implying that he embraces it himself. From the external perspective, such as we might take as legal theorists, we can discuss the ways in which the norms operate on those for whom they are supposedly applicable without thereby implying that we endorse those norms.[13]

The problem of legal normativity can therefore be understood initially to be particularly acute for someone with positivist inclinations. If law is merely a human creation, made by certain events and actions we engage in, then it appears that whether something is a law is merely a matter of fact about a state of affairs in a given jurisdiction. That is, statements of the form "Legally, one ought to φ" are merely asserting the existence of a state of affairs and not necessarily making any claims about what one ought to do, since it is always a separate question whether one should do it for that reason. To get from this fact about the law to the conclusion that "Here, one ought to φ" we need some argument to get us over the apparent fact/value gap.

David Enoch denies this is necessary or that this is a problem for positivists, claiming instead that law merely purports to activate preexisting reasons that we already have.[14] This might often be the case, but it is hard to swallow this claim in its entirety as the law does appear to

[11] Most of the law's directives take the *form* of non-prudential reasons. Where they are legally valid but not authoritatively legitimate, the most they do is trigger a prudential reason by threatening coercion for non-compliance.

[12] Raz, *Practical Reason and Norms* (1975 edn), 175–6. See also Joseph Raz, *The Authority of Law* (Oxford: Clarendon Press, 1979), 156–7.

[13] This is not to say that acceptance of the norms is necessary, since whether consent is necessary for legal norms to apply is a separate question for political philosophy.

[14] Enoch, "Reason-Giving and the Law."

create wholly new reasons sometimes. By denying that the law creates new reasons whole cloth (rather than merely activating preexisting reasons), Enoch solves the problem of understanding the source of law's normativity. But this comes at the cost of going against what certainly seems to happen when the law sets forth how to make a valid will, or gives direction to Hart's "puzzled man,"[15] who is looking to the law for guidance. Take the example of flag law,[16] the set of rules for how to treat the United States flag, which does not have any punishments for noncompliance. We can see that one who merely wants to be law-abiding now has a set of reasons for behaving in a certain way toward the flag. Even someone who had the motivation to be respectful toward the flag needs the law to set forth some of the standards for that respectful treatment. If I were so motivated, I might be able to intuit that I should not burn the flag, or perhaps not let it touch the ground. But how am I supposed to know that "respecting the flag" includes folding it into a triangle with the stars and blue field showing, or that it should be on its right when displayed with other flags? Wherever the law is not capturing preexisting behavioral standards but creating those standards, it creates reasons (rather than merely activates them) for those who are motivated or have good normative reasons to comply. A way to better understand this is to examine Enoch's claims to the contrary.

After distinguishing the giving of normative reasons into three groups: epistemic reason-giving (reminding someone of a preexisting reason that had already been applied), triggering reason-giving (activating a reason that the person already had but was not yet applicable), and "robust" reason-giving (creating a reason that did not exist before),[17] Enoch claims that a legal reason is rather like an imaginary friend, in that the most it can be on its own is a reason in the context of a practice.[18] This is akin to the idea that the rules of a game are only reasons for those already committed to playing the game. This will not be of much use to a greater understanding of law since any practice can create such reasons inside its own context. If we join him in seeing a clear distinction between legal reasons and real (normative) reasons, we can understand the force of

[15] H. L. A. Hart, *The Concept of Law*, ed. Penelope A. Bulloch and Joseph Raz, 2nd edn (Oxford: Clarendon Press, 1994; first published 1961), 40.

[16] Flag Code, 4 *United States Code*, §§3–9.

[17] Enoch, "Reason-Giving and the Law," 4–6. As we will see, he evenutally says that robust reason-giving is really just a special case of triggering reasons. David Enoch, "Giving Practical Reasons," *Philosophers' Imprint* 11 (2011), 1–22, 9.

[18] Enoch, "Reason-Giving and the Law," 18.

Raz's point that legal reasons are claims to impose or reflect normative reasons. Sometimes those claims might be true and sometimes they are false.

Law, seen this way, is a practice-context that has contextually bound reasons for people who are committed to that context in some way. For those already in the game and committed to playing it, the legal rules can be real rules to the extent that their commitment is morally valid or binding. This is not to say that once you are subject to the law in one area you are committed to playing the legal game and therefore must see those contextual reasons as real. Rather, as with many other contexts, you may sometimes be bound and other times you may not be bound. The rules themselves might in some cases be reasons not to participate in the context, especially if they lead one away from what one has good "real" reasons to do.

A context-dependent reason is a kind of putative reason. It becomes a real normative reason when one is in that context and becomes committed to it (which may or may not happen voluntarily). But, *pace* Enoch, contexts are not quite the same as the realm of the imagination. Some putative contextual reasons may succeed in being real reasons regardless of whether one endorses the context. We do not say moral reasons are like imaginary friends precisely because everyone has a real reason to be moral, regardless of whether she has accepted anything about the moral "context." Law is somewhat weird because, seen from outside, it looks more like a context such as a game, while at the same time it appears to be making the claim that it is more like morality in providing real non-prudential reasons. It is that weirdness that is and should be of interest to legal philosophers and calls for our understanding. Why should we take this general claim on the part of law seriously at all, and what about law seems to necessitate this claim?

Enoch argues that robust reason-giving is itself a special instance of triggering reasons. His argument is based on the idea that no one can give a robust reason unless the recipient already has a conditional reason to treat the issuance as a reason.[19] If my telling you to do something can actually give you a reason to do it, this must be because you already have a reason to do that thing if and when I tell you to do it. Hence my telling you to do something merely activates the condition precedent of your preexisting conditional reason. The upshot of this is that even instances

[19] Enoch, "Giving Practical Reasons," 9–10.

of what Enoch thinks can be considered robust reason-giving are actually still merely triggering these conditional reasons.[20]

This view strikes me as problematic in that it appears to suggest that one is born with all the reasons one will ever have in life (at least in some conditional form). There is something trivially true but also unilluminating about the claim in that every reason is conditioned upon *some* conditional precedent being true. To say that all instances of robust reason-giving are merely instances of triggering because one could come up with some antecedent conditional statement that was already true is almost like saying that nothing new ever happens because we can always come up with some statement about the past that was already true and included some conditional causal antecedents about the event in question.

In correspondence, Enoch has clarified that he thinks one is born with all of the "ultimate, grounding reasons" that one has in life, and that this group includes all of one's conditional reasons, with new reasons arriving as a result of those conditions being triggered. This has a number of implications that strike me as strange. One is that the conditional reason "I have a reason to take extra care to ensure the wellbeing of H, if I marry her" and "I have a reason to take extra care to ensure the wellbeing of H" (where H is my wife) are two different reasons. Another one is that I am born with the first (conditional) reason, although admittedly not the second. This seems to imply that I have a conditional reason to take extra care to ensure the wellbeing of everyone on the planet (or at least those I could possibly marry).[21] A third strange implication is that the grounds for any unconditional reason are always therefore a vast number of conditional reasons that have the unconditional reason as a consequent. When I think of the ground for a reason, I think of a more ultimate value that serves as the justification for that reason. I do not see how a tacked-on condition precedent is really a ground for that reason, even if it captures a set of empirical facts that would make the reason valid for me. We need to make a distinction between a more general reason that serves as a ground for more particular ones, and a precondition that must be present for a reason to exist (or apply). It seems reasonable to suppose that I am born with a reason to take extra care to ensure the wellbeing of those with whom I form a close

[20] More on what distinguishes this subclass of robust reason-giving below.

[21] I probably have a non-conditional reason to take some care to ensure the wellbeing of everyone on Earth, but only a reason to take *extra* care of a small subset of them.

relationship. This is the ground for my "conditional reason" to take extra care to ensure the wellbeing of H, if I marry her. But once that condition is met, the reason is not distinct from my reason to take extra care to ensure the wellbeing of H.

I believe what is multiplying reasons here is the assumption that every logically distinct true proposition that describes a reason refers to a distinct reason. But my reason to take extra care to ensure the wellbeing of any woman who becomes my wife and my reason to take extra care to ensure the wellbeing of the woman who does become my wife are the same reason. Of course, there are unique things about the particular woman who became my wife that gave me additional distinctive reasons that are particular to her. But under Enoch's taxonomy, I would have already had an additional conditional copy of those reasons before I ever met her. Consider the following. On Enoch's view the statement "I have a reason to take extra care of H, if I marry her" was true upon my birth, although "I have a reason to take extra care of H" was not true upon my birth. That proves to him that these are two distinct reasons, and that triggering is a form of reason creation. I claim, however, that both propositions refer to the same reason, even though one proposition was true at my birth and the other was not. The first proposition was true at my birth but the reason it described was not yet created. This seems required by some form of metaphysical parsimony about reasons, if the strange implications I noted above did not suffice. Hence a "conditional reason" with an untrue (or not yet true) condition precedent is not (yet) a reason. This should not be so surprising. Assuming I can legitimately give my military subordinate a reason to clean parts of the barracks by ordering her to do so, I have not yet changed her reasons for action by saying to her "You must clean the latrine if I order you to do so." But when I say "I order you to clean the latrine," I have given her a new reason for action, even if that is grounded on preexisting general reasons to follow my orders regarding cleaning parts of the barracks.

While much of what I have to say about the ontology of legal norms may work even if one agrees with Enoch's picture of triggering and conditional norms, I think it is important to note the reasonableness of a picture that allows for the potential for law to create norms entirely anew.

Independently of its relation to triggering reasons, Enoch gives a communicated-intention-based account of robust reason-giving.[22] There

[22] Enoch, "Authority and Reason-Giving," 12–15.

are three parts to the account: I must intend to give you a reason to φ and communicate that intention to you; I must intend that you recognize my intention; and I must intend your reason to φ to depend on your recognition of my communicated intention to give you a reason to φ. The worry then arises whether anything other than "persons or person-like organs can play the role of an authority."[23] That is, the ability to give a robust non-prudential reason such as a moral duty depends on the communication of an intention to do so, which is needed in order to distinguish the possibility of successful creation of duties from merely triggering preexisting non-prudential reasons. But building in this communicated-intention requirement seems to mean that only other people (or bodies) can be authorities, not the law itself.[24] One easy solution to this problem is to say simply that the authority is vested in the lawmaker, whatever person or body that might be, and that talk of the authority of law is merely metaphorical. However, this solution does not sit well when we think of the antiquity of some legal norms that are still apparently binding, especially when some of those legal norms are borrowed directly from jurisdictions we would not think meet our normative requirements for political legitimacy (as is the case with the remaining American legal norms whose legal validity is sourced in medieval English law). This is precisely where the metaphysical questions about law become important. A better understanding of law's ontology will solve the problem of how a communicated intention can exist and possibly be robustly reason-giving when there is no identifiable human being or body we would identify as having the authority to address us directly. Creators' intentions about the content of the law and their communication to us are bound up into the law by its artifactual nature; their applicability across the ages is explained by its institutionality.

Institutions, artifacts, and the communication of intention

As mentioned above, institutions can be understood as a subclass of artifacts, although institutions may be abstract in that they might not be identical to whatever concrete entities they may be associated with.

[23] Ibid.

[24] To be fair, Enoch is agnostic about whether the law can communicate the necessary intentions to robustly give reasons. "Reason-Giving and the Law," 30, says that if the law is capable of robustly giving reasons, it must be carrying the complex intentions of the legislature.

Institutions like universities are not identical to any set of physical entities such as their students, faculty, administrators, buildings, or land. Laws and legal systems are certainly abstract institutions in that they are not identical with the people constituting the legal officials, the words written in books or scrolls of law, or the geographic area of their jurisdiction. Even if abstract institutions frequently confer status on physical objects, the object should not be confused for the institution that conferred the status. Money is an institution; a piece of currency is not, although we can say whether a given piece of paper is money is an institutional fact about the paper. Under John Searle's theory, an institutional fact is created by the collectively intended assignment of a status function by using a constitutive rule.[25] That status function conveys deontic powers, which is to say that the bearer of the status can "provide desire-independent reasons for action,"[26] including non-prudential reasons. The key is the collective acceptance of some set of conditions, which, if fulfilled, brings the institution into existence. The immediate questions are what are the normative grounds for that collective acceptance, i.e. what is a good reason to accept those conditions; how wide must that collective acceptance be; and how the status function conveys deontic powers.

The constitutive rule sets the conditions for membership and hence applicability of the institution's norms. Some institutions are relatively static and do not require much alteration after their creation. In these, there may not be much room for roles or offices. But in other, more dynamic, institutions, there will generally be roles or offices, themselves creations of the institution and which carry deontic powers to alter the (institutionally context-bound) normative space of those subject to the institution. In a legal institution, those deontic powers are themselves legal creations and are to be characterized as such. (The law is a special kind of institution in that one of its key functions is the creation of other institutions; legal systems are therefore institution-generating institutions.) The deontic powers are held by officials, or possibly by individual laws and regulations themselves if they can operate without official

[25] Searle, *Construction of Social Reality*, 23–8. The constitutive rule tends to take the form "X counts as Y in context C." Thomasson broadens this to account for abstract institutional entities, which are not applied to preexisting objects. Thomasson, "Realism and Human Kinds," 587–8. Searle has also broadened his view, in part for the same reasons. John R. Searle, *Making the Social World* (Oxford University Press, 2010), 19–20.

[26] Searle, *Making the Social World*, 23.

intervention.[27] They have a system or practice-based normativity applicable to anyone subject to that system. Again, we can analyze that normativity in two ways. The first way is merely in terms of the system itself as a practice and seeing the normativity it imposes through the creation of its institutional deontic powers. In this way we can analyze legal normativity in an external but engaged fashion, speaking about legal reasons as applying to whomever the system claims they apply to, treating those legal subjects as practice participants. (It is far from unusual for other social institutions and practices to make normative claims upon more people than those who belong to the institution or acknowledge its authority to do so. Organized religions are one example.) The other way to analyze that normativity is to ask what might give someone a robust reason for being bound by those system norms. This is to inquire into the conditions for legitimating the claims that the law makes that all its directives are morally binding on those to whom they are directed. If they are truly morally binding, then those who are subject to them have a good reason to see themselves as bound, whether or not they acknowledge that reason.

Whether the norms are viewed contextually or robustly, however, what is important here is that it is possible for institutions to be created anew, usually by a kind of declaration that is collectively accepted.[28] The new status that is created consists partially in the deontic powers that are conferred by the acceptance of the constitutive rule that creates the new status. This self-referentiality is an important feature of how collective acceptance confers status and creates norms. For something to have the properties of a given institutional kind, it must be believed to be of that kind; the belief that it is of that kind makes it so.[29] Hence, part of what it is to have an institutional status is the ability to create new reasons for those subject to the institution. If the institution persists, then the new reasons it creates for those subject to it may also persist. Since the status and the new reasons created by the deontic powers are so closely linked, we can say that part of what it is for the institution to persist is for the reasons it creates to continue to apply. Conversely, by the time none of its created reasons any longer apply to anyone, the institution has ceased to

[27] I am here imagining some kind of system that automatically generates and sends a violation notice to motorists tripping a camera when running a red light.

[28] Thomasson, "Realism and Human Kinds," 589; Searle, *Making the Social World*, 85–6.

[29] Thomasson, "Realism and Human Kinds," 585, citing Searle, *Construction of Social Reality*, 32.

exist (although other associated artifacts might continue to exist). Hence we have the beginnings of an answer to the question of how reasons created by people long dead and not authoritative in the properties they had when alive can continue to be applicable to us today. Their reasons retain their context-dependent normativity just in case their institutionality is still retained; they retain any robust normativity to the extent they are (now) legitimately authoritative to their addressees. They can continue to address people long into the future so long as the institution itself persists and that persistence depends on continued collective acceptance.

As for the questions of how the institution generates norms and who is in the ambit of collective acceptance, Amie Thomasson has a compelling argument that because an institution is a self-conscious creation, the group that collectively accepts the institutional status cannot be ignorant of or in serious error as to its nature or contents.[30] The collective acceptance of the relevant set of conditions that are declared sufficient for the creation of the institution makes it the case that those conditions are sufficient to create the institution.[31] And we cannot be massively wrong about the instantiation of those conditions since it is generally our perception of those conditions which we declare sufficient for creation of the institution.[32] Since the content of the institutional status is (partially) the desire-independent reasons it purports to create, those parts of the collective acceptance of the institution cannot be massively wrong about the creation of its norms.

This does not tell us anything about the scope or nature of that collective acceptance which creates the institution.[33] It simply states that,

[30] Thomasson, "Realism and Human Kinds," 588–90.

[31] We can be wrong about necessary conditions and other conditions that are not criterial of the institution. Ibid.

[32] The dispute between inclusive and exclusive legal positivists can be understood to be over whether the conditions sufficient for the creation of a legal institution must be perceptions (or beliefs). Both would agree that we cannot be wrong about the conditions sufficient for the creation of a legal institution (i.e. that the legal validity conditions are as the community determines them to be); they disagree about whether we can be wrong about whether those conditions are instantiated (i.e. whether there can be an element of those validity conditions the instantiation of which is beyond our epistemic access). The more serious or massive the error that inclusive positivism allows, the less likely it is consistent with this understanding of the metaphysics of institutions.

[33] Thomasson's theory of artifacts does not depend on collective intentionality (Thomasson, "Artifacts and Human Concepts," in Eric Margolis and Stephen Laurence (eds.), *Creations of the Mind: Theories of Artifacts and their Representation* (Oxford University Press, 2007), 52), although her theory of institutions as a subset does (Thomasson, "Public Artifacts, Intentions and Norms," 54). Nevertheless, this understanding of

where there is an institution, there is some group whose collective acceptance confers that institutional status, thereby implying the power to give reasons and alter the normative space for those subject to it. But that protection from error does not extend to individuals or to groups outside the collective whose acceptance creates and sustains the institution.[34] This opens up the possibility for empirical research or discovery and highlights the importance of social scientific investigation into the conditions creating the institutions we see ourselves and others believing in.

We also have an answer for Enoch: he got the picture partially right but did not allow that questions of what makes legal normativity morally legitimate may still be an apt subject for legal philosophers. The reason that it is an apt subject is precisely that the law is claiming moral legitimacy. Hence, it is certainly within our dossier to comment upon that claim and to investigate the circumstances in which it may be accurate. In doing so, we may be admitting that the law is usually merely activating reasons that already apply, even when it does have moral legitimacy. But by acknowledging its institutional nature, we are open to the possibility that it creates new norms that were not originally present and merely activated by the law. They are sometimes akin to imaginary norms as Enoch claims would be the case with any merely practice-based norms. But where the law's claim to moral legitimacy is accurate (if ever) and where that accuracy coincides with the creation of a new norm that did not already apply to the subject, there is a space for law to make a real normative difference that Enoch does not acknowledge.

One might object here that, insofar as we are seeing legitimacy along Razian lines, in order for just about any legal directive to be legitimately authoritative, it must be based upon preexisting, "dependent" reasons. These are reasons that already apply to the person who is subject to the directive. If that is the case, the objection might go, then Enoch must still be right since the law is merely activating these preexisting dependent reasons. The answer is that, for a directive to be legitimately authoritative

institutions appears compatible with a range of different theories of collective intentionality. See ibid., citing Searle, *Construction of Social Reality*; Michael E. Bratman, *Faces of Intention: Selected Essays on Intention and Agency* (Cambridge University Press, 1999); Margaret Gilbert, *Living Together: Rationality, Sociality, and Obligation* (Lanham, MD: Rowman & Littlefield, 1996).

34 Thomasson, "Realism and Human Kinds," 591.

under Raz, it need not be based directly on these dependent reasons; it need only reflect those reasons.[35] While there must ultimately be underlying dependent reasons that apply to the subject, it is not the case that the law's directive must be directly based on those underlying reasons in order to be legitimate. If it is not based on those underlying reasons but merely reflecting them, then it opens up more space to say that the law is doing more than simply activating existing reasons.

One way to see this is to remember the complexity of reasons and how they are created. In order to be legitimately authoritative, the law's directives must at least reflect those underlying dependent reasons (according to Raz). This means that legal directives must ultimately aid the subject to comply with the correct balance of those reasons that already apply to her: the dependent reasons. Hence, on this model, it is easy to see a view like Enoch's get off the ground: if the law is merely reflecting preexisting reasons when legitimate, then the most it can do is either to remind us of the applicability of that preexisting reason (an "epistemic" form of reason-giving in his taxonomy) or to activate those preexisting reasons, perhaps marshaling them to coordinate behavior or otherwise provide the kind of guidance we need in order to comply with the best balance of all those reasons (a "triggering" form of reason-giving in his taxonomy). Since the law is merely changing social facts, the most it can do is trigger a preexisting normative reason one already had but was not yet applicable.[36] For Enoch, to trigger a reason, a fact need only be "normatively significant,"[37] but to provide a robust reason is for the communication itself to make the normative difference. That is, a robust instance of reason-giving requires, on Enoch's view, the reason's creation merely from facts about the communication, e.g. the intention to create such a reason in the listener and that the communication itself serve as the listener's reason.[38] The idea is to capture the distinction between seeing a request as a reason to comply on its own, and seeing making the requester happy as an instrumental reason given further goals or values of the listener.

Most of the time when we accede to the law's demands of us, we are very likely seeing any reason-giving on the part of the law as triggering in Enoch's sense. But the law does purport to give us reasons merely because it is the law and not by triggering reasons that we already have. Is there a way to say that when it commands compliance merely because it is the law it is robustly reason-giving even if that command is only legitimate where it

[35] Raz, *Morality of Freedom*, 51. [36] Enoch, "Reason-Giving and the Law," 26.
[37] Ibid. [38] Ibid.

reflects preexisting reasons we already have? This depends again on whether one is sufficiently internal to the practice to see the law's reason-giving as robust, which itself depends on whether the directive is legitimate.

Here is where it becomes important to see law as a genre of artifacts. Laws are artifacts in that they are specialized creations of human intentionality that serve specific purposes and are designed in order to be recognized as such. Artifacts themselves are a special case of tools, which would be anything adapted or used for a human purpose. Artifacts are distinct in that they are designed to be recognizable as the specific kind of tool that they are. That means at the very least that the creator of the artifact has in mind that others will see the artifact for the kind of thing it is supposed to do (where, as with law, we are dealing with public artifacts that are understood in terms of the function they are to perform). This is a kind of communication between creator and those who will in the future come into contact with the artifact. Hence, if Enoch is right that communicated requests can be sufficient for robust reason-giving, then it seems that artifact creators can perform a similar kind of communication merely through the creation of objects that are intended to be seen by others in a certain way. This does not mean that they are creating a reason to treat the object in a very precise way such that we are normatively bound not to repurpose those objects. But it does seem likely, as Amie Thomasson notes, that the identity of an artifact as a certain kind of thing does provide some robust norms of treatment.[39]

Imagine I sew the flag of a country in which we happen to be located. (Assume for the sake of simplicity that this country has no laws about how to treat its flag.) There are likely all sorts of norms that are thereby created with regard to this object I have made. They may not be precisely the norms I intended to create. For example, I may hate the government of that country and have created the flag with the intention that you burn it. Nonetheless, I still intend that the object be recognized as the flag and not, for example, as a dinner napkin. That seems to create a reason for you to treat it as a flag, even if one intended treatment in this case is to burn it. Now in making the flag-token I am also calling up its

[39] Thomasson, "Public Artifacts, Intentions and Norms," 51. While Thomasson's aim in this article is to show that artifacts need not have intended functions in order to generalize the theory of the metaphysics of artifacts to include works of art, she acknowledges that some kinds of artifacts are to be understood in terms of intended functions. Ibid. She also agreed in conversation that individual laws have intended functions on her analysis and that law, as a genre of artifact (particularly an institutional one), is therefore to be understood in terms of those functions.

institutional status. Hence, even if I wish you to burn the flag I created, if many norms of the wider institution are legitimate, that could undermine the reason-giving efficacy of my specific intention for you to burn it. (Even if there are no laws against flag burning, saying the norms of the institution are generally legitimate is to say that it is providing a valuable service in the creation of those norms. As a result there may be moral reasons not to burn its flag even if there are no legal reasons not to do so.) Hence, when I create the flag-token, some of my communicated intentions may be successfully norm-creating and others may not be.

On Thomasson's analysis, something is an exemplar of an ("essentially"[40]) artifactual kind

> only if it is the product of a largely successfully executed intention to make [an exemplar of that kind,] where the maker must have a substantive concept of the nature of [those artifacts] that largely matches that of some prior [ ] makers (if any) and intend to realize that concept by making an object with [ ] relevant features [of the kind].[41]

We can broaden this to include institutional entities that are the result of collective creation and recognition. The key for our purposes is to recognize that some of those relevant features are "receptive." That is, they are "intended ways in which the object is to be regarded, used, or treated."[42] This is not to say that the creator of the artifact must create it with the intention that it actually be recognized as a member of that kind. Rather, it is only necessary that (for public artifacts, which are our primary focus) it is intended to be "recognizable" at least to an intended audience.[43] For many genres of public artifacts, the main (sometimes the only) thing that distinguishes them is the norms of treatment they receive and hence the recognizability of the artifact carries with it those norms of treatment.[44] That is, for many such artifacts, what it is to be that artifact

40 "[A]n essentially artifactual kind is a kind that necessarily has in its extension all and only artifacts – considered as intended products of human action." Ibid.

41 Ibid., citing "Realism and Human Kinds," 599–600.

42 Thomasson, "Public Artifacts, Intentions and Norms," 49.

43 Ibid. The limitation to "public artifacts" excludes artifacts that are designed not to be recognizable to anyone, or only to the creator. Institutions, requiring collective acceptance as they do, come within the class of public artifacts.

44 Ibid., citing Roman Ingarden, *Ontology of the Work of Art*, trans. Raymond Meyer (Athens: Ohio University Press, 1989; originally *Untersuchungen zur Ontologie der Kunst*, 1962), 260–1. Thomasson notes that these are genuine norms and not regularities of behavior as "misuse" of the artifact or "improper" behavior with regard to it are subject to "correction or rebuke." Thomasson, "Public Artifacts, Intentions and Norms," 53.

is to bear those norms of treatment, and it is the intention of its creator that it carry those norms, which are thereby at least partially constitutive of its identity.[45]

Now we are closer to seeing how it must be possible to create completely new reasons for action upon creating artifacts and hence law as a species of artifact. Since it is possible to create new artifact types,[46] as well as to create new exemplars of existing artifact types that still differ from their predecessors in some of their structural or receptive features,[47] it must be possible to create new norms of treatment that are constitutive of these new entities. To the extent that the artifact is a public kind, then those norms are addressed to the community that comprises the potential users of the artifact. This is not to say that the creator of a wholly new artifact type is necessarily successful in the particular norms of treatment that she might intend for her artifact. But for her creation to be successful at all, it generally will have to be recognizable as a member of a more general kind that comes with some norms already in place. When people recognize its value as a distinct type they will then start to generate additional norms of treatment that may or may not be in line with her intentions. The key for us to take away from this discussion of artifacts is the possibility of new norms, not from where they come or to whom they might apply. But when we think of institutions as a subclass of these public artifacts then we start to see a clearer picture of how people in certain roles might have privileged places from which to ensure those new norms are what they intend them to be and apply to that group within the institution's ambit.

Conclusion

Law as a genre is a type of institutionalized abstract artifact. That it is a type of artifact means that it has some receptive features, some of which are norms of treatment that its tokens tend to share. The creators of those tokens (legislation, judicial decisions, administrative rules, etc.) intend

45 Thomasson, "Public Artifacts, Intentions and Norms," 56. 46 Ibid.

47 Beth Preston calls this phenomenon of artifacts "reproduction with variation" and it is one of several phenomena characteristic of artifact functions that must be accommodated by any complete theory of artifacts. Preston, "Philosophical Theories of Artifact Function," in Meijers, *Philosophy of Technology and Engineering Sciences*, 216–17. As she and Thomasson both note, even new artifact types tend to be improvements upon existing broader artifact types in some way. Thomasson, "Public Artifacts, Intentions and Norms," 56.

what they create to be publicly recognizable as law and generally to share in those norms of treatment. Since part of what it is to be an exemplar of that type of artifact is that it bears some of those norms, to the extent the creation is successful (determined in law by the criteria of legal validity) the token carries some of those general norms of treatment and possibly creates new ones in terms of what is distinctive about that exemplar. That it is a type of institution means that it confers a special status on some members or other elements within its ambit. That special status tends to include deontic powers to give non-prudential reasons by the institution's own lights. Where those reasons are legitimately authoritative, the institution has successfully created the non-prudential reasons it claims to have created. Where they are not legitimately authoritative, they merely alter empirical facts about how members of the institution are likely to treat actions in compliance and non-compliance with those contextual norms (implying a possible triggering of prudential reasons to comply). This picture therefore holds out the possibility of the law creating entirely new reasons for action and explains the contours of that normativity.

13

American Legal Realism and practical guidance

MANUEL VARGAS AND JOSHUA P. DAVIS

H. L. A. Hart's well-known rejection of American Legal Realism turned in part on the idea that Realism lacked the resources to provide the sort of guidance that we might reasonably seek from a theory of law. Although Hart's criticisms were widely regarded as devastating, in recent years American Legal Realism has undergone something of a renaissance. Brian Leiter has done as much as anyone to bring about its rehabilitation. Primarily because of his efforts, Legal Realism has become a philosophically credible position in contemporary jurisprudence.

On Leiter's account, Legal Realism is principally a theory of adjudication, and not an account of the nature of law more generally. Leiter's reconstruction of Legal Realism holds that all a respectable theory of adjudication can aspire to do is to offer explanations – ideally, predictions – about adjudication. As he sees it, a commitment to philosophical naturalism and philosophical pragmatism, where these are understood as particular methodological commitments concerning theory construction, entails the fruitlessness of a normative theory of adjudication.[1] Consequently, Leiter's reconstruction sidesteps Hart's objection by (1) narrowing the scope of Legal Realism (on the nature of law, Realists are tacit positivists) and (2) rejecting the possibility that a theory of adjudication can satisfy any interest we have in (non-trivial) normative guidance concerning adjudicative matters.

The present chapter takes issue with the important – even crucial – anti-guidance element of Leiter's version of Legal Realism. Despite the considerable attractions of Leiter's reconstruction of Legal Realism, the arguments Leiter offers against a *normative* theory of adjudication

We are grateful to Dan Speak and Brian Leiter for helpful comments on a draft of this chapter.

[1] Leiter has offered independent reasons for skepticism about a normative theory of adjudication in B. Leiter, "Heidegger and the Theory of Adjudication," *Yale Law Journal* 106 (2) (1996), 253–82. We intend to respond to those arguments in a future paper.

and on behalf of Legal Realism do not demonstrate the impossibility of a theory of adjudication providing normative guidance to judges and other legal actors. If we are right, then one of the signal achievements of the new Legal Realism turns out to be less a burying of normative concerns than an example of how difficult it is to insulate normative matters from our practical interests in offering theories of law, especially concerning adjudication.

The picture we offer is an ecumenical one. We argue that the Legal Realist's interest in a predictive theory of adjudication can coexist with a normative theory of adjudication that offers practical guidance for judges and other legal actors. So, Legal Realism's contribution is not that it dissolves our interest in normative matters (for it does not), but rather, that it offers a promising way of responding to one (but not all) of the practical interests we have for a theory of adjudication.

The order of our discussion is as follows. In the first section, we consider the relationship of the Legal Realist's theory of adjudication to more general aspirations for a theory of law. The second section addresses the philosophical core of Leiter's reconstruction of Legal Realism. On that reconstruction, naturalism and pragmatism undermine the possibility of a normative theory of adjudication. We argue that, *pace* Leiter, these arguments do not succeed in ruling out the possibility and utility of a normative theory of guidance. Indeed, in some cases they suggest principled reasons to doubt that the Legal Realist's project of replacing our ordinary understanding of adjudication will succeed. In the third section, we consider some alternatives to the methodological commitments Leiter attributes to his interlocutors. In the fourth and final section we conclude with some brief thoughts about the notion of pluralism in jurisprudence, and what it might mean for the possibility of normative theories of adjudication to coexist with the Legal Realist's interests in a predictive theory.

Aspirations for a theory of adjudication

We can have diverse motivations for developing a theory of adjudication. For example, one reason to develop an account of law arises from an interest in *description*. That is, we might be interested in seeking to explain the nature of legal practices as such from an outsider's perspective and to illuminate how and why law functions as it does. We might even hope that such an account will enable us to predict judgments about cases.

A different reason for developing a theory of law is an interest in *prescription* or *normative guidance*. Among prescriptive approaches, one view of the function of legal theorizing is to offer guidance to those concerned to adhere to the law. A prescriptive account of that sort would, for example, help a judge decide what ruling the law requires in a given case.[2] These aspirations can come apart. For example, a legal theorist might not be particularly concerned to characterize the actual operations of law, but might instead seek to provide guidance or recommendations on how to resolve various legal questions. The aim of such accounts can range from providing guidance under ideal conditions (for example, under full information and with a goal of providing fully determinate answers in the law) to providing various forms of guidance under non-ideal conditions (for example, without full information about the case or about the sources of law that may apply to it).

The textbook version of Legal Realism exploits the fact that prediction and prescription can come apart. On such an account, the Realist is offering an exclusively "predictive" theory of the law. That is, a Realist theory endeavors to offer a description of legal activities that would enable legal actors to make reliable predictions about "moves" in legal space. The paradigmatic case concerns adjudication. By Realist lights, the goal of a theory of adjudication is to offer an account that allows legal actors to make predictions about how judges will decide individual cases. As Holmes put it, "The prophecies of what the courts will do in fact, and nothing more pretentious, are what I mean by the law."[3]

A familiar objection to Legal Realism as a theory of the nature of law, suggested by Hart among others, is that in making legal decisions a judge is not trying to *predict* how she is going to decide.[4] Rather, she is attempting to discern what the law is for the case under consideration. So, as a theory of the nature of law, Legal Realism falls flat.

One of the important contributions of Brian Leiter's work on American Legal Realism (ALR) is that it helps us to see how this familiar dialectic misses a more promising construal of ALR. On Leiter's reconstruction, it is a mistake to understand ALR as offering an account of the

[2] As Leiter notes, "Theories of adjudication, of course, typically make both descriptive and normative claims." B. Leiter, *Naturalizing Jurisprudence: Essays on American Legal Realism and Naturalism in Legal Philosophy* (Oxford University Press, 2007), 24, n. 47. As we discuss below, he is skeptical about the viability of normative claims, however.

[3] O. W. Holmes, Jr., "The Path of the Law," *Harvard Law Review* 10 (1897), 457, 460–1.

[4] H. L. A. Hart, *The Concept of Law*, 2nd edn (Oxford University Press, 1994), 10–11; Leiter, "Heidegger and the Theory of Adjudication," 253–82.

nature of law. Instead, Legal Realism is best construed as a theory of adjudication, functioning as a supplement to positivist accounts of the law.

On Leiter's version, the familiar objection to Legal Realism is simply sidestepped. Given that ALR is not offering a theory of law, it cannot be offering a predictive theory of law.[5] The theory of the law it is attached to is a form of legal positivism.[6] The central aspiration of ALR is to offer a predictive or explanatory theory of adjudication. For philosophical reasons we discuss below, however, ALR dismisses the possibility that an adequate predictive theory must (or even can) be a theory that provides guidance in the context of adjudication. What is left then is an account of ALR that accepts only the descriptive (or explanatory or predictive) aspiration we might have for law.

We take it that the central goal for Leiter's account of adjudication is to provide a philosophical framework for a theory of specifically appellate adjudication. In various places, Leiter suggests that he does not seek to offer a more broad-ranging theory of adjudication.[7] One worry about ALR, were it so narrowly construed, is that its practical and theoretical interest would be comparatively modest. The vast majority of litigated cases settle before they reach trial, and the vast majority of those that are tried never reach a decision on appeal. Moreover, it would not be very ambitious or interesting to claim that a normative theory of appellate adjudication is not tenable but to take no position on the feasibility of a normative theory of non-appellate adjudication or of law more generally.[8]

There are suggestions throughout Leiter's work that the ramifications of naturalistic Legal Realism extend beyond a theory of adjudication.[9] There is also independent reason to think that ALR's significance is somewhat broader than a theory of appellate adjudication. As we will

[5] Unless otherwise noted, we will henceforth use the terms "Realism," "Legal Realism," "American Legal Realism," and "ALR" to refer to Leiter's reconstruction of American Legal Realism.

[6] Leiter, *Naturalizing Jurisprudence*, 121–2. [7] Ibid., 20, 41, 45.

[8] Appellate decisions can have sweeping implications. In the American system of precedent, for example, the rulings of appellate courts claim to bind lower courts and legal officials, as well as lawyers and citizens. So one possibility is to construe Leiter's reconstruction of Legal Realism as staking a claim on appellate adjudication that would include these implications. However, this would transform his position into a much broader theory of adjudication, potentially ramifying into a more general theory of law.

[9] Cf. Leiter, *Naturalizing Jurisprudence*, ch. 6.

see below, the idea of legal indeterminacy (the idea that legal considerations fail to provide a unique recommendation for how a case is to be decided) looms large in Leiter's discussion. Although the most obvious cases where such indeterminacy is operative are appellate decisions, Leiter's reasoning about indeterminacy readily extends beyond those particular cases. Thus, we will take it that Leiter is offering a theory of adjudication that takes appellate cases as a particularly salient example, but not as the only context of legal decision-making in which Realism applies.

In the next section we consider arguments that flow from broadly Quinean commitments Leiter invokes on behalf of his reconstruction of ALR. The Quinean arguments are intended to show why naturalistic commitments preclude a normative theory of adjudication, even for positivists who allow for indeterminacy about legal reasons.

The arguments against normative theories of adjudication are not mere diversions for Leiter's rehabilitation of Realism. On the contrary, they are central to the question of whether a purely descriptive or predictive approach offers everything one might reasonably want – or, at least, reasonably expect – from a theory of adjudication. We will show why these arguments do not succeed.

We now turn to Leiter's account of American Legal Realism.

Naturalism and the Quinean critique

Leiter's version of ALR is a purely descriptive or predictive theory of adjudication. It does not aspire to provide a normative theory of adjudication: that is, one that provides legal actors with guidance on legal decision-making. It can allow that we might have an interest in guidance of that sort, but it maintains that this interest is impossible to satisfy – or, at least, that any ensuing account is not fruitful.

Leiter's arguments against a normative theory of adjudication are rooted in the main features of his version of Realism. In particular, the anti-normative arguments arise from a Quinean picture of naturalism and philosophical pragmatism. Leiter argues that the basic constituents of any normative theory of adjudication – talk of legal reasons of the sort invoked in legal decisions, along with the corresponding practical "oughts" that arise from a rationalist framework of judicial decisions – will be replaced by a naturalistic framework of the "real" causes of the decision. In this section, we evaluate those arguments.

Leiter maintains that the greatest contribution of early forms of ALR was an implicit commitment to two ideas: *pragmatism* and *naturalism*.

By pragmatism, Leiter means to invoke a particular philosophical tradition in which theorizing is worth doing only if it makes a difference to practice or experience. The operative notion of *pragmatism* is also distinguished by a family of commitments: (1) anti-foundationalism about beliefs, or the view that all justification is inferential, and (2) a commitment to "consilient" explanations, or explanations on which the posits converge with the posits of other, independent explanations.[10] *Naturalism*, as Leiter means it, refers to a methodological commitment to continuity with empirical inquiry in the sciences, in virtue of employment of scientific results or "distinctively scientific ways of looking at and explaining things."[11] On this conception, naturalism is an outgrowth of pragmatism; naturalism earns its practical keep precisely because the epistemic norms of science have worked best for various practical purposes.

Naturalism and pragmatism are distinct ideas, but the arguments for them interlock in important ways. For example, ALR's commitment to pragmatism is a commitment to the practical "cash-value" of the theory, which Leiter characterizes in terms of a predictive theory of adjudication. Prediction is appealing because it is a gold standard in the sciences. Consider a predictive theory of adjudication that works entirely by appeal to, for example, the political motivations of the judge. Such an account would earn its theoretical keep in virtue of its continuity with other scientific explanations of action, and its ability to make a difference for our practical interests.

At least in principle, a *normative* theory, or a theory of how one ought to adjudicate, could provide "cash-value" in other ways. For example, a theory that allowed us to make defensible decisions in hard cases in a way that we could not absent the theory would thereby earn its theoretical keep. However, naturalism is supposed to preclude that possibility. So, in the present context, the case against a normative theory of adjudication turns significantly on whether the naturalistic argument against guidance succeeds. According to Leiter, Quine's argument for naturalistic epistemology shows how there is no room left for any interestingly normative form of epistemology. Leiter maintains that similar considerations apply to a theory of adjudication. Given pragmatism and naturalism in jurisprudence, there is no interestingly normative theory of adjudication available to us. The Quinean picture Leiter invokes has

[10] Ibid., 48–52. [11] Ibid., 35.

the following structure. First, there is the pragmatist commitment to anti-foundationalism about beliefs and the idea that evidence always underdetermines which theory we should select. Quine's discussion concerns normative epistemology. Even if we aspire to a theory that tells us which beliefs we should and should not have, such a theory remains perpetually out of reach. Beyond correcting for logical errors, we have no path to generating an account of which theoretical beliefs are *warranted* (or, we might say, normatively preferable) and which are not. Why? Notice that systematizing our mundane intuitions about normative matters achieves very little, because *all* reasonable systematizations of intuitions about normative matters are compatible with the evidence. This just is the underdetermination claim. Moreover, given anti-foundationalism, we cannot get outside our own evidential framework to evaluate the competing systematizations. So, all that is left is *replacement* of our prior ambitions. In the case of the epistemologist, the replacement project is the "naturalizing" of epistemology: the reduction of the epistemological task to providing a description of *how* we in fact form our beliefs.

Leiter runs an analogous argument beginning with legal indeterminacy and concluding with the impossibility of a normative theory. First he invokes what he characterizes as a form of "anti-foundationalism" about legal reasons: in particular, a notion of legal indeterminacy. On that view, legal reasons do not always justify a unique decision.[12] Therefore in those cases (appellate cases, typically) the set of legal reasons underdetermine which decision a legal adjudicator should make. Correspondingly, a normative theory of adjudication remains perpetually out of reach, leaving the (replacement) descriptive project of ALR as the only possible theory of adjudication.

Beyond the pedestrian activity of correcting for logical errors, a normative theory of adjudication is "sterile" or "impossible" because the set of legal reasons will rationally underdetermine which theory we should accept.[13] What is left for the theorist of adjudication is just what the Legal

[12] Leiter's definition of what counts as a legal reason excludes considerations rooted in morality and policy (ibid., 43). One might resist a conception of legal reasons that is this narrow, at least when the law serves as a source of normative guidance. However, for present purposes, we accept Leiter's characterization of legal reasons.

[13] Sometimes, Leiter's remarks suggest that what is at stake is an impossibility claim, such as when he writes that "the foundationalist enterprise of theory of adjudication is impossible" (ibid., 40). Such a reading is consistent with the anti-normative arguments Leiter gives elsewhere ("Heidegger and the Theory of Adjudication"), and we shall reply to those

Realist offers us: a replacement account of adjudication that focuses on description or explanation of what combination of facts and reasons produces what judicial decision.[14]

Indeterminacy and guidance

To put our cards on the table, we think that even – indeed, *especially* – if we grant the point about legal indeterminacy, ALR has not yet offered a compelling case against the possibility and utility of a normative theory of adjudication. If so, then ALR is not the final word on adjudication, even by pragmatist lights. In what follows, our approach grants the idea of rational indeterminacy in legal reasons, but resists the implications Leiter attributes to it for a theory of adjudication.

We begin with Leiter's claim that indeterminacy shows that a theory of adjudication cannot provide practical guidance. At first pass, it is unclear why we should think this is the case. One way a theory can guide our practical deliberations is by narrowing the scope of permissible options. A theory might do this, without offering a single determinate conclusion. Consequently, the mere fact of legal indeterminacy would not suffice to show that we cannot have a guidance-providing theory of adjudication. It would merely show that what guidance is afforded by such a theory would rarely or never be determinate.

Leiter anticipates this reaction. His reply is largely a reiteration of the Quinean rejoinder about normative projects more generally: namely, that they are unfruitful or "sterile" (as Quine puts it). Leiter's remarks are worth quoting at length:

> [A] normative theory that specifies what the anti-foundationalist concedes – namely, that there is more than one (though not simply any) judicial decision that can be justified on the basis of the class of legal

arguments in a future paper. Here, we take it that Leiter is principally interested in the sterility claim.

[14] Leiter identifies two versions of methodological naturalism: Replacement Naturalism [Quine] and Normative Naturalism. The former aims at description or explanation, the latter at regulation of the practice through the promulgation of norms or standards. The replacement naturalist holds that "if no normative account of the relation is possible, then the only theoretically fruitful account is the descriptive/explanatory account given by the relevant science of that domain" (*Naturalizing Jurisprudence*, 37). Leiter favors the replacement version, because he believes that normative theory is "sterile" or "banal" without foundationalism, and without it nothing we have to say about justification will be of much theoretical interest (ibid., 38).

> reasons – must, in some measure, be a theory worth having. Arguably, such a theory might be adequate to deflect the challenge to the political *legitimacy* of adjudication based on the indeterminacy of law, but does it provide the *normative* guidance to judges we want from a theory? Does a theory that tells judges they would be justified (on the basis of the class of legal reasons) in deciding for the plaintiff on theory X *or* the defendant on theory Y (but not the plaintiff or defendant on theory Z!) really provide normative guidance for judges worth having? Indeed, if we take seriously the pragmatic ambitions of the Realists – to enable lawyers to predict what courts will do – then formulating a non-foundational normative theory of adjudication will be inadequate, precisely because it provides the lawyer with insufficient tools for predicting the actual decision in the case at hand. My lawyerly intuition is that normative guidance like this (which underdetermines the final outcome) is not of much value to judges *or to lawyers.*[15]

First, notice that there is an important assumption smuggled in here, namely, that the only pragmatic interest we have is *prediction*. Prediction is certainly one interest we have, and it looms large for clients and those who represent them. Nothing we say here is meant to suggest otherwise. However, for *judges* – or anyone interested in normative guidance – prediction is only one measure of theoretical appeal. Even under conditions of indeterminacy, adjudicators can still want (and benefit from) normative guidance. That clients seek a theory of adjudication for prediction of judicial outcomes does not, by itself, speak for or against a theory with a different goal that responds to the interests of adjudicators (among others) in a theory that provides normative guidance.[16]

Why would indeterminacy – that is, the idea that the class of legal reasons is insufficient to justify only one outcome – preclude "real" normative guidance or normative guidance "worth having"? In the passage quoted above, Leiter simply asserts that it does, and offers his lawyerly intuition as the grounds for concluding as much.

[15] Ibid., 41–2.

[16] One can deny the possibility of normative theories in any interesting form, thereby ruling out normative theories of law (as well as politics and morality). To his credit, Leiter has also argued on broadly Quinean grounds against any endeavor to accommodate substantively normative conceptions of morality in a naturalistic, pragmatist framework (see the essays in part 3 of *Naturalizing Jurisprudence*). These debates remain unsettled, so declaring victory for any view strikes us as premature. Our point is that naturalism and pragmatism as defined by Leiter are compatible with a wider range of theoretical aims than mere prediction. Moreover, as we argue below, limiting one's explanatory focus to causal explanations turns out to be more complicated than his discussion suggests.

We are uncertain how to evaluate the evidential force of Leiter's intuition. Fortunately, other considerations suggest principled reasons for thinking guidance is indeed possible and real under conditions of rational indeterminacy. Where there is a vast range of fine-grained decisions available, the more the theory delimits the range of permissible options, the more helpful it will typically be. A possible source of the need to narrow options in this way arises from the familiar fact, important to a wide range of work in decision theory and the philosophy of action, that real-world agents are deliberators with finite deliberative resources.[17] For real-world agents, a theory of adjudication that restricts the scope of deliberation by identifying some decisions and judgments as off the table are in better shape than deliberators without such guidance. This is so, even if the guiding theory does not provide a single determinate answer about what to do.[18]

So, if a theory of adjudication can provide normative guidance by providing "anchors" for deliberation, either by affecting the weighting of particular options, or rendering some as flatly impermissible, then it does provide an important form of normative guidance. This would be a theory worth having, at least for those of us operating under conditions of limited deliberative resources.[19] Of course, the more a theory is able to delimit the decision space, the more helpful the theory will be. However, the claim of "sterility"[20] for a normative theory of adjudication cannot be derived from indeterminacy alone.

Interestingly, in later work Leiter recognizes something like this point. When discussing the relationship of ALR to positivism, he acknowledges that so long as legal rules provide restrictions on the domain of possible outcomes "even on the Realist picture, the primary rules validated under the Rule of Recognition *guide* decision in some measure for appellate

[17] For classic work in decision theory, see H. Simon, *Models of Bounded Rationality*, vols. I and II (Cambridge, MA: MIT Press, 1982). For an overview of how this work has been important in the philosophy of action, especially via the work of Michael Bratman, see M. Vargas and G. Yaffe, "Introduction," in Vargas and Yaffe (eds.), *Rational and Social Agency: On Themes in the Philosophy of Michael Bratman* (New York: Oxford University Press, 2014).

[18] To be sure, there are some who aspire to a normative theory that provides a unique answer to any legal decision. Our point is that such an outcome is not required for a theory to be guiding or normatively significant.

[19] If the descriptive account of law produces indeterminate results – even for the decision-maker with infinite resources – this point still may hold true. But we have not reached a settled view on this issue.

[20] Leiter, *Naturalizing Jurisprudence*, 38.

judges."[21] In the context of the above passage, Leiter's position is that what normative guidance can be extracted from a theory of adjudication will be extraordinarily limited, providing answers of the sort for which there is plausibly considerable convergence. Answers in harder cases, though, will remain out of reach. That is, no existing or possible normative theory is *sufficiently* guiding as to meet a notion of "fruitfulness" for a normative theory.

We offer two observations about this position.

First, if our analysis thus far is correct, then the "no normative guidance" argument is not robustly propelled by naturalism or pragmatism per se. Instead, it looks like the decisive bit is some notion of just how much guidance counts as providing "real" or "fruitful" guidance. If that is right, then naturalism and pragmatism are simply background presumptions that color the particulars of the argument, rather than sources of the anti-normative argument.

Second, we agree that below some threshold in the scale of deliberative utility, a theory is normatively fruitless in some or another intuitive sense. Nevertheless, so far as we know, *no one has a principled account of that intuition or the corresponding threshold.* Moreover, a pragmatist should think that the threshold for utility will be quite low. If a theory helps guide adjudication, then even if the degree to which it helps is relatively minimal, it thereby provides a *pro tanto* theoretical and practical value. To put it bluntly, any cash value provided by a theory is still cash value. Such value might be outweighed by other costs to the theory, to be sure. If the anti-normative argument turns on exploiting this thought, however, then we need evidence – or, at least, an argument – about why such minimal cash value is outweighed. Leiter offers none.

On the picture we are offering, it is an empirical matter just how much guidance agents get in different contexts from proposed theories of adjudication. Whether a normative theory provides guidance about hard cases, and if so how much, is not anything anyone – especially the most avowed naturalist about law – can determine without serious empirical work on a scale that does not yet exist.

Determinateness and complete explanations

We have argued that acceptance of legal indeterminacy does not entail the impossibility of guidance by a theory of adjudication. Why then does

[21] Ibid., 79.

Leiter think that a normative theory of adjudication cannot survive against the background of philosophical commitments he attributes to Realism?

Perhaps the heart of his naturalistic skepticism about normative theories derives from a view about better and worse explanations. As Leiter sees it, one contribution of ALR is that it seeks to replace rationalizing accounts of adjudication (which appeal to reasons, legal or not) with *causal* accounts of adjudication. According to Leiter, social scientific accounts and their explanations (for example, in terms of economic and social demographics) will supplant law-based explanations of adjudicative behavior.[22]

The picture the Realist seeks to supplant is one where we explain legal decisions in terms of legal reasons, of the sort typically cited in judicial decisions. The radical consequence of the naturalistic replacement of this form of explanation is to undercut the basic constituents of a normative theory of adjudication. Without recourse to a picture of reasons and guidance afforded by the familiar elements of standard legal explanations, there is no obvious way for a normative account of adjudication to arise. In effect, the Realist seeks to cut the normative ground out from under theorists of adjudication.

There are two related motivations for the approach: a view about explanatory completeness and a view about the superiority of causal explanations. The naturalist about adjudication is committed to the view that explanatory completeness is a desideratum of a theory of adjudication. In particular, Leiter notes that the naturalist is "seeking deterministic causes."[23] The aspiration here "is to locate and articulate the real cause of the decision, which requires going beyond the domain of reasons."[24] Explanatory completeness is best achieved by identifying the causal bases of decisions, for the "real" causes are deterministic in a way that allows us to dispense with, or otherwise replace, the ersatz causes offered by rationalizing explanations, which are ineradicably indeterminate, rationally speaking. Naturalism is supposed to preclude a normative theory of adjudication by showing that the rationalizing explanations, on which normative recommendations are premised, will be replaced by causal, deterministic explanations about judicial decisions.

[22] Ibid., 65, 135. [23] Ibid., 42.

[24] Ibid., 44. We take it that the "domain of reasons" Leiter has in mind comprises not reasons per se, but the more restricted class of reasons of the sort cited in typical judicial decisions.

On this picture, the reasons cited in the rationalizing explanations cannot be the "real" causes of the decision. The mere fact of rational indeterminacy demonstrates a kind of explanatory incompleteness in theories of adjudication that invoke legal reasons.[25] In contrast, a deterministic causal theory affords considerably greater explanatory completeness. Moreover, such accounts are interesting and informative to have, because they provide an account of *why* persons respond to the reasons they do.[26] Compared to legal reasons-centered accounts, the Realist's causal replacement account provides for greater explanatory completeness because it offers an explanation of *how* responsiveness to various reasons is the case here and not there.[27]

We are unconvinced by most of this. If there is a unifying theme in what follows, it is that the stuff that provides the basis of a normative theory of adjudication – reasons and guidance – are not obviously left behind just because one embraces naturalistic commitments.

First, prior to the success of a displacing explanation, it strikes us as puzzling how a naturalist can, by his or her own lights, be warranted in concluding that one explanation will displace another. Leiter's remarks above seem to suggest that he is confident that there is a compelling reason to be a (replacement) naturalist in the sense advocated by his (reconstruction of) ALR.[28]

We believe the naturalist should be agnostic about whether rationalizing explanations of the sort commonly deployed in theories of adjudication will persist in some recognizable form upon the arrival of the yet-to-be-achieved causal story of adjudication. To be sure, legal, rationalizing explanations may fail in the face of some yet-to-be-on-hand replacement explanation. However, rationalizing explanations might not be so readily replaced.[29] In the absence of some obviously compelling reason for thinking that rationalizing explanations will be

[25] Ibid., 43. Indeed, Leiter suggests that "even the non-legal reasons (e.g. reasons of 'policy' or 'morality') are rationally indeterminate."

[26] Ibid., 44. [27] Ibid., 45.

[28] In a postscript, Leiter acknowledges that the Legal Realist's hope for an effective science of adjudication is not obviously in the offing. We say more about this below.

[29] Indeed, from our current vantage point we seem to have just as much reason to think rationalizing explanations will persist in some form or another. The rise of cognitive neuroscience, for example, has not yet displaced rationalistic explanations and folk psychological vocabularies. Instead, such developments have generally complemented and informed more familiar rationalistic explanations. At any rate, replacement is not the only naturalistically respectable possibility here.

entirely displaced, agnosticism is the most reasonable position for the naturalist.

Second, it is not clear why indeterminacy entails explanatory incompleteness. Indeed, focusing on just physical causes can help make clear why indeterminacy can be compatible with explanatory completeness. Physicists – and philosophers who work on questions of causation and determinism – are generally prepared to acknowledge that causes can be probabilistic.[30] That is, given some starting conditions and holding fixed all the causes in that set of starting conditions, which effect or effects follow is a matter of a probability distribution. Of course, once an event happens, there is frequently a particular identifiable effect that followed from the antecedent cause. The explanation of what happened, however, can (and indeed, requires) appeal to a probabilistic explanation. That explanation will be as complete as physics allows. What the case of indeterministic causation shows, then, is that the mere fact that some outcome is indeterminate does not by itself show that there is incompleteness in explanation.[31]

The foregoing considerations suggest several conclusions. First, Leiter's commitment to "real" causes being deterministic is something a naturalistically minded philosopher should be reluctant to accept, given mainstream scientific understandings of causation. Second, explanatory indeterminateness can have multiple sources, and therefore we cannot use the fact that an explanation does not provide a single determinate outcome as evidence of explanatory incompleteness. An indeterminate outcome can be a product of either causal/metaphysical indeterminacy that is basic to the involved ontology or of unknown or hidden causes relevant to that explanatory framework. When it is the former, enumeration of the (indeterminate) causes will be as complete an explanation as can exist, but yet the indeterminacy will remain. In short: indeterminacy is not proof of incompleteness of explanation.[32]

[30] C. Hitchcock, "Probabilistic Causation," in Edward N. Zalta (ed.), *The Stanford Encyclopedia of Philosophy* (winter 2012 edn), available at: plato.stanford.edu/archives/win2012/entries/causation-probabilistic.

[31] This is, for example, a standard interpretation of one of the implications of quantum mechanics. Under deterministic causation, then, a probabilistic outcome can have as complete an explanation as is scientifically and metaphysically possible.

[32] The point here is not that rational and metaphysical indeterminacy are the same thing. Rather, the mere fact of indeterminacy (whether causal or rational) can be consistent with completeness of explanation. Once we have identified the rationally indeterminate sources of a decision, there might be nothing explanatorily incomplete about the story – it might just be

The conflation of indeterminateness with incompleteness of explanation is pervasive in Leiter's arguments about the implications for naturalism. For example, he writes that "if legal rules and reasons cannot rationalize the decisions [i.e. provide a unique outcome], then they surely cannot explain them, either."[33] First, as we showed earlier, rational indeterminacy does not preclude guidance. Second, as we have been arguing here, where a phenomenon is genuinely (metaphysically) indeterminate, then a complete explanation of that phenomenon does not entail a unique, determinate outcome.[34]

These considerations help us see why one kind of reply to these criticisms does not succeed. Suppose one were to object that the foregoing has missed the force of the Realist's concern. On this interpretation, the Realist is less motivated by a particular picture of ideal explanation than by the concern that, in the light of indeterminacy, two opposite decisions are possible and equally probable given the class of legal reasons. While this is surely a concern for a predictive theory, it is less obviously an argument against the fruitfulness of a normative theory. Even were both decisions equally probable from a predictive standpoint (which does *not* follow from accepting indeterminacy), it is not clear why this fact would cut against the utility of a theory of normative guidance. Moreover, that the class of legal reasons (assuming Leiter's restricted notion of them) leaves some matter indeterminate does not mean that a theory cannot provide guidance, for a theory can still preclude judgments on some grounds and not others. Again, restricting the domain of the permissible (which decisions on which grounds) can still be valuable, even if it does not always provide a determinate judgment about which way to settle a case.

Suppose the naturalist gives us what is thus far only a promissory note, i.e. a full replacement vocabulary for the rationalizing explanations offered in judicial decision-making. Will the replacement vocabulary be more complete if it is less indeterminate? The issues here are delicate, but here is what any naturalist should say: *from the armchair it is impossible to say.*

For example, suppose the reasons cited in the rationalizing explanations are causal explanations. If they are, any indeterminateness in these

a basic fact about that part of the world that there is no deeper explanation in the framework of those terms.

33 Leiter, *Naturalizing Jurisprudence*, 64.

34 We are considering cases where there is no external overdetermination of the outcome, and where the phenomenon is not subject to masking, finking, and other metaphysical exotica that are mostly tangential to the points we make here.

explanations might be rooted in causal indeterminacy. If so, then reasons explanations can be rationally indeterminate but complete. Suppose, however, that the promised replacement vocabulary admits of cases of indeterminateness, but the indeterminateness is rooted in hidden determinate causes. If so, then the proposed replacement account's comparatively smaller degree of indeterminacy would, compared to the prior case, be symptomatic of *greater*, not lesser, explanatory incompleteness. In the former case, we would have all the causal and rational explanation the world permits. In the latter case, we would have less indeterminacy but greater explanatory incompleteness because the theory would, by stipulation, miss real causal factors that make a difference to what happens.

Third, it is unclear what Leiter's invocation of a "real cause" is supposed to be doing. Leiter argues that the naturalist's replacement account of the rationalizing explanation is more complete, on account of it identifying real causes. We have already seen reason to think that argument turns on confusion about what it means to give a causal explanation. However, the present issue concerns the appeal to some notion of a "real" cause, and whether and how it leaves us room for rationalizing concerns.

Consider a picture of the universe in which science characterizes different aspects of the universe at different levels of granularity. At the most fine-grained level is fundamental physics. At higher levels we have the phenomena of chemistry, biology, psychology, and so on. This is, of course, a very simple picture of the structure of the world, and it is silent on many rich and important questions in the philosophy of science. In what science or sciences of a world thus described might we find Leiter's "real" causes of a legal decision?

Leiter initially thought the answer would be found in the social sciences.[35] However, for an old-fashioned reductionist, the real cause is going to be one or several causes of basic physics. For some really old-fashioned reductionists, there are no real causes because on such views any talk of causation is unscientific.[36] However, Leiter's "relaxed" naturalism is rightly pragmatic about ontology and what counts as a science,[37] so no

[35] Leiter, *Naturalizing Jurisprudence*, 65, 135.

[36] The "no causes at all" position was famously Russell's view about causation, and it seems to have been espoused by Quine as well. See J. Schaffer, "The Metaphysics of Causation," in Zalta, *The Stanford Encyclopedia of Philosophy* (fall 2008 edn), §2.1.2, available at: plato.stanford.edu/archives/fall2008/entries/causation-metaphysics.

[37] Leiter, *Naturalizing Jurisprudence*, 4.

version of his view is plausibly committed to these pictures of the real causes of legal decisions. Nevertheless, what should we regard as the real causes of a legal decision, and are they such that they rule out the possibility of guidance?

At this point, we are inclined to take seriously Leiter's warning against pursuing philosophically parochial jurisprudence.[38] In that spirit, we note that in the broader philosophical literature the question of how to best understand causation and its relationship to basic ontology remains an unsettled matter.[39] In particular, there is an ongoing dispute about whether there are scientifically sensible notions of causes that emerge at relatively high levels of ontological organization (read: at the level at which our folk psychological theories and the empirical social sciences operate).

We take it that the trajectory of late twentieth- and early twenty-first-century analytic metaphysics has been one in which philosophers increasingly take seriously the possibility that causes can be usefully construed as having scientific bona fides in ordinary human practices and within various special sciences. Across the sciences, and within the social sciences in particular, the recent proliferation of pluralist approaches to causation has undermined the hope for a single, causally unified picture of the world.[40] Indeed, it is extraordinarily difficult to predict how these matters will be sorted out. On currently respectable theories of causation, it might well turn out that the "real" causes of legal decisions are best understood at levels of description more fundamental than social science, or at the level of social science (existing or future), or in the terms invoked in familiar (i.e. non-Realist) theories of adjudication – or even in terms given by all of these accounts simultaneously, even if they conflict. This latter idea just is what pluralist theories of causation in the philosophy of science acknowledge as a live possibility.

[38] At one point, he writes that such parochialism is a problem for the "the small, hermetic – and rather incestuous – universe of Anglophone legal philosophy" (Leiter, *Naturalizing Jurisprudence*, 2).

[39] Schaffer, "The Metaphysics of Causation."

[40] For a sample of representative views, see G. E. M. Anscombe and Samuel Guttenplan (eds.), *Mind and Language* (Oxford: Clarendon Press, 1975), 45–65. H. E. Longino, "Theoretical Pluralism and the Scientific Study of Behavior," in S. H. Kellert *et al.* (eds.), *Scientific Pluralism* (Minneapolis: University of Minnesota Press, 2006), 102–31, and see P. Godfrey-Smith, "Causal Pluralism," in H. Beebee, C. Hitchcock, and P. Menzies (eds.), *The Oxford Handbook of Causation* (Oxford University Press, 2010), 326–37. For an overview of pluralism in science more generally, see S. H. Kellert *et al.*, "Introduction: The Pluralist Stance," in Kellert *et al.*, *Scientific Pluralism*, viii, xxx.

In a later postscript, included in *Naturalizing Jurisprudence*, Leiter acknowledges that "there is no robust, hence epistemically credible, social science of adjudication."[41] He goes on to suggest that perhaps theories of law will come to be subsumed under more general accounts of human activities[42] and that all that may be left for jurisprudence is "an exercise in sophisticated conceptual ethnography."[43] We point to scientific pluralism, however, because it suggests a rather different array of possibilities than Leiter emphasizes. In particular, if scientific pluralism is true, it is possible that what will emerge are pictures of adjudication that permit considerably more than austere replacement accounts (whether in the form of social sciences or mere conceptual ethnography).

Here is one possibility: law and/or the theory of legal adjudication may emerge as something like a special science or, at any rate, a field with its own distinctive structure. That is, explanations of legal adjudication might appeal to reasons and explanations that make sense only internally to the practice, and where there is no useful reduction of those elements to other practices. Any attempted reduction of legal reasons and adjudication will, by hypothesis, fail to capture important emergent (and causally significant) aspects of the practice. So, no replacement account would be available.

One motivation for treating this as a live possibility might derive from the thought that an account that is purely descriptive will leave out something important. Parallel remarks hold for a purely normative or guidance-focused account. This dual thought is captured in the familiar, if difficult to reconcile, notions that what we want from the law is both something descriptive and something normative – that we want both explanation and guidance. It also emerges in the idea that immoral law is no law at all (for guidance purposes) and the contrary idea that immoral law is indeed law (for descriptive purposes, minimally); or in the idea that morality and law are both normative practices, the lived experience of which are both susceptible to familiar forms of empirical inquiry.

One way to accommodate this bifurcated picture is to insist that law is *sui generis*, and unlike the sorts of issues readily assimilated by the social sciences. If so, any theory of legal adjudication that takes seriously the thought that adjudication is part of a larger legal practice will need to accommodate the *sui generis* nature of law.

[41] Leiter, *Naturalizing Jurisprudence*, 192. [42] Ibid., 199.

[43] We note that this latter suggestion is not systematically developed in *Naturalizing Jurisprudence*. We make no pretense of directly pursuing its implications here.

A different possibility is this: accounts of adjudication will sometimes not explain away some decision in terms of reasons so much as explain how some decision in terms of reasons was achieved. Rather than *replacement*, the Legal Realist's favored theory might be a *supplement* to our understanding of adjudication.

Not all scientific explanations are displacing. The molecular theory of water did not show the non-existence of water (at one time thought to be one of the four basic, indivisible substances of the universe) so much as it showed what water consists in.[44] Similarly, an account of which reasons for a legal decision can also be construed as the product of a confluence of situational factors and psychological dispositions of the judge might not show anything more than *how* these elements constitute legal reasons. In neither the case of water, nor the instance of legal reasons, does the scientific theory necessarily displace the "cash value" of the higher-level notion with which we began.[45]

To see the implications of this point, consider Leiter's insistence that if legal reasons are indeterminate, and if non-legal reasons are themselves indeterminate (as he thinks), then "any causal explanation of the decision will have to go beyond reasons to identify the psychosocial facts (e.g. about personality, class gender, socialization, etc.) that cause the decision."[46] Importantly, there are two ways of going beyond an existing theory. A molecular theory of water will go beyond a folk theory of water

[44] Similar remarks hold even if we consider cases that are not plausibly natural kinds. For example, many social constructionists about race point out that such accounts do not displace or explain away race, so much as they show something important about the nature of race.

[45] Recent work suggests that the impact of science on socially or practically important categories is complex. For example, contemporary neuroscientific claims that purport to show the non-existence of free will tend to rule out only antecedently implausible views. A. Mele, *Effective Intentions: The Power of the Conscious Will* (New York: Oxford University Press, 2009), E. Nahmias, "Scientific Challenges to Free Will," in T. O'Connor and C. Sandis (eds.), *A Companion to the Philosophy of Action* (Malden, MA: Wiley-Blackwell 2010), 345–56. M. Vargas, "If Free Will Doesn't Exist, Then Neither Does Water," in G. Caruso (ed.), *Exploring the Illusion of Free Will and Moral Responsibility* (Lanham, MD: Lexington Books, 2013), 177–202. For standard *philosophical* views of free will, neuroscientific developments typically constitute complementary explanations. Similar conclusions seem to apply for work in biology that purports to have ramifications for racial categories. Q. Spencer, "What 'Biological Racial Realism' Should Mean," *Philosophical Studies* 159 (2) (2012), 181–204; Q. Spencer, "Biological Theory and the Metaphysics of Race: A Reply to Kaplan and Winther," *Biological Theory* 8 (1) (2013), 114–20.

[46] As Leiter has noted, historical Realists may not have aspired to this much, except in passing asides.

in the sense of having more articulated commitments, but it does not necessarily *replace* the folk theory of water. If, for example, water is that clear, frequently liquid stuff that we drink and that sustains a wide range of life forms, then the molecular theory of water is an "in addition to" explanation rather than a "replacement of" explanation

To be sure, the molecular theory – and the naturalist's theory of adjudication – may fare better than the folk theory of water and adjudication in a variety of ways, both in terms of prediction and consilience with other theories. However, neither may fare as well as the folk theory for everyday guidance under conditions of limited epistemic resources. If I want refreshment, it will usually be enough to know that water reliably refreshes, and I will not need to know the mechanics of H_2O in the human body. If I want a justifiable legal decision, I do not need to know that my perception of legal reasons is partly constituted by the epistemic circumstances afforded to me by social position, education, emotional dispositions, and so on. It will usually be enough to know that an intention to harm justifies a conviction.

So, in advance of seeing how any proposed and reasonably advanced replacement account actually functions, we cannot conclude that the proposed replacement is a replacement for rather than a complement to (or an explanation of) the mechanics of the target phenomenon.

We have sketched two ways we might accept the basic tenets of naturalism without accepting the particular commitments Leiter identifies with Realism. The first is that law may be *sui generis*. The second is to embrace a view on which social-scientific explanations supplement without replacing: for example, by providing partial explanations of the mechanisms of reasons explanations. We do not seek to vindicate either of these strategies. However, we mention them to make clear that, for all that Leiter has offered, a commitment to methodological naturalism need not entail the replacement of core notions of legal theory, including the idea that legal reasons might figure in explanatorily adequate accounts of adjudication – whether descriptive or normative. Simply put, a great deal more work is required before we should conclude that a theory of adjudication faces a choice between, on the one hand, naturalism and, on the other hand, what Leiter calls a "fetish for pedantry" purportedly evident in our concern for legal reasons of the sort offered by judges in their decisions.[47]

[47] Leiter, *Naturalizing Jurisprudence,* 53.

A third possible strategy – which we have hinted at throughout, and can overlap in various ways with those we have already mentioned – is to insist that we can have different explanatory or theoretical interests in a theory of adjudication, each of which will bring its own ontology or primary explanatory categories in tow. Even if adjudication is in some sense an ontologically or explanatorily single thing, our interests in accounting for some or all parts of it may be diverse. As a consequence, the standards or metrics for evaluating theories of some or all parts of adjudication will reflect diverse interests. So what we want from a theory of adjudication in the context of prediction might be something rather different than what we want for a theory of guidance.

One direction in which this approach might take us is to use different theoretical understandings of adjudication (or of law more generally) for different purposes. It is possible that such an approach would reflect a distinction between descriptive and normative purposes, and a correspondingly different set of principles or commitments for each approach. So a theory designed merely to describe or predict would require only explanatory judgments, and a theory designed to offer normative (or moral) guidance would require normative (or moral) judgments.[48] Full exploration of that possibility is a task for another day, but we conclude with some remarks about the presumptions behind such a project.

Sketch of a (realist+) theory of adjudication

In this section, we consider some foundational questions about methodology in a theory of adjudication. Leiter's skepticism about non-realist, non-predictive theories of adjudication arises in part because he rejects a particular jurisprudential methodology common to some normative accounts. Here we argue that there is a middle path available that can accommodate both predictive and guidance interests for a theory of adjudication, without running afoul of the methodological objections Leiter has raised for normative accounts.

We have argued that an interest in a descriptively adequate theory does not, by itself, preclude our having a further interest in possessing a normatively adequate theory of adjudication. The project of describing our (norm-structured) practices and describing a normatively satisfying (norm-structured) practice are not mutually exclusive. Leiter does not

[48] For a preliminary argument along these lines, see J. P. Davis, "Legality, Morality, Duality," *Utah Law Review* 55 (1) (2014), 55–107.

dispute this. He has found fault with standard approaches to the theory of adjudication, however, because he understands them as simultaneously offering a descriptive *and* normative theory. In his words,

> Conceived as both a descriptive and normative account, the theory of adjudication is a strange hybrid, standing almost alone in the philosophical world. For most philosophical theories do *not* aim to discharge both descriptive and normative functions in this way – that is, they do not try to first describe a practice and then use the description as a basis for normative guidance.[49]

As Leiter sees it, there are three important ideas in conventional (i.e. non-Realist, in Leiter's sense) theories of adjudication. The first is a view about the aspirations for a theory of adjudication. The second is a view about the normative status of existing adjudicatory practice. The third is a commitment to normative elements emerging from descriptive aspects of the theory.

On Leiter's account, conventional theories aim to make explicit "the rules that govern and explain judicial decision."[50] This seems innocuous enough, but it is the second commitment that serves as a normative catalyst. The second commitment of standard theories of jurisprudence is the presumption that "current adjudicative practice is *roughly right.*"[51] He calls this "the Presumption." The idea of adjudicative practice being "roughly right" is meant to be understood as a claim about the normative status of the practice – that it is normatively sound, or, as Leiter describes it, "normatively attractive."[52]

Given the presumption that adjudicative practice is roughly right (the Presumption), the articulation of those rules (the theory) yields a third thing: normative guidance. An adjudicative theory obviously describes the rules underpinning adjudication, given the conception of theorizing. However, because those rules are presumed to be normatively attractive, the theory thereby provides normative guidance about how one *ought* to adjudicate.

This conception of the relationship of normative to descriptive projects is something he calls the "Standard Relation."[53] The Standard Relation is just the idea that the normative element of a theory of adjudication is parasitic on the descriptive element. In virtue of

[49] Leiter, "Heidegger and the Theory of Adjudication," 256. [50] Ibid., 258.

[51] Ibid., 257. [52] Ibid.

[53] Dworkin figures prominently in this part of Leiter's jurisprudential landscape. One way of understanding the present account is that one might accept some of the Dworkinian aspirations (for a normative theory of adjudication) without accepting all of the commitments Leiter plausibly ascribes to Dworkin.

accurately describing what judges are doing, one can enable judges to "more explicitly and more consciously" pursue what the descriptive theory describes them as already doing.

Leiter takes his targets to thus be committed to the following: the methodological conviction that a theory of adjudication is an articulation of implicit norms governing the practice, the Presumption that the practice is normatively attractive, and the ensuing view that judges ought to be doing what they are already doing, just more explicitly and consciously.

It is unclear why we should suppose that adjudication as it currently operates in Anglo-American law is normatively attractive. Moreover, on the face of it, it is puzzling why one should think that we can extract a normative, guidance-oriented account from obviously complex and widely variable practices. Still, the success or failure of a normative theory of adjudication does not depend on these assumptions.

First, as a matter of the sociology of jurisprudence, Leiter might be right to declare that conventional theories of (Anglo-American) legal adjudication are committed to the Presumption thus described, i.e. the idea that current adjudicative practice is normatively attractive. Nevertheless, there is a related view available that makes good on the spirit of the Presumption without embracing all of the particulars to which Leiter objects. For example, one could allow that for a theory of adjudication to be a theory of adjudication and not something else, it must be descriptively adequate to some minimally recognizable degree. The point here is that the requisite degree of recognizability required for the ensuing account of adjudication to be a theory of adjudication need not be such that all features of the current practice are captured.

On this alternative conception of the Presumption – call it the Presumption* – a theory of adjudication needs to be committed to the normative attractiveness of only some core features of adjudicatory practice. These features may be essential features of the concept or the current function of the practice, or not. They may be merely contingent, non-essential features that are widely regarded as jointly sufficient for constituting legal adjudication. In calling this the "core" of the practice, we mean to leave it open whether the normatively attractive portions of a practice constitute essential features of adjudicative practice or merely the features of a normatively attractive successor notion.[54]

[54] Elsewhere, Leiter has written that "Philosophy becomes unsatisfying . . . when it turns into intuition mongering and armchair sociology about what is really fundamental to 'our' concepts" (*Naturalizing Jurisprudence*, 133). In light of this, we hasten to note that

One consequence of endorsing the Presumption* is that it permits the resultant theory to issue normative recommendations that can be at some remove from existing practices. How these recommendations might be thought of with respect to the Presumption* might vary. One attractive picture is to insist that the normative prescriptions issuing from the proposed theory of adjudication constitute the best codification of norms that are responsive to one or more subsets of interests that motivate our concern with the practice. The Presumption* is thus distinct from the Presumption in allowing that non-trivial elements of current practice might not constitute the normatively attractive "core" of adjudicative practice, and thus that the ensuing account flowing from the approach is, in some sense, a recommendation for revision or replacement of current practice.

Second, beyond the specified core that is taken to be normatively attractive, theorists committed to the Presumption* need not accept Leiter's characterization that non-realist theories of adjudication must be committed to current adjudicative practice as being "roughly right." Indeed, to the extent that such accounts embrace a revisionist or replacement model of aspects of existing practices, it need not obviously follow that "judges ought to do 'more explicitly and more consciously' what it is that the theory claims as a descriptive matter they largely do already."[55]

It is unclear whether and to what extent contemporary theories of adjudication are committed to the Presumption*, as opposed to the Presumption. However, it is notable that if the Presumption* does a better job of rendering the interests of Leiter's targets, then it cannot be objected that prescriptive accounts are inappropriately parasitic on descriptive accounts of adjudication. As we have already seen, the Presumption* does not entail that adjudicative practice is "roughly right" in any sweeping way – only that some subset of it is. An account committed to the Presumption* might well allow that important aspects of current adjudicative practice are at odds with the normatively attractive dimensions of the practice.

To be sure, the specter of revisionist understandings of theories of adjudication raises familiar questions about how such accounts are to be understood, and the grounds on which such accounts are indeed theories of adjudication. There are also familiar replies to these worries.

this approach is *not* committed to conceptual analysis – certainly not as Leiter characterizes it, and maybe not at all.

[55] Leiter, "Heidegger and the Theory of Adjudication," 258.

Proponents of the Presumption* can offer a theory of the reference-determining aspects of the notion of adjudication, or invoke an account of what is semantically essential, or they can embrace a pragmatic line, appealing to an independent account of the explanatory or practical interests we might have for a theory of adjudication.[56] Indeed, one might wonder whether we need to suppose that there is a uniform story of reference to be told here, across the wide range of explanatory or theoretical goals that might structure proposed theories of adjudication.[57]

The theory of adjudication is, as Leiter rightly notes, typically undertaken in a conservative spirit. Nevertheless, complete conservatism is not a necessary feature of normative or prescriptive accounts in other domains. If so, then there may be good reason to reject the Presumption as stated, and potentially the Standard Relation. Accounts undertaken in the spirit of the Presumption* would have grounds to distinguish more carefully between description and prescription, and, consequently, enable us to accept some degree of revision away from our existing practices, at least in cases where we are interested in questions of guidance. If so, then accounts with more than predictive aspirations need not be hamstrung by the puzzling methodological commitments Leiter attributes to contemporary analytic jurisprudence.

Conclusion

One way of construing Hart's critique of Realism is in terms of the thought that Realists lacked the resources to answer the kinds of questions judges might ask when adjudicating. Leiter's reconstruction of the Realist position rejects the presumption that guidance is something a theory of adjudication must, or even can, provide. However, we have argued that Realists have not yet delivered the goods for even the narrow limits for a theory of adjudication that they favor. In light of this, some might be tempted by the thought that Legal Realists are in a position akin to where they found themselves in the mid twentieth century: saddled

[56] These ideas have been developed in some detail in other contexts, including the philosophy of mind, the philosophy of race, and the philosophy of action, especially concerning free will and moral responsibility. See M. Vargas, *Building Better Beings: A Theory of Moral Responsibility* (Oxford University Press, 2013).

[57] S. Nichols, "Free Will and Error," in Caruso, *Exploring the Illusion of Free Will*, 203–18, contains a helpful overview of this idea with an eye toward debates about free will. He offers a general taxonomy of error theories and their alternatives.

with an unsatisfying theory of adjudication and inadequate grounds for dismissing the practical interests of adjudicators for a theory of law.

We reject that assessment. To be sure, we have argued that crucial parts of Leiter's reconstruction of ALR are seriously problematic. Nevertheless, it seems to us that ALR does show real promise for thinking about one – but *only* one – aim we might have for a theory of adjudication.

Our diverse interests might sometimes favor other conceptions of the explanatory burdens and possibilities for a theory of adjudication. So far as we can make out, Leiter's naturalistic Legal Realism – for all its value – has not given us a compelling reason to abandon the hope for a theory of adjudication that offers practical, normative guidance.

14

The authority of conventions, norms, and law

BRUNO VERBEEK

Introduction

The ubiquity of norms is overwhelming. There are (detailed) norms regulating our behavior and our actions in the community at large, in the schools we attend, in the organizations we join, in the workplace we frequent. There are norms that tell us what to wear, how to eat, and how much real fruit there should be in orange juice. There are norms regulating spoken language, as well as our communications in electronic mail and on paper. The important occasions in life from birth to burial are structured by norms.

Some norms are rules we have set only for ourselves. They determine our individual actions and habits. For example, I have made it a rule never to leave home without my keys. Such personal norms will not be my concern here. Instead, I will be concerned with norms that regulate the interactions between people. These norms are such that we expect each other to observe them. We believe that others expect the same of us. For these reasons we could label such norms as *social norms*.

However, that is still too crude. There are further distinctions possible and, indeed, necessary. When arriving in London one would expect that people will speak English and so one addresses a person one asks for directions in English. If, instead, it turns out that this person does not speak English, one may be surprised, but not outraged, indignant, or resentful. Instances like these concern social norms that are best characterized as *mere conventions*. These norms do seem to have a grip on our lives, but they do not have the same normative "pull" as other norms.

Earlier versions of this chapter were presented at the ECPR Joint Sessions Workshop on Social Norms and Law in Lissabon, April 15, 2009, and at the IFR Session on "Legal Normativity and the Philosophy of Practical Reason" in Frankfurt am Main, August 15, 2011. I want to thank George Pavlakos and Veronica Rodriguez-Blanco, Nic Southwood, Michael Baurmann, and the audiences for their helpful and insightful comments at those two occasions.

Compare this preliminary characterization of conventions with the reactions that most people in our culture have towards an adulterous partner. They feel seriously let down and hurt, and feel that their soon-to-be ex-partner is a terrible cheat who has transgressed some basic norms of sexual fidelity. The authority of the norms of sexual fidelity has a different "flavor" from those of mere conventions. Not only do such norms regulate the interactions among certain groups, perhaps society as a whole, they also come with a battery of social responses that seem somehow connected to its normative force. For want of a better label, I will refer to norms such as those of sexual fidelity as *social norms proper.*[1]

The set of social norms is not exhausted by distinguishing conventions from social norm proper. Law, especially formal law, also contains norms that regulate the interaction between agents. In this chapter, I will argue that law is not just a (set of) mere convention(s). Nor is it just a (set of) social norm(s) proper. Law is a system of norms that is different from either category of social norms. However, law has lots of similarities with the other two categories of social norms. One way in which these differences and similarities show up is when investigating the role social norms of all kinds play in social life, in particular.

Social norms of any kind seem to make a difference to how we behave in our interactions with others. Social norms *require* certain actions from us, they *obligate* us, and *give us reasons* to act in certain ways. What is it about social norms that has that power? What is the authority of social norms? In this chapter, I sketch a framework that allows me to characterize the authority of social norms. This framework is the conventionalist theory of norms.[2] In the next section, I will explain

[1] I tend to believe that a large part of morality falls within this category, but I will not pursue this point here. In what follows, I will ignore questions about the proper characterization of the authority of morality. In B. Verbeek, "The Authority of Norms," *American Philosophical Quarterly* 44 (3) (2007), 245–58, I say a little about how we should understand morality in the theory that I develop here.

[2] This is my favorite label for theories of norms as they have been developed by authors such as A. Schotter, *The Economic Theory of Social Institutions* (Cambridge University Press, 1981); R. Sugden, *The Economics of Rights, Co-operation and Welfare* (Oxford: Basil Blackwell, 1986); K. Binmore, *Game Theory and the Social Contract,* vol. II: *Just Playing* (Cambridge, MA: MIT Press, 1994); B. Skyrms, *Evolution of the Social Contract* (Cambridge University Press, 1996); K. Binmore, *Game Theory and the Social Contract,* vol. I: *Playing Fair* (Cambridge, MA: MIT Press, 1994); G. Den Hartogh, *Mutual Expectations: A Conventionalist Theory of Law* (Dordrecht: Kluwer, 2002); B. Skyrms, *The Stag Hunt and the Evolution of Social Structure* (Cambridge University Press, 2004); A. Marmor,

how I understand the question of whether a norm has authority. Next, I will show how one can understand that mere conventions have authority. I then argue that this cannot fully explain the authority of social norms proper and suggest that special attention to the role of resentment, indignation, and dispositions like trustworthiness and fairness is helpful here. Then, in the final section, I turn to law and argue that if it has any authority of its own, this presupposes the existence of certain social norms proper in the society in which it is valid law.

Authority

People often act in accordance with existing social, legal, and moral norms. Often they do so out of habit. Sometimes they are tempted to break these norms but fear the response of others. They wish to avoid the formal and informal sanctions that disobedience to norms provokes. Alternatively, sometimes people seek the positive sanctions that are attached to acting in accordance with the norm, such as the esteem and respect of others. In all these cases, the agent's motivation to act in accordance with the norm is independent of the norm itself but is derived from other considerations. However, sometimes it is not habit or the fear of sanctions that motivates such behavior but the very fact that it is the norm. That is, agents recognize that a norm has *authority*. The fact that the norm requires certain behavior is sufficient reason to act in accordance with it. In those cases, the motivation to act in accordance with the norm depends on the norm. If agents recognize the authority of the norm, they *comply* with the norm rather than *conform* to it.

Many authors, most notably Joseph Raz, believe that authority has two distinct features.[3] A norm is authoritative if, first, it gives (sufficient) reason to the agent to act in accordance with it. Authority makes a difference in the deliberation of the agent independent of the formal and informal sanctions that accompany it.[4] Second, a norm is considered

Social Conventions (Princeton University Press, 2009). For my own version of the theory, see B. Verbeek, *Instrumental Rationality and Moral Philosophy: An Essay on the Virtues of Cooperation* (Dordrecht: Kluwer, 2002); Verbeek, "The Authority of Norms."

3 J. Raz, "Authority and Justification," *Philosophy and Public Affairs* 14 (1985), 3–29; J. Raz, *The Morality of Freedom* (Oxford University Press, 1986). For an overview of the alternatives to Raz's view, see H. M. Hurd, *Moral Combat* (Cambridge University Press, 1999), ch. 2.

4 See also J. L Coleman (ed.), *Hart's Postscript: Essays on the Postscript to "The Concept of Law"* (Oxford University Press, 2001), introduction, for a characterization of the "difference thesis": the claim that (legal) norms make a practical difference.

authoritative if it is – to use Raz's terminology – *preemptive*. The reason for action that a norm gives excludes other reasons for action from consideration. There is much discussion about the question of how any reason for action, including those issued by an authority, can be preemptive at all.[5] In this chapter, I will only consider the first part of this Razian notion of authority. How can it be the case that norms in and of themselves give reasons for action, which are not present in the absence of those norms? That is, I am interested in the difference that norms make.[6]

If this is how I propose to think of authority, the question comes up whether it exists. More precisely, do social norms, whether conventions, social norms proper, or legal norms, have authority? A well-known skeptical answer to this question has been put forward by the philosophical anarchists. William Godwin (1756–1836) argued that governments could never have authority:

> To a government therefore, that talked to us of deference to political authority, and honour to be rendered to our superiors, our answer should be: "It is yours, to shackle the body, and restrain our external actions; that is a restraint we understand. Announce your penalties; and we will make our election of submission or suffering. But do not seek to enslave our minds. Exhibit your force in its plainest form, for that is your province; but do not seek to inveigle or mislead us. Obedience and external submission is all you are entitled to claim; you can have no right to extort our deference, and command us not to see, and disapprove of, your errors."[7]

We can apply the same criticism to the idea that social norms, conventional or proper, have authority. The criticism takes the form of a dilemma – the *compliance dilemma*:[8] suppose that a norm N requires from an agent A an action Φ in circumstances C. When C is the case, there is either a better option than Φ available or there is not. Suppose there is a better alternative than Φ. Then it would be *irrational* to comply

[5] E.g. M. S. Moore, "Authority, Law and Razian Reasons," *Southern California Law Review* 62 (3–4) (1989), 827–96; S. R. Perry, "Second-Order Reasons, Uncertainty and Legal Theory," *Southern California Law Review* 62 (3–4) (1989), 913–94.

[6] S. Shapiro, "Authority," in Jules L. Coleman and Scott Shapiro (eds.), *The Oxford Handbook of Jurisprudence and Philosophy of Law* (Oxford University Press, 2002), 382–439.

[7] W. Godwin, *Enquiry Concerning Political Justice, with Selections from Godwin's Other Writings*, ed. K. Codell Carter (Oxford: Clarendon Press, 1971).

[8] I adapted this formulation of the dilemma from E. F. McClennen and S. Shapiro, "Rule-Guided Behavior," in Peter Newman (ed.), *The New Palgrave Dictionary of Economics and the Law* (London: Macmillan, 1998), 363–9.

with N. Suppose, on the other hand, that there is no better option than Φ. Then Φing is supported by the balance of reasons, and A is justified in Φing but not because Φing is required by N but because rational agents should always choose options which have better alternatives. N is *irrelevant* to the deliberations of A. Therefore, compliance to norms is never rational and norms do not have authority.

Note that the notion of rationality that I employ in formulating the dilemma is the standard kind of instrumental rationality, which gets a theoretical expression in contemporary rational choice theory, especially in evolutionary game theory. Many, mostly Kantian, authors have argued that this conception of rationality is problematic and that if we abandon it for a more encompassing notion of rationality, the compliance dilemma will look very different and avoidable.[9] I do not think it necessary to attack the compliance dilemma at such a fundamental level. As I will demonstrate in the next section, the dilemma can be avoided within a conventionalist theory of norms that does not question this conception of rationality.

The authority of conventions

Imagine a crossroads where two vehicles, A and B, approach each other at the same time. Both drivers have the usual preference of going their way as quickly, efficiently, and safely as possible. However, this is only going to be achieved if one of them gives way to the other, for if they do not a terrible accident is bound to happen. On the other hand, if both give way, they will both come to a stop and inch their way over the crossroads and lose a lot of time in the process. Clearly, it would be best if one of them simply gives way to the other while the other maintains speed. Finally, while both prefer this last outcome to be realized, each prefers to be the one who maintains speed. What are they going to do? How can they resolve this?[10]

Suppose that B gives way. In that case, A has good reason to maintain speed. If A maintains speed, B has reason to give way. Therefore, A's

[9] C. M. Korsgaard, *The Sources of Normativity* (Cambridge University Press, 1996); C. M. Korsgaard, "The Normativity of Instrumental Reason," in Garrett Cullity and Berys Gaut (eds.), *Ethics and Practical Reason* (Oxford: Clarendon Press, 1997).

[10] In Verbeek, *Instrumental Rationality and Moral Philosophy*, I give a formal analysis of this situation. In this chapter, I try to avoid all formalisms, but for those who yearn for some, the situation of A and B is that of an impure coordination game.

reason to maintain speed depends on B's reason to give way. And B's reason to give way depends on A's reason to maintain speed. A and B's reasons refer to each other; they are *interdependent*. Notice that these are all the reasons that they have. Neither A nor B has independent reasons to give way or maintain speed. Independent, that is, of each other. Both A and B have reason to move quickly and efficiently through traffic, but that reason does not inform them whether to maintain speed or give way at all.

Given this interdependency of reasons, should A then maintain speed and B give way? Of course not, as there is an alternative outcome possible in which A gives way and B maintains speed. This is no surprise, as interdependence of reasons occurs only if there is at least one alternative pair of reasons for action. Note, furthermore, that interdependence of reasons only occurs when neither A nor B has an independent reason to give way or maintain speed. Suppose that A has no reason to stop, regardless of what he believes B will do (suppose A is driving in an armored vehicle and is unconcerned about what will happen to B, whereas B is riding a bicycle). That is, A has an independent reason to maintain speed. Then, of course, B has reason to give way. Since A's reasons do not depend on those of B in that case, their reasons are not interdependent.

Suppose that this is not the only crossroads in this part of the world. Suppose, moreover, that there are many drivers like A and B who regularly meet at crossroads like this one.[11] Second, suppose that A and B can learn from past experiences and adjust their choice of action in the light of what they have come to believe about the expected choices of others in this part of the world. Suppose, furthermore, that drivers such as A and B notice asymmetries between them. For example, A and B could notice who comes from the right. Evolutionary game theory teaches us that under such circumstances individuals could adopt asymmetrical strategies, such as "if I come from the right, I will maintain speed; otherwise, I will give way." What is more, such asymmetrical strategies are remarkably successful.[12] Individuals will recognize this success and adjust their choice in the light of this success and adopt

[11] In the jargon of evolutionary game theory, anonymous agents from a finite population are randomly paired in each round in a repeated game.

[12] Formal proofs of this success can be found in most texts on evolutionary game theory, e.g. J. Maynard Smith, *Evolution and the Theory of Games* (Cambridge University Press, 1982), and Sugden, *The Economics of Rights, Co-operation and Welfare*.

the same strategy. In short, after some time, individuals such as A and B will expect that people in this part of the world will maintain speed when coming from the right. This expectation will give them reason to do the same, thus reinforcing the expectation in that population. Once it is there, it is best for each individual agent to follow it. This asymmetrical strategy is stable. Occasional deviations do not cause the whole pattern of expectations to shift. Rather, occasional deviations reinforce the belief of all concerned that they should conform to the asymmetrical strategy.[13] Note that this is not the only possible stable strategy. The population could have settled on the strategy as "if I come from the left, I will maintain speed; otherwise, I will give way." A stable strategy in a situation where there are more stable strategies possible points to the existence of a *convention.*

Many social theorists, especially economists, claim that the existence of such stable strategies should be identified with conventions, rather than taken as evidence for a convention's existence.[14] This claim is misleading for a number of reasons. One reason is that the identification of conventions with combinations of strategies that are stable implies that one thinks of norms as convergent patterns of *behavior*. However, such a convergent pattern may be an indication that agents are following a convention, but it is not itself a convention. Therefore, I propose that we think of a convention in terms of the *reasons* of the agents that lead to such a convergence.[15] To be precise, I propose that we think of a convention as the stable pattern of *interdependent expectations* that supports this convergent behavior. Thus, the claim that "when coming from the right, maintain speed; otherwise, give way" is a convention, and is to be understood in the sense that there is a stable pattern of interdependent expectations to this effect.

[13] "Maintain speed when coming from the right; otherwise, give way" is an evolutionary stable strategy in this population (Maynard Smith, *Evolution and the Theory of Games*, 10). Occasional deviations from this course of action will immediately be corrected as individuals find out on each occasion that had they followed the same rule, they would have done better.

[14] E.g. Sugden, *The Economics of Rights, Co-operation and Welfare*; Skyrms, *Evolution of the Social Contract*; Skyrms, *The Stag Hunt and the Evolution of Social Structure.*

[15] Therefore, though my theory is clearly related to the standard evolutionary game-theoretic analysis of norms, I deviate in two ways from this analysis. First, on my theory, norms are patterns of convergent expectations rather than patterns of convergent behavior. Second, the agents that have these expectations are capable of reasoning in a strategic fashion about these expectations, whereas the agents in contemporary evolutionary game theory are often portrayed as a-rational creatures.

The compliance dilemma answered

This gives us the answer to the compliance dilemma according to which norms never have authority. First, notice that a typical individual in such a population will have good reasons to follow the convention that requires her to maintain speed when coming from the right. She will expect others to be prepared to give way when they come from the left, and therefore she does best by maintaining speed. Similarly, when this individual comes from the left, she can expect the other to maintain speed, and hence she does best by giving way. In general, individuals in such a society will conform to the convention to give priority to the right.

Second, conformity is not the same thing as compliance. It is not enough to demonstrate that people will conform to a convention. We also need to know *why* they follow the convention. A typical individual will give way when coming from the left because she expects the other driver to maintain speed. What warrants her expectation? The answer is that she expects that the other driver expects her to give way. What supports that expectation? The answer is that the other driver expects that she expects that the other maintain speed – and so on. What emerges here is that the expectation of each of the drivers is supported by the expectations of the other. This is true for all the relevant expectations of all members of this group. The reasons of each individual for following the convention are determined by the reasons of the other members of the group. No single member of this group can work out for herself, independently of others, whether she ought to give way or maintain speed. Her reason for action is not accessible independently of those of others. It is only against the background of existing patterns of expectations that she can determine what to do. An individual in this group has reasons to follow the convention only insofar as she takes others to have similar reasons. These interdependent reasons are self-enforcing. Once the members of this group expect each other to act according to the convention, they have no reason to stop expecting this from each other. These expectations form a stable pattern of interlocking expectations. This pattern is the reason for each individual agent to do as the convention prescribes. Since conventions are nothing but such patterns of expectations, we have a solution to the compliance dilemma: the convention itself is the reason for doing as the convention prescribes.

At this point, it may be objected that such a pattern of interdependent expectations that give these reasons is ultimately ungrounded. When such a pattern of expectations is in place, each individual has reason to do as the convention requires, but that does not justify the "first" of these expectations upon which the others are grounded. Therefore, so the objection continues, the authority of conventions is not justified.[16]

This objection rests on a confusion. The reasons for compliance with a particular convention are not the reasons for that particular convention itself. What is more, these reasons need not depend on each other in any way. The reason that "when coming from the right, maintain speed; otherwise, give way" is the accepted convention in this community has to do with contingent developments in the history of the interactions of the members of that community. The reason for individuals to comply with this convention is that there exists this more or less stable pattern of interdependent expectations about how to behave when approaching a crossroads. Thus, even if the convention itself were ultimately arbitrary and ungrounded, it can still give individual agents reasons to comply (i.e. have authority).

Another objection to the theory thus far is the following. Consider a typical driver in this community. She will have prudential interests in driving safely and will want to avoid (the risk of) a collision at the crossroads. It is only given such interests that the existence of a convention makes a difference. Hence, so the objection goes, what is really grounding the authority of the conventions are these interests. There are two responses to this objection. First, this objection commits

[16] As a corollary to this objection, it now turns out that the agents cannot all be rational believers, contrary to what rational choice theory presupposes. There are roughly four strategies to meet this challenge. First, one can give up on the assumption that all agents are rational all the time. This is typical for the evolutionary game-theoretic approach to institutions and social norms in general. This approach assumes that the first agents to adopt the strategy to give priority to traffic from the right had no particular reason for doing so. Having done so, however, they created an environment where this became the rational course of action. The second strategy assumes full rationality of the agents, but claims that the grounding of those "first" expectations comes from brute psychological facts like salience. T. Schelling, *The Strategy of Conflict* (Cambridge, MA: Harvard University Press, 1960), and, perhaps, D. Lewis, *Convention: A Philosophical Study* (Cambridge, MA: Harvard University Press, 1969). The third strategy assumes full rationality but instead of seeking grounding in salience or lower-order beliefs, it assumes that the grounding comes from higher-order beliefs. See G. Den Hartogh, "A Conventionalist Theory of Obligation," *Law and Philosophy* 17 (1998), 351–76; Den Hartogh, *Mutual Expectations*. This type of strategy reverses the usual direction of justification of beliefs. Finally, one could abandon the traditional individualism of rational choice theory and argue that the grounding of that first belief is due to other "social facts." M. Gilbert, *On Social Facts* (London: Routledge & Kegan Paul, 1989), ch. 4. I think all four strategies are flawed, but the flaw in the first strategy is tolerable, whereas this is not the case in the other three. See Verbeek, "The Authority of Norms."

a fallacy akin to the fallacy of composition. It assumes that since without such interests the pattern of expectations that forms the convention will not provide reasons, therefore, all reason-giving power comes from the interests that typical individuals have in this community. This is a mistake because, as I argued above, if you remove the pattern of interdependent expectations altogether, there are no particular reasons to give priority or to maintain speed. So, at the very least, the authority of conventions is grounded in the combination of background interests and the stable interdependent expectations.

Furthermore, in the example of the conventions I outlined above, the interests of the individual agent play a role very different from the convention itself in the reasoning of the compliant agent. The interests in question – that one safely negotiates the crossroads – provide a background against which deliberation about what to do makes sense in the first place. It is against the background of the interests of the agents concerned that a stable pattern of interdependent expectations can emerge and provide reasons to give priority or maintain speed, respectively. In other words, the objection that the interests of the individual concerned ground the reason to comply misunderstands the role that the convention plays in the individual deliberations of the agent.

However, this indirect dependency of the authority of conventions on background interests gives rise to another objection. The authority of such conventions as described so far is quite limited and is not like that of most, if not all, social norms. It is to this objection that I turn in the next section.

Social norms and resentment

Given that we have shown one kind of social norms – mere conventions – to have authority, it is tempting to see if we can extend this account to other social norms: in particular, social norms proper and law. Perhaps *all* social norms are conventions in the sense described above. This is too quick. The authority of mere conventions is quite limited. Stable patterns of interdependent expectations can only give reason to agents such as A and B if they have an interest in traveling safely and efficiently. Once this interest changes, it no longer need be the case that such patterns of interdependent expectations continue to give reason. Similarly, if one person in such a network has an independent reason, the expectations may shift and new regularities in behavior and expectations that are not conventions may emerge. In Kantian terms, conventions bind only hypothetically.

Furthermore, if a person deviates from the convention (perhaps she made a mistake, or perhaps her particular interests give her independent reasons for action), on the model presented so far, the response of others will be surprise and perhaps the adjustment of expectations. However, social norms proper, like the example of sexual fidelity I mentioned in the introduction, are not like that at all. First of all, the reasons for fidelity that this norm gives often seem stronger. They cannot be ignored as easily as mere conventions can. Second, social norms proper remain valid even if on occasion one feels tempted and it is not in one's interest to comply. That is, social norms proper seem to bind categorically, unconditioned by our particular ends and desires. In general, this seems true of many social norms proper. We judge in terms of them without it being the case that "I had no interest in complying" is accepted as an apology. Third, social norms in the proper sense differ from mere conventions in that deviation is not met with surprise and adjustment of expectations. Instead, violations of such norms provoke strong emotional responses like resentment and indignation: if your partner has an affair with another, then, other things being equal, you will experience hurt, anger, and a deep resentment towards your partner. Other people will, if they learn about this, also feel some form of indignation toward your partner.

The key to understanding how social norms proper differ from mere conventions lies in these emotions. Resentment and indignation help explain the stronger authority of social norms proper. They also show that an account of social norms proper presupposes networks of interdependent expectations, just like conventions. That is, at the heart of social norms proper lie conventions. Further, these emotions show that the authority of social norms proper presupposes a kind of virtue among the norm-followers. Finally, resentment and indignation, as well as the virtue that is presupposed in this theory of social norms, help us explain the above-mentioned features of social norms proper: their strength and that they seem to bind categorically. So it is to the analysis of resentment and indignation that I now turn.

Resentment and indignation made a comeback to the philosophical scene in 1962 when Peter Strawson published his famous essay "Freedom and Resentment."[17] In this essay he distinguished between two kinds of

[17] P. F. Strawson, "Freedom and Resentment," *Proceedings of the British Academy* 48 (1962), 1–25. Of course, resentment and indignation are a major concern for the British

attitudes we take toward others: the participatory stance and the objective stance. In the participatory stance we regard others as agents. We respond to their actions with praise or blame, resentment or gratitude, indignation or admiration. Strawson called these responses "reactive attitudes" and their existence shows that, at least sometimes, we take others somehow as fellow agents – as beings like us. The objective attitude, on the other hand, does not take others as agents. Instead, when we take the objective attitude we regard others as causally determined input–output systems that do not merit any of the reactive attitudes (those would be beside the point). For example, we do not resent a psychopath who harms someone. Instead, we hospitalize such a person and try to treat her. Perhaps we are annoyed at the trouble she is causing us, but resentment would be out of place. Recently, Stephen Darwall has argued that the participatory attitude somehow marks the realm of morality.[18] Resentment is the appropriate response of the victim of a norms violation. Hence, to claim that an action wrongs a particular person (is wrong to that person) means that the action is such that it is appropriate for that person to resent the agent. Indignation, on the other hand, is the proper response for those who are not victims of the violation, but share the participatory attitude. Hence, to claim that an action is wrong, *period*, is to claim that it is appropriate to be indignant towards the agent.[19]

We can apply Darwall's analysis of the duties that moral norms impose on us to the realm of social norms proper. Then we will not be discussing whether it is in some absolute, ideal sense appropriate to resent someone's actions or be indignant. That is, we are sidestepping any issue of whether the social norm can be justified or is correct. Instead, we will look at those cases where the people concerned *believe* it to be proper to resent the agent or to be indignant.

With that last caveat in place, I will argue for the following claims about resentment: (1) resentment or indignation concerns other agents

sentimentalist school of thought and figure prominently in the writings of philosophers such as David Hume and Adam Smith.

[18] S. Darwall, *The Second-Person Standpoint: Morality, Respect, and Accountability* (Cambridge MA: Harvard University Press, 2006), refers to the participatory attitude as the "second person perspective" for reasons that need not concern us here.

[19] The main difference between an action that is wrong *to* a person and an action that is wrong, *period*, is that in the former case it is up to the victim to resent the agent. The victim has the prerogative to resent or indeed forgive the agent. However, this prerogative is not available to the indignant person.

and their actions; (2) resentment or indignation implies that the one who is resented (or is an object of indignation) knows this to be the case; (3) resentment or indignation implies the existence of interdependent expectations; and (4) resentment or indignation presupposes certain virtuous motives, in particular trustworthiness and fairness.[20]

Claim (1) is easily verified. One does not feel resentment against the outburst of a volcano, no matter how much damage it has done or the degree in which one's expectations about the likelihood of the event was reasonable.[21] Claim (2) seems equally platitudinous, when we consider how ignorance can function as an apology. If I park on your spot without realizing it, you will resent my action and, when aware of this resentment and its cause, I can excuse myself by saying that I did not realize that this was your spot and move my car away (assuming, of course, that there are social norms governing the allocation of parking spots). Then my parking on your spot is no longer resented, though my ignorance might be.[22]

The third claim introduces the expectations of the agents concerned. Resentment follows deviance from a social norm proper. Deviance implies that the deviant did not act as was expected. However, not just any failed expectation gives rise to resentment; it is only those expectations that somehow warrant taking the participatory attitude. That is, only if the expectation is taken to be legitimate will resentment be forthcoming. To analyze when such expectations are legitimate we can appeal to the analysis of conventions in the previous section. There we saw that when a pattern of interdependent expectations exists among all in the collective in question, each agent has a reason to expect that others will comply. What is more, when a convention is in place, my expectation that you will act according to the convention is (part of) your reason to comply. Therefore, once we are in this web of interdependent expectations, our expectations about the actions of others

[20] I am agnostic on the question of whether these conditions are necessary, sufficient, both, or neither. I simply assume that they tell us something about the phenomenon of resentment.

[21] Except, of course, when one lives in an animistic culture where one's worldview allows for personification of such things as volcanoes.

[22] To be sure, often the angry feeling will not subside immediately. Resentment is "sticky" in this sense. Sometimes people continue to bear a grudge even when proper apologies and reparations have been made. Most contemporary theorists of the emotions, however, agree that a crucial component of resentment is the belief that you have been wronged. N. H. Frijda, *The Emotions* (Cambridge University Press, 1986); R. De Sousa, *The Rationality of Emotion* (Cambridge University Press, 1987).

become legitimate for they are based on reasons. What is more, this shows to a large extent that the participatory attitude is not a non-cognitive attitude we happen to take or not. Instead, it has cognitive components since it depends on interdependent beliefs (expectations). Therefore, just as is the case with reactive attitudes like resentment and indignation, we can determine whether or not the participatory attitude itself is reasonable. We can determine, in other words, who is the relevant "us" to whom the social norms in question apply.

This leads me then to an intermediate conclusion about social norms proper. For resentment and indignation to function the way they do in the context of social norms, social norms are conventional patterns of interdependent expectations such that they draw those under their scope into taking the participatory attitude towards each other, making resentment and indignation appropriate responses toward violations of the norm. Roughly and in a nutshell: social norms proper are conventions plus reactive attitudes where the conventions warrant taking the participatory attitude.[23]

Before tackling the final claim I made about resentment and indignation, I wish to signal two implications of this rough and preliminary idea. First, this explains in large part why there are very few mere conventions. Almost any convention – that is, any pattern of interdependent expectations – draws individuals into taking the participatory attitude and makes them suitable candidates for the reactive attitudes of resentment and indignation. In other words, most conventions quickly become social norms, as their existence draws people into taking the reactive attitudes toward each other. The example of the crossroads above demonstrates this. In all societies I am familiar with, an accident that occurs as a result of violating a pattern of interdependent expectations is a suitable occasion for criticizing the perpetrator, including resentment and indignation, and sympathy and solidarity with the victim.[24]

[23] At this point it could be objected that the reactive attitudes of resentment and indignation do not do any additional normative work, as their appropriateness is determined by the underlying pattern of interdependent expectations (a mere convention). This commits the fallacy of composition that I signaled above, again in a different form. I argue that reactive attitudes are a necessary ingredient of the "deep" authority of social norms proper. While it is true that those attitudes are appropriate only against a background of mere conventions, it does not follow that, therefore, these attitudes are normatively inert. Both elements – conventions and reactive attitudes together – account for the authority of social norms.

[24] Not that resentment necessarily follows such accidents. It is up to the victim to determine whether or not he will be upset and how upset he will be. This is a general point about reactive attitudes. When legitimate they not only entitle the victim to resent a wrong; they

There is a further aspect of social norms proper that is explained by resentment and indignation. As I stipulated above, social norms proper seem to generate stronger reasons for action than mere conventions. Various authors have argued that we have intrinsic desires to avoid the resentment of others, and instead seek their praise, admiration, and gratitude.[25] Thus, the prospect of resentment gives us additional reason to comply. It might be objected that the avoidance of resentment at best gives us reason to conform rather than comply. However, since we are to understand social norms proper as interdependent patterns of expectations plus reactive attitudes, it follows that the avoidance of resentment triggered by violations of interdependent expectations is just compliance with the norm. Note that the presence of these interdependent expectations is crucial in this argument. It is not the case that indignation and resentment do all the work.

Social norms and moral motives

However, this cannot be the whole story of social norms proper. For we still have to account for the fact that they bind categorically. So the very least we need to establish is that social norms bind even on those occasions when it is not in one's interest to comply. We saw that interdependent patterns of expectations only give reasons when a certain background configuration of interests is in place. Moreover, only in such circumstances is resentment reasonable, and therefore legitimate.[26] The answer is to be found in other sources that contribute to the legitimacy of the expectations upon which the reactive attitudes are based. These sources can be found in what can loosely be referred to as *moral motives*. The idea is that if, on occasion, it is not in your interest to comply with a social norm, it can still be the case that others rely on you

also entitle the victim to forgive and to withdraw resentment. Darwall, *The Second-Person Standpoint.*

25 Most notably, again, D. Hume, *A Treatise on Human Nature,* ed. David Fate Norton and Mary J. Norton (Oxford University Press, 2001), and A. Smith, *The Theory of Moral Sentiments*, in D. Raphael and A. Macfie (eds.), *The Glasgow Edition of the Works and Correspondence of Adam Smith* (Oxford University Press, 1976). An interesting contemporary defender of this view is Sugden, *The Economics of Rights, Co-operation and Welfare*. In Verbeek, *Instrumental Rationality and Moral Philosophy*, I cast doubt on this view, arguing that only reasonable expectations matter.

26 Remember that I am not talking of ideal, objective, or "real" legitimacy – rather I take these to be conditions under which agents come to believe the legitimacy of their expectations.

to comply. Their interests are at stake. They depend on you. This reliance is of a specific kind.[27] That is, the kind of reliance at stake here is not the sort of attitude you have towards an ATM when you rely on it to function well in order to retrieve money from your bank account. Neither is the reliance the sort of attitude one takes when one relies on the independent motives or interests of others. For example, it is not the attitude you take toward a second-hand car dealer on whom you depend to get a good car when you rely on this car dealer's concern for his reputation. What is it then that others rely on when you comply with a social norm even if it is not in your direct interest on this occasion? It has to be that they rely on your *trustworthiness*, on your *fairness*.[28] They rely on you not to let them down precisely *because* they are vulnerable and rely on you. In other words, in addition to the background of interests, dispositions of trustworthiness and fairness provide the additional background sources that justify compliance with a norm and the resentment with which deviations from the norm are met.

At this point, one might object that if such moral motives are introduced, the whole idea of interdependent expectations giving reasons can be abandoned, for now it seems that the categorical authority of social norms proper derives from such moral motives and not from the interdependence of reasons.

This, however, is a mistake. Motivational dispositions such as trustworthiness and fairness are insufficient to guarantee compliance on their own. For trustworthiness and fairness to give reasons to comply with a norm when it is not in your interest to do so, there have to be interdependent expectations about one's actions. Here is why. First, without relevant expectations, trustworthiness and fairness are "blind." They would be motivationally ineffective. Typically, if one is trusted to act in accordance with a norm, which is a pattern of interdependent expectations, the trusted agent needs to know of the existence of this norm. If not, the trusted agent cannot figure out what she is trusted to do. She has to know what the relevant expectations are. Second, these

[27] See A. Baier, "Trust and Anti-Trust," *Ethics* 96 (1986), 231–60. Trust is the reliance on the other to comply when you are vulnerable to his performance.

[28] Here I use the terms "trustworthiness" and "fairness" almost interchangeably. Roughly, trustworthiness is the disposition to act as one is trusted to act; fairness is the disposition not to let others down when they rely on you and are vulnerable. Both dispositions are such that they can motivate compliance on occasions when it is not in one's interest to comply. For a more elaborate discussion of trustworthiness and fairness, see Verbeek, *Instrumental Rationality and Moral Philosophy*.

relevant expectations cannot be arbitrary. When I trust you, when I rely on you to treat me in a certain manner, this trust, this reliance has to be reasonable. Suppose you and I are unfamiliar with one another. Then it is unreasonable for me to rely on you to unconditionally give me your life savings. I might hope or fantasize that you will donate these to me, but it seems odd to suppose that if you fail to do so you are guilty of unfairness and fraudulent untrustworthiness. Again, the prime resource that makes such expectations reasonable is the existence of interdependent patterns of expectations. So trustworthiness and fairness alone are not enough to account for the categorical authority of social norms.

The introduction of moral motives at this point is plausible. It explains the categorical authority of social norms in that there are sources other than pure interests to explain the authority of social norms. What is more, it helps us understand how resentment and indignation could be legitimate. Therefore, social norms proper presuppose that at least a substantial number of those following the norm are characterized by such moral motives.

Notice that this also shows that a social norm that is absolutely not in your interest ever to comply with does not have authority. For if this fact is well known, others will refrain from relying on you and they cannot appeal to considerations of fairness or trustworthiness to entice you to comply. In such a case, you would truly be out of the scope of the social norm.[29]

Finally, all this helps to make good on the fourth claim I made about resentment and indignation: namely, that these reactive attitudes presuppose the presence of moral motives, i.e. trustworthiness and fairness, among the followers of the norm in addition to the existence of interdependent expectations. These moral motives explain the reasonableness or legitimacy of the expectations that ground the reactive attitudes in those cases where other considerations (such as the interests of those concerned) give out. They explain why, even if it turns out to be the case that your interests on occasion are not served by compliance with the pattern of interdependent expectations, it can be reasonable to nevertheless expect you to comply. And if it is reasonable, resentment is an appropriate response to violations of social norms proper.

[29] G. Den Hartogh, "Politieke Verplichting: Gronden en Grenzen," *Algemeen Nederlands Tijdschrift Voor Wijsbegeerte* 80 (1988), 231–58, Den Hartogh, "A Conventionalist Theory of Obligation," and Den Hartogh, *Mutual Expectations*, develops this thought into a theory of political obligation.

This leaves us then with a final refinement over the rough and ready characterization of social norms proper. A social norm proper exists in a society when:[30]

(1) there is a stable pattern of interdependent expectations;
(2) this pattern generates reasons for compliance and not just conformity;
(3) this pattern draws people into taking the participatory attitude towards others;
(4) this pattern of interdependent expectations is supported by moral motives, such as trustworthiness and fairness;
(5) reactive attitudes of resentment and indignation are perceived to be proper responses to deviations from these expectations by those concerned;
(6) these responses, as well as these moral motives, provide additional reasons for those concerned to comply with the norm.

What emerges here is a "layered" account of the authority of social norms.[31] Each step creates additional normative pressure on agents to comply. Together these steps explain the nature of the reasons of agents to comply with a social norm and demonstrate how social norms can come to have a kind of categorical authority.[32]

The authority of law

With this rather elaborate analysis of social norms proper and their authority, we can finally turn our attention to law. Just as it was tempting to assume that social norms proper are mere conventions, it is similarly tempting to assume that law is completely reducible to social norms. Formal law is nothing but the codification of mere conventions and

[30] This list of conditions for the social norms closely resembles that of H. L. A. Hart, *The Concept of Law* (Oxford University Press, 1961); P. Winch, *The Idea of a Social Science and its Relation to Philosophy*, vol. II (London: Routledge & Kegan Paul, 1990); and Den Hartogh, *Mutual Expectations*.

[31] Thanks to George Pavlakos and Veronica Rodriguez-Blanco for this characterization of my view.

[32] Again, just because moral motives add to the authority of social norms and just because these moral motives explain the categorical nature of social norms, it does not follow that these motives do all the normative grounding. All three elements are necessary: stable patterns of interdependent expectations, reactive attitudes, and moral motives. To single out one of them as the most basic commits the fallacy of composition mentioned above.

social norms proper. Common law – informal law – consists of mere conventions and social norms proper that have not been codified.

This idea has certain advantages. If (formal) law is nothing but a set of (codified) social norms, we can explain why legal rules oblige. For example, traffic laws, just like the rules of the road, give drivers reasons to give way and stop at certain signs, just as social norms proper and mere conventions would. Law, on this picture, is nothing but a sign, a reminder, that in this society certain patterns of interdependent expectations exist.

Second, we can explain the authority of laws that do not seem to oblige. For example, a legal requirement that a will be signed does not impose a duty. It does not require you to make a will, nor does it require you to sign the document. All it stipulates is what makes a certain document a will. It is, in the words of Rawls, a constitutive rule.[33] Such a legal rule can be interpreted as a convention: it generates a pattern of interdependent expectations as to which documents are recognized as a will.

Third, it throws an informative light on the function of legislation. Legislation need not just be the codification of what is already there. It could also be the starting point of new patterns of interdependent expectations. For example, when back in 1969 the Swedish government changed the traffic law such that, instead of driving on the left, people had to drive on the right from then on, the entire country complied. The fact that parliament enacted such a law was enough to shift the whole pattern of interdependent expectations from expectations of driving on the left to expectations of driving on the right. Legislation on this view is a process whereby patterns of interdependent expectations come into being or shift.

Finally, we can explain why some law (but not all law) comes with sanctions. Just as social norms proper come with reactive attitudes, criminal law has its own responses to violations.

In spite of its many virtues, this picture is too simple. Law does not just contain norms that oblige its subjects. In addition to the obligations *in* the law, there is an obligation *to* the law. More precisely, many authors

[33] J. Rawls, "Two Concepts of Rules," *Philosophical Review* 64 (1) (1955), 3–32. For a conventionalist theory of social norms, this distinction is not fundamental. Both regulative rules, i.e. rules that impose duties, and constitutive rules, i.e. rules that do not oblige, but instead constitute certain practices (e.g. the rules of the game) or artifacts (e.g. money, or indeed a will), are patterns of interdependent expectations.

believe that there is an obligation to obey the law because it is the law. That is, law requires compliance to itself and not to other norms. So if the law is nothing but a set of (codified) social norms, whether conventions or social norms proper, the law has no independent authority. It would merely be an archive of the social norms that operate in a society. This mischaracterizes existing law in many places. Law is itself a source of new norms and corresponding obligations.

I must confess that I am not sure about this objection, as it seems to run together two claims. First, there is the claim that law is itself a source of norms as opposed to being a mere depository of norms. Second, there is the stronger claim that we have an obligation to the law *qua law*. In what follows, I will leave out extensive discussion of this second claim.[34] Instead, I will show how a conventionalist theory of social norms could deal with the first claim.

Again, I turn to the idea of interdependent expectations. Suppose that you live in a well-ordered society with a decent and relatively well-functioning legal system. In such a society there exists a well-entrenched social norm that one conforms to the law. I believe that some western democracies are societies where such a norm exists (most notably, the USA with its obsession with legal correctness).[35] Such a social norm *confers* authority to the law. It tells subjects that they need to look to the law for practical guidance in certain matters. With such a social norm

[34] If only because the claim that we have an obligation to the law *qua law* is far too broad and imprecise. First, there is a question of the scope of this alleged obligation. Are subjects obliged to comply with *everything* that is in the law or with most laws? Or are subjects obliged to comply with whatever would be law (i.e. could any legal dictate become a legal obligation)? The latter reading is probably too strong (could there be an obligation to obey a law that dictates the scratching of your little toe on Tuesday mornings?). Second, it is easy to interpret the claim that there is an obligation to the law *qua law* as the claim that there is an independent (moral) obligation to obey. For example, John Simmons thinks this obligation is like that and argues that it cannot be justified. A. J. Simmons, *Moral Principles and Political Obligations* (Princeton University Press, 1979). On the other hand, many authors have pointed out that the law could have an authority of its own without it being the case that there is a (moral) obligation to obey the law, Shapiro, "Authority"; Shapiro, *Legality* (Cambridge, MA: Harvard University Press, 2011). In short, this second claim requires a lot of disambiguation and argument that would take us to the core of current debates in legal philosophical thought. A defense of the first claim – that law can be a source of new obligations – is enough to illustrate the place of law in the realm of social norms.

[35] I am not claiming that only in western democracies (minus Italy?) such a social norm could exist. I do think that if it exists anywhere, chances are it would be a well-functioning democracy.

in place, law becomes a source of reasons of its own: it makes a difference in the reasons of subjects.[36] In other words, because and only because in such a society we expect from each other that we conform to the law, the dictates of law provide reasons that are independent of mere conventions and social norms proper. Law is then not just the institution that passes on reasons stemming from existing social norms. It will be a source of reasons of its own. If such a pattern of interdependent expectations exists, can we accept the claim that law has authority that is derived from the authority of social norms and at the same time extends beyond the authority of social norms?[37] If all the above is correct, we have the beginnings of a general theory of all social norms – mere conventions, social norms proper, and, finally, legal norms.

[36] In the sense of the practical difference thesis of Shapiro, "Authority."

[37] It is a matter of empirical debate whether such a social norm exists. It is also a matter of debate what the scope of such a norm would need to be. Hart, *The Concept of Law*, famously believed that only judges would have to be part of such a social norm.

SELECT BIBLIOGRAPHY

Alexander, Larry. "All or Nothing at All: The Intentions of Authorities and the Authority of Intentions," in Andrei Marmor (ed.), *Law and Interpretation: Essays in Legal Philosophy* (Oxford University Press, 1995).

"Telepathic Law," *Constitutional Commentary* 26 (2010), 139–40.

Alexander, Larry and Prakash, Saikrishna. "Is That English You're Speaking? Why Intention Free Interpretation is an Impossibility," *San Diego Law Review* 41 (2004), 967–95.

Alexander, Larry and Sherwin, Emily. *The Rule of Rules: Rules, Principles, and Dilemmas of Law* (Durham, NC: Duke University Press, 2001).

"Interpreting Rules: The Nature and Limits of Inchoate Intentions," in Jeffrey Goldsworthy and Tom Campbell (eds.), Legal Interpretation in Democratic States (Aldershot: Ashgate, 2002), 3–28.

Demystifying Legal Reasoning (Cambridge University Press, 2008).

Anderson, Elizabeth S. "What is the Point of Equality?" *Ethics* 109 (1999), 287–337.

Anscombe, G. E. M. "Causality and Determination," in E. Sosa and M. Tooley (eds.), *Causation* (Oxford University Press, 1993; first published 1971), 88–104.

Intention, 2nd edn (Cambridge, MA: Harvard University Press, 2000; first published 1957).

"Action, Intention, and 'Double-Effect,'" in M. Geach and L. Gormally (eds.), *Human Life, Action and Ethics: Essays by G. E. M. Anscombe* (St. Andrews: Studies in Philosophy and Public Affairs, 2005; first published 1982), 207–26.

Aquinas, Thomas. *Summa Theologiae*, trans. Thomas Gilby, Latin and English text, paperback edn (Cambridge University Press, 2006).

Aristotle. *Nicomachean Ethics*, trans. H. Rackham (Cambridge, MA: Harvard University Press, 1934).

Baier, Annette. "Trust and Anti-Trust," *Ethics* 96 (1986), 231–60.

Binmore, Ken. *Game Theory and the Social Contract*, vol. I: *Playing Fair* (Cambridge, MA: MIT Press, 1994).

Game Theory and the Social Contract, vol. II: *Just Playing*. Cambridge, MA: MIT Press, 1998).

Bork, Robert. "Neutral Principles and Some First Amendment Problems," *Indiana Law Journal* 47 (1971), 1–35.

Bradley, Ben. "Against Satisficing Consequentialism," *Utilitas* 18 (2) (2006), 97–108.

Bratman, Michael. *Intention, Plans, and Practical Reason* (Cambridge, MA: Harvard University Press, 1987; Stanford: CSLI Publications, 1999).

Faces of Intention: Selected Essays on Intention and Agency (Cambridge University Press, 1999).

"Temptation Revisited," in M. Bratman, *Structures of Agency: Essays* (New York: Oxford University Press, 2007), 257–82.

Broome, John. "Normative Requirements," in J. Dancy (ed.), *Normativity* (Malden, MA: Blackwell, 2000), 78–99.

"Are Intentions Reasons? And How Should We Cope with Incommensurable Values?" in C. W. Morris and A. Ripstein (eds.), *Practical Rationality and Preference: Essays for David Gauthier* (Cambridge University Press, 2001), 98–120.

Byron, Michael. "Simon's Revenge: or, Incommensurability and Satisficing," *Analysis* 65 (288) (2005), 311–15.

Cohen, Gerald Allen. "Political Philosophy and Personal Behavior," in *If You're an Egalitarian, How Come You're So Rich?* (Cambridge, MA: Harvard University Press, 2000), 148–79.

Rescuing Justice and Equality (Cambridge, MA: Harvard University Press, 2008).

On the Currency of Egalitarian Justice and Other Essays in Political Philosophy, ed. Michael Otsuka (Princeton University Press, 2011).

Coleman, Jules L. (ed.). *Hart's Postscript: Essays on the Postscript to "The Concept of Law"* (Oxford University Press, 2001).

Darwall, Stephen. *The Second-Person Standpoint: Morality, Respect, and Accountability* (Cambridge, MA: Harvard University Press, 2006).

Davis, Joshua P. "Legality, Morality, Duality," *Utah Law Review* 55 (1) (2014), 55–107.

De Sousa, Ronald. *The Rationality of Emotion* (Cambridge University Press, 1987).

Den Hartogh, Govert. "Politieke Verplichting: Gronden En Grenzen," *Algemeen Nederlands Tijdschrift Voor Wijsbegeerte* 80 (1988), 231–58.

"A Conventionalist Theory of Obligation," *Law and Philosophy* 17 (1998), 351–76.

Mutual Expectations: A Conventionalist Theory of Law. Law and Philosophy Library (Dordrecht: Kluwer, 2002).

Dipert, Randall R. *Artifacts, Art Works, and Agency* (Philadelphia, PA: Temple University Press, 1993).

Donnellan, Keith. "Proper Names and Identifying Descriptions," *Synthese* 21 (1970), 335–58.

Dworkin, Ronald. *Justice in Robes* (Cambridge, MA: Harvard University Press, 2006).

Justice for Hedgehogs (Cambridge, MA: Harvard University Press, 2011).

Enoch, David. "Intending, Foreseeing, and the State," *Legal Theory* 13 (2) (2007), 69–99.

"Being Responsible, Taking Responsibility, and Penumbral Agency," in Ulrike Heuer and Gerald Lang (eds.), *Luck, Value, and Commitment: Themes from the Ethics of Bernard Williams* (Oxford University Press, 2011).

"Giving Practical Reasons," *Philosophers' Imprint* 11 (2011), 1–22.

"Reason-Giving and the Law," in Leslie Green and Brian Leiter (eds.), *Oxford Studies in Philosophy of Law*, vol. I (Oxford University Press, 2011).

"Authority and Reason-Giving," *Philosophy and Phenomenological Research*, doi: 10.1111/j.1933-1592.2012.00610.x.

Estlund, David M. *Democratic Authority: A Philosophical Framework* (Princeton University Press, 2009).

Falvey, Kevin. "Knowledge in Intention," *Philosophical Studies* 99 (1) (2000), 21–44.

Fara, Michael. "Dispositions and Habituals," *Noûs* 39 (2005), 43–82.

Ferrero, Luca. "Can I Only Intend My Own Actions? Intentions and the Own Action Condition," in D. Shoemaker (ed.), *Oxford Studies in Agency and Responsibility*, vol. I (Oxford University Press, 2013), 70–94.

Finnis, John. "Law and What I Truly Should Decide," *American Journal of Jurisprudence* 48 (2003), 107–29.

"Foundations of Practical Reason Revisited," *American Journal of Jurisprudence* 50 (2005), 109–31.

"On Hart's Ways: Law as Reason and as Fact," in M. Kramer, C. Grant, B. Colburn, and A Hatzistavrou (eds.), *The Legacy of H.L.A. Hart* (Oxford University Press, 2008), 3–27.

Fish, Stanley. *Doing What Comes Naturally: Change, Rhetoric and the Practice of Theory in Literary and Legal Studies* (Durham, NC: Duke University Press, 1989).

"There Is No Textualist Position," *San Diego Law Review* 42 (2005), 629–50.

Flikschuh, Katrin. "Justice Without Virtue," in Lara Denis (ed.), *Kant's Metaphysics of Morals: A Critical Guide* (Cambridge University Press, 2010), 51–7.

Foley, Richard. *Intellectual Trust in Oneself and Others* (Cambridge University Press, 2001).

Foot, Philippa. "The Problem of Abortion and the Doctrine of the Double Effect," *Oxford Review* 5 (1967), 5–15.

Frijda, Nico H. *The Emotions* (Cambridge University Press, 1986).

Gans, Chaim. "Mandatory Norms and Exclusionary Reasons," *Philosophy* 15 (1986), 373–94.

Gardner, John. "The Legality of Law," *Ratio Juris* 17 (2004), 168–81.

Gardner, John and Macklem, Timothy. "Reasons," in Jules L. Coleman and Scott Shapiro (eds.), *The Oxford Handbook of Jurisprudence and Philosophy of Law* (Oxford University Press, 2002), 440–75.

Gilbert, Margaret. *On Social Facts* (London: Routledge & Kegan Paul, 1989).

Living Together: Rationality, Sociality, and Obligation (Lanham, MD: Rowman & Littlefield, 1996).

Godfrey-Smith, Peter. "Causal Pluralism," in H. Beebee, C. Hitchcock, and P. Menzies (eds.), *The Oxford Handbook of Causation* (Oxford University Press, 2010), 326–37.

Godwin, William. *Enquiry Concerning Political Justice, with Selections from Godwin's Other Writings*, abridged and ed. K. Codell Carter (Oxford: Clarendon Press, 1971).

Green, Leslie. "Law as Means," in R. Cane (ed.), *The Hart–Fuller Debate in the 21st Century* (Oxford: Hart Publications, 2010), 169–88.

Greenberg, Mark. "How Facts Make Law," *Legal Theory* 10 (2004), 157–98.

Hanser, Matthew. "Intention and Teleology," *Mind* 107 (1998), 381–401.

"Permissibility and Practical Inference," *Ethics* 115 (3) (2005), 443–70.

Hart, H. L. A. "Legal and Moral Obligation," in Richard E. Flathman (ed.), *Concepts in Social and Political Philosophy* (New York: Macmillan, 1973).

"Commands and Authoritative Legal Reasons," in H. L. A. Hart, *Essays on Bentham* (Oxford University Press, 1982), 243–68.

The Concept of Law, 3rd edn (Oxford University Press, 2012).

Hatzistavrou, Antony. "Instrumental Rules and Motivation," *Legal Theory* 12 (2006), 315–45.

"Reconsideration, Motivation and Exclusionary Reasons," *Ratio Juris* 25 (2012), 318–42.

Heuer, Ulrike. "Intentions and the Reasons For Which We Act," *Proceedings of the Aristotelian Society* 114 (3) (2014), 291–315.

Hitchcock, C. "Probabilistic Causation," in Edward N. Zalta (ed.), *The Stanford Encyclopedia of Philosophy* (winter 2012 edn). Available at: plato.stanford.edu/archives/win2012/entries/causation-probabilistic.

Holmes, Jr, Oliver Wendell. "The Path of the Law," *Harvard Law Review* 10 (457) (1897), 460–1.

Hume, David. *A Treatise on Human Nature*, ed. David Fate Norton and Mary J. Norton (Oxford University Press, 2001).

Hurd, Heidi M. "Sovereignty in Silence," *Yale Law Journal* 99 (5) (1990), 945–1028.

"Interpreting Authorities," in Andrei Marmor (ed.), *Law and Interpretation* (Oxford University Press, 1995), 405–32.

Moral Combat (Cambridge University Press, 1999).

"Living in the Past: Burkean Conservatism and Originalist Interpretation," in Jeffrey Goldsworthy and Tom Campbell (eds.), *Legal Interpretation, Judicial Supremacy, and Democracy* (Aldershot: Ashgate, 2001), 173–206.

"Liberty in Law," *Law and Philosophy* 21 (2002), 385–465.

"When Can We Do What We Want?" *Australian Journal of Legal Philosophy* 29 (2004), 27–69.

"Tolerating Wickedness: Moral Reasons for Lawmakers to Permit Immorality," *Philosophia Practica Universalis (Annual Review of Law and Ethics)* (2005), 167–94.

Hurka, Thomas. "Two Kinds of Satisficing," *Philosophical Studies* 59 (1) (1990), 107–11.

Husak, Douglas. "The Costs to Criminal Theory of Supposing that Intentions are Irrelevant to Permissibility," *Criminal Law and Philosophy* 3 (2009), 1–70.

Ingarden, Roman. *Ontology of the Work of Art: The Musical Work, the Picture, the Architectural Work, the Film*, trans. Raymond Meyer (Athens, OH: Ohio University Press, 1989; originally *Untersuchungen zur Ontologie der Kunst*, 1962).

Jackson, Frank. "Decision-Theoretic Consequentialism and the Nearest and Dearest Objection," *Ethics* 101 (1991), 462–82.

Joyce, James M. *The Foundations of Causal Decision Theory* (New York: Cambridge University Press, 1999).

Kamm, Frances. "The Doctrine of Triple Effect and Why a Rational Agent Need Not Intend the Means to his End," *Proceedings of the Aristotelian Society*, supplementary vol. 74 (1) (2000), 21–39.

Kant, Immanuel. *Kants gesammelte Schriften*, Deutsche Akademie der Wissenschaften (formerly Königlich Preußische Akademie der Wissenschaften) (Berlin: Walter de Gruyter, 1902–).

The Cambridge Edition of the Works of Immanuel Kant (Cambridge University Press, 1995–).

Practical Philosophy, trans. and ed. Mary J. Gregor (Cambridge University Press, 1999).

Kaplan, Mark. *Decision Theory as Philosophy* (New York: Cambridge University Press, 1998).

Kellert, Stephen H. *et al.* "Introduction: The Pluralist Stance," in S. H. Kellert *et al.* (eds.), *Scientific Pluralism* (Minneapolis: University of Minnesota Press, 2006), vii–xxx.

Kenny, Anthony. *Aristotle's Theory of the Will* (London: Duckworth, 1979).

Kolodny, Niko. "Why Be Rational," *Mind* 114 (455) (2005), 509–63.

"Scanlon's Investigation: The Relevance of Intent to Permissibility," *Analytic Philosophy* 52 (2) (2011), 100–23.

Korsgaard, Christine. *The Sources of Normativity* (Cambridge University Press, 1996).

"The Normativity of Instrumental Reason," in Garrett Cullity and Berys Gaut (eds.), *Ethics and Practical Reason* (Oxford: Clarendon Press, 1997), 207–31.

"Acting for a Reason," in Christine Korsgaard (ed.), *The Constitution of Agency* (New York: Oxford University Press, 2008), 207–31.

Self-Constitution: Agency, Identity, and Integrity (New York: Oxford University Press, 2009).

Knapp, Steven and Benn Michaels, Walter. "Not A Matter of Interpretation," *San Diego Law Review* 42 (2005), 651–68.

Kripke, Saul. *Naming and Necessity* (Cambridge, MA: Harvard University Press, 1980).

Lehrer, Keith. *Self-Trust: A Study of Reason Knowledge and Autonomy* (Oxford University Press, 1997).

Leiter, Brian. "Heidegger and the Theory of Adjudication," *Yale Law Journal* 106 (2) (1996), 253–82.

Naturalizing Jurisprudence: Essays on American Legal Realism and Naturalism in Legal Philosophy (Oxford University Press, 2007).

"The Demarcation Problem in Jurisprudence: A New Case for Scepticism," *Oxford Journal of Legal Studies* 31 (2011), 663–77.

Lewis, David. *Convention: A Philosophical Study* (Cambridge, MA: Harvard University Press, 1969).

"Finkish Dispositions," *Philosophical Quarterly* 47 (1997), 143–58.

Lillehammer, Hallvard. "Scanlon on Intention and Permissibility," *Analysis* 7 (3) (2010), 578–85.

Longino, Helen E. "Theoretical Pluralism and the Scientific Study of Behavior," in S. H. Kellert *et al.* (eds.), *Scientific Pluralism* (Minneapolis: University of Minnesota Press, 2006), 102–31.

Manley, David and Wasserman, Ryan. "On Linking Dispositions and Conditionals," *Mind* 117 (2008), 59–84.

Markovits, Julia. "Acting for the Right Reason," *Philosophical Review* 119 (2) (2010), 201–42.

Marmor, Andrei. *Social Conventions* (Princeton University Press, 2009).

"Can the Law Imply More Than It Says? On Some Pragmatic Aspects of Strategic Speech," in A. Marmor and S. Soames (eds.), *Philosophical Foundations of Language in the Law* (Oxford University Press, 2011), 80–104.

Maynard Smith, John. *Evolution and the Theory of Games* (Cambridge University Press, 1982).

McClennen, Edward F. and Shapiro, Scott. "Rule-Guided Behavior," in Peter Newman (ed.), *The New Palgrave Dictionary of Economics and the Law* (London: Macmillan, 1998), 363–9.

McMahan, Jeff. "Intention, Permissibility, Terrorism, and War," *Philosophical Perspectives* 23 (2009), 345–72.

Mele, Alfred. *Effective Intentions: The Power of the Conscious Will* (New York: Oxford University Press, 2009).

Moore, Michael S. "Authority, Law and Razian Reasons," *Southern California Law Review* 62 (3–4) (1989), 827–96.

Mourelatos, Alexander P. D. "Events, Processes, and States," *Linguistics and Philosophy* 2 (3) (1978), 415–34.

Murphy, Liam B. "The Demands of Beneficence," *Philosophy and Public Affairs* 22 (1993), 267–92.

"Institutions and the Demands of Justice," *Philosophy and Public Affairs* 27 (1998), 251–91.

Moral Demands in Nonideal Theory (New York: Oxford University Press, 2000).

Nagel, Thomas. *The Possibility of Altruism* (Oxford University Press, 1970).

"Libertarianism without Foundations," in Jeffrey Paul (ed.), *Reading Nozick* (Totowa, NJ: Rowman & Littlefield, 1981), 191–205.

Nahmias, Eddy. "Scientific Challenges to Free Will," in T. O'Connor and C. Sandis (eds.), *A Companion to the Philosophy of Action* (Malden, MA: Wiley-Blackwell, 2010), 345–56.

Nichols, Shaun. "Free Will and Error," in G. Caruso (ed.), *Exploring the Illusion of Free Will and Moral Responsibility* (Lanham, MD: Lexington Books, 2013), 203–18.

Owens, David. "Promising Without Intending," *Journal of Philosophy* 105 (2008), 737–55.

The Shaping of the Normative Landscape (Oxford University Press, 2012).

Parfit, Derek. *Reasons and Persons* (Oxford University Press, 1986).

Pavlakos, George. "Practice, Reasons and the Agent's Point of View," *Ratio Juris* 22 (2009), 74–94.

"Legal Obligation in a Global Context," in *EUI Working Papers*, Robert Schuman Centre for Advanced Studies 2012/16 (2012). Available at: http://hdl.handle.net/1814/21758.

Perry, Stephen R. "Second-Order Reasons, Uncertainty and Legal Theory," *Southern California Law Review* 62 (3–4) (1989), 913–94.

"Political Authority and Political Obligation," in Leslie Green and Brian Leiter (eds.), *Oxford Studies In the Philosophy of Law*, vol. II (Oxford University Press, 2012).

Pettit, Philip. "Satisficing Consequentialism," *Proceedings of the Aristotelian Society*, supplementary vol. 58 (1984), 139–76.

Pogge, Thomas. "On the Site of Distributive Justice: Reflections on Cohen and Murphy," *Philosophy and Public Affairs* 29 (2000), 137–69.

Postema, G. "Positivism, I Presume? ... Comments on Schauer's Rules and the Rule of Law," *Harvard Journal of Law and Public Policy*, 14 (1991), 797–822.

"Implicit Law," *Law and Philosophy* 13 (1994), 361–87.

Preston, Beth. "Philosophical Theories of Artifact Function," in Anthonie Meijers (ed.), *Philosophy of Technology and Engineering Sciences* (Amsterdam: Elsevier, 2009), 216–17.

Putnam, Hilary. "The Meaning of 'Meaning,'" in *Mind, Language and Reality: Philosophical Papers*, vol. II (Cambridge University Press, 1975), 215–71.

Ramsey, Frank P. "Truth and Probability," in *The Foundations of Mathematics and Other Logical Essays* (New York: Harcourt, Brace, 1931), 156–98.

Rawls, John. "Two Concepts of Rules," *Philosophical Review* 64 (1) (1955), 3–32.

A Theory of Justice (Cambridge, MA: Belknap Press, 1971).

Political Liberalism (New York: Columbia University Press, 1996).

Raz, Joseph. "Promises and Obligations," in P. M. S. Hacker and J. Raz (eds.), *Law, Morality, and Society: Essays in Honor of H. L. A. Hart* (Oxford University Press, 1977), 210–28.

The Authority of Law (Oxford: Clarendon Press, 1979).

"Authority and Justification," *Philosophy and Public Affairs* 14 (1985), 3–29.

The Morality of Freedom (Oxford University Press, 1986).

"Postema on Law's Autonomy and Public Practical Reasons: A Critical Comment," *Legal Theory* 4 (1) (1998), 1–20.

Engaging Reason (Oxford University Press, 1999).

Practical Reason and Norms, 2nd edn (Oxford University Press, 1999; first published London: Hutchinson, 1975).

"The Problem of Authority: Revisiting the Service Conception," *Minnesota Law Review* 90 (4) (2006), 1003–44. Reprinted in *Between Authority and Interpretation* (Oxford University Press, 2009), 126–65.

"The Guise of the Good," in S. Tenenbaum (ed.), *Desire, Practical Reason, and the Good* (Oxford University Press, 2010), 111–37.

Ripstein, Arthur. *Force and Freedom: Kant's Legal and Political Philosophy* (Cambridge MA: Harvard University Press, 2009).

Rodriguez-Blanco, Veronica. "Claims of Legal Authorities and 'Expressions of Intentions': The Limits of the Philosophy of Language," in M. Freeman and F. Smith (eds.), *Law and Language* (Oxford University Press, 2013).

Law and Authority Under the Guise of the Good (Oxford: Hart Publishing, 2014).

Roth, Abraham. "Shared Agency and Contralateral Commitments," *Philosophical Review* 113 (2004), 359–410.

Scalia, Antonin. *A Matter of Interpretation: Federal Courts and the Law* (Princeton University Press, 1997).

Scanlon, Thomas M. "Reasons: A Puzzling Duality?," in R. J. Wallace, P. Petit, S. Scheffler, and M. Smith (eds.), *Reason and Value: Themes from the Moral Philosophy of Joseph Raz* (Oxford University Press, 2004), 231–46.

Moral Dimensions (Cambridge, MA: Harvard University Press, 2008).

Schaffer, Jonathan. *Playing by the Rules* (Oxford University Press, 1991).

"The Metaphysics of Causation," in Edward N. Zalta (ed.), *The Stanford Encyclopedia of Philosophy* (fall 2008 edn). Available at: plato.stanford.edu/archives/fall2008/entries/causation-metaphysics.

Schauer, Frederick. *Playing by the Rules* (Oxford University Press, 1991).

"Rules and the Rule of Law," *Harvard Journal of Law and Public Policy* 14 (3) (1991), 645–94.

Scheffler, Samuel. *The Rejection of Consequentialism* (Oxford University Press, 1982).

Schelling, Thomas. *The Strategy of Conflict* (Cambridge, MA: Harvard University Press, 1960).

Schmidtz, David. "Satisficing as a Humanly Rational Strategy," in Michael Byron (ed.), *Satisficing and Maximizing: Moral Theorists on Practical Reason* (New York: Cambridge University Press, 2004), 30–58.

Schotter, Andrew. *The Economic Theory of Social Institutions* (Cambridge University Press, 1981).

Searle, John. *The Construction of Social Reality* (New York: Free Press, 1995).

Making the Social World: The Structure of Human Civilization (New York, Oxford University Press, 2010).

Shapiro, Scott. "Authority," in Jules L. Coleman and Scott Shapiro (eds.), *The Oxford Handbook of Jurisprudence and Philosophy of Law* (Oxford University Press, 2002), 382–439.

Legality (Cambridge, MA: Harvard University Press, 2011).

Simchen, Ori. *Necessary Intentionality: A Study in the Metaphysics of Aboutness* (Oxford University Press, 2012).

"Token-Reflexivity," *Journal of Philosophy* 110 (2013), 173–93.

Simmons, A. John. *Moral Principles and Political Obligations* (Princeton University Press, 1979).

Simon, Herbert A. "A Behavioral Model of Rational Choice," *Quarterly Journal of Economics* 69 (1) (1955), 99–118.

Models of Bounded Rationality, vols. I and II (Cambridge, MA: MIT Press, 1982).

Sinnott-Armstrong, Walter. "'It's Not My Fault': Global Warming and Individual Moral Obligation," in Walter Sinnott-Armstrong and Richard Howarth (eds.), *Perspectives on Climate Change: Science, Economics, Politics, Ethics* (Amsterdam: Elsevier, 2005).

Skyrms, Brian. *Evolution of the Social Contract* (Cambridge University Press, 1996).

The Stag Hunt and the Evolution of Social Structure (Cambridge University Press, 2004).

Slote, Michael. "Satisficing Consequentialism," *Proceedings of the Aristotelian Society*, supplementary vol. 58 (1984), 139–63.

"Two Views of Satisficing," in Michael Byron (ed.), *Satisficing and Maximizing: Moral Theorists on Practical Reason* (New York: Cambridge University Press, 2004), 14–29.

Smilansky, Saul. "On Practicing What We Preach," *American Philosophical Quarterly* 31 (1994), 73–9.

"The Paradox of Beneficial Retirement," in *Ten Moral Paradoxes* (Oxford: Basil Blackwell, 2007), 23–32.

Smith, Adam. *The Theory of Moral Sentiments*, in D. Raphael and A. Macfie (eds.), *The Glasgow Edition of the Works and Correspondence of Adam Smith* (Oxford University Press, 1976).

Smith, Michael. "Internal Reasons," *Philosophy and Phenomenological Research* 55 (1995), 109–31.

Smith, Tara. "Originalism's Misplaced Fidelity: 'Original' Meaning is Not Objective," *Constitutional Commentary* 26 (2009), 1–57.

Spencer, Quayshawn. "What 'Biological Racial Realism' Should Mean," *Philosophical Studies* 159 (2) (2012), 181–204.

"Biological Theory and the Metaphysics of Race: A Reply to Kaplan and Winther," *Biological Theory*, 8 (2013), 114–20.

Strawson, Peter F. "Freedom and Resentment," *Proceedings of the British Academy* 48 (1962), 1–25.

Sugden, Robert. *The Economics of Rights, Co-operation and Welfare* (Oxford: Basil Blackwell, 1986).

Tenenbaum, Sergio. *Appearances of the Good: An Essay on the Nature of Practical Reason* (Cambridge University Press, 2007).

"Akrasia and Irrationality," in T. O'Connor and C. Sandis (eds.), *A Companion to the Philosophy of Action* (Malden, MA: Wiley-Blackwell, 2010), 74–82.

"The Vice of Procrastination," in Chrisoula Andreou and Mark White (eds.), *The Thief of Time* (New York: Oxford University Press, 2010), 130–50.

Tenenbaum, Sergio and Raffman, Diana. "Vague Projects and the Puzzle of the Self-Torturer," *Ethics* 123 (1) (2012), 86–112.

Thomasson, Amie L. "Realism and Human Kinds," *Philosophy and Phenomenological Research* 67 (2003), 580–699.

"Artifacts and Human Concepts," in Eric Margolis and Stephen Laurence (eds.), *Creations of the Mind: Theories of Artifacts and their Representation* (Oxford University Press, 2007), 52–73.

"Artifacts in Metaphysics," in Anthonie Meijers (ed.), *Philosophy of Technology and Engineering Sciences* (Amsterdam: Elsevier, 2009), 191–202.

"Public Artifacts, Intentions and Norms," in Maarten Franssen *et al.* (eds.), *Artefact Kinds: Ontology and the Human-Made World* (Heidelberg: Springer 2013), 63–84.

Thomson, Judith Jarvis. "Self-Defense," *Philosophy and Public Affairs* 20 (4) (1991), 283–310.

"Physician-Assisted Suicide: Two Moral Arguments," *Ethics* 109 (3) (1999), 497–518.

Normativity (Chicago: Open Court, 2008).

Van Parijs, Philippe. "The Disfranchisement of the Elderly, and Other Attempts to Secure Intergenerational Justice," *Philosophy and Public Affairs* 27 (1998), 292–333.

Vargas, Manuel. *Building Better Beings: A Theory of Moral Responsibility* (Oxford University Press, 2013).

"If Free Will Doesn't Exist, Then Neither Does Water," in G. Caruso (ed.), *Exploring the Illusion of Free Will and Moral Responsibility* (Lanham, MD: Lexington Books, 2013), 177–202.

Vargas, Manuel and Yaffe, Gideon. "Introduction," in M. Vargas and G. Yaffe (eds.), *Rational and Social Agency: On Themes in the Philosophy of Michael Bratman* (New York: Oxford University Press, 2014), 1–11.

Vendler, Zeno. "Verbs and Times," *Philosophical Review* 66 (2) (1957), 143–60.

Verbeek, Bruno. *Instrumental Rationality and Moral Philosophy: An Essay on the Virtues of Cooperation* (Dordrecht: Kluwer, 2002).

"The Authority of Norms," *American Philosophical Quarterly* 44 (3) (2007), 245–58.

Waldron, Jeremy. "Legislators' Intentions and Unintentional Legislation," in Andrei Mormor (ed.), *Law and Interpretation: Essays in Legal Philosophy* (Oxford University Press, 1995), 329–54.

Walen, Alec. "Choosing Your Reasons for an Action," available at: http://papers.ssrn.com/sol3/papers.cfm?abstract_id+1447042.

Wallace, R. Jay. "The Publicity of Reasons," *Philosophical Perspectives* 23 (2009), 471–97.

Weber, Michael. "A New Defense of Satisficing," in Michael Byron (ed.), *Satisficing and Maximizing: Moral Theorists on Practical Reason* (New York: Cambridge University Press, 2004), 77–105.

Wedgwood, Ralph. "Defending Double Effect," *Ratio*, special issue on Deontological Ethics, ed. Brad Hooker, 24 (2011), 384–401.

"Scanlon on Double Effect," *Philosophy and Phenomenological Research* 83 (2011), 464–72.

Willaschek, Marcus. "Which Imperatives for Right? On the Non-Prescriptive Character of Juridical Law in Kant's *Metaphysics of Morals*," in Mark Timmons (ed.), *Kant's Metaphysics of Morals: Interpretative Essays* (Oxford University Press, 2002), 65–87.

"Right and Coercion: Can Kant's Conception of Right Be Derived from his Moral Theory?" *International Journal of Philosophical Studies* 17 (1) (2009), 49–70.

Willer, Malte. "Dynamic Thoughts on Ifs and Oughts," *Philosophers' Imprint* 14 (2014), 1–30.

Williams, Bernard. "Internal and External Reasons," in Bernard Williams, *Moral Luck* (Cambridge University Press, 1981), 101–13.

Williamson, Timothy. "Knowledge, Context and the Agent's Point of View," in G. Preyer and G. Peter (eds.), *Contextualism in Philosophy: Knowledge, Meaning and Truth* (Oxford University Press, 2005), 91–114.

Winch, Peter. *The Idea of a Social Science and its Relation to Philosophy*, vol. II (London: Routledge & Kegan Paul, 1990).

Wood, Allen. "The Final Form of Kant's Practical Philosophy," in Mark Timmons (ed.), *Kant's Metaphysics of Morals: Interpretative Essays* (Oxford University Press, 2002), 1–23.

INDEX

Lightning Source UK Ltd.
Milton Keynes UK
UKHW02f1353110318
319235UK00009B/147/P

9 781107 642928